THE LANGUAGE OF VALUE

THE LANGUAGE OF
VALUE

EDITED BY RAY LEPLEY

1957 NEW YORK

COLUMBIA UNIVERSITY PRESS

PUBLISHED IN GREAT BRITAIN, CANADA, INDIA, AND PAKISTAN

BY GEOFFREY CUMBERLEGE: OXFORD UNIVERSITY PRESS

LONDON, TORONTO, BOMBAY, AND KARACHI

LIBRARY OF CONGRESS CATALOG CARD NUMBER: 55-9096

PUBLISHED 1957, COLUMBIA UNIVERSITY PRESS, NEW YORK

MANUFACTURED IN THE NETHERLANDS

PREFACE

THOSE familiar with the book *Value: A Cooperative Inquiry* will recognize that the present volume follows the same general plan of organization: a short Introduction; Part I, consisting of constructive essays on issues formulated in preliminary study; and Part II, composed of critical discussion of the essays. Further comparison will disclose, however, that the present essays do not seek to answer one common set of questions, as did those of the earlier book, but rather, that each essay considers a different aspect or group of aspects of a common subject matter: The Language of Value.

The unity of Part I (Essays) of the present volume is consequently a unity such as results when an individual or group of individuals views an extremely complex object from different standpoints and can carefully examine or consider, at any one time, only one or a few of the many aspects or facets of the total object. Taken together, the Essays afford a broad survey and panoramic view of the semantic or linguistic aspects of value theory and open some new lines of study in this area. Part II (Coments and Responses) effects a more organic unity of the volume. Here the Essays are examined, individually and en masse, from viewpoints held by various contributors and in relation to certain general perspectives. The Comments and Responses are particularly fruitful in suggesting issues which invite further discussion and research.

The following, though not direct contributors to the present volume, have assisted by comments and suggestions, especially in the preliminary phases of the study: H. D. Aiken, V. C. Aldrich, G. M. Boas, M. W. Boyer, C. E. Bures, R. G. Chisholm, I. M. Copi, C. J. Ducasse, H. O. Eaton, A. Edel, F. B. Fitch, J. S. Fulton, L. Garvin, D. W. Gotshalk, L. E. Hahn, B. E. Jessup, A. Kaplan, P. G. Kuntz, S. K. Langer, H. S. Leonard, A. I Melden, A. E. Murphy, R. B. Perry, P. B. Rice, D. Rynin, H. G. Schrickel, W. S. Sellars, V. Tomas, G. Vlastos, M. G. White, D. C. Williams, and G. Williams. Though their assistance is gratefully acknowledged, these persons are in no way responsible for any defects or deficiencies of the present volume. Many members of the study group helped select the essays included in Part I, and all members whose essays appear there were consulted with regard to inclusion and revision of the two sets of concluding Comments. But responsibility for inclusion of papers throughout the volume and for some points of form rests finally with the editor, and responsibility for the contents of each paper lies with its author.

Thanks for aid in the preparation of the present book are due especially to those who contributed the constructive Essays. In addition to the labors of drafting and revising their own papers, these members have assisted in the revision of Essays and Comments by others. They have also from time to time made helpful suggestions to the editor and generously expressed appreciation for stimulation received through cooperative study. To each of his fellow contributors to the Essays, the editor wishes to express deepest gratitude. He desires, similarly, to thank Feigl, Lafleur, and Stevenson, who kindly consented to comment on the Essays by Adams, Pepper, and Brandt, respectively, and to thank Hartman, who, in addition to contributing an Essay and a Response, accepted the arduous task of commenting on all the papers from a comparatively formal point of view.

We are also glad to acknowledge financial aid to publication by grants from Bradley University, Tulane University, and the University of North Carolina; to thank holders of copyrights for permission to quote, as indicated in footnotes; and to express gratitude to Mrs. Ada Morlock Emme, whose careful reading of the manuscript, the galleys, and the page proof has very greatly assisted in removing mechanical errors and inconsistencies.

R.L.

Peoria, Illinois
May, 1956

CONTENTS

A SECOND SEQUEL ON VALUE

Part II: Comments and Responses
RAY LEPLEY, BRADLEY UNIVERSITY

INTRODUCTION

RAY LEPLEY

O F ISSUES basic for human survival and cooperation, perhaps none are more important today than those concerning the nature and status of value in a world of scientific fact and force. And few issues are more troublesome than those with regard to the functions and status of value terms and sentences. The present volume results from a cooperative study of some of these linguistic, semantic, or semiotic problems.

The issues considered in the study were encountered particularly in the final phases of work on the book *Value: A Cooperative Inquiry*[1] and in numerous other recent writings in value theory. In the summer of 1950 a number of persons whose publications indicated interest in semantic or linguistic problems of value responded favorably to a proposed plan of study. It was agreed that as a first step members of the group would submit references to books and articles which state or suggest the most crucial problems that might be considered in the study, and after each reference or group of references would state briefly the main issue or issues in the form of topics or questions, with comments indicating why these were felt to be important. The references, topics, questions, and comments would be combined in one list by the editor and sent to all members. Next, each participant would write a constructive essay on one or more of the issues which he considered most important. After exchange of criticisms and suggestions, the essays chosen for inclusion in a proposed volume would be put into final form. Lastly, comments and responses would be prepared for a concluding part of the book.

The references, topics, questions, and comments submitted at the outset were organized, supplemented, and summarized by the editor and presented to all the members. These materials appear in the Appendix.[2] The Summary of Issues was as follows:

[1] New York, 1949.   [2] Pages 395-401, below.

I.   What different functions are performed by signs? What are the various modes of reaction to or as sign stimulation? Can and should a distinction be made between the modes in which signs signify and the uses which signs serve?

II.   If there is justification for distinguishing valuative signs, sentences, problem solvings, or judgments (valuations, evaluations), on the one hand, from factual signs, sentences, or judgments (cognitions, descriptions), on the other hand, are the modes of sign response (possibly the interpretants) different in the valuative as compared with those in the factual? And if there are differences in mode in the valuative as compared with the factual, are they differences of kind or of degree?

III.   Are emotive elements always present in valuative terms, sentences, judgments, but not in factual terms, sentences, or judgments? And why and how are they present or absent? Are emotive factors *basic* in the valuative but not in the factual?

IV.   Under what, if any, conditions is it possible to use "factual" and "valuative" signs or sentences interchangeably or to translate the one into the other? Is this possible in the case of extrinsic or inherent values but not possible in the case of intrinsic values?

If translation or interchange can occur, to what extent is it possible? What if any light does this throw upon the basic logical and ontological relations of fact and value?

When the summary of materials was presented, the participants in the study were assured that they were free to consider in their essays any or all the questions listed or any other point or points suggested by these or other materials. Each contributor was urged to address himself to the linguistic ("semantic") issue or issues which he felt to be particularly important for value theory at the present time. Consequently, few of the Essays which follow (in Part I) discuss directly the questions as formulated in the Summary of Issues. The reader will note, however, that each Essay considers an issue or issues which from the perspective of its author are central or basic for one or more topics, questions, or comments submitted or summarized.

Although there was no attempt to attain or impose any one conception of "semantic of value" or to subdivide the field of study into areas or phases for special consideration by different members of the group, there is among the various Essays substantial agreement with regard to the goal of the study and very little duplication of content. In nearly all cases "semantics" or "linguistics" has been considered more as an aspect or phase of the subject matter to be investigated and as a mode of approach to the problems of value than as a special isolated subject matter or standpoint. The attempt has been to view value language, sentences, and terms within the context of total transactions or situations; to give special but by no means exclusive attention to the nature and functions of linguistic ("semantic") elements in total behaviors; and to utilize, so far as may be possible at the present time, distinctions and conceptions which have developed from linguistic studies in recent decades, for the purpose of probing further into issues of value theory, many of which rise perennially but now present themselves especially in semantic, or semiotic, form.

This volume does not of course consider all problems or points of view with regard to the "language of value" in the broad sense in which the term is here conceived. It does, however, cover a wide range of issues, at various levels of abstraction or generality. Some of the Essays are devoted mainly to description and analysis of instances in which valuings and valuations occur, with particular attention to the language or sign phenomena involved. Others consider more general problems as to the nature and functions of the signs which occur in value situations, the bases of the distinction between factual and valuative terms and sentences, and the place of emotive, cognitive, and other elements within total human adjustments or problem-solving courses. A few seek, on even a higher level of abstraction, to discover how the language of value theory differs from other types of language and how it is related to the language of sign theory, or to determine systematically the types of logical relations or of normative justifications involved in various kinds of value sentences or situations.

The contents within the several individual Essays, and indeed in some measure that in entire Essays compared with each other, may be said to vary—much as Hartman has suggested with regard to value language generally—from EMPIRICAL ANALYSIS ("analysis of value experiences and value phenomena in terms of everyday language"), through CONCEPTUAL ANALYSIS ("analysis of the language used by value theorists about value situations"), to FORMAL ANALYSIS ("an analysis which does not interpret value language but creates it—autonomously defining it in its own terms").[3] Though of course other distinctions among and characterizations of "levels" within value language

---

[3] R. S. Hartman, "Levels of Language," in *Dianoia: Anuaria de Filosofia* (Yearbook of Philosophy) (Center of Philosophical Research, National University of Mexico, 1956), pp. 254-69. See also pp. 352-55, below.

may be made,[4] it would appear in the perspective of Hartman's analysis that parts of each of the Essays are at the "empirical" level, other parts at the "conceptual" level, and still others at the "formal" level; that the Essays considered collectively are in the main at the "empirical" and "conceptual" levels; and that Hartman's own Essay is perhaps most conspicuously at the "formal" level. Thus from the standpoint of the diversity of the levels of analysis and the wide range of semantic issues considered, the Essays and other papers which follow may be viewed both as strands in a richly variegated fabric of value language and as different parts or phases of the study of that language.

The order in which the Essays are presented is, consequently, somewhat arbitrary. Moore's is put first because it gives an over-all view of the place of language in total value situations, both personal and social. Robinson's is second, for it considers the relation of the language of value theory to other kinds of language, especially the language of sign theory. The next nine Essays deal with rather specific issues within the semantics, or semiotic, of value theory, the arrangement being somewhat from the more specific to the more general and with regard to a certain amount of continuity or logical sequence of topics from one Essay to another, though almost any other order might be defended. The last Essay is so placed because it considers rather systematically all the questions in the Summary of Issues and is in this respect the most inclusive.

In Part II is presented one special set of Comments on each Essay, written by a member of the study group other than the author of that Essay, and a Response by the author of the Essay. The order in which the Essays are considered is the same as that in which they appear in Part I. The Essay discussed in each case is indicated in the table of contents and in the running heads of Part II by the name of the person who makes the Response (for example, "Comments by Adams; Response by Moore" signifies that the Essay considered is that by Moore). At the close of Part II are two sets of Comments—those by Hartman and those by the editor—which summarize and appraise the several Essays and the study as a whole from somewhat divergent points of view.

---

[4] See, for instance, the analyses and characterizations by Moore, pp. 16-27, and by Robinson, pp. 35 ff. Questions may of course be raised, particularly as to the sense in which, according to Hartman's analysis, value language can (at the "formal" level) "create," or "autonomously" define, in its own terms; see p. 392.

PART I: ESSAYS

THE LANGUAGE OF VALUES

WILLIS MOORE

A STUDY of the language of values may properly be described as a process of clarification of concepts, provided it is not assumed that such clarifying activity may be confined to the translation of the relatively obscure and ambiguous into the simpler and less ambiguous. In this, as in most such areas, our disagreements are not a function solely of verbal haziness or even of discrepancy in assignment of sign-vehicle, but are often a consequence of differences as to what is found in the referent situation, or more subtly, as to how this factor we call *language* operates within the context which includes its referent and its users. Inasmuch as language is a natural derivative of a more fundamental, nonverbal form of human behavior and experience, the structures embodied in it are intrinsic or peculiar neither to it nor to the thought of which it is said to be an expression but are, rather, the skeletal character of the gross experience whence language evolved. This being the case it is not simply permissive but even imperative that a study of the language of values penetrate beyond the stratum of mere rhetoric to the level of the nonverbal referent of such language and, perhaps more importantly, to the very nature of language itself.

An assumption of this Essay, one some students might debate, is the actuality of a value situation that is both chronologically prior to and logically independent of the use of language of any kind. The rejection of this assumption would involve the assertion that the experience of speechless animals, including our primitive ancestors and all human infants, is devoid of value situations. Such an assertion seems ridiculous in the face of close observable analogies between the behavior of these forms of life and those of developed human beings in admitted axiological relations. More seriously, the assumption that value experience is a function of the use of language would assign to linguistic behavior a magical creative power far in excess of what one would expect to find in an instrument. For these reasons I shall feel free to speak in terms of a prelanguage and non-language level axiological situation.

The initial guideposts to the area in which our problem situation lies must of necessity be the relatively rude indications of common language usage. These suggest, first, simply by reason of their non-inclusive application, that value terms are relevant, not to just any kind of situation, but only to certain ones, namely, those involving an organism, usually man, in some sort of experiential relationship with an object. Common language has no truck with the theory that there are value phenomena in a context in which the place of the organism is occupied by some other order of entity. A second limitation indicated in common usage but disputed by certain philosophers is that this organism must be in a special sort of experiential relation with its object. Common sense seems to require something more of such an organism than mere attention or interest with regard to its object. This something more seems to be an affective involvement. Whereas mere interest or attention is taken to represent a tentative or noncommittal position, the value attitude is thought of as signaling a deeper implication on the part of the organism. Attentive interest is assumed to come first, but common language sanctions the use of value terms only after the experiential factor has gone beyond this affective neutrality to the deeper reaction of approval or disapproval, of acceptance or rejection, of the object involved. On the basis of common language, therefore, I should roughly define a value situation as one in which an organism is affectively committed to an object of its experience.

Furthermore, it seems impossible to square the common use of value language with the behavioristic convention which would limit the reference of such phraseology to what can be reported by a non-participating observer of an axiological situation. For instance, when a person expresses linguistically his approval of an apple he is eating by saying, "I like it," he intends something different from what he would be referring to were he to say, as the objective observer also could say, with appropriate changes in grammar, "I grasp and eat it." The person eating the apple would insist that, however finely dissected, the behavior components represented in the second statement comprise a phenomenon related to but not identical with what is referred to in the first. In other words, the "I like" and the "I grasp and eat" are, for common language, renditions of associated but not identical structures within the same general situation.

If this subjective interpretation of "affective commitment to an object" is accepted as a defining character of the value situation, we are compelled to assume the perspective of the participating organism for descriptive detail going beyond the crude outline so far indicated. The adoption of the subjective approach means further that any such additional detail is, fundamentally and primitively, descriptive of the personal experience of the analyst himself, detail which, however, may, through ordinary analogical procedures, be divested of a portion of its initial privacy and relativity.

From the perspective of the participating organism, admittedly myself in this case but I believe experiencing approximately as do others, the value situation seems a sort of polar arrangement with the organism and the gross sensory object as the two extremes of a continuous, though momentary, organic strand. It is as if the participating organism, by varying the focal length of his discernment, may attend to various intermediate segments of the total strand stretching from his end of the axis to that of the object. This figure of a continuum represents a felt depth or richness in the total experience, one aspect of which may be expressed in terms of value language.

To render descriptively all that may be experienced in this total continuum the organism needs a wide range of sentence type, each representing a sort of focal node in the strand. These range from the relatively objective to the relatively subjective. For example, a focal node near the object end of the axis is described in terms of language reflecting the relationship of the object with other objects, in what many people are accustomed to call the language of science. Value language is descriptive of what appears at a node near the subject end of the same polar line. Any single sentence type used in such describing activity explicitly represents what appears in a limited segment of this axis; but, as the product of attentive focus in this continuous depth, this content never completely excludes the fuller, richer experience shading away peripherally in either direction. Hence we may say that in the most clearly objective language the subject is present in at least a penumbral fashion and that the most intensively subjective types of expression suggest at least vaguely their outlying objective complements.

To illustrate this description concretely we may imagine a person in experiential relation with a candy bar. This person may have a concern which is appropriately rendered verbally as, "Here is something," an expression that is little more than an indication of experienced objectivity; or his focus of interest may be spoken as, "This object is larger than that one," a sentence representing the crude ancestral type of the language of physical science. But there are other focal nodes along this continuum whcih may be expressed as, "This bar is brown"; "It is sweet"; "It is good"; or just, "U-m-m-m" —the last an expression of something close to pure subjective feeling. I have arranged these sentences in an order beginning with the relatively objective and ending with the relatively subjective; but it is important that we see that each is a description of a portion of one continuous line, that each, if you please, is a selective rendition of an aspect of one rich, integrated experience.

These sentence types seem to be clearly though not sharply distinguishable. Their distinctiveness is a function, not simply of attentive focus, but, jointly with this, of a sort of natural bunching of characters along the axis. Obviously these bunchings are in part represented physiologically by our various sensory modalities; but even with these we have the feeling that at least a tenuous thread connects one modality with another. For instance, the passage from "This is sweet" to "This is brown" is felt not like the crossing of a gulf but more like a sliding along a line.

Regardless of the proper way of explaining physiologically or otherwise the felt continuum of such an experience I think it may be held that the various types of sentence used in connection with it share the function of description. Every expression from a sheer "U-m-m-m," a primitive or incomplete way of saying "I am pleased," to "Here is something" is a form of description. A simple exclamation of gustatory pleasure may be relatively difficult to test for truth value; the statement "This bar is larger than that one" may be more simply and directly tested; but the principle involved in the two extremes, and in all intermediate cases, is the same: a symbol arrangement claiming to represent accurately something beyond itself must be checked against what it allegedly represents to determine accuracy of representation. One sort of checking may involve indirection and inference, the other a relatively simple process of conventional manipulation and inspection; but there is no difference in principle between the truth test relevant to the various types of sentence used. So, a sentence which says, "I like X," is just as descriptive as one which reads, "Y is brown," or "X is larger than Y." If there can be a science of any area which yields to descriptive sentences, then, in principle, there can be a science of likes and dislikes, of approvals and disapprovals, of acceptances and rejections. Further, if such sentences as these, indicating as they do a degree of affective commitment to an object, may be termed *value* sentences, then there can be a science of value. Such would be a *descriptive* science consisting of tested propositions about men's valuings and would probably be considered a part of social psychology.

There are some students of value who would admit that such sentences as those just listed are descriptive but who would insist either that these are not *value* sentences at all or that they are not ones involving a certain especially important and distinctively axiological element of the total value experience. It makes no great difference how we denominate sentences expressive of likes, approvals, acceptances, and so on, except that there is some obligation on our part to stick to common language usage, which I believe myself to be following in this instance. In the absence of any weighty reason for violating convention I shall continue to denominate these as *value* sentences. The insistence of these students upon the presence of a further and distinctive value element, at least in certain kinds of value sentences, one that renders such sentences unamenable to ordinary processes of testing for truth value and hence one that makes them nonscientific sentences, deserves serious consideration.

For one school of thought the simple type of experience so far described is not a value experience but one of a more primitive sort, that of "taste." The sentence "I like apples" is thus an expression of "taste," not *value*. The additional element necessary to render this type of situation a value is the judgmental act of comparison. "I like apples" is not a value sentence, but "I prefer apples to pears" *is* such. As George Geiger puts it, "[the taste] x becomes a value after it has been chosen over taste y."[1]

The obvious objection to this proposal is that it violates common usage, which would call these more complex sentences *evaluative* or *preferential* rather than valuative. Although language terms are in a

[1] G. R. Geiger, "Values and Social Sciences," *Journal of Social Issues*, VI (1950), No. 4, 9.

sense arbitrary there is some compulsion to conform to the conventional, the penalty for refusal to do so being the danger of being misunderstood. Anyway, I see nothing to be gained by using *value* in this fashion; for the suggested advantage of thus being able to insist that values necessarily involve a rational, hence scientifically accountable, factor would be a victory by definition only. Moreover, if my earlier conclusions are sound the end Geiger seeks by this dubious definitional procedure is more properly attained simply by noting that a science of "tastes" is possible. If we can have a descriptive science of these elementary "tastes" or values then we can certainly have such of evaluations. We can test empirically these statements of preference. In fact descriptive psychology, by means of the rating scale technique, has already accumulated a considerable body of reliable data about preferences among human beings.

So far we have considered value situations and consequent descriptions only insofar as they involve a single person. Although there are such simple situations it must be admitted that most value situations are considerably more complex by reason of the inclusion of social factors. It is in the social context that some students find this further value element allegedly unamenable to scientific procedure.

This social dimension affects the value experience and its descriptions in various ways. The individual who likes a candy bar may note that others of his kind behave outwardly in the presence of one much as he does under similar circumstances; so he may come to say, "We like candy bars." If agreement in this matter is widespread, though not necessarily universal, he and most others of his kind may finally come to say, in a sort of shorthand fashion, "Candy bars are *good*." This gustatory "good," or equivalent, so used, is simply an expression of assumed or noted general agreement in liking. The objective form of sentence is a reflection of the tendency to celebrate general agreement by means of the type of expression customarily used with regard to the segments of the polar axis near the object pole, where general agreement is most frequent. As a summation of general agreement in liking, this type of sentence is still descriptive. It describes a liking, indicating further that men generally agree in this particular reaction. Being descriptive this type of sentence is subject to ordinary empirical tests, and hence, is scientific. It is probable that this summary function is operative in every general value statement of the form "x is good," "x is beautiful," "x is right,"

and so on. The portion of descriptive psychology mentioned earlier
would actually consist in such generalizations as these rather than
in statements only of the experience of this, that, or the other
individual.

But the addition of the social dimension to the individual axiological situation does more than simply to pluralize singular instances.
The social factor, in the form of opinion of others, may so operate as
to affect the intensity or even to change the direction of the value
component of the individual's experience. In effect, society is looking
over our shoulders down that same continuum, its value reactions so
merging with ours as to alter appreciably the character of our individual reactions. Usually, and within limits, the consciousness that
others feel about *x* as we do serves to *heighten*, and an awareness that
they disagree with us to *depress*, our feelings about that same object.
When the difference between the felt general attitude and our own
initial reaction is great, the values of the group tend to replace our
individual ones.

There are limits to the modifying power of this social factor, else
we should all value alike, which we do not. Native physiological
differences and contextual variations, including, among other things,
variations in the effectiveness of communication among us, constitute
individuating forces with respect to valuings. Furthermore—and this
difference is a part of the explanation of the rebel against current
social attitudes—individuals differ considerably in what they are
sensitive to as social opinion. They differ as to the breadth of the
group to whose opinion they react, some being sensitive only to the
attitudes of family and close friends while others respond to the
opinions of wide groups. They differ also as to the defining
character of such a group, being sensitive to the attitudes of some
types of associate and insensitive or even negative to those of others.
The social rebel is probably reacting partially in terms of the real
or anticipated approval of an uncommon or a relatively remote
group. These various differences in circumstance make for such
variety in socially influenced value attitude that we need never fear
drab uniformity in axiological perspective.

There is nothing in a sentence expressing a socially influenced
value experience to make it semantically different from those reflecting the simpler individual situation. There is a difference in the
total situation, of course; but this difference lies not in the verbal

rendition of the felt value experience, but in the external, causal nexus resulting in the type of valuing thus described. Therefore, such sentences, like those describing the valuings of the nonsocial situation, are empirically testable and hence eligible for inclusion in a descriptive science. But there *is* a factor in the social situation, which, should it ever occur as a functioning part of a value sentence, would constitute a radically different semantic element.

This situational factor is an imperative element, a pressure to conform both in outer behavior and in attitude to the standards of the other person or persons involved. Its primitive, sub-language form is overt action to the end of keeping the individual in contact with the herd and within the limits of behavioral patterns of survival value for the species concerned. As such overt action, this pressure is simply coercion; and coercion it remains on up through its various levels of complexity to the plane of speech itself. At the brute level the application of such coercive pressure may affect only outer behavior, achieving, perhaps, overt compliance but leaving untouched the relevant covert attitudes of the individual thus coerced. At the human level this pressure is often less directly, more subtly applied, and with the design of eliciting a deeper affective consonance within the group. The importance to the human race of such agreement in attitude lies in the superior reliability of a behavior pattern proceeding from internal rather than from merely external motivation.

By reason of structural similarities among members of a species making up a group and patterns of similarity among their experiential situations, a workable degree of behavioral and affective consonance is often achieved with little or no pressure. In situations where, for reasons aforementioned, this automatic agreement in attitude does not occur, and where such agreement is felt to be necessary, society may attempt to bring it about by one or the other of two ways. It may maneuver the recalcitrant individual into behaving as the pattern indicates, with the possible consequence of his discovering, contrary to his earlier belief, that he really does value the experiences to which he is thus being introduced. The most effective instrument for inducing this agreement in valuings, however, is not brute force or any kind of manipulation of behavior but the gentle persuasion of the almost universal tendency to do and be as the group desires and expects us. As indicated earlier, this deep appreciation of the approval of others usually so invades the individual situation as to deflect any divergent individual attitude in the direction of that of the group or even to cause the latter to supplant the original one.

This factor of "society looking over the shoulder of the individual" is present in the vast bulk of axiological situations as at least a potential coerciveness, the degree of its felt force varying from nearly zero under certain circumstances to one so great under others as to overwhelm the motive force of the strongest individual attitude. These variations in felt social pressure are a function of degree of agreement already achieved on the items involved and the importance for group efficiency of conformity in the area concerned. In matters upon which the individual already agrees with group opinion little or no force is felt; and in areas in which it is of relatively little importance that he agree, as for instance, in aesthetic taste, group pressure is light. But in instances in which individual and group valuings differ greatly, especially when these are in areas where experience has emphasized the superior need for conformity, as for example, in the matter of respect for truth and for human life, the felt force of public opinion is very strong.

These areas of strong social pressure, actually differing from most other axiological situations only in degree of pressure involved, are, nevertheless, usually set off from others under the name of *moral* situations. It should be noted that the adjective *moral* in such usage simply indicates that society is or seeks to be a causal factor in the determination of the character of any behavior involved, usually including valuings. It should be noted further that it is at least theoretically possible that this social pressure be operative only with respect to the *behavior* of the individual target of that pressure. Our concern in this study is not, however, with this last type of situation but rather with one in which moral pressure is being exerted upon *valuings*. And, we must keep in mind that it is, again, at least theoretically possible—I am sure, *actually* the case—that there be axiological situations which are, for practical purposes, completely uninfluenced by this social factor, hence ones not at all "moral." We may, therefore, distinguish the moral factor rather sharply from the axiological, even though we must recognize that in some degree it invades and influences the great bulk of value situations. We must not take the common phrase "moral values" to mean a type of values completely set off from all others by reason of some initially different generative force. They are, rather, those originally individual human valuings that have proved to be of general concern, which, however greatly smoothed off through social compromise or expanded through group application, remain the valuings of individuals. So, though the moral factor may operate upon and influence the affective attitudes of men, it is over and above, independent of, and, in a sense, external to them. Finally, we must conclude that sentences expressing such socially influenced valuings, as could be the case with "I approve of peace," are simple descriptions, just like individual ones, and as is the case with them, subject to empirical verification.

So far we have dealt with this imperative factor only as it occurs at the sub-language level of experience, where it constitutes no semantic problem. The moment it makes its appearance in sentences, however, it becomes an object of semantic concern. There is one type of such appearance which may be disposed of rather shortly. From the viewpoint of the recipient of such social pressure this factor is simply one fact among others of this experience and may thus become a component of ordinary descriptive sentences, for example, "I feel obliged to do so and so," or "to try to appreciate such and such." Such sentences are certainly amenable to empirical testing.

The imperative element may appear in a sentence "in person," so to speak, not as part of a simple description but as a symbol functioning as an operator. Such an operator may be directed to behavior, as in an imperative of the type, "Johnny, eat your spinach," which is functionally quite different from "Johnny is eating his spinach." The latter is, in Wittgensteinian language, a "picture" of a portion of the world, a picture sketched for us by the producer of the sentence. For the reason that "pictures" may be more or less accurate renditions of their intended objects we may test the truth-value of assertions which proffer them by comparing the picture with the pictured. Such is not the case with the imperative form. It is not an assertion of a fact, the presentation of a certified picture of a portion of the world, but an order, a directive with regard to behavior. It is in function, therefore, not a picturing but a pushing or a pulling; and we do not test pushings or pullings for degree of resemblance to something. Commands are, thus, not "scientific sentences."

Theoretically we could have simple axiological imperatives. Just as we say, "Johnny, *eat* your spinach," we could say, "Johnny, *like* your spinach." Occasionally a parent in complete exasperation may actually speak in some such fashion, but the hopelessness of this type of approach to the modification of the valuings basic to voluntary behavior is soon apparent. Backing up the mother's order to *eat* the spinach is her ability so to manipulate the fork and arm of the boy as to cause him to consume the food, but there is no such possibility of direct enforcement of an order to *like* spinach.

Does the impossibility of using verbal commands in the modification of individual valuings rule out as ineffectual in this regard any and all forms of imperative behavior? I think not. We know, as already indicated, that the individual is influenced in his axiological tendencies by group attitudes felt as pressure, and we know that human beings can and do so manipulate situational elements as to make this pressure operative. In doing so they are attempting, often successfully, to accomplish in an indirect way what they cannot do by means of direct command. This indirect means of influencing valuings may be carried out wholly in terms of nonverbal behavior. Simply through the "language of action" a group may advertise its value attitudes and so indirectly affect those of the individual. Our concern, however, is with those modificatory situations in which verbal structures have a role.

There is a way of influencing valuings through the use of value sentences without any *verbal* suggestion of coercion. For example, Johnny's mother may say, "*I* like spinach," and thus, by reason of the son's desire to be like Mother, influence his affective reaction to spinach, without any attempted overt application or even any mention of coercion. The situation is not, however, devoid of an imperative factor. In this instance it lies outside the verbal structure, operating as a contextual adjunct of it but not as an element in it. In spite of the fact that such a sentence is functioning as an element in a wider, partly nonverbal structure which *is* intentionally manipulatory with regard to valuings, it is, just as a sentence, purely descriptive.

But the mother may, in our sample situation, be somewhat more direct than just indicated and yet not so direct as in an axiological imperative. She may say, "Johnny, you *ought* to like your spinach; Mother likes it; and you want to be like Mother." In this manner of speaking she is, as in the previously described instance, utilizing an instrumentality already internally influential with regard to Johnny's overt behavior and valuings, namely his desire to be like

Mother. She is here, however, raising the whole contextual adjunct to the level of language: the boy's assumed desire to be like his mother and in the *ought*, as we shall see later, a verbal reference to a coercive context. Note that the source of this indicated coerciveness lies not in the mother but in something presumably already present in the boy. The mother's language merely triggers this potentially imperative factor. Discourse which seeks to modify behavior or valuings in this indirect way is spoken of as persuasive or hortatory; and if our analysis is so far correct, it is the only type of imperative we may expect to be effective in the modification of valuings.

The source of coerciveness in all instances of the hortative situation, whether it be action or valuings which we seek to control, is some already functioning internal affective factor. Such situations may be subdivided in a roughly dichotomous fashion into those in which this internal affective urge is moral, that is, ones in which the individual is being persuaded through his desire to live in accord with the desires and expectations of others, perhaps as summarized in a moral code, and those in which the inner urgency thus being utilized is a desire to obtain some state or object other than social approval. The two types of persuasion may be illustrated as follows: "Johnny, you ought to eat your spinach; see, Mother does"; and, "Johnny, you ought to eat your spinach so you can go play." Both types are commonly used in our attempts to control action; but only rarely do we try the second as a means of influencing valuings, probably because only a powerful, pervasive urge, such as is the moral one, is efficacious in modifying another urge, and the desire of most ordinary ends is not this strong. In the case of actions there is always present in the background, for possible use as a reinforcing factor, direct behavioral manipulation, an aid we cannot call upon in our attempts to influence valuings.

Occasionally the hortative sentence may appear without any verbal indication of the reason for the described behavior, as in "Johnny, you *ought* to like spinach." Such sentences I believe always to be elliptical. The speaker is saying that some unspecified factor is here coercive. If Johnny, when thus addressed, should ask "Why?" the speaker would be expected to complete the exhortation by mentioning some supporting reason. This being so it follows that all hortative sentences, moral or not, are a special case of means-ends sentences. In fact, they are sentences so presenting a set of means-ends relations as to modify in the intended direction the affective or behavioral reactions of the person to whom they are addressed. Specifically, they are sentences which assert that a given reaction or course of action is a means to an end to which the person addressed is already committed. Thus for the person doing the persuading the other person's attachment to a given end serves as a tool or instrument whereby the persuader may maneuver this other person into accepting some desired attitude or action.

All value sentences previously discussed, with the exception of the axiological command, which is probably always ineffectual and seldom or never seriously employed, have been found to be descriptive and hence empirically testable. Now what of the hortative sentences that seek to influence valuings? To many people they seem to fall somewhere between simple descriptive sentences and commands, which are admittedly nondescriptive in function. Their grammatical form is the same as that of the descriptive type, yet their function seems to be at least partly imperative.

As asserted earlier, the hortative sentence always includes, either explicitly or implicitly, supporting reasons for the assertion made in the initial "ought" clause. At least these supporting clauses are descriptive, for example, "Mother likes spinach, and you want to be like Mother." They are descriptions of two simple valuing situations and are, thus, subject to empirical tests. But what of the crucial clause, "You *ought* to like spinach"? We have already noted that there seems to be a difference between such a sentence and one which reads, "You are eating spinach." The latter is obviously a "picture" of a portion of the world, hence purely descriptive in function, just as obviously the former is persuasive in function; but—and this is important—this fact does not preclude its being descriptive also.

A possible answer to the question as to the status of the hortative sentence is that it is both descriptive and persuasive. Sentences that are descriptive in their first-level functioning may be used for various second-level purposes. For example, a sentence describing the rich aroma of a cup of coffee may be used by an advertiser to persuade a reader to go out and buy some coffee. In such a case one person is constructing a picture of a portion of the world, a picture that may be tested for truth value. However, he is using the picture not simply to convey information but, beyond this primary function, to modify the attitudes or behavior of another through the natural affectiveness of the situation pictured. Although this single sentence is both descriptive and persuasive, no functional conflict is involved because the two functions occur at different contextual levels. A sentence so used may contain no internal sign of the second-level role it is playing, the indication that it has a hortative function lying in the wider context that includes the speaker, his accompanying behavior, and intentions, as well as the affective tendencies of the receiver. We have already noted that purely descriptive axiological sentences may have these persuasive effects by reason of non-verbalized contextual adjuncts. Our present question is: May we treat an "ought" sentence as such a purely descriptive construction used persuasively?

The apparent objection to this solution is that the verb "ought" has no obvious nonlanguage referent. In such a sentence as, "Johnny *eats* spinach," the symbol for the verb has an observable action as its intended object; but this seems not so in the case of the "ought" in "Johnny *ought* to eat spinach." If this latter is a descriptive sentence, a "picture," the verbal element must refer to something "in the world." There are two difficulties here: (a) What is "the world" in this case? and (b) To what factor in this "world" does the *ought* refer? First, we must recognize that "the world" is not restricted to what can be sensibly observed or physically manipulated. In an "ought" sentence "the world" includes, besides the ordinary sensible constituents, the so-called ideal factors of intentions, anticipations, expectations, standards, codes, and so forth. An investigation of the root meaning of "ought" may give us a suggestion as to the nature of its contemporary referent in this broad, inclusive "world." The word comes from a Middle English verb meaning "to owe," "to be indebted to," "to be under obligation to restore, pay, or render." Apparently it was initially used to symbolize the pressure factor in a concrete debt situation. What we have done is to retain this symbol to render the less concrete, the more ideal form of obligatory force investing situations in which some standard is operating as a partial determiner of attitude or behavior.

When we say that Johnny *ought* to eat his spinach we mean that he is under obligation to eat it. Like the debtor of old he is an element in a situation an integral part of which is a standard which tends to pervade and to determine the structural pattern of its context, including the behavior of the person involved. For the debtor

of the root situation that coercive standard is an agreement to which
he and the lender are parties; for Johnny it is social opinion, perhaps
in the limited sense of the wishes or expectations of one person, of
a few such, or of the Deity, expressed, possibly, in the form of an
ideal or a code and given force by reason of Johnny's fundamental
desire to achieve social approval. All this, I believe, is the referent
of the "ought" in a hortative sentence. Verbs as well as nouns may
be abstract and just as an abstract noun may appear in a sentence
without benefit of a simple referent so may it be with a verb. In
short, we need not look for an observable or simple "ought" in the
hortative situation. The referent of this verb is a situation, a certain
type of situation, a sort of field of force in which a person is subject
to the structuring tendencies of a social norm. An axiological exhortation is, therefore, at its first level of functioning, factual, informative, descriptive, and scientific.

To test such a sentence we should have to determine whether or
not the person mentioned is, in attitude, actually subject to this
coercive pattern, and also, of course, whether or not the pattern
involved is as described or even in existence at all. To test the truth
value of the sentence "Johnny ought to like spinach," we should
have to determine whether or not there exists a coercive context for
liking spinach and if Johnny is at present a part of it. If, as suggested
in an earlier paragraph, this sentence may be expanded to include
the reasons there indicated for the initial clause, this test would
attempt to discover if Johnny has a coercive urge to be like Mother
and if Mother does in fact like spinach.

But what of the admittedly imperative aspects of these exhorta-
tions? The direct imperative or command is so constituted that the
coercive element appears, in person, so to speak, in the sentence
itself. It is not a description used indirectly to coerce, but a symbolic push or pull. You cannot confirm or disconfirm pushes or pulls;
you simply experience them. The hortative sentence contains no such
coercive element within the picture itself. The nudge or tug of the
exhortation is external to the "picture"; it operates in the broad
context of which the "picture" is a part, through contextual associates
of the "picture" rather than through elements present in it. The
"picture" in the exhortation serves to remind the person to whom
it is presented of a coercive force operative on him; the "picture"
does not itself coerce; the coercion is accomplished by the sug-

gested situation as held in the memory of the person concerned.

In addition to this coercive force which is triggered by the description carried in an exhortation there is the desire or expectation of the speaker as sensed by the person spoken to. The speaker is felt to be using the exhortation purposely to influence our reactions; so, again, by reason of our desire for approval of others, including the speaker, we feel the force of his attitude added to that of whatever portion of society may be suggested in the description itself. This force, also, is outside or external to the "picture" of the sentence. It is another part of the contextual adjunct. Neither this nor the force aroused or triggered by the picture itself, as a nudge or a tug in the direction of a certain pattern of reaction, is subject to empirical test. All this means is that a hortative sentence in its second level function of persuasion cannot be confirmed or disconfirmed; this level must simply be observed.

What are the implications of this total analysis with regard to the central problem of the possibility of a science of values? I have argued that this may be put in the form of a question as to the possibility of rendering value sentences as descriptions. If this way of putting the problem is correct then my conclusion is that we not only may have an axiological science but that we already do have at least the rudiments of such. Let us summarize: The basic form of value sentence is one expressing the affective reaction of the speaker to some object, for example, "I like spinach." This is a simple assertion of fact subject to empirical test. Extended through analogical procedures and pluralized so as to include the valuings of others, such sentences become, "People like spinach," or "Spinach is good." Though the necessary verificatory techniques are more complex for such sentences they remain essentially empirical and testable. Evaluative sentences, ones asserting comparative valuings, introduce no new principle insofar as testing procedures are concerned. It is not difficult to test sentences reporting that spinach is better than chard. Psychologists, using the rating scale technique, have successfully accumulated considerable data on human preferences. Even when the social dimension is added to our initial, oversimplified value situation no problem is created in the matter of testing the resulting value sentences. A socially influenced valuing is reported in sentences structurally and functionally identical with the ones reporting on those of a simple individual situation. All of this holds regardless of the type of valuing involved, the so-called moral values differing from aesthetic and other values only in the degree of importance of general agreement in their resultant behavior patterns.

We have spent considerable time in the analysis of hortative discourse because it is often held that hortative value sentences contain an essentially unverifiable element and hence are not subject to scientific testing. We have found them to be descriptive in their basic-level functioning and consequently amenable to scientific treatment. It must be emphasized, however, that though an exhortation may be an attempt to influence the valuing act and may stem from a set of values in the mind of the exhorter it is, as a form of discourse, logically independent of valuings. You can have a study or even a science of valuings without anything more than an incidental mentioning of persuasion. Exhortation may be a way of dealing with valuings, but it is not itself a valuing.

But, someone may object, the type of value science herein suggested can yield nothing but a set of generalizations as to how people do value and evaluate aspects of experience whereas it is the very essence of a value system that it tell us how people *should* value or evaluate things. How can a description of what men do ever be considered normative? If you grant two supportable hypotheses, functioning in this area roughly as does the assumption of the uniformity of nature for the natural sciences, namely, that human beings are similar in nature and that widespread and long term agreements in this field are at least fair approximations to satisfactory choices, an individual may even expect to be able to direct his own behavior fairly successfully in terms of such generalizations. In fact, I believe that this is just what men do more or less consciously insofar as they pattern their living, including their valuings, after the mores of the group; and they do not do too badly in so acting so long as they stick to broad generalities and so long as conditions are not appreciably different from those of ages gone by. This means that in broad outlines what is or has been in regard to human valuings may be a justified set of guiding principles.

In terms of this view both actual and ideal valuings are human in origin. This is a thoroughgoing naturalism but not a vicious relativism, for though it ties values to the human situation it does not contend that they are relative to the individual. Human likings and preferences are not individually arbitrary or transitory. They are what they are because man's structure is what it is and that of the world in which he lives is what it is. Such a theory is, therefore, a modest sort of naturalism, one that does not rule out the possibility that all that man and nature are may be the responsibility of something beyond both. It simply says that insofar as anything like scientific knowledge is concerned—and this holds likewise of physics, astronomy or any other natural science—men must be content at this level with a system of values whose justification, if you please, lies in the fact that its constituents necessarily follow from the structure of the universe, of which the structure of man is an integral part.

This view may be charged with being a rationalization of conservatism in that it emphasizes the dependence of the individual upon the group and of any specific group upon the past insofar as valuings are concerned. No such defense of ordinary conservatism is intended. The appearance of being such a defense is a function of omission of a discussion of the nature and role of the rebel and the pioneer in axiological areas. It is certainly possible for progress in valuing and evaluating to take place, just as it is still possible for man to make progress in the field of an established science though he knows full well that everything he will learn in the future will probably be consistent with and actually built upon the broad structures already erected by others. This view is not incompatible with those so-called "process philosophies" which see creation ever going on, particularly at the point of human invention. A full account of the value experience would include a discussion of man's ability to discover, create, or otherwise expand the value possibilities in human living. Space limitations permit me to say here only that such a discussion would center about the origin, nature, and function of ideals in experience.

A criticism voiced by one colleague in this study is that this treatment of values could be strengthened by the inclusion of a definition of "value." I have purposely omitted such a definition because I do not believe there is any object called "value." Although I have occasionally lapsed into the language of those who believe in a substantive value, I have intentionally spoken, for the most part, in terms of a "valuing situation." With this sort of language I expected to convey the twin beliefs that the value experience is basically verbal in character and that the referent of much of our value terminology is the total situation rather than any simple element in it.

There is a sense in which we *can* define such high-level abstractions as "value," but it is not the traditional one in which we equate a simple term with an analytically complex one describing the location of the definiendum in a classification scheme. The sense I have in mind is a kind of clarifying process in terms of which we may show, through a combination of genetic and functional explanation, the how and why of a term's usage. Such a clarification of the meaning of the term "value" would go somewhat as follows. The situation with regard to which value terminology is relevant is that in which an organism for our purposes *man*, is responding affectively to some object. The first-level linguistic rendition of this experience is in terms of such sentences as, "I like (or dislike), approve (or disapprove), enjoy (or find not enjoyable) this object." The verbal element of this type of sentence has been generalized in terms of the one verb, "value," so that we can say, generally, "A *values* x." The adjective form of the verb "to value" is secondary, derivative, and is used to characterize an object of the valuing act, as in the sentence, "X is a valuable object." Men usually mean by this type of sentence to say not only that A values x but that generally, or perhaps in accordance with a norm, men value x.

The genesis of the noun form of the value terminology can best be understood in terms of an example of nominalization that is closer to first-level verbalization. For instance, we speak of men having "freedom" when we are thinking, not of some distinguishable simple character like height or weight, but of a sort of character of characters or character of a complex of first-order characters. First we say that a man is "free," in this, that, or another circumstance. By his being free we mean that he can behave in certain specifiable ways without restriction. Then, desiring to single out for attention and for communication this character of being without restraint (an aspect of an organic situation), we turn the adjective into a noun. We do the same sort of thing for verbs. The nominalization of what are primarily adjectival or verbal aspects of situations is the linguistic equivalent of turning the spotlight of attention on such aspects. Doing this does not change the status of an adjectival or verbal aspect; it does not create a first-level substantive object where before there was only an adjectival or verbal factor; it merely singles out such for attention and communication.

So it is with the noun "value." I take its use to be our way of signaling a certain type of situation, one whose defining character is a specifiable verbal appearance. It is not meant to refer to some distinguishable object or element in the first order experience. There is no "value" in the sense in which there may well be an apple in a valuing situation. If we insist that defining means equating then I should equate a *sentence* in which the term "value" appears with another sentence. For example, I should say that the sentence "Equality is a value" may roughly be equated with "Men like or find desirable a certain degree of sameness in participation in human affairs." Acceptance of these conclusions does not entail the elimination of the term "value" from sophisticated usage. It means that as a form of symbolic ellipsis it should be used wherever such shorthand saves us more in effort than it loses us in ambiguity. We should, however, always use such ellipses with the primarily verbal equivalence uppermost in mind and never in such a way as to suggest that the noun form refers to some element of the basic situation, to some thin earthly essence pervading the total context, or to a heavenly Idea hovering over it.[2]

[2] For the Comments and Response which relate to this paper see pp. 261-67, 365-66, and 376-77, below.

THE LANGUAGES OF SIGN THEORY
AND VALUE THEORY[1]

EDWARD SCHOUTEN ROBINSON

ANY ATTEMPT to study the language of value theory is bound to raise many problems. Among them are two which I shall consider in this paper: (a) How does the language of value theory differ from other kinds of language? (b) How is it related to the language of sign theory? I shall not attempt to answer these questions with equal thoroughness. I feel that the term "value theory" is rather loosely used at present; and while a number of definitions have been proposed, I doubt whether any of them is widely enough accepted to be taken as standard. It is not my intention to provide a new definition in any final form, still less to show *precisely* how the language of value theory does differ from other languages. Indeed, I think that the expression "value theory," like the expressions "science," "philosophy," "logic," and many others, is far more useful if we respect its vagueness and allow it to remain vague. I shall, however, provide a rough classification of what I choose to call "value-theoretical terms." This will enable me to point out some of the ways in which I think the language of value theory may differ from other languages; it will also indicate roughly and partially how I intend to use the term "value theory" and how I think that term is generally used today. I hope, of course, that my own usage coincides with the most general usage, but if my guess is wrong, I shall not be seriously distressed.

The question of how the language of value theory is related to that of sign theory raises the further problem of how the term "sign theory" is defined. Very likely there is no more unanimity here than in the case of "value theory." But ever since Charles Morris published

---

[1] An abbreviated early version of this paper was presented before the Southwestern Philosophical Conference as the address of the president for 1952. A more expanded version was presented before the First New Zealand Philosophical Congress in May, 1953.

his pamphlet *Foundations of the Theory of Signs*,[2] it has been fairly customary to think of sign theory, or semiotic, as involving three branches of study which may be labeled with his now familiar terms —"semantics," "syntactics," and "pragmatics." Not all writers are willing to use these terms in this way, and those who have used them, including Morris himself, have vacillated considerably in deciding precisely how they should be defined and how the fields of investigation corresponding to them are related. But most of the studies which I like to think of as included in sign theory fall within these three fields, whether we delimit them according to Morris's earlier or later versions or according to those which Carnap has proposed. Morris's own later work in *Signs, Language, and Behavior*,[3] remains perhaps the richest, maturest, and best-informed contribution to sign theory in all the theory's long history, even if it may not be the most original or the most rigorous; it will probably be taken as a point of departure for other contributions for some years to come. I shall accordingly approach the general question of how the language of sign theory is related to that of value theory by considering the terminology which Morris has there proposed. This will certainly not provide a final answer to the general question; but it will raise several issues which other students should consider, and this is as much as I can hope to do at present.

I

To return to my first problem, I believe that if we were to make an inventory of writings which might plausibly be counted as contributions to "value theory," we should find in them a number of words and other expressions which might be classified as falling into a few roughly distinguishable groups. I shall present a number of examples for each group, and provide each group with a name, which will thus be ostensively defined; I shall then adopt the general

[2] C. Morris, "Foundations of the Theory of Signs," in *International Encyclopedia of Unified Science* (Chicago, 1938), Vol. I, No. 2. Excerpts from this source are reprinted in this Essay by permission of the University of Chicago Press, publishers. I am extremely indebted to Morris not only for the great stimulation I have received from his writings, but also for his penetrating criticisms of an earlier version of the present Essay.

[3] C. Morris, *Signs, Language, and Behavior* (New York, 1946). Excerpts from this book are reprinted in this Essay by permission of Prentice-Hall, Inc., publishers.

expression "value-theoretical term" as characterizing the entire class of which these groups are subclasses. I shall approach the definition of "value theory" by making some suggestions as to the role which value-theoretical terms may play in the language of value theory, and shall answer my first question to this extent, and to this extent only. The rest of the paper will be largely devoted to studying the role which value-theoretical terms have played in the language of Morris's book and to considering the bearings which a system such as Morris's may have upon value theory as a whole.

I am not sure just what it takes for a term to deserve the title of *value-theoretical*, but I suggest that membership in any of certain subclasses should be sufficient, though I am not sure that my list of subclasses is complete enough. First we have what I shall call (1.1) *valuative* terms, and these may be of either (1.11) *relatively high* or (1.12) *relatively low generality*. Among those of higher generality are such words as "good," "bad," "right," "wrong," "valuable," "valueless," "worthy," "worthless," "optimal," "praiseworthy," and "blameworthy." I must add, however, that while each of these terms is a valuative term in some of its senses, it is not necessarily valuative in all of its senses, and that for reasons which I shall specify later, I hesitate to tell what these critical senses are. Among the valuative terms of relatively low generality will be such words as "beautiful," "ugly," "just," "unjust," "tasteful," "tasteless," "virtuous," "vicious," "kind," "cruel," "honorable," "dishonorable," "harmless," "harmful," "brave," "cowardly," and so forth. Obviously the generality of valuative terms may vary considerably in degree.

Next there are terms which I shall call (1.2) *motivational*, and which I shall divide into four main subclasses. First there are (1.21) *affective* terms, such as "pleasure," "displeasure," "pain," "embarrassment," "shame," "enjoyment," "admiration," "fear," "love," "anger," "worry," "anxiety," "despair," "preference," "sympathy," "antipathy," and so on. Then there are (1.22) *conative* terms, such as "motive," "drive," "instinct," "interest," "appetite," "will," "volition," "willingness," "want," "desire," "avoidance," "conscience," "superego," "id," "libido," "appraise," "prize," "assess," "like," "dislike," "accept," "reject," "approve," "disapprove," and the like. Thirdly, there are (1.23) *telic* terms, such as "goal," "goal-gradient," "valence," "requiredness," "object of interest," "final cause," "purpose," "object of choice." And fourthly, there are (1.24) *teleutic* terms, such as "satisfy,"

"achieve," "attain," "succeed," "fail," "fall short of," "fulfill," and
"gratify."

Obviously these classes may be further subdivided in many interesting ways. It should be noticed, for instance, that while most
affective terms represent enduring psychological states, many can
indicate occurrents in W. E. Johnson's sense; moreover, while some
of the enduring states may be dispositional, this is not always the
case. Many of the conative terms represent enduring dispositions;
some, however, may represent nondispositional enduring states (for
example, "avoidance") or even occurrents. Whether telic and teleutic
terms can be similarly divided is not so clear. But as many motivational terms can be used in all three ways, I have not attempted a
further breakdown.

In addition to valuative and motivational terms, there are some
which at present I can do no better than to lump together as (1.3)
nomological—for example, "law," "precept," "command," "authority,"
"legislative," "social pressure," "permitted," "permissible," "forbidden,"
"tabu." These nomological terms are presumably those which some
other writers have classified as "sociological." However, I prefer the
term "nomological" so as to be able to include terms describing commands and pressures which one gives to oneself as well as commands
which one gives to others or receives from others. Here, too, we may
distinguish many subvarieties.

It should be clear by this time that my classification is a bad one,
perhaps a very bad one. This is one of the most important things
about it, as we shall see later. In the first place, it is not properly
representative even for my own purposes. I have, for instance, overloaded my list of valuative terms with adjectives and my list of
motivational terms with nouns and verbs. This is largely an accidental product of my own associational habits. It would not be hard
to extend all these lists by including cognate expressions in other
parts of speech, and my present listings are not intended to preclude
such extensions. But if this is a flaw, it is a trivial one compared
with others. I have already pointed out that my classification is not
exhaustive, for I have left open the possibility that other subclasses
should be included.[4] It also fails to satisfy the traditional rule that

---

[4] Professor William Anderson of the Auckland University College has called my
attention to my failure to give a special place in this list to expletives. I am inclined
to believe that the only kinds of expletives which should be classed as value-

subdivisions should be mutually exclusive; for many of the words I
have listed are ambiguous enough to warrant placing them simultaneously in more than one subdivision, and many are so vague as to
defy exact classification. Furthermore, the very headings which I
have used these examples to "define" are themselves vague and
ambiguous, like any terms for which only ostensive definitions are
given; and there are many words which indisputably play an important role in value theory but which can be interpreted in so many
ways that it is not at all clear where we should put them. Sometimes
this is because we can find various distinguishable senses which fall
under different headings rather clearly; in other cases it is not at all
obvious that we are dealing with different senses; we seem rather to
be dealing with different interpretations of what purports to be the
same sense. It is not always easy to keep these distinguished. For
instance, such words as "instrumental," "means," "expedient," might
be counted as valuative terms of rather high generality, as telic terms,
or even as teleutic terms. "Right," as is well known, may be either
valuative or nomological. The adjective "perfect" is normally a
valuative term nowadays, but there was a time when it was properly
teleutic, and it still has its telic uses. (The verb "perfect" seems unmistakably teleutic.) "Desirable" may be either telic, affective, or
simply valuative, or perhaps even conative, depending on how one
chooses to analyze it. "End" and "aim" have significations which I
would not care to call value-theoretical at all, but they also have
their telic, conative, and even valuative uses. The word "need" has
all these uses, and can also be used affectively. "Ought" perhaps
started as a nomological term, as Nietzsche has suggested,[5] but it
soon became telic as well and can also be used valuatively or even
teleutically. Whether it has any uses which fall outside my classification is a matter over which there may well be controversy. The

theoretical terms are either valuative or motivational terms, and that most of those
to which other writers have devoted special consideration in this context are
valuative terms. But there is room for controversy about this. Even if we should
decide that all relevant expletives are valuative or motivational, they may well
belong in a very important subclass of their own and deserve special treatment.

[5] For Nietzsche's treatment of "ought" see his *Genealogy of Morals*, Book II, § 4.
I am reluctant to assign "ought" the special status which Garnett has given it in the
paper he has contributed to this volume (see p. 122 below). Accordingly I have
provided no subclass for what he would call "normative terms," even though it is
quite possible that they are entitled to one.

word "value" itself is especially rich in its meanings; I am convinced that it has at least one distinguishable sense in each of my subdivisions and probably as many distinct interpretations. This is one of the reasons why I am willing to call all these terms value-theoretical and why, for instance, I do not like to think of value theory as confined to the analysis of valuative terms.

On the other hand, few, if any, of these terms are peculiar to value theory. Many of them turn up constantly in our everyday conversation, especially when we might be said to be expressing *value judgments* like "Lemons give me pleasure," "Stealing is wrong," "I like cookies," "We aim to please." Though valuative terms are perhaps those most likely to turn up in expressing value judgments, they have no monopoly, and value judgments can be expressed quite effectively with terms from my other groups. Value judgments are certainly an important part of the subject matter for value theory, and I am sure that value theories sometimes take the form of genuine value judgments; but this does not mean that the class of value judgments coincides with value theory as such. One important point of difference is that while value-theoretical terms such as we have mentioned are often *used* in value judgments, they are often *mentioned* in value theories and subjected to some sort of semiotical analysis. This by no means gives us a sharp criterion for distinguishing between value theories and value judgments; but it does give us a convenient rule of thumb for making some such distinctions.

It is important to notice that these value-theoretical terms also have a way of turning up in other sciences, such as psychology, sociology, economics, and jurisprudence. These sciences are certainly not as free from value judgments as some writers like to think, and all of them are concerned rather often with the analysis of value judgments and the interpretation of value-theoretical terms. I believe, however, that one of the principal differences between value theory and these other sciences is that in value theory the semiotical study of value-theoretical terms is a *major* concern, and that in the works of some writers (though surely not in all) it is even *the* major concern, while in other sciences it is seldom more than incidental at best. This does not mean that value theory cannot play a part in the other sciences. I believe that important portions of sociology, psychology, jurisprudence, economics, and political science are strictly value-theoretical, and that it is a preposterous abstraction to think of value theory as the private preserve of philosophy teachers. Surely this is a region where disciplines overlap and where it is absurd to dispute about priority rights.

But even if we recognize this overlapping, we can still maintain that the language of value theory *as such* is at least in part distinguishable from the languages of these other sciences *as such*, not in that they use distinct vocabularies, but in that certain words common to both vocabularies are not used with the same frequency; we can say much the same for the distinction between value theories and value judgments. And I think that there are several kinds of value-theoretical terms not included in my earlier listings which occur with much greater frequency in value theories than in value judgments, in value theory than in the other overlapping sciences, and in the value-theoretical portions of those sciences than in their non-value-theoretical residues. First there are (2.1) the *names* of the value-theoretical terms already classified. To provide examples one need only put quotation marks around any of the words in my previous lists (just as I have done above) or adopt some similar device. Then there are (2.2) certain specialized semiotical terms which may be used to describe other value-theoretical terms. My own terms "valuative term," "motivational term," "conative term" are examples; so are Garnett's "normative term," Morris's "incitive use," "prescriptive mode," "appraisive mode," Hare's "neustic," and the term "imperative" in some of its senses.[6] While terms from groups 2.1 and 2.2 will most often be *used* in value theory, they will also be mentioned and discussed, just as they are in this Essay; and this can happen in the value-theoretical portions of the other sciences too. Our classification must therefore include (3.1 and 3.2) the names of the terms of Groups 2.1 and 2.2; these names are semiotical value-theoretical terms on a higher level, and it is obvious that this hierarchy may be extended indefinitely. There is clearly such a thing as semiotical value theory,

---

[6] For Morris's terms, see *Signs, Language, and Behavior*, Glossary, *s.v.* For Garnett's, see p. 122, below. For Hare's "neustic" see his *The Language of Morals* (London, 1952), p. 18. While the term "imperative" as used by contemporary writers in this field is perhaps most often a semiotical term, it is frequently used as a nomological term. In the philosophy of Kant it is probably best interpreted as telic or conative, though I am not sure which. Whether neustic expressions in Hare's sense deserve a special place in my classification as a subdivision of Group 1 is by no means clear; I am inclined to look upon them as nomological. The term "neustic" itself is unmistakably semiotical.

and this itself can have many levels, which in turn are higher levels of value theory as a whole. On the first level of value theory we find terms from Group 1 but not from the higher groups. On the second level of value theory, which is the lowest level of semiotical value theory, terms from Group 2 are used to mention or describe terms from Group 1. On the third level of value theory, which is the second level of semiotical value theory, terms from Group 3 are used to mention or describe terms from Group 2. Probably value theory need not go much further up the hierarchical ladder than this, but it is important to recognize that it must go at least this far.[7]

In pointing out this hierarchical structure I have no illusion that I have provided an adequate basis for distinguishing sharply between value theory and the other sciences or between their value-theoretical and their non-value-theoretical portions, or even between value theories and value judgments; but I think it will *help* us in making these distinctions. At any rate it has enabled me to show, after a fashion, how I am using the expression "semiotical value theory," and to indicate that where semiotical value theory is present I am willing to say that value theory itself is present too, even if we should sometimes find it in one of the so-called "sciences" rather than in what university catalogues call "philosophy." But the presence of semiotical value theory is only a sufficient condition for the presence of value theory and not a necessary condition, and the nature of value theory as such deserves further consideration.

First, however, I want to call attention again to the difficult problem of the relations between value theory and value judgments. One might suppose that all value judgments are confined to what I have called the first level and enter into value theory only as its

---

[7] It might be tempting to suggest that such words as "ethics" and "morals" are definable as referring to bodies of value judgments involving terms from Group 1 but none from the higher groups. I feel, however, that this would be out of line with most present usage. Surely the average textbook in "ethics" includes a great deal of what I should call "value theory" and will utilize terms from the higher levels, while many first-level value judgments (for instance, most aesthetic ones) will not be called "ethical" at all. Of course when we speak of a man's "morals" or the "morals" of a tribe or community, we probably are referring to bodies of first-level value judgments, though not to *all* the man's value judgments or to *all* the value judgments which occur in the community; but when we venture into "morals" as a field of research, we almost certainly will find ourselves employing terms from Group 2 even if we make first-level value judgments our primary object of study and take pains to avoid using terms from Group 3 and the higher groups.

subject matter, never as value theories in any proper sense. This, I think, would be a mistake. Clearly one can say such things as "Conative terms are more useful than teleutic terms," or "The word 'imperative' is pleasanter than the word 'threat,'" though probably one will not do this sort of thing very often. I think it is plausible to say that both these sentences express value judgments, but value judgments on the *second* level; I should also like to classify them as semiotical value theories, minor ones, to be sure, but theories nonetheless. If so, we must concede that value judgments are not confined to the first level and that value judgments and value theories can overlap. On the other hand, it is obvious that there are many value judgments which neither I nor anyone else would care to describe as value theories or even as theories at all, and that this is the case with most of our first-level value judgments about ordinary things, experiences, processes, occurrences, dispositions, and states, and even certain classes of these. I think that when one says, "I like cookies," or, "Stealing is wrong," or, "My hunger is not yet satisfied," one is usually expressing a value judgment but hardly a value theory, in spite of the fact that each of these sentences employs some value-theoretical expression from my first group. Furthermore, there are many sentences involving terms from Group I which can hardly be said to express either value judgments or value theories: for instance, "John seldom obtains the kind of food he likes" or "Rats motivated by hunger will not cross an electric grid as frequently as rats motivated by thirst" or "If Helen's maternal instinct is not gratified, she may not find married life as pleasant as she expects." This is not to say that these sentences might not be called "theoretical" in a good sense; at least one can make out a case for calling them "theories about value judgments." I feel, however, that nobody would be likely to call them "theories of value" or even "theories about value," and I would hesitate long before calling them value-theoretical at all. Certainly these would not normally be counted as value judgments either. On the other hand, there are many first-level statements which might plausibly be called value-theoretical or theories about values, even if one would hardly call them theories of value: for instance, "All good things come from God," "Pleasure occurs whenever a desire is satisfied," "When profligacy and drunkenness are openly permitted, respect for the laws is diminished." (Perhaps the first and third of these might also be interpreted as value judgments;

the second could be construed as a second-level definition of the word "pleasure." All three, however, are easily interpretable as simple first-level theories.)

We thus have three kinds of statements involving terms from Group 1: (a) sentences expressing value judgments; (b) sentences which do not express value judgments and which are not value-theoretical; (c) value-theoretical sentences. At present I do not see how to distinguish between these except by giving examples. It is clear that there will be ambiguous cases and borderline cases, and it is hardly likely that we can deal with these adequately until our semiotical value theory on the higher levels has been better developed than it is at present.

But what, after all, is value theory? Many writers, including several of the contributors to this symposium, have rightly pointed out that value theory is something in which definitions are important. I think it is obvious, however, that this is not the whole story. *Some* value theories may boil down to mere persuasive definitions, as Arthur Pap has hinted;[8] *some* value theories may be *primarily* sets of definitions, as Gardner Williams suggests;[9] and surely Stephen Pepper is right in saying that many value theories "pivot" on definitions of "value."[10] One can find classical examples of definitions of value-theoretical terms in Plato, Aristotle, Epicurus, Hobbes, Spinoza, Kant, Bentham, Marx, and any of the writers whom G. E. Moore has accused of committing the "naturalistic fallacy."[11] But semantics involves more than mere definitions; it also involves speculation as to the kinds of entities which signs stand for, so that most of the traditional theories which we have in mind when we speak of the controversies over nominalism, conceptualism, and realism here find their place, as do Ogden and Richards's theory of "referents," Morris's theories of "designata" and "significata," and, of course, much of the literature on *Sinn* and *Bedeutung* from Frege to Schlick and beyond. Similarly, semantical value theory includes more than definitions of "value" or other value-theoretical terms; it also includes speculative theories as

[8] A. Pap, *Elements of Analytical Philosophy* (New York, 1949), p. 50. I am indebted to Paul Kuntz for calling my attention to this passage.

[9] See his unpublished paper Words and Values.

[10] P. 78, below.

[11] Pepper has rightly pointed out (p. 79) that Moore himself is deeply interested in the semantics of the word "good" in spite of his declaring it to be indefinable.

to what sorts of entities values "are." But it would be a grave mistake to suppose that all value theory or even all semiotical value theory is simply a semantical exercise. Even a definitional value theory has its syntactical side as long as it involves definitions which coordinate one term or set of terms with others. And there are important value theories where the syntactical development is carried to a point of systematization far beyond mere definition. I have in mind such studies as Hofstadter and McKinsey's "On the Logic of Imperatives" and Von Wright's "Deontic Logic."[12] Moreover, it is not hard to find works plausibly describable as value theory which are as much concerned with the pragmatics of value-theoretical terms as with either their semantics or their syntactics. For instance, Nietzsche's *Genealogy of Morals*, Thurman Arnold's *Folklore of Capitalism*, and Lasswell and Kaplan's *Power and Society* consider not only the "significations" of value-theoretical terms but also the purposes for which different persons and groups of people have used them and the roles which they play in society.

But even semiotical value theory is by no means the whole of value theory. While Spinoza's *Ethics* might well be interpreted as an exercise in the semantics, the syntactics, and even the pragmatics of value theory, it is also an exercise in theology, metaphysics, epistemology, and psychology; and these disciplines are here so ingeniously integrated that it is almost impossible to disentangle the value-theoretical portions from the rest. Similar difficulties occur in most of the great philosophical masterpieces which are in any way concerned with the study of values. Kant's value theory is inseparable from his epistemology and his psychology, just as Whitehead's is inseparable from his metaphysics. I myself would say that value theory in general, as we think of it today, has its semiotical, its speculative, and its systematic aspects, and even its value-judgmental aspects, as I have hinted above,[13] though I am by no means prepared to say that these four aspects are entirely independent. It is concerned with the study of value-theoretical terms, with description of the things they stand for (whatever these may conceivably be), with speculation as to how these are related to each other, and to anything else which the theorist may see fit to consider in the same

---

[12] A. Hofstadter and J. C. C. McKinsey, "On the Logic of Imperatives, *Philosophy of Science*, VI (1939). G. H. von Wright, "Deontic Logic," *Mind*, LX (1951).
[13] P. 37.

context. I hesitate to say that these are the only activities which value theory involves, but I feel that any of them may properly be called a value-theoretical activity. Moreover, as a body of theory, value theory includes many specific theories of value or theories about values, which may take any of these forms, singly or in combination. Even if these special theories turn out sometimes to be no more than would-be analytical definitions, I think that they are still worthy to be called "theories" in the generous sense in which I am using this term, and that they have a place in value theory as a whole. But if value theory really is a whole, it is at present a very complex and amorphous one, with many subdivisions whose interrelationships are none too clear, and with ramifications in many directions, trailing off into other fields which are usually none too well defined. It is a serious oversimplification to think of this as a purely semiotical discipline, still worse, a purely semantical one. Nevertheless, semantical value theories do occur, and they deserve our attention.

Most semantical value theories, I believe, have been chiefly concerned with the meanings of *valuative* terms; many of them—perhaps a majority—have attempted to show that valuative terms are definable by motivational ones and are thus "reducible" to these. This reductive approach has been very clearly analyzed by Philip Blair Rice,[14] who distinguishes between conative and affective value theories and discusses some of their subtypes. But other kinds of reductive semantical theory are quite possible. One might claim, for instance, that all valuative terms, when properly analyzed, will prove to be basically nomological, that all (or at least some) telic terms are definable in a conative or affective vocabulary, or that the very distinction between conative and affective terms is a questionable one.[15] It is still by no means clear whether the so-called "naturalistic fallacy" is really a fallacy, whether non-normative definitions of valuative terms are possible, or whether these may be defined in terms of imperatives, as Hare suggests.[16] It is possible that some value-theoretical terms are not analyzable at all, or at least not reductively (though I am not

---

[14] See R. Lepley (ed.), *Value: A Cooperative Inquiry* (New York, 1949), pp. 265 ff.

[15] See Lee's Essay in the present volume, p. 186.

[16] See Garnett's Essay in the present volume; and Hare, *The Language of Morals,* Chap. 12.

sure what this would mean). I feel, however, that *all* kinds of value-theoretical terms are deserving of some attempt at analysis, and that value theory has not finished its work until this has been done. It is not enough to confine one's attention to valuative terms, important though this may be. The very fact that valuative terms have been analyzed reductively, whether correctly or not, requires us to examine the terms into which they may conceivably be "reduced." Here one might object that this is a job for the psychologist, the sociologist, or the political scientist rather than for the philosopher or the value theorist. But I think this is to overlook the extent to which different disciplines properly overlap. Surely, neither philosophical analysis nor philosophical speculation nor philosophical system-building nor even philosophical appraisal is a technique reserved for the professional philosopher, nor has he any right to lay claim to the territory of value theory as his private domain; on the other hand, the practitioners of the other sciences have no better claim, and it would be sheer folly for them to block off their respective spheres of influence with iron curtains between.

It is important, however, to recognize that reductive semantical value theories *do* occur and will probably continue to do so, and that as long as this remains possible, any classification of value-theoretical terms such as I have proposed is easily open to challenge on the ground that terms from any of my groups may conceivably be definable by terms from others. I think this is a much more serious difficulty than the mere technical difficulty of classifying value-theoretical terms which happen to be vague or ambiguous; it is more serious than any vagueness or ambiguity in the system itself which may result from my own ostensive procedures, perhaps even more serious than the difficulties which arise from attempting to classify terms "as such" rather than simply to classify the various functions which they may perform.[17] For here we have come up against one of the most striking aspects of philosophy itself—the fact that not only are alternative speculative hypotheses and alternative

[17] Morris has quite properly called attention to a similar difficulty in the attempt to distinguish between "pragmatical signs," "semantical signs," and "syntactical signs" rather than between three kinds of relationships which signs can have. See *Signs, Language, and Behavior,* p. 218. His own distinction between various "modes of signification" and "uses," which is essentially a distinction between various ways in which signs can function, avoids a difficulty which is rather crucial for my own classification of value-theoretical terms.

systems possible, but also alternative *analyses*. Just as there are alternative ways of setting up the undefined terms and underived principles of a mathematical or logical system, there presumably are alternative ways of setting up the undefined terms and underived principles of value theory, and any systematization of them which we are likely to propose will have an arbitrary character which is properly challengeable. Not to recognize that this is the case—at least for our own era—is to fail to take philosophy as seriously as I think it deserves. We must bear this in mind when we consider the relations between value theory and semiotic.

An adequate descriptive semantics might indeed be expected to throw light on value theories if it could be assured some logical priority with respect to them. If semiotic were an unchallengeable propaedeutic for any philosophical theorizing whatsoever, or even for any theorizing about values, we might be able to devise a classification for value-theoretical terms which would provide independent semantical criteria throughout. This might result in an enormous simplification for value theory as a whole, for any specific theory which disputed the independence of these criteria might then be rejected as false or at least confused, and many reductive theories could perhaps be eliminated in this manner. But it is by no means clear that semiotic has any such priority over value theory or over the other sciences.

To be sure, some such priority seemed to be conceded when Morris's pamphlet *Foundations of the Theory of Signs* was given the place of honor as the first special monograph of the *International Encyclopedia of United Science*. At that time Morris did not hesitate to write that while

semiotic is a science co-ordinate with the other sciences, studying things or the properties of things in their function of serving as signs, it is also the instrument of all sciences, since every science makes use of and expresses its results in terms of signs. Hence metascience (the science of science) must use semiotic as an organon... It is possible to include without remainder the study of science under the study of the language of science, since the study of that language involves not merely the study of its formal structure but its relation to objects designated and to the persons who use it. From this point of view the entire *Encyclopedia*, as a scientific study of science, is a study of the language of science. . . . Semiotic supplies a general language applicable to any special language or sign, and so applicable to the language of science and specific signs which are used in science.[18]

Similarly, in his later book, *Signs, Language, and Behavior,* he writes that semiotic is "indeed a prolegomena to any future philosophy" and that "semiotic ... becomes in its expanded form the essential organon of philosophy."[19] On the other hand, in his article, "Scientific Empiricism," in the introductory fascicle of the *Encyclopedia,*[20] he had already written more conservatively that "the elaboration of the syntactics, semantics, and pragmatics of science may rightly be regarded as the natural extension and completion of the scientific enterprise itself." And in other passages of *Signs, Language, and Behavior* he has even tried to show that the language of semiotic is itself largely definable in terms of a behavioristic psychology, so that semiotic now appears merely as a branch of psychology. We shall see furthermore that those portions of his work on sign theory which are most obviously relevant to value theory employ many value-theoretical terms, and could hardly be conceded a complete priority over value theory if Morris were so rash as to claim it.

Morris himself approaches the problem of value theory rather gingerly. While he does not hesitate to write in "Scientific Empiricism" that for the program he envisages, "Logic is grounded on semiotic" and "metaphysics is replaced by sign analysis and unified science," he says no more about value theory than that "axiology becomes the scientific study of values and judgments of values,"[21] and he apparently makes no effort to establish value theory on a semiotical basis, surprising though this may seem. He is even more explicit in his recent article "Axiology as the Science of Preferential Behavior,"[22] where he writes: "A scientific axiology will have as its task the development of a verified theory of preferential behavior ... Axiology so conceived is a part of behavioristics ... a behavioral axiology, as a science of valuation, will be the scientific study of valuing and evaluation." These passages suggest that Morris prefers to think of value theory not as subordinate to semiotic but as a more or less parallel discipline, similarly grounded in a behavioral

[18] Morris, "Foundations of the Theory of Signs," pp. 2-3.
[19] *Signs, Language, and Behavior,* pp. 233, 237.
[20] *International Encyclopedia of Unified Science* (Chicago, 1938), I, No. 1, 70.
[21] *Ibid.,* p. 71.
[22] In *Value: A Cooperative Inquiry,* p. 212.

psychology. This would, not, however, rule out the possibility that both disciplines might have some portions in common, or that these portions might be as extensive and important as I have suggested. Indeed this seems to be essentially Morris's position in his Essay in the present volume.

It is, of course, quite conceivable that other approaches to both semiotic and value theory are possible; the mere fact that one of their more competent students has chosen a behavioristic approach does not require other investigators to choose likewise. But the very fact that signs and values are normally signs and values *for* someone, suggests that it is not easy to build up either a sign theory or a value theory in complete disregard of psychology, and that any such theory would be open to the charge of unwarranted abstraction.[23] It also remains questionable whether any semiotic adequate for handling problems of value theory can be constructed until certain portions of value theory itself have been developed enough to point the way.

II

In attempting to answer the question of how the language of value theory differs from other types of language, we have already given a partial answer to our second question: "How is the language of value theory related to the language of sign theory?" We have seen that since value theory is concerned with certain words and with what they stand for, its language must contain not only those words but also their names, and may also contain certain general semiotical terms such as "conative term," "valuative term," and so forth. And we have seen that value theory may tackle various semantical, pragmatical, and syntactical problems. To this extent we are justified in holding that an important portion of value theory actually coincides with an important portion of sign theory.

If this is the case, one might well dismiss as trivial or misguided such questions as "What can sign theory *contribute* to value theory?" and "What can value theory contribute to sign theory?" But it is still significant to ask how extensive are the nonoverlapping portions of these two disciplines, and whether they have any important bearing

---

[23] Even Carnap has recognized this in the case of sign theory, though some of his critics have not yet discovered it. See his *Introduction to Semantics* (Cambridge, Mass., 1942), pp. 3-15.

on those which overlap.[24] I shall not try to answer these questions
in full detail. I have already given a tentative answer to the question
of how semiotical value theory is to be distinguished from the rest
of value theory.[25] But it is still important to ask how it is related to
the rest of semiotic. Here, Morris has suggested some ways of
dividing up semiotic which deserve our attention and might perhaps
be expected to give us some clues. We have already examined his
distinction between semantics, syntactics, and pragmatics, and shown
that semiotical value theory does not fall exclusively into any of
these subdivisions.[26] But Morris proposes another threefold distinction—between pure, descriptive, and applied semiotic—which cuts
across his other classification and looks somewhat promising. "Pure
semiotic," he claims, "elaborates a language to talk about signs,
descriptive semiotic studies actual signs, and applied semiotic utilizes
knowledge about signs for the accomplishment of various purposes."[27]
Morris does not make it entirely clear, however, (a) whether applied
semiotic is to be distinguished from both pure and descriptive
semiotic as another variety coordinate with these, (b) whether it is
merely a subdivision of descriptive semiotic, or (c) whether it is a
subdivision of semiotic as a whole, with both pure and descriptive
components. I have tended to favor the third of these interpretations,
but if this is correct, one might well ask whether applied semiotic
as a whole may not coincide with the whole of semiotic, even though
specific applications can at best be merely subdivisions of that whole.
At any rate, semiotical value theory has its pure and its descriptive
aspects, and is not without applications. This is especially well
illustrated by Hartman's contribution to this volume, which is surely
an exercise in both pure and descriptive semiotic, no matter what
other purposes it may be intended to fulfill; it may also be regarded
not unplausibly as an application of semiotic to value theory. One
can say the same for the work of Spinoza and Bentham and many

[24] The very fact that these questions can be raised suggests that H. N. Lee may
have oversimplified matters when he writes (this volume, p. 183) that "the semantic
scheme and the logical scheme of theory are the obverse and reverse of the same
medal."

[25] See p. 30, above.

[26] See pp. 29-30, above.

[27] *Signs, Language, and Behavior*, pp. 353-54. Contrast *Signs, Languages, and
Behavior*, pp. 219-20, where Morris's presentation seems somewhat different.

of the classical authors. It is clear that we must find some other
way of subdividing semiotic if we are to discover just where
semiotic value theory fits in. My own proposal is a very simple
one. I should like to say that semiotical value theory is that portion
of semiotic which is concerned with value-theoretical terms. If so,
semiotical value theory is to be distinguished from the rest of
semiotic simply by its subject matter rather than by any peculiar
techiques or procedures, and no further breakdown of semiotic as
a whole is required.

One might ask, however, whether Morris's semiotical system may
not provide us with a better method of classifying value-theoretical
terms than that which I have proposed. Here we must consider his
distinction between the "uses" of signs and their "modes of signifying," and the various forms which these may take. One may also ask
whether he can provide a more illuminating way of describing what
goes on in value theory, and here we must consider his classification
of "types of discourse"; for among the names of these types we find
such words as "Critical," "Moral," "Legal," "Religious," "Political,"
and "Propagandistic," and one might well suspect that even if value
theory as a whole should not fall under any one of these types, its
own subdivisions may do so. But the classification of types is based
upon the distinction between "modes" and "uses," to which we must
now turn our attention.

Morris seems to have great difficulty in providing a suitable definition for his term "mode of signifying,"[28] but he assures us that

[28] In his glossary (Signs, Language, and Behavior, p. 351) Morris defines "mode
of signifying" as, "A differentiation of signs in terms of the most general kinds of
significata." But this involves the difficult term "significatum," which is in turn
defined as, "The conditions such that whatever meets these conditions is a denotatum of a given sign" (Signs, Language, and Behavior, p. 355). This definition
has been sharply criticized (for example, by M. Black in his Language and Philosophy, Ithaca, N.Y., 1949, pp. 180 ff.), and Morris himself seems to have trouble
in sticking to it. In "Foundations of the Theory of Signs" (p. 5) he defined the
analogous term "designatum" as follows: "The designatum of a sign is the kind of
object which the sign applies to, that is, the objects with the properties which the
interpreter takes account of through the presence of the sign vehicle." And later
in the pamphlet (p. 50) he wrote: "The designatum of a sign is the class of objects
which a sign may denote in virtue of its semantical rule." But on page 4 he wrote:
"What is taken account of are designata." There is considerable ambiguity in these
passages; but they suggest that in "Foundations of the Theory of Signs," Morris is
not quite sure whether he wants to treat designata as objects taken account of, as
classes or "kinds" of objects taken account of, or as properties which the members
of such classes possess. Similarly in Signs, Language, and Behavior he soon aban-

there are five such modes altogether: identificative, designative, appraisive, prescriptive, and formative. He considers the last four of these fundamental for classifying the types of discourse. In attempting to differentiate the five modes, he builds up an interesting set of correspondences. He states that to each mode there corresponds (a) a special relationship to the environment, (b) a special kind of interpretant (or "disposition in an interpreter to respond, because of a sign, by response-sequences of some behavior-family"),

---

dons the obscure term "conditions," and describes significata as "the properties something must have to be denoted by a sign" (p. 67). In his Essay in the present volume, even this definition is watered down when he writes: "By the signification of a sign will be meant the properties something must have for the sign to apply to it" (p. 59, below).

Most of these definitions, however, involve some such word as "denotatum," "denote," or "apply," and here Morris is again in trouble. I suppose we could construct a contextual definition for "applies" on the basis of my first quotation from "Foundations of the Theory of Signs," and write that a sign is said to "apply" to certain objects if and only if those objects have the properties which the interpreter of that sign takes account of. But this is not what Morris has done. In "Foundations of the Theory of Signs," page 4, he writes: "Where what is referred to actually exists as referred to the object of reference is a denotatum." He then goes on to say that the denotata of a sign are the members of the class of objects which constitutes its designatum (*ibid.*). In *Signs, Language, and Behavior*, however (p. 17), he writes: "Anything which would permit the completion of the response-sequences to which the interpreter is disposed because of a sign will be called a *denotatum* of that sign. A sign will be said to *denote* a denotatum." It seems obvious that these definitions don't quite match. It is also obvious that the definitions in *Signs, Language, and Behavior* lead to paradoxes.

Let us suppose, for instance, that I tell you that Morris's book is a *good* one, as indeed I believe it is. If the word "good" is here an appraisor, as it would seem to be, and if we are to determine its significatum according to Morris's definitions, we must then ask what conditions are such that whatever meets these conditions is a denotatum of the word "good" as here employed; and we must remember that such a denotatum may be anything that would permit the completion of the response-sequences to which you as an interpreter would be disposed because of that appraisor. Let us suppose that you have been annoyed by Morris's book (as many people have been), and that my remark immediately disposes you to the preferential behavior of retorting, "No, it's not!" but that your respect for my feelings prevents you from completing that response. In such a case a *lack* of respect for my feelings would have permitted the completion of your response, and would thus be a denotatum of the word "good" by Morris's definition. Any conditions which a lack of respect for my feeling would meet would then constitute a significatum for the word "good"; I suppose that among these conditions we would find such properties as "failure to possess," "psychological state," "relationship to feelings," and so forth. But this is obviously not the sort of thing that Morris has in mind. Fortunately his treatment of the terms "signification" and "denotation," while a serious minor blemish, does not corrupt his work as a whole.

(c) a special kind of significatum, and (d) a special kind of sign.[29] In the light of remarks in his glossary[30] and other passages it would seem that he is here giving the significata the priority in the definition of "mode," as compared with the other factors. On page 64, for instance, he writes that "the modes of signifying will correspond to the major kinds of significata." But he follows this immediately by a statement which suggests that interpretants are more fundamental still: "A significatum, however, as the condition under which something is denoted by the sign, always involves an interpretant...; hence the major kinds of significata must be distinguished in terms of distinctions between interpretants, that is, in terms of differences in dispositions to respond." Apparently these dispositions in turn are to be distinguished in terms of the relations between organism and environment, if we may judge by the remainder of the passage.

Be that as it may, it should be noted that I have already included the terms "appraisive mode" and "prescriptive mode" among my examples of semiotical value-theoretical terms, and it is interesting to see how Morris defines them. He writes[31] that the appraisive mode is a factor or component in sign-behavior corresponding to "the *import* or *relevance* of this environment for the *needs* of the organism" (italics added), and that the prescriptive mode corresponds to "the ways in which the organism *must* act upon this environment *in order to satisfy* its *needs*" (italics added). He does not describe the corresponding interpretants for these modes in such general terms, but contents himself with adducing typical laboratory examples. To illustrate the appraisive mode he describes a hungry dog in a situation where a stimulus, A, arouses a disposition "to respond *preferentially* to food at one place rather than another" (italics added) or

---

[29] *Signs, Language, and Behavior,* pp. 62-65. For Morris's definition of "interpretant" see *Signs, Language, and Behavior,* pp. 17, 349, and "Foundations of the Theory of Signs," p. 34. This dispositional definition should be sharply contrasted with his earlier definition in "Foundations," p. 4, where he describes an interpretant simply as a "taking-account-of."

[30] For the passage from Morris's glossary see footnote 28, above. This definition has led V. C. Aldrich (*The Journal of Philosophy,* XLIV, [1947], pp. 325 ff.) to complain that "since Morris makes the mistake of supposing that modes of signifying are to be distinguished in terms of things signified ('significata'), he in effect gives us no analysis of the ways of signifying or mean*ing* .... the only difference so far is in kinds of things signified ..., all apparently *designated* by their respective signs .... We are left with only one mode of signify*ing.*"

[31] *Signs, Language, and Behavior,* p. 62.

to "*seek* food" (italics added) at one place rather than another.[32] Corresponding to the prescriptive mode there might be in this case "another stimulus *P* such that when and only when *P* is introduced in combination with other stimuli . . . the response-sequence of the dog includes some such specific response as turning in a circle three times when it goes for food," *that is,* that it is disposed "to perform certain response sequences *rather than* others"[33] (italics added). The stimulus *A* is called an "appraisor," and has for its significatum a "*preferential status*" which Morris decides to call a "valuatum." The stimulus *P* is called a "prescriptor," and has for its significatum "the *requiredness* of specific responses" (italics added), which is to be called an "obligatum."[34]

In citing these passages I have italicized a number of words which I look upon as value-theoretical. I would classify "needs," "seek," and "preferentially" as conative terms in their present usage, "requiredness" and "preferential status" as telic. The phrase "must . . . in order to satisfy" is clearly teleutic. It is hard to say whether "rather than" is conative or telic, but I suspect that it is one or the other. In this context "import" and "relevance" are perhaps best classified as telic terms, but they might also be construed as teleutic and their status is by no means clear; in many other contexts they are probably not value-theoretical at all.

At any rate, Morris has succeeded in framing these definitions without making use of any unmistakably valuative, affective, or nomological terms; and as the distinction between appraisors and prescriptors may well help us in analyzing terms of these types, this is no mean achievement. On the other hand, to the extent that his account utilizes some conative, telic, and teleutic terms, it is obvious

---

[32] *Signs, Language, and Behavior,* pp. 65-66. In his later essay "Axiology as the Science of Preferential Behavior" (in *Value: A Cooperative Inquiry,* p. 217) he writes: "An appraisive sign signifies the position of something within a series of objects or acts ordered in terms of its interpreter's preferential behavior." Morris has refined this definition considerably when he writes in the present volume (p. 68) that "appraisive terms signify the significances of objects (that is, their capacities to satisfy needs)," and defines the teleutic term "satisfaction of a need" as "the doing of what one needed to do, that is, doing what there was a tendency to do." But here we still find the conative term "tendency," even though the conative terms "respond preferentially," "seek," "preferential behavior," and "need" have all been eliminated.

[33] *Signs, Language, and Behavior,* pp. 65-66.

[34] *Signs, Language, and Behavior,* pp. 66-67. See also pp. 79, 84, *et passim.*

that this portion of his sign theory still includes certain value-theoretical terms as part of its basic vocabulary and might even be said to "presuppose" a descriptive semantic of them. This is not to say that it is "based upon" value theory as a whole or upon any specific "theory of value," but merely that it takes for granted whatever simple semantical lore the naïve usage of these familiar terms involves. It does not "presuppose" any *sophisticated* analysis of them except in the sense that it requires such analysis for its own full clarification.

This naïve semantical lore is presumably part of what Morris would call "descriptive semiotic," and is to be distinguished from the "pure semiotic" which he is attempting to develop. Obviously the descriptive semantic here proposed is common to both semiotic and value theory and is not to be assigned arbitrarily to one rather than to the other. The important point is that in order to develop the theory of the appraisive and prescriptive modes, which is a contribution to pure semiotic, Morris has apparently taken for granted a naïve descriptive semantic of certain value-theoretical terms, which might well be considered a portion of second-level value theory, even if it is of a very rudimentary sort.

At any rate, it is important to notice that Morris's definitions enable him to construct a very useful classificatory system for certain value-theoretical terms which differs in important respects from the one I have proposed in this paper. He suggests that such highly general valuative terms as "fine," "good," "better," "best," "bad," "worst," "preferable," "rather good," "fair to middling," "rather bad," and "very bad" may often operate as appraisors, though they may sometimes have strong designative and prescriptive components, and that this also holds for such valuative terms of lower generality as "wise," "far-sighted," "prudent," "hesitant," "indecisive," "cowardly."[35] He claims that such expressions as "should," "must," "required," "Come here!," "Keep the wind ahead!," "ought," and "ought not" will often operate as prescriptors, though this does not prevent them from having designative or appraisive components.[36] (These expressions are all rather hard to classify in my system, but some of them might be counted as nomological, others as telic or teleutic, some perhaps as all three.) He also proposes that both appraisors and prescriptors

---

[35] *Signs, Language, and Behavior,* pp. 64, 69-82.
[36] *Signs, Language, and Behavior,* pp. 64, 83-86.

may themselves be subdivided in various ways: he states, for example, that "appraisors signify along a positive-negative continuum, and so may be classified as positive or negative";[37] that they may also be classified as "utilitators" or "consummators," depending upon whether the objects appraised are subordinate or superordinate goal-objects;[38] that both prescriptors and appraisors "have various degrees of generality";[39] and that prescriptors themselves fall into three types—categorical (for example, "Come here!"), hypothetical (for instance, "If your brother phones, come here!"), and grounded (as, "Come here so I can give you the note!").[40] Morris does not, of course, provide *definitions* for any of the value-theoretical expressions from my Group 1 which he is here classifying; he does, however, provide definitions for the terms which designate these subdivisions, and these are all semiotical terms belonging in my Group 2.2. The classification is a useful one, and there is no reason why we should expect a contribution to pure semiotic like Morris's book to serve also as an exercise in descriptive semantic for the terms of my Group 1.

Morris's account of the *uses* of signs is also pertinent to our investigation. He writes: "A sign S will be said to be *used* with respect to purpose *y* of an organism *z* if *y* is some goal of *z* and if *z* produces a sign which serves as a means to the attainment of *y*."[41] This definition contains the important telic terms "goal" and "purpose" and the teleutic expression "serves as a means to the attainment of." Morris does not define the terms "goal" and "means," though he does define "goal-object" and "means-object." That these are not intended to be synonyms for "goal" and "means" is suggested by the fact that he uses the word "means" when he defines "means-object" as "an object that serves as a means toward the attainment of a goal-object."[42] The term "goal-object" is defined without employing the word "goal"; but this definition does employ the term

---

[37] *Signs, Language, and Behavior,* p. 82.

[38] *Signs, Language, and Behavior,* p. 83, and footnote 43, below.

[39] *Signs, Language, and Behavior,* p. 86.

[40] *Signs, Language, and Behavior,* pp. 85-86.

[41] *Signs, Language, and Behavior,* p. 92. A somewhat similar definition is given in Morris's glossary, p. 356, *s.v.* "Use of a sign."

[42] *Signs, Language, and Behavior,* p. 351. See also p. 83, where it is characterized as "subordinate goal-object."

"response-sequence," which, as Smullyan has pointed out,[43] is itself defined in terms of "goal-object," so that an obvious circularity is involved. (The definition of "goal-object" also involves the term "motivates" in an unmistakably conative sense.) Apparently the terms "goal," "means," and "attainment" must be regarded as primitives in Morris's vocabulary.

He next proceeds to distinguish four primary sign uses. He writes:

> To attain its goals the organism must take account of the environment in which it operates, select for its concern certain features of this environment, respond by response-sequences which will attain an environment suitable to its needs, and organize its sign-provoked responses into some pattern or other. Each of these stages of its activity may be facilitated by the use of signs, and the four primary usages of signs correspond to these four aspects of behavior.
>
> Signs accordingly may be used to inform the organism about something, to aid it in its preferential selection of objects, to incite response-sequences of some behavior-family, and to organize sign-produced behavior (interpretants) into a determinate whole. These usages may be called in order the *informative,* the *valuative,* the *incitive,* and the *systemic* uses of signs . . . They are the purposes for which an individual produces signs as means-objects in the guidance of the behavior of others.[44]

It should be noticed that this passage contains the telic terms "goal" and "purpose," the conative terms "need" and "preferential selection," the teleutic term "attain," and the questionable terms "means-object" and "response-sequence," which we have just discussed; probably "select" and "selection" should be classed as conative terms, while "suitable to," "facilitated by," and "aid . . . in" should be classed as teleutic expressions; whether the terms "guidance" and "incite" should be regarded as telic or conative or teleutic I leave for the reader to judge. All of these terms (with the exception, of course, of "means-object" and "response-sequence") seem to be undefined in Morris's system. Again it is noteworthy that he has

---

[43] *Journal of Symbolic Logic,* 1947, p. 50. The definition of "response-sequence" in Morris's glossary (p. 353) reads as follows: "Any sequence of consecutive responses whose first member is initiated by a stimulus-object and whose last member is a response to this stimulus-object as a goal-object (an object that partially or completely removes the state of the organism that motivates the sequence of responses)." Whether the term "response-sequence" is itself definable without the benefit of any telic or conative terms is a question which I leave to the psychologists.
[44] *Signs, Language, and Behavior,* p. 95.

apparently succeeded in constructing his definitions without recourse to valuative, affective, or nomological terms; but this passage is amply stocked with motivational terms from Group 1, and to this extent may still be said to presuppose a descriptive semantics of certain value-theoretical terms.[45]

By this time the reader may wonder why I have taken the pains to build up an admittedly unsatisfactory classification of signs, when Morris has already provided one which, with all its shortcomings, avoids the difficulties of ostensive procedures and enables us to say some important things about certain kinds of value-theoretical terms without any obvious circularity. As a matter of fact, I consider Morris's mode-use classification an extremely valuable one and preferable to mine in several respects, especially in its cleancut emphasis on important functions which signs may be said to perform. I feel, however, that a classification such as mine is perhaps a little better adapted for a discussion of what happens in value theory in general; it also has the further advantage of enabling me to talk about Morris's definitional system without presupposing that system and exposing myself to the charge of circularity. Whether it exposes me to the charge of setting up a straw man of my own in order to show that my adversary is himself a straw adversary is more debatable.

At this point it is well to call attention to the problem of how the language of value theory is related to that of psychology. In *Signs, Language, and Behavior* Morris is attempting to base his semiotical vocabulary upon a psychological vocabulary that is essentially behavioristic.[46] It is not too clear that he has succeeded, and the frequency with which he has taken advantage of familiar value-theoretical terms suggests that he has not. He has chosen, however, not to adopt a simple stimulus-response behaviorism such as Watson advocated, but

---

[45] It should be noticed that Morris's behavioristic approach in *Signs, Language, and Behavior* makes trouble for him in maintaining these distinctions; for his definition of the *incitive usage* seems broad enough to cover all the others. He tells us, for instance, that "in the informative use of signs, signs are produced in order to cause someone to act as if a certain situation has certain characteristics" (p. 97); that "the use of signs to cause preferential behavior to certain objects, needs, preferences, responses, or signs, is to use signs valuatively" (p. 99); that "the systemic use of signs is the use of signs to systematize (organize) behavior which other signs tend to provoke" (p. 104). In each of these cases, however, it would seem plausible to say that signs are being used "to incite response-sequences of some behavior-family," which would bring them all under the incitive use.

[46] *Signs, Language, and Behavior*, p. 2 *et passim*.

rather a far less rigid behaviorism more comparable to the "purposive behaviorism" of E. C. Tolman or the "social behaviorism" of his own teacher, G. H. Mead. I think it is characteristic of all behaviorisms and indeed of most psychological systems that they avoid the inclusion of valuative terms in their primitive vocabularies; and in this respect the portions of Morris's system which we have investigated are clearly successful. But whether it is proper for psychological or behavioristic systems to include conative terms, affective terms, telic terms, or teleutic terms is still a matter of controversy. Indeed there is room for questioning whether these are primarily psychological terms which happen to be employed in value theory, primarily value-theoretical terms which happen to be employed in psychology, terms from a common metalanguage, or merely terms from everyday language which it is up to the psychologist and the value theorist to explicate. A value theorist who is eager to establish the verifiability of value judgments, or a semiotician who is trying to build up a comprehensive classification of signs, is easily tempted to treat them as psychological; and many psychologists are willing to employ them in their official language without questioning their status. It is conceivable, however, that these terms have entered psychology as a residue from a naïve value theory, and that they should either be eliminated entirely, or defined entirely in non-value-theoretical language, or introduced explicitly as standing for "hypothetical constructs" or other putative entities. A great deal depends, of course, on whether a psychologist is willing to assign psychology some primitive terms of its own, or whether he will insist upon defining all psychological terms either (a) in a purely physiological vocabulary, (b) in a vocabulary directly applicable only to observable overt behavior, or (c) in a vocabulary which combines terms from one or the other of these with terms drawn from sociology. Here, there is still plenty of room for controversy. But there is room for similar controversy among value theorists: for while many writers may be interested in defining value-theoretical terms in what they suppose to be a psychological vocabulary, others would prefer a sociological, a theological, or even a logical[47] vocabulary; and, as the work of G. E. Moore suggests, it is possible that some important value-theoretical terms may be entirely *sui generis* and not to be defined

---

[47] See, for instance, Hartman's remarkable paper in this volume, pp. 197-231, below.

in the language of any alien disciplines.[48] It is thus conceivable that some value theories will have virtually nothing in common with certain psychological theories except their mutual irrelevance; but I think we must grant that if we take psychological theory *as a whole* and value theory *as a whole*, there will surely be a region in which they overlap, and that at least part of this region will coincide with a portion of semiotic.

But it is time to return to Morris. By distinguishing the various modes and uses, he feels that he has provided an adequate basis for classifying the main types of discourse, and it is interesting to ask what light this may throw upon works in value theory. He states that a "type of discourse is characterized both in terms of a dominant mode of signifying and a primary usage."[49] He intimates that the "dominant" mode in a piece of discourse is the one which most frequently characterizes the statements (or "ascriptors") in that piece of discourse, while its "primary" usage is the chief purpose which it is intended to achieve as a whole. I do not think the methods he proposes for ascertaining the dominant mode and the primary usage are satisfactory. But even if they were, it would seem absurd to try to subsume such vast achievements as Plato's *Philebus*, Spinoza's *Ethics*, or the *Critique of Practical Reason* under any of the mode-use rubrics; and while it might well be possible to classify certain important portions of them in this manner, these works are so intricately organized that I doubt whether this analysis would yield enough useful information to be worth the trouble. It is perhaps enough if the reader can form rough piecemeal estimates of mode and use as he needs them, comparing his own immediate reactions with conjectures as to what the author intended; but this has long been a standard procedure for any well-trained student of philosophy or literature, and is a very gentle mouse to emerge from Morris's mountain.

[48] See, for instance, Von Wright ("Deontic Logic," *Mind,* LX [1951]), who takes the nomological term "permitted" as undefined, and Hofstadter and McKinsey ("On the Logic of Imperatives," *Philosophy of Science,* VI [1939]), who take the imperative operator "Let it be the case that . . ." as undefined. Of course the mere fact that these terms are taken as primitive does not mean that the authors consider them absolutely undefinable in *any* system, or that they have any illusion that they have here constructed *complete* theories of value.

[49] *Signs, Language, and Behavior,* p. 125. The other passages discussed in this paragraph are all to be found in *Signs, Language, and Behavior,* pp. 123-26, unless otherwise noted.

While many works on value theory undoubtedly have their valuative and incitive aspects, I suspect that the informative and systemic
uses are just as characteristic. I also suspect that while works on
value theory are often concerned with appraisive and prescriptive
signs, they are somewhat more likely to mention them than to use
them; I think their own ascriptors are more likely to be designative.
But it is not easy to classify even a relatively simple work which one
knows very well. Though I am sure that this paper, as an exercise
in semiotical value theory, is intended to be informative and systemic
rather than valuative or incitive, I am at a loss to decide whether
the systemic intention or the informative intention is uppermost, and
I should distrust any statistical content analysis of it, no matter what
units are employed. I surmise that the members of the rather small
community to which this paper is addressed will interpret it as
designating and perhaps as organizing certain signs which in turn
designate certain value-theoretical terms, and that some of these
value-theoretical terms will ordinarily be interpreted as appraisive
or incitive, while others will ordinarily be interpreted as designative.
But whether the dominant mode of signifying is designative or
formative as registered in the actual experiences of my interpreters
is for them, not for me, to decide.

Let us suppose, however, that these problems can be satisfactorily
solved, and that works on value theory can be classified with some
precision under the sixteen combinations of dominant mode and
primary usage which Morris discusses. This still is not enough to
enable us to classify them under such rubrics as "scientific discourse,"
"religious discourse," "metaphysical discourse," "critical discourse,"
and so forth. For while Morris treats these types of discourse as
illustrating various mode-use combinations, he takes pains to point
out that these types are merely examples of such combinations and
are not strictly definable by them. Moreover, it is quite evident that
even when these types fall properly under the mode-use combinations
to which Morris assigns them (and this is not always the case), one
cannot define them properly without introducing other components
besides mode and use, such, for instance, as subject matter.[50]

---

[50] *Signs, Language, and Behavior,* Chap. V, *passim.* It is surely obvious, for example, that what we would usually call "religious discourse" and "poetic discourse" do not fall exclusively under the mode-use combinations "prescriptive-
incitive" and "appraisive-valuative" to which Morris assigns them, and that these

The upshot of our investigation is not especially encouraging. We have seen that Morris has succeeded in building up a nomenclature which enables us to say some important things about value-theoretical terms and others, and that he has managed to do so without utilizing any obviously valuative or affective terms. But he has not been able to do this without using a number of value-theoretical terms of other kinds. He has not succeeded in giving us a semiotical framework which can properly claim any systematic priority over value theory, nor has he given us a satisfactory technique for classifying works in this field.

But my own contributions are not satisfactory either. While I have perhaps succeeded in distinguishing several levels of value theory and showing how semiotical value theory fits in, I have not been able to do so with much precision. For my definition of "semiotical value theory" involves all the drawbacks of a purely ostensive definition of the expression "value-theoretical term," and my classification of value-theoretical terms not only suffers from similar drawbacks but is also vulnerable from the standpoint of any reductive value theory which might be employed to challenge it. As long as such theories are available, and as long as the basic language which we use to talk about value theory must itself employ value-theoretical terms either as ostensive examples or as components in explicit definitions, we must admit that the relations of value theory and sign theory are still in a tangle.[51]

---

combinations can presumably be found in many documents which we would hesitate to call either "religious" or "poetic," such as the coach's pep-talk before the game or the Boy Scout oath if these are reasonably effective in carrying out the purposes intended. Similar counterexamples can be given for nearly all the types and combinations which Morris discusses.

[51] For the Comments and Response which relate to this paper see pp. 268-73, 355-56, and 377-78, below.

SIGNIFICANCE, SIGNIFICATION, AND PAINTING[1]

CHARLES MORRIS

I

THE WORD "meaning" is double-faced. If we ask what is the meaning of life, we may want a definition of the word "life," or we may be seeking wisdom for the conduct of life. Questions about meaning move back and forth ambiguously between the two poles of signification and significance, of sign and value. This ambiguity causes trouble, and contemporary thought has found it expedient to put asunder what the god of language has united. But ambiguities have their own merits, and this one is an invitation to explore the relation between signification and significance which the existence of the ambiguity suggests.

Every sign in its actual functioning occurs within a process of action, and since action is goal-oriented, every sign occurs in a context of significance. My former colleague, Manuel Andrade, one day greeted his friends as he met them on the street with the words, "Man is mortal," and said nothing more. The bewilderment of those so greeted, and the diverse ways they tried to find out why he had made this isolated utterance, showed vividly the normal embedment of signs in a context of significance. Further, since signs are produced or attended to for a purpose, signs themselves always have some degree of significance depending upon the adequacy with which they fulfill purposes for which they are used. Signs, then, both minister to significance and have significance because of this ministry. But of course significance is not restricted to signs.

Robert F. Bales, in his *Interaction Process Analysis*,[2] has suggested

[1] The material of this study, up to the Supplement, was presented to the Thirteenth Conference on Science, Philosophy, and Religion, New York City, September, 1952. The Conference topic was "Symbols and Values."
[2] Cambridge, Mass., 1950.

that there are four "functional problems" which action must meet. Stating these in a form that applies both to individual and group action, they are as follows: action must be adaptive to conditions of the external situation, must manage and express the sentiments and tensions of the actor or actors, must obtain instrumental control over parts of the situation in order to move toward the goal of action, and must preserve its integration as a system. Bales calls these the adaptive, the expressive, the instrumental, and the integrative problems. My book, *Signs, Language, and Behavior*,[3] had catalogued the four main uses of signs as those of giving information, directing preference to some objects rather than others, selecting one course of action rather than another, and organizing the behavior induced by other signs. These four uses were called in turn the informative, the valuative, the incitive, and the systemic uses of signs. While the parallelism with Bales's four functional problems is not exact, it is very close, and illustrates how signs are used to further every basic phase of human conduct.

Nevertheless, to speak of the uses of signs (and so of their significance) does not in itself tell us what signification is or discriminate the various kinds of signification. A cigarette manufacturer wants to use signs to incite the act of purchasing his particular brand of cigarette, but he may attempt to do this by comparing the nicotine content of his cigarettes with that of other brands, or by affirming that his cigarette is the most satisfying of all cigarettes, or by direct admonitions to buy the cigarette he is advertising. In all these cases signs are used for a single purpose, and the statement of the purpose throws no light upon the differentiation of the various kinds of signs which may be employed.

Hence it is common in the study of signs to approach the problem of signification directly and in its own terms. And this we will do. By the signification of a sign will be meant the properties something must have for the sign to apply to it. Looked at psychologically, the signification of a sign is what is "expected" (or "imagined") about something when the sign is said to apply to that something.[4] Thus if a given person applies the term "banana" to an object if and only

---

[3] New York, 1946.
[4] This is not a second definition. The signification of a sign does not include the psychological processes of expectation and imagination, but only *what* is expected or imagined when something is a sign.

if the object has properties a, b, and c, then the set of properties a, b, and c, constitute for him the signification of the term "banana." In that case if he is told that there is a banana on his desk he will expect to find there (or imagine that he would find there) an object with those properties.

Under this criterion for signification it is in principle, and often in practice, possible to find out by objective methods the signification which a sign has for an individual or group of individuals (and in the latter case to find the degree to which the signification of the sign is interpersonal or common to the members of the group). One would present an individual, for instance, with a number of objects and ask which ones were bananas (that is, those to which the term "banana" applied). Then one would study the objects so named, and seek for the properties these objects shared in common. The induction would then be made that this set of properties constituted the signification of the term "banana" for the person in question. Such an induction is of course only probable; it is in effect a hypothesis, with a given degree of verification. It can be subjected to further test by enlarging the group of objects which are presented to the individual being studied.

All statements as to what a given sign signifies to an individual or group of individuals are inductive generalizations. This is true even if the generalization is made about one's own signs. One can of course "define" or "lay down" what a sign is to signify, and a stipulation is not an induction. But whether in fact the sign does have this signification in one's own actual behavior can only be determined by the study of one's own behavior, whether by oneself or by others, in the way indicated. To make a resolution does not in itself guarantee that one does or will act in accordance with the resolution.

What is the implication of this analysis for determining the signification of such words as "good" and "bad"? These words signify not merely in a context of significance; they signify significance directly. Such terms we will call appraisive signs, and our concern will be them. (Prescriptive terms, such as "ought," will not be considered in the present paper.) There are three major alternatives as to the signification of appraisive signs, and all are currently proposed and defended. Assuming that appraisive signs do signify, the determination of their signification may involve (a) reference only to the object reacted to and not to the actor, (b) reference only to the actor and not to the object reacted to, or (c) reference to both the actor and the object reacted to. These three positions may be called the objectivist, the relativist, and the objective relativist positions.

If those who hold one or another of these alternatives are merely proposing definitions of appraisive terms then there is no empirical problem involved, as no factual statement is being made. But this is presumably not their intent; rather they are saying that such and such is the actual signification of appraisive terms commonly held by themselves and by others. But if this is the case, the questions at issue should be open to empirical investigation in the manner suggested for the term "banana." It is a strange commentary on contemporary discussion of the signification of "value terms" that such empirical investigations are almost never made. The next section of this paper will present part of one attempt to carry out such an investigation.

II

The data to be considered come in the main from thirty college men at Harvard University, and were secured in the spring of 1951. They are supplemented by material from ninety men from the University of Chicago and the Chicago Institute of Design, gathered in 1946 and 1947. These persons were shown, one at a time, numbered (but unnamed) colored reproductions of classic and contemporary paintings, and were asked to indicate how much they liked each picture by putting after the number of each picture shown one of the following seven marks:

7 I like it very much
6 I like it quite a lot
5 I like it slightly
4 I am indifferent to it
3 I dislike it slightly
2 I dislike it quite a lot
1 I dislike it very much

The ratings so obtained are called P-ratings (preference-ratings). The subjects were told explicitly that they were not to judge a picture as a work of art, but were simply to indicate the strength of their own liking or disliking for each picture.

The thirty subjects were also given an additional task. They were asked to appraise twenty of the pictures as works of art. In doing this they had no access to their earlier P-ratings. The marks by which they were to indicate their appraisal of a painting as a work of art were as follows:

> 7 It is very good
> 6 It is quite good
> 5 It is somewhat good
> 4 It is indifferent
> 3 It is somewhat bad
> 2 It is quite bad
> 1 It is very bad

Such ratings are called A-ratings (appraisal-ratings).

The Harvard subjects were also asked whether or not they were interested in painting, the minimum criterion being whether they had collections of paintings or of reproductions of paintings. By this criterion 43 percent of the subjects were interested in painting. The Harvard subjects were also asked to write down what standards or criteria they seemed to be using while appraising the pictures as works of art. Both of these questions were asked after the ratings had been made.

Such A-ratings and P-ratings, when used in connection with an analysis of the material rated, give important data for the study of values. They give a means of finding out, for instance, the relative strength within a group of persons of the preferences and appraisals of various items, in this case of paintings. They allow a comparison of the consistency or discrepancy of preferences and appraisals in individuals and in groups. They can be used for comparing the preferences and appraisals of various groups or subcultures or cultures.

But for our more limited purpose it is only necessary to note that in the data obtained from the Harvard students there was a very wide range or spread of both A-ratings and P-ratings. While a few of the twenty paintings were generally liked and positively appraised, and some others generally disliked and negatively appraised, all of the paintings were liked by some persons and disliked by others, and all of the pictures, except one, were positively appraised by some persons and negatively appraised by others.

This fact suggests the untenability of the first alternative with respect to the signification of appraisive terms, namely, that they signify properties of objects independently of the relation of the objects to persons. For since nineteen of the twenty paintings were signified as both aesthetically good and bad, there can be no observable property or properties of the paintings alone which would constitute the signification of "aesthetically good" or "aesthetically bad." The analogue for the term "banana" would be a situation where nineteen out of twenty objects were signified as being bananas and also signified as not being bananas. No inspection of objects signified as not being a banana or not being good can determine the properties necessary to call something a banana or to appraise it as good.

The term "good" apparently does not signify objects in the way the term "banana" does. Either it has no signification, or it is very ambiguous in its signification (differing from person to person), or it signifies in some different manner than does a designative word such as "banana." If this last alternative can be established the first two alternatives are ruled out. So let us examine the data from this point of view.

The simplest hypothesis would be to say that while the term "good" says nothing about objects, it does signify (or "express") something about a person who uses the term. But if this is so, there should be a very close relation between the A-ratings and the P-ratings of the twenty paintings. There is in fact a correlation of .50 between the two sets of ratings, and this is statistically significant.[5] But it is not a "very close" relation; it shows a connection somewhere between preferences and appraisals, but also a considerable discrepancy between them. The problem posed is to explain both the positive correlation between the A- and the P-ratings and why the correlation is not higher.

The correlation between the two sets of ratings differed widely from subject to subject, spreading all the way from .99 to -.05. Does the relation, however, differ with different kinds of person? As a first approach to this problem, it was decided to see if such differences manifested themselves at the simplest and most manageable level of personality, namely, at the level of physique. Twenty-four

[5] The phrase "statistically significant" is here used in a technical sense to indicate that the likelihood of a result being due to chance is less than 5 in 100.

of the subjects were somatotyped according to William H. Sheldon's method, and classified into five groups: those predominantly endomorphic with mesomorphy as the second component; those predominantly mesomorphic with endomorphy as the second component; those predominantly mesomorphic with ectomorphy as the second component; those predominantly ectomorphic with mesomorphy as the second component; those who differed only slightly in the strength of the three components. These five somatotype classes will be referred to as Groups I, II, III, IV, and V. The number of members are in order 3, 4, 3, 8, 5. One subject did not fall in any of these groups.

Though the number of subjects is too small to permit many statistically significant comparisons, a number of facts are suggestive. The average correlations between the A-ratings and the P-ratings for the five groups were as follows: .87, .75, .58, .51, .44. This suggests that different kinds of person differ, even at the level of constitution, in the closeness of their A- and P-ratings, the relation being significantly closer for the more endomorphic groups than for the more ectomorphic groups.

It was also found that the differences between the A-ratings and the P-ratings within each of the five groups was less than the difference obtained when the members of any one group were paired with the members of any other group. This suggests that the positive correlation between the two sets of ratings is not due to a direct relation between them, but is connected in some way with underlying factors in the personality system which are reflected in both sets of ratings.

The correlation between the A- and P-ratings was significantly higher for those interested in painting than for those not interested: .63 in the former case, and .39 in the latter.

There was furthermore a significant difference in the correlations in the case of those who adopted a "subjective criterion" for making appraisals in contrast to those who adopted an "objective criterion." A subject was regarded as using a subjective criterion if he stated that his basis for judging the value of pictures as works of art was determined by the effect of the picture upon himself; otherwise he was classified as using an objective criterion. Obviously no perfectly sharp distinction could be made here, for the same subject at times used both kinds of criteria. But when the most doubtful cases were left aside, the average correlations of preference and appraisal ratings for those using subjective criteria of appraisal (29 percent of the group) was .67 as contrasted to .43 for those who stated that they judged the pictures on the basis of objective criteria. There was no significant relation between being interested or not interested in painting and in choosing a subjective or an objective criterion.

Do these considerations show that the second of the alternative analyses of the signification of appraisals is correct, namely, that appraisals signify only in the sense that they express something about the person, or kind of person, making the appraisal?

I think not. The data do show that appraisals vary to some extent with the kind of person making the appraisal, and to this extent they may be said to "express" the appraising person. But we must not forget that the appraisals were made about the paintings, and that the members of the different groups of persons tended to agree among themselves as to the paintings which they appraised positively and negatively. This suggests that an appraisal involves, or is a "function of," both objects and persons, and of neither alone. If this is so, the data that have been examined throw doubt upon both the purely objectivistic and the purely relativistic views as to the nature of appraisive signification. And in doing so they speak in favor of some version of the objective relativist position that appraisals signify objects as being in some specific relation to persons. What this relation is in the case of appraisals will perhaps become clearer if we ask of our empirical data a final question: What kinds of persons like what kinds of paintings? An answer to this may furnish a clue as to the unique feature of appraisive signification needed to differentiate it from other signs (such as the term "father") which also require an objective relativist analysis.

For this purpose we turn now to the larger group of ninety Chicago men. Unfortunately from this group only P-ratings were obtained, because the study of that group was completed before the present problem was formulated. But under the hypothesis that the results for the smaller Harvard group are correct (that is, that the correlation of A- and P-ratings on paintings is positive and of the order of .50), we can make use of the P-ratings of the larger Chicago group where there is less doubt about questions of statistical significance.

The Chicago subjects gave P-ratings to eighty-seven colored reproductions, among which were the twenty so far considered. From this data three sets of paintings were formed: those distinctively favored by endomorphs, those by mesomorphs, and those by ectomorphs. As examples of the pictures, it may be mentioned that Redon's *Vase of Flowers* and Rouault's *Christ Mocked by Soldiers* were in the first set, Marsh's *High Yaller* and Bellows's *Stag at Sharkey's* were in the second set, and Picasso's *Two Harlequins* and Seurat's *La Parade* were in the third set. The three sets were then given to three professional art critics who were not told the basis of selection of the sets; they were asked independently to describe what the pictures of each set had in common and how the sets differed from each other. The comments of the three critics were very similar, so that the remarks of only one of them need be referred to here.

Concerning the first set (pictures differentially favored by the endomorphic group), the critic noted that the paintings "used color as color," that one must "go along with them to enjoy them," that the paintings were "decorative, imaginative, nonrealistic, without spatial depth." Of the set differentially favored by the mesomorphic group, he noted that the paintings were "athletic, muscular, tactual," that they were realistic presentations of sturdy objects in three-dimensional space, that "the colors were not used as color but to accentuate the vitality of the pictures." Of the set differentially favored by the ectomorphic group, he remarked that "horizontal and vertical axes were used in the design," that the compositions were "self-contained," that persons portrayed showed "sensitivity and self-awareness."

As previously mentioned, the critics did not know that the three sets of pictures were favored differentially by predominantly endomorphic, mesomorphic, and ectomorphic persons. Their general agreement in the comparison of the three sets suggests that there is a tendency for persons to prefer and to appraise positively paintings which symbolize a situation that would satisfy their constitutional needs, that is, which portray a situation of a sort that is congenial to themselves, and if persons are portrayed, in which persons act as they themselves prefer to act. Thus the vigorous, muscular, mesomorphic persons tend to prefer and appraise positively paintings that show mesomorphic persons in a realistic situation in which they are actively dominant. The relaxed, receptive, endomorphic persons tend to prefer and appraise positively paintings that are imaginative

CHRIST MOCKED BY SOLDIERS,
BY GEORGES ROUAULT
Collection Museum of Modern Art

TWO HARLEQUINS,
BY PABLO PICASSO
Courtesy New York Graphic Society,
Original—Collection of Stephen Clark

STAG AT SHARKEY'S, BY GEORGE BELLOWS
The Cleveland Museum of Art—Hinman B. Hurlbut Collection

and meditative, and in which persons and things are in close rapport, neither isolated from each other nor struggling against each other. The sensitive, self-protective, ectomorphic persons tend to prefer and positively appraise paintings in which persons and objects keep their distance, neither pressing upon each other nor merging with each other. The Rouault, Bellows, and Picasso photographs, and the material tabulated on pages 70 and 71, serve to make more concrete these relations between somatotype and preference for certain paintings.

III

The data that have been examined support the thesis that appraisive signs do not signify objects in isolation from persons or persons in isolation from objects, but objects in their capacity to satisfy needs. The data of course tend to confirm this general thesis only with respect to a limited area of constitutional needs. The general thesis sets no limit to the range of human needs nor their forms of satisfaction. Whether further study would support the general thesis only further study can say.

Three terms in the preceding formulation require some elaboration: "object," "need," "satisfaction of a need." "Object" is intended to include whatever can be reacted to directly or by symbols. Anything so attended to can be signified appraisively—qualities, pleasures, signs, needs, images, paintings, internal organs, parts of the body, persons, the other side of the moon, and so on, without end.

By "need" is meant a tendency or a readiness to preferential behavior, that is, a tendency to act toward certain kinds of objects in a certain kind of way. Similar conceptions of need are found in the writings of Henry A. Murray, Edward C. Tolman, Donald O. Hebb, and Gardner Murphy. "Need," in this sense of the term, is to be distinguished from the processes which give rise to the need, whether the processes be nonsymbolical or symbolical. Thus, to use Hebb's illustration in *The Organization of Behavior,*[6] to be hungry, to need food, is to tend to eat. Conditions of the stomach and the blood influence this need, but so may symbolic processes, such as being told by a friend that he has just brought a steak. Appraisive symbols in particular influence the need or motivational system. For to signify something as good sets up a readiness or tendency to favor

[6] New York, 1949.

that something, to give it a preferential status in action, and so changes to that extent the need system. Hence while appraisals are made with respect to needs, the needs themselves may be due in various degrees to earlier appraisals.

By "satisfaction of a need" is meant the doing of what one needed to do, that is, doing what there was a tendency to do. Whatever makes possible this action has, with respect to the need in question, significance, and it is such significance that appraisive terms signify. The "feeling of satisfaction" is perhaps a person's own experience of the process of satisfying a need; the relation of P-ratings to constitutional needs in the study of paintings would suggest this, but the matter deserves more explicit consideration than can here be given it.

The view that appraisive terms signify the significances of objects (that is, their capacities to satisfy needs) explains why the same paintings can be called good by one person and bad by another without contradiction, for as persons differ with respect to needs, so does the significance of an object differ. In this way the term "good" can have the same signification to a number of persons even though the objects to which the term applies differ with the persons. This could not be the case if "good" were a designative term such as "banana." As an appraisive sign "good," when claimed to apply to an object, leads to tendencies to favor the object in action and to expectations that the object will be found satisfying. The claim is directly confirmed to the degree that these expectations are fulfilled in commerce with the object, and indirectly confirmed to the degree that there is evidence that the expectations would be confirmed if there were to be such direct commerce with the object. Thus, in the last analysis, the evidence for the applicability of an appraisive sign, in distinction from a designative sign, consists in finding the object appraised to be satisfying or unsatisfying with respect to the need or needs for which the appraisal was made.

It is now possible to see why, in the data studied, there was a positive correlation of A-ratings and P-ratings and also why this correlation was not higher. The correlation was positive because to like an object is to find it satisfying, and objects which have this property are in general appraised positively.

The human being, however, has many needs, and the need which is involved in a preference-rating of an object may not be the same need, or the only need, which is controlling the appraisal-rating of that object. Then, too, a person may at a moment prize an object and yet doubt if the object has the capacity to sustain such prizing; hence the appearance of such distinctions as prizing and prizable, desire and desirable, preference and preferable, the latter terms of these pairs suggesting the "ableness" of an object to continue to give satisfaction. And, finally, human beings, to varying degrees, have needs to consider the needs of other living beings. Some of the students, asked to give the criteria they believed were operating in their appraisals, said they considered the painting in terms of the number of people who would like it, or whether a museum director would want the painting in his museum, and so on. We noted that the correlation of A- and P-ratings was lower for individuals who professed such objective criteria, and that such individuals seemed on the whole to be more ectomorphic than individuals professing a subjective criterion. Regardless of physique, however, the fact that some individuals need to consider the needs of others gives one more reason why preference- and appraisal-ratings, though related, do not coincide.

To shift the example, consider a dietician appraising diets for various persons. Diet X may be better than diet Y for one person and less good than diet Y for another. This may even be true with respect to the same person if different needs are the point of reference. A given person might prefer the taste of diet Y to that of diet X and yet agree with the dictician that diet X is better for him with respect to his need of regaining health. The dietician himself may not like either diet, and yet claim that his appraisal is correct or true, for the needs with respect to which the diets were appraised were needs of other persons. His own need in this situation was to make a correct appraisal, and to the extent that he believes his appraisal was correct he will be satisfied with it, and call it good.

In terms of such considerations we can see how A-ratings can be regarded as signifying the capacity of objects to satisfy needs, and yet differ to some extent (and in some persons more than in others) from P-ratings of the same objects. This was the main problem which the data posed.

In conclusion, let us return for a moment to the general question of the relation of signification and significance. Signification is to be distinguished from significance, even in those cases where it is significance that is signified. In principle at least, anything may

PREFERENCE-RATINGS OF TWENTY PAINTINGS*
(Listed in order of liking)

Painting number	Artist	Title	Mean of P-ratings
20	Vermeer	The Milkmaid	5.35
9	Renoir	Self-Portrait	5.11
5	Manet	Le Bon Bock	5.03
39	Marsh	High Yaller	4.97
52	Crawford	Overseas Highway	4.95
13	Kroll	Figure Outdoors	4.69
83	Van Gogh	The Starry Night	4.69
59	Cezanne	Stockade	4.68
30	Rousseau	The Waterfall	4.62
18	Curry	John Brown	4.57
77	Bellows	Stag At Sharkey's	4.50
85	Rouault	Christ Mocked by Soldiers	4.45
37	Corbino	Flood Detail	4.37
1	Picasso	Two Harlequins	4.36
28	Seurat	La Parade	4.36
2	Lautrec	Portrait of Dethomas	4.24
6	Modigliani	Woman with a Necklace	4.10
87	Redon	Vase of Flowers	3.96
79	Klee	The Twittering Machine	3.66
47	Monet	Carnival	3.41

* Made by the Chicago subjects (90 men).

have significance and anything may be signified, whether the "anything" be a sign or something other than a sign. Things have significance in their capacity to satisfy needs, and they have signification in their capacity to control expectations.

Signs in general serve to guide all phases of human action. The appraisive sign in particular assesses the significance of objects with respect to the needs that are operative, and so focuses action selectively upon some objects rather than others.

Appraisive signs are true or false in the same way as other signs: they are true if the object has the significance it is signified to have, and otherwise, false. But since the significance of an object is a property of the object relative to beings with needs, it is important to be clear as to what needs and whose needs are to be taken as the point of reference. There is a strong tendency to ignore this, partly

PREFERENCE-RATINGS OF TWENTY PAINTINGS[*]
BY SOMATOTYPE GROUPS[†]

(Listed in order of liking)

Group I (7 men)	Group II (16 men)	Group III (22 men)	Group IV (30 men)	Group V (15 men)	Group II+Group III (38 men)
85	39	5	20	9	39
87	18,20	9	52	5	20
13,9,20	9	20	1	59,20	9
59	5	39	9	13	5
83	83	52	30,5	52	18
39	77,13	77	39	83	77
52	52	18	28	18	52
5	37	59	2	39,77	83
30,6	79	30	59	30	13
28	30	37	83	85	37
77	28	85	13	37	30
37	2	13	85	6	59
79	1	83	18,37	2,1	28
18	6	28,6	77	87	85
1,2	59	47,2	79,6	28	6
47	85	1	87	47	2
	87	87	47	79	1
	47	79			47
					87
					79

[*] Indicated by their key number as shown in the table above.
[†] A classification of the Chicago subjects (90 men). For explanation of somatotype groups, see page 64.

because the person making an appraisal usually takes himself as the point of reference. And because, by what Talcott Parsons calls a "transfer of cathexis," a person tends to find satisfaction in signs which signify a state of affairs in which he would find satisfaction (a tendency confirmed in the present study), the temptation is very strong simply to cherish our appraisals and not subject them to the test of validation. Even where the needs of other persons are claimed to be the point of reference, it is very easy mistakenly to attribute to other persons the needs which we ourselves have.

But if we are to move toward responsibility in the making of appraisals, we must make clear the needs with respect to which things are appraised, and be clear that it is only the satisfaction or frustration of those needs that is evidence for the truth or falsity of the appraisal.

Such are some—and only some—of the complex interrelations between signification and significance, between sign and value. The term "meaning" hints at the complex interrelation, but does little to clarify the difference or to specify the relations. It is hoped that focusing upon concrete data has made our thought on these matters more concrete, and has indicated a method for further advance.

SUPPLEMENT

I

During the summer of 1952 certain additional data were secured to supplement, and so to check, the argument of the preceding pages.

A correlation of .63 between A- and P-ratings was obtained when 23 more men rated the 20 pictures used for the Harvard group (7 of the 23 rated only 14 of the pictures). This correlation is higher than the original .50. But whereas only 43 percent of the 1951 group were interested in painting, 59 percent of the 1952 group were interested; and we noted previously that the relation between the two ratings was higher for those interested in painting than for those not interested. This is also the case with the 1952 data.

For Pictures 1, 13, and 39 the P-ratings of "liking very much" or "liking quite a lot" were counted for 99 persons, 22 of whom were women. The differential liking for these pictures by the five somatotype groups was statistically significant. Also significant was an analysis of variance made on the P-ratings on pictures 1, 13, and 18, by 14 men, half of whom were ectomorphs and half endomorphic mesomorphs. For these two groups the variance estimate for the interaction of som totype group and pictures was statistically significant.

Preferences for Pictures 1, 13, and 39 were compared for students in China, India, and the United States (approximately 90 men from each country). In all three cases, the average ectomorphy of those who liked Picture 1 very much was above the average of their group in ectomorphy; the average endomorphy of those who liked Picture 13 very much was above the group average in endomorphy; and the average mesomorphy of those who liked Picture 39 very much was above the group average in mesomorphy. This suggests that for at least some pictures the relation of P-ratings to personality differences extends across cultures.

The P-ratings of 39 American women on the twenty pictures showed an over-all similarity to that of American men, the rank order correlation being .66; the women, however, liked Picture 1 much more than did the men, and liked Pictures 18 and 77 considerably less.

The question has sometimes been asked as to the stability of P-ratings over time. This problem needs careful study. In terms of available data, the stability seems to be high. Mr. Richard Gedney informs me that on five retests which he made, using 50 pictures out of an original set of 295, the percent of cases where the new P-rating equalled or differed by only one point from the original P-rating was respectively 76, 88, 80, 82, 84. Two of the retests were seven weeks apart; three of them were eleven months apart.

It is felt that the new 1952 data agree substantially with the earlier data in respect to the relation of A- and P-ratings. The statistical analysis of the relation of somatotype to P-ratings, and the indication of the stability of such ratings in time, seem to strengthen some of the more general statements made in the original presentation.

The 1952 material, however, forces caution on one interesting point, though one not essential to the main argument. The earlier material seemed to indicate that the agreement between A- and P-ratings was higher for the more endomorphic men and lower for the more ectomorphic. But when the data from 13 of the 23 men studied in 1952 is added to the 1951 data, the correlation between endomorphy and the average difference of the subjects' A- and P-ratings is only .27; while this is in the direction of the earlier suggestion, it is not sufficient to be statistically significant for 36 subjects.

If, however, only the extremes of the average differences of 56 subjects' P- and A-ratings are used (those of 1.30 or above, or .90 or below), and if these are compared with respect to differences in endomorphy (3.5 or above, or 2.5 or below), then the results are statistically significant by the chi-square test.

This perhaps indicates that at least the more extreme agreements of A- and P-ratings are found in those higher in endomorphy, and the more extreme disagreements in those lower in endomorphy (and hence on the whole higher in ectomorphy).

In both sets of data (1951 and 1952) the just noted relation of the two ratings to differences in physique tends to drop sharply for those interested in painting, the relation being in the same direction but no longer statistically significant. Thus as technical skill and knowledge develop, new interests and needs develop, and preferences and appraisals are not so directly a function of the constitutional level of personality.

In the present study attention has been directed primarily to constitutional factors in order to simplify the problem for initial study and to make clear the basic line of argument. The concern has been to show that even at this level the needs of the personality system reveal themselves to a significant degree in preferences and appraisals. An investigation of the temperament and character levels of the self from this point of view would be another task.[7]

II

In the original part of this paper comments of one art critic were given with respect to the sets of pictures favored, respectively, by the predominantly endomorphic, mesomorphic, and ectomorphic persons. It may be of interest to clarify somewhat one point, and to add the comments of the other two critics.

The three sets of pictures submitted to the three critics were not limited to the twenty pictures so far referred to. The set that contained Redon's *Vase of Flowers* and Rouault's *Christ Mocked by Soldiers* also contained Kroll's *Figure Outdoors*, Modigliani's *Woman with a Necklace*, Miro's *Harlequin's Carnival*, and Rousseau's *The Waterfall*. In the set with Marsh's *High Yaller* and Bellows's *Stag at Sharkey's* were also Corbino's *Flood Detail*, Sloan's *Main Street—Gloucester*, Waugh's *The Big Water*, Rubens's *Wolf and Fox Hunt*, and Degas's *Jeunes Spartiates*. The third set included, in addition to Picasso's *Two Harlequins* and Seurat's *La Parade*, Cezanne's *Stockade*, Bellini's *The Doge*, and Homer's *Fog Warning*.

The subjects were not limited to men, so that there are some minor differences in the liking of these pictures from the figures given earlier in this paper. And the pictures were not chosen in

---

[7] See the Ph.D. thesis of Jean Cardinet, Esthetic Preferences and Personality (University of Chicago, 1952).

terms of the average P-ratings of the various somatotype groups, but in terms of the average endomorphy, mesomorphy, and ectomorphy of those who liked a given picture very much. Hence the sets commented upon by the critics, while very similar, are not identical with those obtained by choosing pictures in terms of the highest average P-ratings for each somatotype group.

Concerning the pictures in the set where the endomorphy of those who liked the pictures very much was high, Critic II reported as follows: The line is serpentine, flowing, effortless. There is considerable abstract quality to the paintings. There is good design, good decoration, and enjoyment in letting paint flow about on the surface. There is a sensuous voluptuousness in many of the pictures. From Critic III: The colors are warm, and their values (relative lightness) are in the upper range. There is a note of meditation, mysticism, often of a religious quality. There is a tendency to parallelism in design—a repetition, mimicry, or mirroring of forms.

In the set where the mesomorphy of those who liked the pictures was high, Critic II made these observations: The lines zigzag, are full of tensions, impinge upon and butt into each other. The composition is much more in turmoil than in the first set of pictures. The forms overlap and cut each other up. The paintings are much more representational and photographic than those of the first set. He added that he would need a "shot of adrenalin in his arm" to paint such pictures. Critic III: There are many horizontal formats, and the reproductions are fairly large in size. A fuller palette is used than in the other two sets, with a great range of values in the same picture and with many contrasts of color. The composition has a tendency to instability. Impulsive movements are shown in the pictures. The whole is an expression of will.

In the set where the ectomorphy of those who liked the pictures very much was high, Critic II noted that the pictures showed a premeditated and arranged kind of painting, that they had a stationary quality, and that the persons represented were repressed and inhibited. Critic III remarked that the pictures were not as a whole intense, that the colors were cool and in a balanced middle range of values, and that the composition was based on stable horizontal and vertical axes.

It is clear that the analyses of Critics II and III are in substantial agreement with each other, and with the analysis of Critic I.

III

The procedures adopted in this study show it is possible to combine the experience of the humanist and the methods of the scientist in studies which have both philosophic and scientific significance. It would of course be possible to go much further in this direction than has here been done.[8] The material and the content of the pictures could be analyzed according to a number of categories, and the amount of agreement upon the application of these categories by various judges could be ascertained. Then in terms of the preferences and appraisals of the pictures by various persons, quite specific knowledge of their values could be obtained. Also, material relevant to aesthetics could be secured, such as insight into the number and organization of various styles of art. And the methods applicable to the study of paintings could be extended to other arts, and indeed to the study of all domains of human value.

Our problem, however, has not been the study of particular values, nor the field of aesthetics, but the analysis of a certain group of appraisals. And even here the basic interest was not a defense of specific results, but the indication of a method. In the serious study of values we are just beginning to roll balls down an inclined plane. In axiology we are of the time of Galileo, not that of Newton.[9]

[8] See in this connection *Varieties of Human Value,* to be published in the fall of 1956 by the University of Chicago Press.
[9] For the Comments and Response which relate to this paper see pp. 274-80, 371-74, and 378-79, below.

EVALUATION AND DISCOURSE

STEPHEN C. PEPPER

An EVALUATION is a judgment about the presence or amount of value of any sort in an object or event. All judgments about value are not evaluative judgments. Analyses of value situations, historical or anthropological statements about values are not necessarily evaluations. An evaluative judgment involves reference to some criterion in virtue of which the presence of a value is established or the amount of it measured.

There are two principal sorts of criteria: qualitative criteria by which the presence of some sort of value is established, and quantitative criteria by which the amount of some sort of value is determined. In discourse a qualitative criterion always turns out to be ultimately a definition of the sort of value judged to be present. Theoretically there might be no values except those instituted by definition. If this were taken as the case, then there would be no qualitative criteria of value other than definitions of value. But if definitions of value are formulated to correspond with certain fields of facts, and some of these facts are selective or regulative of others, then the principles of selection among the facts act as natural norms. The definitions of value would then be expected to conform to the facts and to reflect in discourse the selections discovered in fact. Whether definitions of value are final, however, or conform to natural norms, in either case so far as evaluations *in discourse* are concerned the judgment of the presence or absence of any sort of value is performed by reference to a definition. A definition of value is thus the ultimate criterion of value in discourse.

By discourse is meant symbolic expressions through which communication goes on. All discussions about values, or expositions or analyses of values necessarily go on in terms of language. An evaluative judgment is thus often conceived as an explicit symbolic expression, an item of discourse. A convenient distinction, however,

is sometimes made between implicit and explicit evaluative judgments. By this is ordinarily meant that an act of choice has occurred
which if expressed in symbols would appear as an explicit judgment.
An implicit evaluative judgment is an act of choice which when
described appears as an explicit evaluative judgment. For instance,
a shortstop throws to first and puts the batter out, allowing a man
on second base to reach third. This act appears to be an implicit
evaluative judgment, which, if expressed in words as an explicit
evaluative judgment, is to the effect that as a means of winning the
game a throw to first in this situation is better than a throw to third,
and the winning of the game is an item of value for the shortstop. By
the very nature of the study of value (as of any subject matter), the
communication of evaluative judgments has to be made by means of
symbolic expressions in discourse. And once this is understood, then
it appears that the basic criterion of value in discourse is a definition.

Only after it has been established that some sort of value is present
can it be determined what the quantity of that value is. Let us call
a criterion of the quantity of any sort of value a "standard" of value.
In discourse, then, a definition of value is the qualitative criterion of
value, and a standard the quantitative criterion. A standard then
depends upon a definition. For unless one knows by reference to a
definition that an item has value, one cannot estimate how much
value it has. A value must be established first before it can be
quantified. Or once more, in discourse a definition of value is the
basic criterion for evaluative judgments, and standards of value
depend upon definitions.

The pivotal position of a definition of value in discourse is still a
matter of surprise and demur for many students of the subject. Most
attention has been given to standards on a sort of presumption that
anyone can intuit an instance of value, and that the problem is how
much value should be granted a given intuited instance in comparison
with other values in a situation. It is not noticed that the setting up
of the item as an instance of value is the basic evaluation without
which the quantitative judgment relative to other items would be
empty.

And yet every student of value knows that the big issues in value
theory are not over standards of value but over the definitions of
value. This fact indicates where the basic problem of value lies. It
lies in the basic evaluative criterion. Let any student of the subject

ask what is the most vulnerable part of any value theory. It is that theory's definition of value. What is the most upsetting argument that can be brought against the hedonistic value theory? Not the difficulties in the hedonistic calculus in making out how much pleasure *versus* pain can be anticipated from a given act, but evidence leading to the denial that pleasure and pain are constitutive of value. Such an argument becomes decisive if it can take the form of showing conclusively that there is no such thing as pleasure and pain at all as conceived by the traditional hedonists.

Likewise the most upsetting argument against G. E. Moore's "indefinable good" is evidence that what he defines as an "indefinable good" cannot be constitutive of value because no such quality appears to exist. To "indefinable good" in his discussion, G. E. Moore, of course, gives a peculiar meaning of his own. "My point is," he says, "that 'good' is a simple notion, as 'yellow' is a simple notion." That is to say he defines "good" as a simple notion. This point is his basic point, his qualitative evaluative criterion, his definition of value. This is the most vulnerable point in his theory, which his critics have been quick to perceive.

And so on, with every value theory. The definition of value is that upon which the whole theory pivots, and discussions of standards, and the details of the application of values to objects and situations, are all beside the point if the basic criterion of evaluation has not been established, the definition of what is a value.

How is such a definition established? The answer will prove less difficult if some other questions about the nature of evaluation are cleared up first. Two questions immediately suggest themselves: (1) What is the relation of a standard to a definition? (2) How can a definition as a value criterion be made responsible and kept from being a mere arbitrary stipulation?

So first, what is the relation of a standard to a definition? The problem here is that an indefinite number of standards can be applied to a defined field of values, but many of these are immediately regarded as irrelevant, and some as doubtfully relevant. How determine the relevancy of a standard to a definition of value? For instance, in evaluating the worth of a picture, we sense that the social standing of the painter, the political convictions he holds, the price the picture brings, its size, the popular vote it gets, and so on are all more or less irrelevant standards. Yet they are standards often applied, and easily applicable. If they are irrelevant, or only partially relevant, how is relevancy determined?

Very easily, as it turns out. Let us make a distinction between intrinsic and extrinsic standards. The intrinsic standards are the basically relevant ones. These consist in the quantification of the defining characters of the definitional criterion of value. If the definition of value contains among its defining characters any that are capable of quantitative differentiation, the modes of measuring these characters are intrinsic standards for the values defined. These standards are clearly relevant because they apply to the defining characters, and they are intrinsic to the values defined because they are quantitative criteria of the values themselves as defined.

It should be added that if there are any other characters of the values defined which might be used as defining characters of them but may not be included in some given definition because they are not necessary for practical identification, these also would be sources of intrinsic standards if they are quantifiable. That is to say, if the class of value items M is defined by the characters a, b, c, d and it is found that all the items in the class which have the characters b or c also empirically have the character d, so that the class can be defined for purposes of empirical identification in terms of a, b, and c with d left out, nevertheless d would be an intrinsic character of the class defined and its mode of quantification an intrinsic standard.

In contrast, an extrinsic standard is one that is more or less reliably correlated with the intrinsic characters of the definition so that a high or low quantification of the extrinsic standard may be taken as a symptom or fairly predictable condition for the appearance of a value as defined.

To illustrate the principle for determining the intrinsic relevancy of a standard, the following passage from R. B. Perry's *General Theory of Value* states the matter with great clarity:

If one object is better than another, it must be better in respect to the same condition that renders it good, or worse in the same respect that renders it evil ... This would hold whatever the definition of generic value. If good is pleasure and evil pain, then the more pleasure the better and the more pain the worse; if good is wholeness and evil partiality, then the more whole the better and the more partial the worse; if good is union with God and evil the fall from God, then the nearer God the better, and the remoter the worse; so, if good is favor and evil disfavor, then the more favorable the better, and the more unfavorable the worse.[1]

To illustrate still further in detail with respect to pleasure. If value is defined in terms of pleasure and pain, then, as Perry says, the more pleasure the better, and there are three respects in which pleasure is directly quantifiable—in respect to intensity, duration, and number (since a single individual may have pleasure from several sources at once, so that number of pleasures is not reducible to duration). Similarly with pain. There are these three intrinsic hedonic standards.

With respect to these three intrinsic hedonic standards, such standards as health and wealth would be extrinsic. Health would unquestionably be a relevant extrinsic standard, since health seems clearly to have a high correlation with a capacity for joy in life. At the same time, it does not seem to be in perfect correlation with the intrinsic standards, so that it cannot be suggested for an additional intrinsic standard in its own right. As for wealth, the correlation with the intrinsic standards is much lower, so much so that even though it is widely regarded as a sign of happiness its use as an extrinsic hedonic standard is much open to question. But however difficult it may be in practice to determine the relevancy of this standard to the hedonic criterion of value, in principle the mode of determination is perfectly clear—namely, the degree of empirical correlation, if any, between wealth and happiness in hedonic terms. If the correlation is low or negligible, then the standard is irrelevant to hedonic value. Of course, people can still be measured for their wealth, just as they can be measured for their height, but this will be no indication of their hedonic goodness or badness.

It should not be assumed that all the defining characters of a definitional criterion are open to quantification. Santayana in his Sense of Beauty[2] defines aesthetic value as "objectified pleasure." In this definition pleasure is quantifiable, yielding intrinsic standards, as we have just observed. But objectification, as Santayana describes it, seems to be incapable of quantification. In a given experience pleasure either is or is not objectified. There are no degrees of objectification. Accordingly there are no intrinsic standards of objectification.

[1] New York, 1926, pp. 599-600; reprinted by permission of Harvard University Press, which now holds the copyright.
[2] G. Santayana, The Sense of Beauty (New York, 1896).

By way of further illustration, it can be seen that in terms of Santayana's definition of aesthetic value the standards mentioned earlier for evaluating a picture would all be extrinsic and largely irrelevant. The artist's social standing would obviously be irrelevant to the capacity of a picture to give objectified pleasure. So also his political convictions, unless some correlation could be found between the conformity of an artist to the prevailing beliefs of his time and the hedonic aesthetic value of his production. Santayana does take up the standard of cost, and makes out a distant, highly qualified relevancy. The size of a work of art may also be shown to have some relevancy to its aethetic value if carefully qualified; that is, if a work of art can be shown to have a capacity for objectified pleasure, then there is some correlation between physical bigness and amount of intrinsic aesthetic value. A cathedral may be regarded as a greater object of beauty than a jewel box because of its size and inclusiveness and so, capacity for aesthetic satisfaction. As for popular vote, if this is taken as a gauge of the capacity of a work of art for giving discriminating satisfaction, it is clearly irrelevant. As a gauge of capacity to give undiscriminating objectified pleasure, it would be hard to say, but from ordinary observation of such voters, it would appear to be irrelevant. But this judgment is on the belief that discriminating perception is a reliable extrinsic criterion of hedonic aesthetic value. A popular vote is definitely not an intrinsic standard of aesthetic satisfaction.

From the above, it can be seen that it is theoretically possible for a field of values to be defined for which there would be no intrinsic standards. If all the defining terms of a definition of value were incapable of quantification, there would be a qualitative criterion for determining whether a value was present or not, but no intrinsic quantitative criterion. Croce's definition of the aesthetic field in terms of intuition is an instance of this. On his view no measurement is possible of the amount of an aesthetic intuition. This is an immediate unique qualitative experience for each occurrence. Whether a spectator has it or not can be determined, but not how much of an intuition it is.

So now it is clear how the relevancy of a standard to a definition can be made out. Our next question was how a definition as a value criterion may be kept from being arbitrary and irresponsible. If a definition is a stipulation about the meaning of a term, how can the definition of value be other than an arbitrary stipulation of the person making the definition.

Occasionally one comes upon a writer who practically says this. He defines value in a certain way and tells his reader that this is this writer's personal stipulation for the meaning of the term, which the reader is free to accept or not. The writer proceeds to develop his theory, but always, so far as I have observed, he nevertheless expects his reader to be convinced.

It is evident, however, that if a writer's stipulated definition of the term "value" or "good" or an equivalent were very far off the range of usage for these terms, it would not receive any attention from the body of students working in this field. In fact, the reference to a common use of the term "value" in mathematics, which is in no sense equivalent with the meanings of "good," is systematically discarded by students of value theory. In other words, a definition of "value" which showed no respect for its rough equivalence with meanings of "good" would be regarded as irrelevant to the subject matter of this field of study and discarded as irresponsible in respect to this area of study.

It is then tempting to say that the criterion of responsibility for a writer in this subject is that he should respect the usage of the term. Then the danger is that the study of value should turn into a branch of linguistics and that then a writer on value would seek to define the field definitively in terms of common usage. Actually a considerable group of contemporary writers seems to be submitting to this restriction. Probably few of them realize just what they are doing. They are subordinating the basic criterion of evaluation to the current criterion of linguistic usage. This is something like subordinating our Constitution and the Supreme Court to the committee of scholars selected to edit the Oxford Dictionary.

Just to have one example of this sort of procedure in mind, consider an argument advanced by C. A. Campbell for rejecting as a moral standard one that evaluates the contents and effects of an act in favor of a standard that evaluates the motive or conscientiousness of the agent. The justification of one or the other of these standards as primary in ethics is beside the present point. The point here is the use Campbell makes of the argument from common usage. If a moralist does not accept the conscientiousness standard as *the* moral standard, then this man according to Campbell expresses "a paradox

... of that inexcusable kind which arises from using old words with new meanings," something that "would seem to the ordinary man to be an abuse of the convention of language," and so would violate "the elementary duty of respecting the normal usage of words."[3] Notice the *caveat* against using old words with new meanings. Campbell does allow for "refinements" in a later sentence, but the weight of his argument still falls on the meaning for "the ordinary man" and conformity to this takes on a sort of intrinsic moral sanction of its own as an "elementary duty." The argument is the more astonishing since Campbell speaks of the meaning of the moral criterion according to the view he is opposing as that of the "orthodox" and "traditional" view. There is then another culturally sanctioned usage recognized by him for the moral criterion, that is, the usage of the experts, of the recognized students in the field of moral values, so that in effect he himself legislates which usage shall take precedence over the other—namely, the usage of the ordinary man (if indeed that is the only usage, or the preferred usage, of the ordinary man) over the usage of the experts in the field.

This brings out another characteristic of writers in the modern common sense school, who seek to make their value criteria responsible by reference to the usage of the "ordinary man." If they were studiously interested in the usage of the "ordinary man," they would appeal to the lexicographer who is an expert in this field. But, so far as I have observed, they never do this. Instead they appeal to their own intuitions of the common man in them. These intuitions usually check up with my own so far as they go. But usually I find they do not go along all the mazy paths of common sense. Practically all the common words in the dictionary have a large number of meanings. It appears to be the practice of the common sense analysts to select the one of the common sense meanings which appeals to them, and to set this up as the authoritative meaning of the ordinary man for them. So, for instance, Campbell arbitrarily selects the standard of conscientiousness and rejects that of the content or consequences of an act as the standard for the "ordinary man," though both are prevalent common sense standards. The method of the common sense analyst is thus one of concealed arbitrary stipulation. Instead of frankly stipulating a definition without claims of factual

[3] "Prolegomena to a Theory of the Moral Criterion," quoted from W. Sellars and J. Hospers (eds.), *Readings in Ethical Theory* (New York, 1952), p. 637.

support, these men stipulate an arbitrary definition behind the screen of common usage. A genuine appeal to common usage would be an appeal to the conclusions reached by the expert lexicographer. These conclusions in the value field would be ambiguous and contradictory and obviously inadequate for the fundamental concept of a carefully considered theory of value.

The appeal to usage, therefore, as a final criterion of responsibility for a definition of value is either inadequate or arbitrary. However, as a tentative test by reference to which a student can locate through ordinary language the rough boundaries of a field of subject matter, the common sense definition, or set of definitions of a term may be exceedingly useful. As already pointed out, a definition of value which departed far from its synonym "good" or *vice versa* would be regarded as irrelevant to the traditional field of study. It may be said then that a responsible definition of value to serve as the basic evaluative criterion is expected to conform roughly to the facts referred to by common usage and the tradition in the area of study so named.

The final criterion of responsibility thus passes through the common meanings of a term to the subject matter meant. It is the facts referred to by a definition which ultimately give firmness and responsibility to a definition employed as an evaluative criterion. This means that it is not sufficient for a definitional criterion that it should stipulate the meaning to be given to a term. It must also stipulate that the defining symbols shall be truly descriptive or clearly indicative of identifiable facts. This twofold stipulation—(a) that a term shall have a specific reference and (b) that what it refers to shall be truly descriptive or indicative of fact—constitutes a kind of definition deserving a special name. It may aptly be called a descriptive definition.[4] Such a definition is by stipulation responsible to the facts referred to.

Now, any definition that can be applied to empirical subject matter may be regarded as a descriptive definition. And every descriptive definition functions as a criterion in discourse for the identification of the facts it refers to. Thus, a descriptive definition of a conifer is a criterion by which one can determine whether a tree under observation is of the sort described or not. How, then, can one tell whether

[4] For a fuller treatment of this type of definition, see my *The Basis of Criticism in the Arts* (Cambridge, Mass., 1949), pp. 27-32.

a descriptive definition functions as a value criterion or not? The answer is: It is a criterion of value, if it describes value facts. For precisely what the definition does then is to determine whether an item in question is a value or not, or whether it is a value of the sort defined.

But here the question is sure to arise as to how we may be confident that the facts defined by the definition we employ are actually value facts. Does not this require another definition as a criterion for this judgment, and so on in an infinite regress? The answer to this objection is that a descriptive definition of the sort here considered is hemmed in by two bounds which keep it from dissolving into an infinite regress. On the one side is the test definition of usage which roughly demarcates the field of relevant subject matter, and on the other side are the facts referred to by stipulation which unequivocally determine the form of a description which shall truly descriptively define them.

The situation in respect to value is not different in principle from that in the procedure of descriptively defining a conifer. An evergreen is an ancient common sense term. The technical botanical synonym is a "conifer." The term evergreen gave the rough area of subject matter. If botanists had started studying daisies as conifers and offered a refined description of daisies as a definition of conifers and suggested that this should be accepted as the definition of the common sense evergreen, the "ordinary man" and even the botanists would have protested that the areas of subject matter referred to were quite different and seemingly irrelevant to each other. The common sense definition of evergreen would have served effectively to direct the observations of botanists to the relevant field of subject matter. But the botanists have not felt confined to the common sense descriptions of this field of facts. The botanists, for example, come upon some peculiar trees called larches which have all the characteristics of evergreens except that they drop their leaves periodically and are not ever green. But since these trees are from the evidence more closely related to pines and spruces than to birches and maples, the students of the field believed the facts compelled them to include them among the conifers. Thus the relations among the facts determined the refined descriptive definition of conifer in spite of the limitations of the common sense definition of its synonym "evergreen." There is no infinite regress.

The reason there is no infinite regress is that there is a process of successive refinement (what Lenzen in discussing the concepts of physics calls "successive definition"[5]), and that this process is rigidly controlled by the facts. In entering upon a confused or a novel field of subject matter, inquiry begins with what is cognitively available, and this is the persuasions of common sense. When these are given their first rough refinement through an analysis of their common sense meanings according to the sense of the "ordinary man," we have a common sense definition of the field. (If a seal of intuitive certainty is now placed upon these initial results, as semantic analysts like Campbell, Ross, Moore, and others would have us do, the progress of inquiry is blocked off at the start.) But in undogmatic empirical inquiry, these common sense definitions then function as test definitions for further refinement in this field of subject matter. The content of the definitions does not legislate over the content of future more refined definitions of the same general field of subject matter. But it gives the reference to the factual field which does thereafter legislate over the content of the descriptive definitions offered for the discrimination of that field in human discourse.

There is no infinite regress of criteria because the facts stop it. It is the facts referred to tentatively in the common sense definition which thereafter legislate as to what details are or are not relevant to the successive refinements of the description and definition of that field. The stipulation in a descriptive definition that the description be true automatically makes the facts themselves the ultimate criterion of what details are or are not relevant to the field of subject matter concerned.

Moreover, when a descriptive definition of sufficient refinement is achieved, so that there is a firm cognitive grasp of the field of subject matter, then the need to refer to the common sense test definition for a bearing becomes less and less pressing and may be completely abandoned. The common sense idea of magnetism of Gilbert's era, for instance, is almost completely gone today and the description of the physicist is implicitly accepted. The significance of this sort of thing is that once an inquiry can get well started, the facts are quite adequate to take over and do not need a directive definition. The facts control the definitions, not in any degree the reverse.

[5] V. F. Lenzen, *Nature of Physical Theory: A Study in Theory of Knowledge* (New York, 1931), p. 48.

Now, to apply these principles to the evaluative problem. The conclusion to which it is leading must already be apparent. It is that the facts referred to by a descriptive definition of the field of value subject matter themselves ultimately legislate over the definitions which are the basic evaluative criteria in discourse. The basic evaluative criteria in discourse are, in other words, subject to correction by the field of value facts which thus function as natural norms and as the ultimate criteria of value.

I see no way of avoiding this conclusion (nor indeed have I any wish to avoid it), so long as a theory of value is accepted as an empirical theory. This conclusion may be arbitrarily and dogmatically blocked off at a variety of points by appeals to self-evidence for some ethical principles or to indubitable certainty for some arbitrary or half verified definition of "value," "good," "obligation," or whatever. But if these typical dogmatic devices are eschewed, and the inquiry into the nature of value is allowed to follow the evidence of the facts referred to as this evidence guides the way, the facts themselves will furnish the norms for responsible evaluations.

We asked the question, how can a definition of value as a basic criterion be made a responsible instrument of evaluation? The answer appears to be: by first seeing that it squares with the common sense definition of value for a reference to an area of subject matter; that being determined, then by describing the nature of that subject matter as faithfully as possible. The laws descriptive of the operation of that empirical material will then be found to yield the evaluative norms required. In so far as the definitions of value employed in discourse truly reflect the operation of the natural norms they describe, these definitional criteria will be empirically responsible.

Let me give a couple of examples. Suppose we take a hint from common sense and the usage of the "ordinary man" and define value (in at least one of its accepted meanings) as the achievement of a purpose. We may call it achievement value and define it roughly as the attainment of a desired goal. Since this is a definition in discourse referring to activities ordinarily considered as values, it has the sanction of usage as a definition of values of the sort specified. It is a responsible definition in the initial sense that it conforms to usage. It is not an arbitrary personal stipulation of the man who formulated the definition. It is thus a serviceable test definition for the location of a subject matter widely recognized as a field of value facts.

From this common sense test definition we can then proceed to an examination of the facts referred to—actual instances of purposive achievements—for a more refined descriptive definition of these activities. We then find that such activities are constituted of an impulse or drive directed upon a terminal goal and of a sequence of subordinate acts instrumental to the attainment of the goal. We then refine our rough common sense definition by defining achievement value in terms of this more detailed description. Achievement value is now defined as an activity by which a drive charging a succession of subordinate acts attains a succession of goals leading to a terminal goal which brings the drive to quiescence. And now out of an examination of these facts the standards of achievement reveal themselves. The significant point to notice here is that the evaluative standards come out of the facts themselves. They legislate over the descriptive definition as natural norms to which the definition as a factually responsible criterion of value in discourse truthfully conforms. These standards of evaluative achievement are quantitative features of selective activity revealed in the processes themselves. It is found as a general law of such activities that a subordinate act which attains its goal but fails to bring about a superordinate goal anticipated by the subordinate act, is dropped out of the activity as an error. This selective process goes on till the terminal goal is attained. That is to say, every superordinate goal functions as a natural norm over subordinate goals within a purposive activity. If a subordinate goal brings about a superordinate goal it is good; if not, it is bad. A definition in discourse descriptive of the superordinate goal would thus be a value criterion in respect to this stage of a purposive act. Moreover, such a definition would not be an effective and responsible criterion unless it truly described the goal actually anticipated by the organism impelled by the drive which charges the anticipatory references for this particular goal. The drive-charged anticipation of the superordinate goal is the actual selective agent in this process and the *ultimate factual criterion* for the achievement value of subordinate goal objects. The descriptive definition of this anticipated goal is only the evaluative *criterion in discourse,* and must truly describe the factual criterion in order to be effective and responsible to the value facts it refers to.

Here we can plainly see the pattern of any empirically responsible evaluative procedure. A descriptive definition of some sort of value is the basic criterion in discourse for the value concerned, but this definition only becomes effective and responsible if it is truly descriptive of a selective process among the value facts referred to.

But this is only part of the story for achievement value. Another selective law comes to light as we observe the results of a series of successful achievements motivated by a drive under similar environmental conditions. An organism learns, as we say, the succession of correct choices for the attainment of a terminal goal, and eliminates the incorrect choices. The learning process is itself a selective activity which can be described as that of selecting for the succession of acts which will bring the organism most speedily (or by the shortest path) to the terminal goal of a drive, and against acts which delay or are wasteful of effort towards this achievement. Translated into terms of "good" and "bad," the shorter and speedier the attainment of the terminal goal the better, and the longer and slower the worse. Acts or objects which slow down or block the attainment of a goal are called frustrating. The opposite of successful achievement is thus frustration. Frustration is negative achievement value. Here again a descriptive definition of this selective feature of the achievement process affords the criterion in discourse for evaluating degrees of successful achievement, but this definitional criterion depends for its effectiveness and responsibility upon the facts of the learning process as a natural norm of achievement.

So we say of a person who makes a wrong choice in respect to some goal that he *ought* not to have chosen that way. We now see why this statement was factually justified in terms of the person's own acts. He acted in such a way as to frustrate his own achievement. The act was opposed to the natural norm of selection revealed in the learning process by which an organism eliminates acts which reduce the speed of attainment of the goal of a drive. The laws of learning are properties intrinsic to any purposive act, so that the drive for a goal is at the same time a drive for the speediest attainment of the goal. Thus a purposive drive institutes two natural norms on its emergence—that of its terminal goal or conditions of quiescence, and that of the shortest path or quickest completion of the learning process. These two norms become manifest in the selection and elimination of acts actually performed. And they determine the truth and effectiveness of the definitions of instrumental and achievement value which function as basic criteria for these values in discourse.

One more example, in case a reader might think these instances are exceptional. Another criterion of value that has the strong support of usage and tradition is that of harmony or integration. There seems to be much evidence of a tendency to harmonize or integrate the dispositions composing a personality structure. If so, here is another selective system which serves as a ground for intelligent human decisions. A disposition which is out of harmony with the other dispositions of a personality tends to be eliminated. The dynamics of this process seems to be the frustrating effect of the obstructive disposition in relation to the drives for the satisfaction of the other dispositions. The relatively harmonious dispositions tend to squeeze out the obstructive disposition. A man convinced that his smoking habit has reached a stage where it is affecting his health, and so most of his other life aims, is already in the process of eliminating that disposition. When this integrative tendency is blocked off for any reason so that a frustrating disposition is temporarily or permanently (in the form of an addiction or repressed complex) frozen into a personality, we speak of the personality as so far disorganized and in a "bad" state. It is too "bad" so and so has such an addiction. It is here just as it is with a purpose whose achievement is temporarily or permanently blocked. Someone wants to be President and fails. That is too "bad," we say, for this man's ambition. As with achievement value, the criterion for the evaluative judgment in discourse is a descriptive definition of the characteristics of personality integration. But this criterion is effective and responsible only in so far as it is true of the actual process of personality integration and the natural norm of a harmony of dispositions implicit in the process. I will go further and point out that the criterion of the worth of an integrated personality would be empty and ineffective if the dynamic selective process it describes were not verifiable in fact.

The same sort of thing, I should maintain, is the ground of justification for criteria of value in reference to interpersonal and social relations. In so far as such justification can be found, the criteria of evaluation are verifiable and open to scientific investigation. In so far as they cannot be found, evaluative criteria are arbitrary and open to the winds of doctrine and the breezes of personal fancy. In either event, evaluations are made from basic definitional criteria in discourse. The only question is whether these criteria are irresponsible, or are open to factual verification. In the face of the evidence for the natural norms of achievement and instrumental value (to go no further), the utterly skeptical theory of the complete factual irresponsibility of evaluative criteria would be very difficult to maintain. Most writers approximating this view appeal to self-evidence, indubitability, the intuitive certainty of the meanings of the "ordinary man" to block off cognitive inquiry at that point, but allow for factually verifiable criteria below that point. There are many, for instance, today who assume or assert that the satisfaction of interest is indubitably value, and then factually verify instrumental value under that definition. But by their assumption of indubitability they block off inquiry and verification of selective systems that work upon satisfactions. Of the integrative criteria, for instance, they say, "But suppose somebody does not want to be integrated!" That attitude blocks off (or is supposed to) inquiry as to whether there is not a selective system which could be verifiably shown to have a tendency to reject such a want, and so evaluate it as "bad." On what ground can a tendency to satisfy interest be set above a tendency to integrate a personality? Either both are equally arbitrary and so equally justified by default of evidence either way; or it can verifiably be shown that one of these tendencies legislates always, or under certain conditions, or never over the other. In short, there seems to be plenty of evidence for natural norms of value which empirically determine the justification of our definitional evaluations in discourse. The only question is, just what are they and how do they operate or legislate in reference to one another. This is an empirically rational and scientific problem. It is not a question at the mercy of arbitrary nominal definitions or of emotive eruption except in so far as an emotive impulse can be verifiably shown to be involved as a selective feature in many empirically described natural norms of evaluation. It is a question of straightening out certain somewhat more than usually complicated factual relationships. Evaluation appears to be a scientific type of procedure subject to all the usual criteria of inductive inference and observational control.

Let me now briefly summarize the principles of evaluation as these have been developed in the previous pages:

1. The basic criterion of evaluation in discourse is the *definition of value*, which determines whether a thing is a value and of what kind—the qualitative criterion

2. A quantitative criterion or *standard* depends for its relevancy on the definitional criterion. It is intrinsically relevant if it consists in the quantification of a defining character of the definition. It is extrinsically relevant to the degree that it is correlated with a defining character

3. The initial relevancy of a definitional criterion to the subject matter of value is determined by *usage*. But an initial common sense *test definition* is open to cognitive refinement in relation to the subject matter referred to

4. A cognitively responsible definitional criterion is a *descriptive definition* stipulating the verifiability of its content

5. The facts described in a descriptive definition of value, as these facts are indicated by usage, are selective systems, which thus become *natural norms* of value, since they determine the content of the definition of value

6. Cognitively irresponsible definitions of value are possible which neglect or deny reference to fact (4), or reference to usage (3), or both. These would be arbitrary stipulations of meaning, or *nominal definitions*. Theoretically, the term "value" could be entirely so defined. Such stipulations would be entirely uncontrolled and evaluations by them completely arbitrary. Actually, such definitions are rarely made in the value field without at least covert reference to usage or fact or both. Only through such references do nominal definitions of value have any cognitive appeal. But such definitions are irresponsible just in proportion to their failure to accept final factual control

In responsible evaluations, then, quantitative standards of value depend upon qualitative descriptive definitions of value which in turn depend upon natural norms of value, or selective systems, that factually verify the legitimacy of the evaluative judgments derived from the definitions.[6]

---

[6] For the Comments and Response which relate to this paper see pp. 281-86, 362-64, and 380, below.

EMPIRICAL VERIFIABILITY THEORY OF FACTUAL MEANING AND AXIOLOGICAL TRUTH

E. MAYNARD ADAMS

THERE HAS BEEN a significant development in the philosophy of value of logical empiricism within the past several years. I refer to the new emphasis on the role of reason in value decisions.[1]

Logical empiricists have for the most part emphasized the emotive aspects of value sentences and claimed that they are noncognitive in meaning and without truth-values. Consequently it was concluded that they were not subject to being reasoned about since reasoning was conceived as showing evidence in support of either the truth or falsity of a statement. In this way value sentences were believed removed from the realm of rationality to the province of irrationality or non-rationality. Value sentences in statement form were said to be merely expressions of feelings or sentiments of the speaker or evocative of similar feelings or attitudes in the hearer or reader.

The new emphasis on the role of reason in the field of values is characterized by a shift from the analysis of value language to a consideration of practical decisions. The questions asked are not the meaning of the sentence "X is good" or "X is right," or what evidence would tend to confirm and what would tend to disconfirm the given sentence; but rather what facts considered by a man in a given problematic situation would warrant the decision expressed by the

[1] See R. Carnap, "Empiricism, Semantics, and Ontology," *Revue Internationale de Philosophie*, IV (1950), 22 ff.; H. Feigl, "De Principiis non Disputandum . . . ?," M. Black (ed.), *Philosophical Analysis* (Ithaca, N.Y., 1950), pp. 119 ff.; C. L. Stevenson, "The Emotive Conception of Ethics and its Cognitive Implications," *The Philosophical Review*, LIX (1951), 49 ff.; W. A. Wick, "The Political Philosophy of Logical Empiricism," *Philosophical Studies*, II (1951), 49 ff. There has been considerable activity among the Oxford philosophers (Hampshire, Toulmin, Hare, and others) along somewhat similar lines, but we are here concerned with those more or less clearly in the fold of logical empiricism.

sentence "X is right." The shift is from rationality in the form of warranted assertability of a statement to rationality in the form of warranted practical decision. Feigl, in the article referred to above, makes the distinction in terms of cognitive and pragmatic justification; Carnap between theoretic questions and questions of practical decisions, which are respectively questions of truth and questions of advisability; Wick, in writing about Carnap's distinction, suggests that Carnap has made a distinction as important as his distinction between formal and material modes of speech and suggests that language expressive of practical decisions be christened the "deliberative" mode. This modification or new way of stating the position of logical empiricism by Carnap, Feigl, Stevenson, and others on value questions reflects the influence of pragmatism, especially Dewey's version, and indicates that the two movements are becoming more closely related.

But in spite of this new emphasis on the role of reason in value decisions, it is still uncompromisingly maintained by these same writers that value sentences in statement form fall outside the domain of truth-values and hence that axiological inquiry is not a cognitive search for truth.

I believe that even the "deliberative mode of speech" version of logical empiricism's value theory, which is far more adequate than the pure emotive variety, excludes value sentences from the domain of truth-values because of a presupposition which stands in need of fresh examination. The presupposition in question is what might be called the monistic theory of factual truth, the theory that there is only scientific truth (or knowledge) about the object world.

It is believed by many that this monistic theory of factual truth follows from the logical empiricist's theory of meaning and that, therefore, everyone who accepts the empirical verifiability theory of meaning is logically obligated to accept a value theory which excludes value sentences in statement form from the domain of statements or propositions and thus from the domain of truth-values. Therefore, the focal point for critical attention is the thesis that the empirical verifiability theory requires the theory that there is only scientific factual truth (or knowledge).

The meaning of a sentence, according to my interpretation of the empirical verifiability theory,[2] consists of a conceptual representation

---

[2] I am aware that the orthodox logical empiricists would not express it this way.

of its truth conditions, the *experienciable conditions* which obtain if it is true and which do not obtain if it is false. From this it follows that all factually meaningful sentences in statement form are empirically verifiable. But, in order to derive the conclusion that only scientific factual statements can significantly function as subjects of truth-value predicates, a further assumption is required, namely, that all empirically verifiable statements are scientific.

Having derived the conclusion that there is only scientific factual truth, that only scientific statements may significantly function as subjects of factual truth-value predicates, and accepting a further thesis that value sentences in statement form are not scientific statements, it follows that value sentences in statement form do not express propositions and thus are not proper subjects of truth-value predicates.

The argument may be formulated in the following manner:

1. The Cognitive meaning of a sentence in statement form consists of a conceptual representation of its truth conditions, which constitutes a proposition. Thus for a sentence in statement form to be cognitively meaningful is for it to express a proposition

2. Only propositions may significantly function directly as subjects of truth-value predicates, but a sentence which expresses a proposition may indirectly function as the subject of truth-value predicates

3. All propositions are either analytic or synthetic

4. Analytic propositions are the only proper subjects of formal truth-value predicates

5. Synthetic propositions are the only proper subjects of factual truth-value predicates

6. All synthetic propositions are empirically verifiable since they are conceptual representations of *experienciable conditions* which obtain if they are true and which do not obtain if they are false

7. All empirically verifiable statements are scientific

8. From Theses 6 and 7 it follows that all synthetic propositions are scientific

9. From Theses 5 and 8 it follows that only scientific propositions are proper subjects of factual truth-value predicates and thus the monistic theory that all factual truth is scientific

10. All scientific sentences in statement form are descriptive

11. Value sentences in statement form are not descriptive

12. From Theses 10 and 11 it follows that value sentences in statement form are not scientific statements

13. From Theses 9 and 12 it follows that there is no factual axiological truth

Theses 9 and 12 are central both for theories that maintain that there is not and those that maintain that there is factual axiological truth. As we have observed above, those who maintain that there is no axiological truth do so because they accept both Thesis 9 and Thesis 12. Naturalistic theories usually accept Thesis 9 and reject Thesis 12. This of course means that axiological truth is reduced to or incorporated within the domain of scientific truth. While many naturalists claim this as a virtue of their theories, many nonnaturalists reject naturalism for this very reason and label it a fallacy of reductionism. Intuitionists such as G. E. Moore and A. C. Ewing reject Thesis 9 and accept Thesis 12. Some metaphysical theories would reject both Thesis 9 and Thesis 12. In this paper we shall attempt both to refute the nihilistic theory of axiological truth and to defend a naturalistic value theory by rejecting Theses 9 and 13 while at the same time accepting Theses 1 through 6, which we believe to embody the essential theses of logical empiricism. In other words, we hope to show that the nihilistic theory of axiological truth is not essential to logical empiricism and that an adequate naturalistic theory, freed from objections directed against other naturalistic versions, is possible.

Let us examine Thesis 9 first. We have seen that it follows from Thesis 5 and Thesis 8. We have stated our intention to accept Theses 1 through 6. Therefore, if we are to reject Thesis 9, we must do so because we reject Thesis 8. Thesis 8 follows from Thesis 6 and Thesis 7. Therefore, accepting Theses 1 through 6, any rejection of Thesis 9 must be based on a rejection of Thesis 7. Let us examine it carefully.

Thesis 7, which states that all empirically verifiable statements are scientific, I interpret to be a functionally analytic statement more appropriately stated in the following definitional form: "Scientific" statement means a statement that is empirically verifiable. We are assuming that a definition of this type is not a stipulated shorthand symbolization, but the discovery through logical analysis of an identity of meanings of two linguistic expressions each of which had a meaning (or meanings) in use prior to the formulation of this definition. Also we should assume that this definition is either analytically true or false. Therefore, our examination is conceived as an inquiry into its truth or falsity by logical analysis.

We would readily admit that empirical verifiability is a necessary

condition for a statement's being scientific. In fact we agree with
logical empiricism in its fundamental thesis that all meaningful
factual sentences in statement form are necessarily empirically verifiable. But this does not establish empirical verifiability as a sufficient
condition for a statement's being scientific. It certainly leaves open
the possibility of there being nonscientific statements which are
empirically verifiable.

The definition of "scientific" statement in terms of empirical verifiability is a consequence of identifying science with its method of
verification, which seems inadequate to me. There is more to science,
more that is essential. Science is a type of inquiry which is to be
defined in terms of that towards which it is directed as well as the
method or methods employed in attaining the desired goal.

If it should be maintained that the goal of scientific inquiry were
factual truth (or knowledge) as such and that the only method for
attaining factual truth were the empirical method of verification, then,
accepting the position that science is to be defined in terms of its
goal and method, we would by the definition of science directly
establish the monistic theory of factual truth. However, it seems to
me that more careful reflection upon the goal of scientific inquiry
would lead to the conclusion that its theoretical or cognitive goal is
not simply factual truth or knowledge, empirically verified factual
statements, but *descriptive-explanatory truth or knowledge*, empirically
verified descriptive-explanatory statements. Simply to state the goal
of science in terms of factual truth or knowledge would not preclude
science's being limited to purely descriptive knowledge.

The ultimate goal of scientific inquiry in every situation is an
answer to the question *why*?, which constitutes an explanation, the
reason or reasons for something being as it is and not otherwise.
However, all the statements functioning in an explanation are also
descriptive. But it does not hold that descriptive statements are
per se also explanatory. The explanatory relation is one that obtains
between statements because of certain logical relations that hold
between or among the statements in question. No single statement
in isolation can be explanatory. Description, on the other hand, has
to do with a relationship that is internal to a statement and hence a
statement in isolation may be descriptive. Thus descriptive-explanatory
knowledge consists of empirically verified descriptive statements
arranged in a logical order such that some, descriptive of certain

states of affairs, are explanatory of others which are descriptive of other states of affairs.

The cognitive goal of descriptive-explanatory knowledge is forced upon man by the necessity of having to make reflective adjustments to a problematic environment. Such adjustments require (1) an understanding of the environment, knowledge of the reasons for situations being as they are and not otherwise, which constitutes descriptive-explanatory knowledge; and (2) predictions of what is to follow, which not only require but constitute descriptive-explanatory knowledge since the logical structure of a prediction is exactly that of an explanation, the only difference between the two being that in a prediction the event or state of affairs concerned lies in the future.

The conceptual scheme of science, the set of concepts out of which scientific statements are formulated, is not a set of simply descriptive concepts. They are descriptive-explanatory concepts since their formation or derivation is a function of both the structure of the given in sensory experience and the scientific goal of descriptive-explanatory knowledge.

This fact may be made clear by a brief consideration of the nature of concepts and how they are derived. We may say that a concept is the intensional meaning of a nonsentential linguistic expression. This intensional meaning is a property or set of properties. By "property" we mean quality, characteristic, relation, and so forth—anything that can be said meaningfully about or attributed to an individual. These properties are *designated* by linguistic expressions, whereas individuals having these properties are *denoted* by them. Concepts are formulated by certain properties being selected from experienced aggregates or clusters of properties and being given the special status of being designated by some linguistic expression. A property as such is not a concept. It becomes one by virtue of being made the intensional meaning of a nonsentential linguistic expression. The selection of properties to be designated by linguistic expressions is of course partially determined by the properties experienced objects possess. But the selection is determined also by the purpose for which the selection is being made. Thus if the purpose were to construct a descriptive-explanatory conceptual scheme, certain properties would be selected and given the status of concepts of the descriptive-explanatory conceptual scheme. Furthermore, the linguistic expressions used to designate the selected properties may be distinctively descriptive-explanatory and thus indicative of the goal sought. In like manner, if the over-all purpose should be something other than constructing a descriptive-explanatory conceptual scheme, like constructing a conceptual scheme of some other type, a different set of properties might be selected and designated by linguistic expressions peculiar to its type.

In light of our discussion, we now see the inadequacy, yes, the falsity, of the definition: "Scientific" statement means an empirically verifiable statement. We are forced to modify it in the following manner: "Scientific" statement means an empirically verifiable statement formulated out of concepts from the descriptive-explanatory conceptual scheme and used in the descriptive-explanatory context.

We have noted that in the argument of the monistic theory of factual truth Thesis 7 functioned as an analytically true statement. However, our definition of "scientific" statement forces us to reject it as *analytically* true. This does not preclude its being factually true, but it does leave open the possibility of its being false, a possibility which our later discussion will show to be an actuality. In any case, no one has shown it to be factually true. And if it has not been established, neither has Thesis 8, since Thesis 7 is a premise of Thesis 8. Furthermore, since Thesis 8 is a premise of Thesis 9, the monistic theory of factual truth, it remains unestablished also. If Thesis 9 has not been established, Thesis 13, the thesis that there is no factual axiological truth, remains unestablished, since Thesis 9 is a premise of Thesis 13.

Having shown the inadequacy of logical empiricism's argument for the monistic theory of factual truth and its argument for the thesis that there is no axiological truth and thus reestablishing the possibility of axiological truth within the general framework of logical empiricism, we must now determine what can be said positively for axiological truth while accepting the general framework of logical empiricism as formulated in Theses 1 through 6.

We accept Thesis 12, which states that value sentences in statement form are not scientific statements, but not for the reasons given in Theses 10 and 11. While accepting Thesis 10, of course, we reject Thesis 11, which states that value sentences in statement form are not descriptive. It has been held by many other than logical empiricists that value sentences, especially ethical sentences, are normative, whereas scientific statements are descriptive. It is our contention that value sentences of the type "X is good" or "X is right" are descriptive, but not descriptive-explanatory. Thus they are both descriptive and nonscientific.

Just as man's attempt to make reflective adjustments to a problematic environment forces upon him descriptive-explanatory inquiry, his attempt to make reflective intrapersonal and interpersonal adjustments among conflicting interests forces upon him a different type of inquiry, axiological inquiry, search for *descriptive-justificatory* knowledge. Reflective adjustment requires that an act performed to satisfy a particular interest be *justified* in terms of its relation to a wider group of interests, whether the actor's own or those of others of his group. Descriptive-justificatory inquiry is just as much a bona fide type of cognitive inquiry as is the descriptive-explanatory. Reflective living requires true explanations of events. Also, reflective living requires *justifications* of acts.

An analysis of axiological inquiry, just as in the case of scientific inquiry, requires a consideration of its cognitive goal, its conceptual scheme, and its method of verification.

An analysis of the cognitive goal of axiological inquiry requires an analysis of justification. Herbert Feigl, in the article referred to in the beginning of this essay, distinguishes between two types of justification: one he calls "validation" and the other "vindication." Validation consists of giving reasons, as distinct from causes or purposes, for a belief or proposition; vindication consists of showing that something is a necessary or efficient means for attaining some given end.

According to this view, the validating type of justification in mathematics consists of deducing the justificandum, the proposition to be justified, from other propositions which are called the justificans. A justificandum that is a proposition about an empirical event is justified, according to Feigl, by showing that it has a certain probability-value deducible from certain other empirical propositions which constitute the justificans. Hence, a justification, according to this view, consists of a justificandum and justificans with the truth or some probability-value of the justificandum being deducible from the justificans.

However, we need to distinguish between two aspects of both the justificandum and the justificans. In regard to the justificandum, there is that which is to be justified and the proposition describing it.

We shall call that which is to be justified the "justificate" and the proposition describing it a "descriptor." The justificans needs to be divided into the propositions, which we shall call "justificators," and that which is described by them, which we shall call "justificatives."

Let us apply this analysis to a concrete case. Suppose that an economist should assert that we were going to have a depression within two years. He might be called upon to justify his assertion or statement and proceed to assert other statements such as: (a) production has already surpassed existing market demands; (b) this overproduction necessitates the laying off of employees; (c) increased unemployment is going to curtail market demands even more; (d) whenever these conditions obtain the result is a depression within a year or two.

In this example, Statements a, b, c, and d are justificators. What do they justify? It is clearly not the pending depression. However, if the justificators justified the proposition that there would be a depression within two years, the proposition would be the descriptor and the state of affairs described by it, a depression within two years, would be the justificate. Hence the justificators, in so far as they were true, would justify the depression. But this is obviously absurd. The confusion which gives rise to this absurdity is the ambiguity of the word "assertion," which means both the proposition asserted and the act of asserting the proposition. The justificators justify the assertion in the sense of the *act of asserting*, but they are assumed to justify the assertion in the sense of the *proposition* asserted. A similar ambiguity appears when we use the words "judgment," "statement," or "belief" instead of "assertion."

In the above example, the justificate would be the economist's act of asserting that there would be a depression within two years. The descriptor would be the statement describing this state of affairs: "The economist, Mr. X, asserted that there would be a depression within two years." The justificators provide evidence in support of the truth of the proposition asserted by Mr. X and in this way justify his act of asserting the proposition. The proposition asserted may be in need of verification, confirmation, or explanation, but it seems inappropriate to speak of its being justified.

This kind of justification may be called "cognitive" because the act is justified in relation to a cognitive interest, an interest in knowledge. Methodological rules of inquiry constitute the criteria by which we judge whether an act of asserting a proposition is cognitively justified. These rules specify the conditions which must be met if our cognitive interest is not to come to grief.

Our analysis has shown that Feigl's validation type of justification actually reduces to his vindication form. This was accomplished by demonstrating that in his validating form it is an *act of asserting*, not the proposition asserted, that is justified, and that the justification consists of showing that the act is a satisfactory means of attaining a cognitive goal.

All justifications are of acts of persons or social institutions (which are also acts of persons but with a difference), and they are all of the means-end type. Justification as such consists of showing that some act is a relatively efficient means of satisfying some interest or set of interests. An economic justification consists of showing that some act satisfies or tends to satisfy some economic interest or set of interests; a military justification consists of showing that some act satisfies or tends to satisfy some military interest, and so forth.

Axiological inquiry concerned with justification in relation to some given specific, limited goal may be called "technological." The questions asked in this kind of inquiry are not those of science, such as: What is X? Why did X occur? If X occurs, what will follow? and so on. To be sure, answers to questions of this type are pre-supposed and used in technological inquiry, but the unique questions asked are: Given a specific, limited end to be achieved, what is the *best* way to do it? How *ought* it to be achieved? What is the *right* way to achieve it? and so forth. The italicized words do not appear in the scientific conceptual scheme.

Since an act is said to be militarily justified if it is shown to contribute more than any of its alternatives to the satisfaction of military interests, economically justified if it is shown to contribute as much or more to the satisfaction of economic interests, and so forth, it should follow that an act is *ethically* justified if it, of all alternatives, contributes as much or more to the satisfaction of the ethical interest. But what is *the ethical interest*? There are several ethical interests, namely, honesty, truthfulness, benevolence, justice, and so forth. However, there is one ethical interest that is dominant over all others and may be referred to as *the* ethical interest, namely, *good will*, an interest which has for its object the maximum net satisfaction of all relevant interests in any given situation. We must not confuse *the*

maximum net satisfaction of all relevant interests with the satisfaction
of the maximum number of interests. The former involves an organization of interests in such a way that a resultant interest—an interest
the satisfaction of which all relevant interests concur in—can emerge
from a set of conflicting interests. In such a situation the satisfaction
of the resultant interest cancels or at least mitigates the dissatisfaction
of the sacrificed but concurring interests.

It is now clear that the fundamental distinction between technological and ethical justification is that the former is in relation to some
specific, limited interest or end, whereas the latter is in relation to all
revelant interests or goals. In technological inquiry, whether the
given end *ought* to be achieved is not questioned or investigated. The
only questions asked concern how it can best be achieved. In ethical
inquiry, the statement that the maximum net satisfaction of all relevant
interests ought to be achieved is an analytic statement and thus true
by virtue of its meaning alone.[3]

The cognitive goal of axiological inquiry, whether technological
or ethical, is, as we have been maintaining, descriptive-justificatory
knowledge. Our axiological conceptual scheme is a function of both
the experienced structured qualities and relationships of acts and the
cognitive goal of axiological inquiry. With the goal of axiological
inquiry our purpose, we abstract from the complex of experienced
qualities and relationships of acts and forge value concepts out of
which value statements can be formulated and empirically verified.
Rational living in a social or private environment requires it. In no
other way could we make rational, reflective adjustments to problematic
situations involving conflicting interests.

Tied to the monistic theory of factual truth is a monistic theory of
description. Logical empiricists have assumed that to describe is to
do so in terms of the scientific conceptual scheme. But this thesis
follows from the assumption that the distinctive mark of science is
empirical description when in fact its distinctive feature is its descriptive-explanatory character. They have not seen the possibility of
different kinds of descriptive conceptual schemes.

We have shown that value sentences in statement form do express

---

[3] We are not attempting within the scope of this paper to consider the nature of
ought-statements. Our attention is limited to value sentences containing value terms
as predicates. These we hold to be both factual (is-statements) and descriptive but
not scientific.

propositions which are empirically descriptive, but in terms of the axiological, they express the descriptive-justificatory, conceptual scheme. But they are nonetheless factual, empirically verifiable, and proper subjects of factual truth-value predicates. Axiological knowledge, empirically verified (or confirmed) statements formulated out of concepts from the axiological conceptual scheme, is no more of a mystery nor mystical than scientific knowledge. Both are completely compatible with each other and with the empirical verifiability theory of factual meaning. Both are twin products, as well as necessities, of reflective living.[4]

[4] For the Comments and Response which relate to this paper see pp. 287-95, 356-58, and 380-82, below.

THE THIRD MAN

IAN MCGREAL

How is the significance of a word determined?" young Professor Sam N. Tassist asked his pretty friend Jean L. Monodogma. "How, in particular, is the significance of the word 'good' determined?"

"That question again!" Jean replied irritably. "As far as I'm concerned, that question is settled—in my own mind, at least."

"Then let me stir it up again, dear, but within the context of a larger question," Sam said soothingly. "I'm not particularly interested, at the moment, in your theory of value—although I hope that before we've finished talking you'll have told me something about it. What I want to know is how one finds the significance of a word."

"Then I suppose you're not interested in *created* definitions—that is, in verbal definitions. If so, my answer is that one discovers the significance of a word by studying how it is used."

"How do you do that, Jean? I don't mean to ask how it is done, as if all philosophers employed the same method. This is a personal question. How do *you* do it?"

"I'm not sure I trust you," Jean whispered, half to herself. "To be sure, all methods are devised or chosen by persons and are, in that sense, personal—but some are better than others. If your question is merely personal, Sam, it's not philosophical."

"It isn't *merely* personal, Jean."

"Then I'll tell you what you want to know, although I suppose I'm about to become a victim of your criticism. This is how I work: since the word 'good' is often used in sentences of the form 'X is good,' I begin by asking what the significance of 'good' is, as used in sentences of that form. Having determined the significance of 'good' as so used, I am then prepared to determine whether the significance of 'good,' as used in the sentences of other forms, or as used in non-sentence form, has the same significance. That ought to satisfy *you*, Sam N. Tassist!"

"You are suggesting, I suppose," Sam said agreeably, "that in order to determine the significance of the word 'good' as used in sentences of the form 'X is good,' you must substitute, or find substituted, for the variable 'X' a value of the variable, for the form 'X is good' is not itself a sentence."

"Of course, Sam! How tiresome to emphasize fundamentals. But, then—sometimes I think you are more a teacher than a philosopher. Now, of course, I realize that the significance of the word 'good' may be affected by the significance of the other words in the sentence. It may be that the significance of the word 'good' is determined, at least in part, by the significance of the value of X. Thus, the question whether 'good' always has the same significance should be left open —until, as a result of inquiry, it can be closed."

"I should remind you," Sam said gently, "that if you substitute a word for X, you will have the problem of resolving the ambiguity of that word. Prior to the resolution of ambiguity, a word is itself a kind of variable."

"Oh, I know that!" she replied. "What I meant is illustrated by the following: suppose someone says, 'This hammer is good.' We want to know the significance of 'good' and we are wondering whether it is affected by the significance of the word 'hammer.' Well, whatever may be the exact significance of 'hammer,' provided its significance is a usual one for that word, 'good' probably signifies 'instrumentally good.' Of course, it would be silly to suppose it signified 'morally good!' But if the speaker had said, 'This is a good hammer,' the word 'good' might have signified 'good of its kind.' However, since we are limiting ourselves initially to sentences of the form 'X is good,' we don't have to worry about that.

"Now, if someone were to say, 'This feeling is good,'" she continued, "we should be inclined to suppose that 'good' signified 'intrinsically good.' Further investigation in each of these cases would be necessary, but this preliminary survey should be enough to show that the word 'good' may vary in its significance relative to the value of X.

"However—" she went on, holding her thin hand before Sam's open mouth, "we should realize that although the phrases 'morally good,' 'instrumentally good,' 'good of its kind,' and 'intrinsically good' may express the significance of 'good' in various sentences, the word 'good,' *as used in these phrases*, probably signifies a generic character the discovery of which would resolve our problem of definition. To summarize: although 'good' may vary in its significance relative to the value of X, it probably has a common core of significance—its generic sense—which we are concerned to discover."

"Doesn't a problem arise in connection with the word 'is' in the sentence 'X is good'?" Sam asked, noticing that Jean was getting her breath. "The ambiguity of 'is' is notorious. In fact, a whole school has been built about it. If the word 'is' may vary in its significance, so may the word 'good' which follows, for the significance of 'good' in a particular sentence may be determined, at least in part, by the significance of the word 'is.'"

"Well, Sam, we *are* progressing!" Jean cried. "I was just about to make that point. After all, it certainly is important to know whether, when a philosopher says, 'Pleasure is good,' he is using the word 'is' in the sense 'is identical to' or in the sense 'is characterized by' or in some other sense.

"Not only that—but there is the further possibility that the significance of the word 'good' may be relative to the circumstances of the utterance of the sentence having the form 'X is good.' I suppose that it is by reference to the circumstances that one most often resolves the problem of deciding what kind of goodness is being attributed to an entity. Two sentences of the form 'X is good'—as, for example, 'This steak is good' and 'This steak is good'—may be identical in the arrangement of the words, in the significance of 'is,' and in the significance of whatever is substituted for X—in this case, 'This steak' —but differ in the significance of 'good' because of a difference in the circumstances. The one sentence might mean that the steak is good because it tastes good; the other might mean that it is good in virtue of being safe to eat."

"I can offer another example," Sam murmured graciously. "When a person who loves his sensations says, 'This feeling is good,' he means it is worth having for the sake of the thrill. But when a moralist who despises joy (or says he does) says, 'This feeling is good,' he means it is *morally* good, worth having as an incentive to virtuous conduct."

"Thank you, Sam. May I conclude? In order to discover the significance of 'good'—or, rather, *a* significance of 'good'—one must discover the significance of the word assigned as a value of X, the significance of 'is,' and the circumstances involved. Then one must analyze the entities denoted by 'good' and find their common and exclusive features, or, at least, come as close as one can to finding them—and there you are!"

Sam N. Tassist hesitated, and then, with patently false modesty said, "I must confess that I seem to have lost the trail. I am not sure, from your account, how one goes about discovering the significance of a word. For, in order to discover the significance—or *a* significance, as you say—of the word 'good,' one must first of all determine the significance of other words—namely, of the word in the place of X, and of the word 'is.' But how are the significances of those words determined? It will not do to talk about analyzing 'the entities denoted' until one has specified how one determines which entities are denoted by a word. Your answer amounts to this: in order to determine the significance of a word, determine the significance of some other words, and then analyze the entities signified, or denoted, by the word in question. And I want to know, 'How does one determine which entities are signified by a word in question?'"

"I'm sorry, Sam," Jean L. Monodogma replied, patently lying, "but I must confess I can't understand your question."

"I don't blame you," Sam responded honestly, "for the question is itself ambiguous. And the word that is causing the trouble is 'signify.' We might be able to progress, as you put it, if we could find someone uttering a sentence of the form 'X is good.'"

The two philosophers wandered hand in hand until they found two men talking. One of the men uttered (much to the gratification of the philosophers) a sentence of the form "X is good":

"Pie is good."

"So is cake," answered the other.

"Here is our chance," Sam whispered to Jean. "Let's try to find out what 'good' signifies as used in the sentence just uttered, and then we may be able to decide what we were doing in trying to find out."

He tapped the first speaker on the shoulder. "Pardon me," he said. "What does the word 'good,' just uttered by you, signify to you?"

"I like pie."

"No—no," Sam replied patiently, "We are interested in what the word 'good' signifies in the sentence 'Pie is good.' Now, we can't substitute the phrase 'I like pie' for the word 'good,' because, if we did, we would then be left with the preposterous sentence, 'Pie is I like pie'! Perhaps you would be willing to say that the word 'good' signifies 'liked by me' because if we substitute that phrase for the word 'good,' we then have the neat sentence, 'Pie is liked by me.' How about it?"

"O.K.," said the man, shrugging his shoulders.

"Well, that's fine," Sam replied, thinking over the situation, and remembering how the speaker (whom he had named "A") had licked his lips and smiled, and acted as if he would gladly polish off a pie, were a pie present. "You certainly seem to like pie. You behave in a manner I should be willing to specify as a manner definitive of liking pie. So it seems likely that the sentence 'Pie is good' signifies 'Pie is liked by me.'"

Sam then turned to the second person present, the fellow addressed by A, and (thinking of him as "B") asked, "What did the word 'good' in the sentence 'Pie is good,' uttered by A, signify to you?"

"Worth eating," B answered abruptly.

"Come, come!" Sam replied agreeably. "You got the point concerning the necessity for a phrase that could be substituted for the word 'good,' but you mustn't use the synonym for 'good' in your definition. Let's see now—what would you be willing to say that 'good' signifies to you, if you are not permitted to use the word 'good' or 'worth' or any other word synonymous with 'good'?"

"All right, then," B answered after some thought. "I was going to say that 'Pie is good' signifies 'Pie is able to cause good taste sensations'—but that would be using the word 'good,' and you won't let me do that—so I'll say that 'Pie is good' signifies to me 'Pie is able to cause taste sensations of a pie-kind.' But, somehow, that seems wrong," he concluded, shaking his head.

"Never mind," Sam responded cheerfully, "You're doing fine. In case you're interested, your friend A has probably used the word 'good' valuatively, in the appraisive mode, and it signifies in the designative mode to you."

"Ummm," B murmured uncommittedly, still shaking his head.

"Look here!" Jean said to Sam, "Are we being scientific about this? I mean, here we are asking these untrained observers to interpret the word 'good'! Maybe we're even forcing answers upon them to some extent. I'm not satisfied, personally, with their answers. The word 'good,' it seems to me, signifies neither 'liked by me' nor 'able to cause taste sensations of a pie kind.' That's fantastic, come to think of it! Think of all the good things there must be which I haven't come across and haven't had a chance to like! Think how many things I have found to be good which were good before I liked them! Think of the good things that aren't able to cause taste sensations! And think of the things able to cause taste sensations that aren't good!

"No—we're going at it the wrong way," she continued. "We can't find the significance of 'good' by asking the man who uses the word, and we can't find it by asking another man who happens to hear the word used. After all, to us philosophers, what difference does it make how Tom, Dick, A, and B interpret symbols? The mode of significance *to them* is irrelevant *to us*! *We* want to know *the* significance of the word 'good,' and that's the long and short of it!"

Sam shrugged his shoulders. "Oh, I was simply using a short cut in getting verbal reports—that's all," he said. "What I'm really interested in is the behavior responses of these fellows to the utterance of the word 'good.' Incidentally, if we're going to be scientific, we should remember to say *a* significance of the word 'good.' Perhaps the word 'good' is used in various senses."

"So is the word 'science,'" Jean replied laconically. "Very well, then, in order to determine the significance of a sense of the word 'good'— if you will permit my rephrasing it—it doesn't seem fruitful to ask A and B, who may very well either not understand our questions or not be able to recognize the significance of the words they use. Further, even if we don't ask A and B, but examine the situation, observing the behavior of A and B in an attempt to understand what the word signifies to them, irrespective of what they think or say it signifies, it might nevertheless turn out that what the word 'good' signifies to A and B is not what it *really* signifies."

"And what is its *real* significance?" Sam N. Tassist asked in a challenging and impertinent way.

"I don't know—I don't like the word 'real' either. But, somehow or other, although I suppose a word must be significant *to* someone, when I want to know a significance of the word 'good,' I don't care to know what the term signifies to A, who uses it, or to B, who hears it. It's as if there must be a third man to whom the word 'good' is significant, and whose point of view is the one that interests me."

"Ah-ha!", Sam responded. "Now we're getting somewhere! And who is *the third man*?"

After a long moment Jean answered: "Why, *I* am the third man! I am a person to whom the words of other men are significant, and I am *the* person whose interpretative point of view interests me most. And you—*you* are a third man, too. Each of us has his own particular criteria by reference to which he determines what is significant *to him*! We should not even speak of *the* significance of *a* sense of the word 'good,' but, rather, of *a* significance of *a* sense of the word 'good.'"

Sam commented enthusiastically: "Then if the behavioral response of A is, to me, *the* significance of the word 'good,' the responses of B, or other persons, are irrelevant. So that you were not quite right in implying that the response of A is not relevant to a question of significance."

"I think I suggested that it was not relevant *to my question*. I meant that *I don't care* what A's response is; that isn't what I *want* to know. But I realize that if the behavioral response or some other kind of reaction is what interests an observer, a student of signs, a third man —then, certainly, study of such responses or reactions is relevant to his inquiry."

"But if you're not interested in the responses of persons, Jean, what are you interested in? For it seems to me that if one is concerned with the *significance* of a word—with its sign status—then one must study the causal relationships between the utterance of the word and the behavior of the person using it, or hearing it."

"I shouldn't have said simply that I don't care what A's response is. I should have said that A's response does not constitute the significance of the word 'good' as far as I am concerned. Suppose, for example, that the utterance of the word 'good' disposes a person to preferential behavior—suppose, that is, that upon hearing the word 'good' such a person becomes a sort of person who could choose that which is then called 'good' in preference to something else. I should not be inclined, on the basis of that observation, to decide upon the significance of 'good.'

"And I believe I am not alone in this," she continued. "I believe that I am interested in the kind of significance which interests most philosophers."

"How rash of you to say so!" Sam protested.

"But we must be rash—otherwise, the truth will never break out! Whether or not I am correct in saying that most philosophers share my interest in a certain kind of significance, let me try to explain what that kind of significance is.

"When I wonder about the significance of a word, I wonder about its *symbolic import*. Often, if not usually, words are used to refer to something, to some individual, some character, some set of characters.

some place, some time. But in studying words *as used*, I am interested in finding that to which the word actually refers, whether or not its user intended it to have the kind of symbolic import it acquires as used. It doesn't matter, then, how a person defines a word. After all, he may not use it as he defines it. The question is how to find that to which a word most often refers—that is, how to find its symbolic import.

"Let me say, parenthetically, that although the mode of analysis I am about to explain applies to most of the terms with which philosophers concern themselves—words such as 'beauty,' 'truth,' 'real,' and 'cause' —it does not apply to such a word as 'God' which, for most persons at least, has no discoverable denotation. Such a word acquires its meaning in much the same way that a word acquires its meaning by definition, but in fragments, and sometimes indirectly. Thus, someone writes, 'God is all-wise,' and we infer 'all-wise being' as part of the symbolic import of 'God.' Since we are talking about 'good,' a word used in such a way that part of its denotation is known to us, I shall not dwell on the deductive kind of analysis to which I have just referred. The mode of analysis appropriate to the problem of significance which interests me in the case of a word such as 'good' is better called 'inductive.'

"I have not defined 'symbolic import.' I think that you will understand what I intend by that phrase if I give you an example of the kind of analysis I have called 'inductive.' But before I do that, I am willing to say that by the 'symbolic import' of a word *whose denotation is in part known to us*, I mean its '*usual causal significance.*' But what that *latter* phrase means—" she continued laughingly, "the following example is designed to show!

"Suppose, then, that a child wants to discover the symbolic import of the word 'dog.' He begins by finding instances of the usages of the word. He comes to realize that an animal of a certain kind is *often* present when the word 'dog' is used, that no other kind of thing is present as often, that it is seldom the case that someone says, 'That's a dog!' or something of the sort when no animal of the kind noticed is present, and that different kinds of things, including some animals somewhat like the kind he has noticed but distinguishable from them, are sometimes referred to as 'not dogs.'

"He finds that he is usually able to call animals of the kind he has noticed 'dogs' and win understanding. A habit of word usage is developed even though the child may not be able to define the word 'dog.'

"Is the word 'dog' *always* used in the sense in which the child probably comes to understand it? No. For example, horses are sometimes called 'dogs' by disgruntled gamblers. The child probably learns to use the word as it is *usually* used in virtue of noticing that utterances of the word causally signify a certain kind of animal more often than they signify anything else.

"Well, then, is it the case that every time the word 'dog' is used, it is used in such a way that it may be understood to be causally related to the existence of some dog? In other words, is a symbol, when used, always a causal sign of what it symbolizes? No, for even when a word is used in its usual sense—and it need not be—it may be used erroneously, as when someone mistakes a large cat for a dog, or it may be used fictitiously, or in such a way that no discovery of a causal connection between *that* utterance and some particular signified entity is possible for any interpreter.

"Nevertheless, *within* the class of utterances of the word 'dog,' there are those utterances which are causally related to the existence of animals of a certain kind more often than to any other kind of thing. It is by reference to the distinguishing character of such animals that the significance—that is, the symbolic import—is finally discovered. Thus, I say that to find this kind of significance, that is, *symbolic import*, one must find what is *usually causally signified* by utterances of the word. Since such an investigation is not likely to be completed, the most one should say is that a certain word *probably* symbolizes whatever, by the utterances studied, has been signified causally more often than other entity.

"Now, Sam, you remember that we decided that there are many kinds of significance. To each third man, his own. But this is mine. This is the kind of significance I seek, and this is the kind most philosophers have sought in attempting to define 'truth,' 'beauty,' 'goodness,' and other terms common (or nearly so) to the understanding of men."

"I'm not quite sure, Jean," Sam said quietly, almost overcome by Jean's volubility, "what you mean by a 'causal sign.' Apparently, by the symbolic import of a word, you mean the defining character of the entities usually causally signified by utterances of a word. It is important, then, to know what a causal sign is."

Jean nodded. "All right. If X is a causal sign of Y to person Z, then X is causally related to Y or coexists with Y as part of a cause or effect, and, in virtue of knowing this, Z infers the existence of Y from knowledge of the existence of X, or would infer the existence of Y if he had knowledge of the existence of X.

"One may realize from an understanding of this definition of 'sign' why a symbol is not always a sign in this sense of the word. In the first place, a symbol need not be used. It is not then a sign. Secondly, even if it is used, the utterance need not signify a discoverable member of the class symbolized. Of course, one may choose to call symbols 'signs.' I have sometimes used the word 'significance' in that sense and sometimes in the sense related to the causal sense of 'sign.' If one chooses to mean by a 'sign' a 'symbol,' then a symbol is always a sign."

"There is at least one other sense of the word 'sign' relevant to our discussion," Sam said patiently. "In this third sense of the word 'sign' (for we have the 'causal connection' sense and the 'symbol' sense), X is a sign of Y to Z (to use your mode of explanation) if Z believes X to be causally related to Y or to coexist with Y as part of a cause or effect and, in virtue of this belief, infers the existence of Y from belief in the existence of X. If a 'third man' were interested in the significance of a word in the sense of 'significance' related to this third sense of 'sign,' he would get different results from those obtained by your kind of philosopher. And those results would vary according to the 'Z' involved—that is, according to the person to whom the utterance of the word is significant in this sense.

"In effect, then," he continued, "we have *four* senses of the word 'sign' to contend with, for your 'causal connection' definition contained an alternative.

"The significance of a word, then, varies according to the sense of the word 'significance' and there are at least four different senses of the word 'sign' which may be related to the word 'significance.'

"The significance of a word also varies according to the 'Z' who might be the speaker, the listener, or a third man. (Of course, the speaker or listener may, as an observer with criteria of significance, be a third man himself.) Since these persons vary in their interests, there is a resultant variation of significance.

"Even if the 'Z' is constant, and the sense of 'sign' is constant—say, the 'causal connection' sense—the significance may vary according to the causal connection Z settles upon as the connection relevant to his sense of 'significance.' The utterance of a word might be a sign of the existence of a dog, but the sign aspect of interest to Z might be the *emotional effect* of the utterance. The significance of the word, then, would vary according to the kind of causal relationship noted, provided the significance were related to that interest, as it often is.

"To make the matter more complicated, there are ambiguities in the definitions of 'sign' we have offered, and ambiguous words in the sentences of the form 'X is good,' as we pointed out at first. It is not surprising, then, that men argue about *the* significance of the word 'good'—and about every other word!"

"I am afraid that this discussion has convinced me that the situation is at least as involved as that," Jean said soberly. "Perhaps I have not been as charitable to persons having other interests and, hence, other kinds of significance, as I ought to have been."

Sam smiled sympathetically. "Nor have I been friendly in the past to your efforts to find 'common and exclusive characters' of entities signified by utterances of a term. Perhaps we can be entirely friendly if you give me an example of how, prior to analysis of signified entities, you could eliminate cases in which a word is mistakenly applied."

"Of course," Jean L. Monodogma replied. "For example: Suppose A says, 'That pie is good,' and I ask, 'To whom, and in what respect?' and he answers, 'To me, in respect of its taste.' 'How do you know, if you haven't tasted the pie?' I ask. 'I *don't* know,' he replied, 'but it looks quite a bit like pies I have liked in the past.' He tastes the pie, spits part of it out, wrinkles his nose, moans, and says, 'I don't like it! It's a terrible pie!' 'Is it a good pie to taste—that is, is it good-tasting to you?' I ask. 'No, of course not!' 'But you said it was.' '*I take it back*,' A says; 'it's bad.' 'Was it bad even while you were saying it was good?' I ask. 'Of course, you don't suppose it changed while I was talking, do you?' 'But you *did* like it, prior to tasting it?' 'I liked it because I *thought* it would taste good. But now I know I made a mistake. It was bad even while I was thinking how good it was.'

"It should be clear from the example," Jean continued, "that you can't assume something has a characteristic simply because, by means of words, a characteristic is attributed to it. Grass doesn't become blue because someone says it is so. Nor does a thing become good because it is called 'good.' Since we can't know, in every case, when a person knows enough to know that a thing is good, we can begin our effort to discover defining characteristics by emphasizing those instances in which existential judgments are confidently made in situations in which the person making the judgments *seems* to know what he is talking about and does not later retract his judgment. In that way, we may be better able to frame an initial hypothesis concerning the defining characteristics of the largest class of entities *probably* causally signified by utterances of the word. In so far as the members of such a class have a common and distinguishing character, such a character constitutes the probable significance to us (relative to our criteria of significance) of the word. We can be mistaken about that significance; the significance to us is not simply a matter of opinion. But it is a matter about which we choose to have an opinion."

"All right," Sam said patiently. "What does the word 'good' signify to a person like you?"

"When 'X is good' is uttered by a person A, it probably signifies that X is such that if, under certain specifiable circumstances, A were to have knowledge of, or about, the entity X, he would favor it (that is, he would be disposed to reach for or retain, not to escape from or reject it). In other words, in so far as a thing is such that, if known by some person it would be favored on account of the respect known, it is good in that respect, to that person, under the circumstances.

"This accounts for the judgment about the pie. We can understand how a person, believing a pie to be such that if he tasted it, he would have a taste experience to his liking, might favor a pie on that account, and call it 'good.' The fact that such a person sometimes 'takes back' the word 'good' *after* having tasted the pie suggests that a thing is good only if it can win, or retain, favor upon examination.

"It might be interesting to draw an analogy," Jean continued, managing by the persuasiveness of her discourse to retain Sam's attention. "Instead of considering a judgment of the kind 'X is good,' let us consider one of the kind 'X is green.' What does 'green' signify? Again, in order to answer that question, we must study the third man. *What are the interests of the person who studies symbols?* What features in the situation in which a word is uttered are relevant to his inquiry?

"One man might be interested in the difference the utterance of the word 'green' makes to the behavior-disposition of the person uttering (or hearing) the word. He would probably decide that 'green' as used in sentences of the form 'X is green' usually signifies a disposition to expect a certain particular kind of visual sensation were the person concerned to observe visually the entity referred to as being 'green.' The word may signify such a disposition even if the case is such that were the person to observe X, he would be surprised to find that he did not receive the kind of sensation he expected.

"Another kind of third man might be interested in the emotions that arise in persons who use the word 'green.' The emotion would be the significant feature to him. (Note how the ambiguity of the word 'significant' in the preceding sentence emphasizes the relationship between word significance and interest.)

"A third kind of third man might be interested in what the word 'green' signifies to a person interested in the defining character of those entities most often causally signified by utterances of the word. He might hear someone say, 'That car is blue,' while the speaker is looking at a car under blue lights. The following day, looking at the car in daylight, the same speaker might be heard to say, 'No—the car is green.' 'It is true that the car was blue?' 'No. I thought it was blue —but it was green all along. I take it back—the car was *not* blue even though I said it was. At the time I didn't know that the lights made things look blue.'

"The student of symbols might decide, if he were to come across similar instances, that 'X is green,' as ordinarily used, symbolizes 'X is such that, under normal lighting conditions (daylight), if a person having normal vision (like most persons) were to observe X visually, he would receive a particular, unique kind of visual sensation called "green."' The word 'green' in the latter part of the definition is not a word having the same significance as the word 'green' being defined. The word being defined symbolizes a causal property definable only by reference to the intuitable character 'green.'

"Another third man might want to discover the significance (in some specifiable sense of the term 'significance') to him of 'green' as used by a scientist reporting his observations of light waves by means of instruments.

"And, of course, there are innumerable other possibilities. Any one of these persons can be mistaken in his hypothesis if he arrives at one. Whatever 'significance' signifies to him, he might err in his selection of relevant data, or in drawing conclusions from the data. But *no one of these persons—these 'third men'—is correct in assuming that what a word signifies to him, even when his investigation is careful and complete, is* THE *significance of the word.*

"Let us compare 'green' and 'good.' The word 'green' may signify a certain kind of behavior-disposition to a person interested in behavorial response to the utterance of a word. Such a response is definable without reference to the characteristics of the object said to be 'green.'

"Similarly, the word 'good' may signify a certain kind of behavior-disposition to such a 'third man,' and such a response would be definable without reference to the characteristics of the object said to be 'good.'

"Or, the word 'green' may signify an emotion to a person interested in emotions. And the emotion is distinguishable from any characteristic of the object said to be 'green.'

"Similarly, the word 'good' may signify an emotion, to such a person, without signifying (to such a person) a characteristic of the object said to be 'good.'

"Or, the word 'green,' as ordinarily used, may signify a causal characteristic to a student of symbols interested in discovering the defining characteristic of entities usually causally signified by utterances of the word. An object may be green (such a person would contend) even though no one is looking at it, in the sense that it may be such that *if* some specifiable kind of person were to look at it, under certain specifiable circumstances, *then* he would receive certain sensations called 'green' (or respond in a manner said to be 'responding to green').

"Similarly, the word 'good' may signify a causal characteristic to a student of symbols interested in discovering the defining characteristic of entities usually causally signified by utterances of the word. An object may be good (such a person would contend) even though no one is acquainted with it, in the sense that it may be such that *if* some specifiable kind of person were acquainted with it, under certain specifiable circumstances, *then* he would favor it (or respond in a manner said to be 'favoring')."

"I suppose," Sam said wearily, "that the reason why some philosophers offer one kind of definition for 'green' and another kind of definition for 'good' is that they switch third men in midstream. There's no law against it, of course, but if they don't tell us about it,

it can be terribly confusing trying to figure out what kind of philosopher is scrambling out of the water."

"Especially if it's over his head!" Jean laughed.

"One more thing—" Sam said abruptly, "some of my friends have
been wondering whether the word 'good' is a designator, or an appraisor, or a prescriptor (to use Morris's terms), and whether, when
the term is used, it is used informatively, valuatively, or incitively.
May I venture an answer, based upon our discussion?"

Jean nodded her head demurely.

"The mode of signification is relative to the third man. If a person
chooses to ignore the entities usually causally signified by utterances
of the word 'good' and chooses to confine his attention to the behavior
and intention of the word-user, then the word 'good' can signify to
him only in the appraisive or prescriptive modes, depending upon
the intentions of the users. 'Good,' then, signifies either that something has preferential status for behavior, or that certain response-
sequences are required.

"But if a student of signs turns his attention to the entities ordinarily
called 'good' and studies them, the word 'good' signifies to him in
the designative mode. 'Good,' then, signifies a characteristic, that is,
a stimulus-property of stimulus-objects, if one does not limit stimulus-
properties to those definable only in terms of sense responses.

"Or, since the word 'good' ordinarily signifies (in your sense of
'signifies') that a certain object is preferred by someone, it may, in
that sense, be regarded as being ordinarily, an appraisor as well.

"As to its uses, the word 'good,' even in the designative mode, may
be used as the user wishes—to inform someone concerning the value
property of an object, to lead someone to favor an object, or to give
someone a ground for acceptance of the object."

"Yes, I should be inclined to agree that, as I use the word 'signify,'
the word 'good' usually signifies in the designative and appraisive
modes, and is used informatively and, almost as often, valuatively and
incitively—although I'm not sure that I see the difference in the latter
two uses as far as the term 'good' is concerned."

"Nor am I," replied Sam. "We'll have to ask Morris about that."

"I must go now, Sam," Jean said. "You know—you are the most
understanding semanticist I have ever known. You seem to realize
that one studies method in order to use it."

"And you, Jean, are the most genial dogmatist I have ever known.

You seem to realize that although one may settle upon a single sense of significance, that decision is not the only one possible. I think that we ought to get married!" he concluded enthusiastically.

"When you say 'ought' Sam, do you mean that we *would* get married *if* we were interested in doing what probably, according to the evidence available to us, would be such that no alternative would be better (to us) in virtue of the value of its consequences, and such that some alternative would be worse?"

"Probably."

"I think we are married now, Sam," she said smiling. "If not, we can be."[1]

[1] For the Comments and Response which relate to this paper see pp. 296-302, 361-62, and 382, below.

A NON-NORMATIVE DEFINITION OF "GOOD"

A. CAMPBELL GARNETT

A NORM is a standard whereby we decide what is right, what ought to be approved, or ought to be done. "Right," "ought," and "duty" are normative terms. They *entail* the notion of a norm, or standard. It is not immediately clear, however, whether "good" is a normative term or not. Statements as to what is good or bad are, certainly, commonly assumed to be relevant to decisions as to what is right, but there is some confusion as to whether the relevance is one of entailment or whether a proposition about what is good is merely a non-normative premise in a syllogism from which, with the help of a normative premise, a conclusion is drawn concerning what is right.

In an earlier paper[1] and in a recent book[2] I have offered a non-normative definition of "good" and have shown how, by its use, a number of important distinctions in ethics can be clarified. In the present paper I wish to defend this definition against alternatives offered by our contemporaries. I shall also briefly suggest an approach to a naturalistic definition for "right," though the development of this argument would require more space than is here available, as it involves an analysis of the moral personality. The definition of good which I shall here defend was stated as follows in the article referred to above:

"X is good" is equivalent to "X is a reasonable object of a favorable attitude," or more fully, "X is an object toward which it is reasonable to adopt a favorable attitude." By a "favorable" attitude we here mean an attitude inclined to keep, preserve, or promote the thing, or the kind of thing, in

[1] "Distinctions and Definitions in Ethics," *Philosophy and Phenomenological Research*, XII (1951), 74. Excerpts from this paper are reprinted in the present Essay by permission of the editors.
[2] *The Moral Nature of Man* (New York, 1952).

question. By saying that an attitude is reasonable we mean that the attitude is such as would arise from an enlightened understanding of the
object and of oneself and of the relation of the object to oneself. We might
express this by putting the above definition in a third alternative form.
"X is good" means "X is an object toward which enlightened understanding tends to develop a favorable attitude."[3]

Various equivalents of the sentence "X is good" have been offered
by philosophers as clarifications of its meaning in accord with common
usage. Some of these are offered as analytical definitions, others as
synonyms. I think it is possible, and will be useful, to classify them
as follows:

1. Factual statements with affective, conative, or attitudinal predicates, for example:

   X is pleasant
   X is an object of desire, interest, or need
   X is an object which satisfies desire, interest, or need
   X is an object of approval

It is obvious that equivalents of this type do not entail norms. In
order to derive normative judgments from them it is necessary to add
a normative proposition such as the greatest happiness principle of
the utilitarians. But how are we to support such a normative proposition? Few philosophers today will follow Sidgwick in claiming
intuitive insight in support of it. Yet the proposition must be one
assumed in the general background of thought or it would not be
assumed in general usage (as it is) that "good" carries normative
implications. It cannot be claimed, however, that there is any such
general assumption of the greatest happiness principle or of any
similar principle to the effect that one ought always to promote
pleasure, or satisfaction of desire, or objects of approval. There is
therefore no generally assumed normative principle from which the
generally assumed normative implication of "good" could be derived
through definitions of "good" of this first type. For instance, there is
no general assumption of the major premise in the following syllogistic
argument:

   Whatever satisfies desire ought to be generally promoted.
   Good is that which satisfies desire.
   Therefore good ought to be generally promoted.

[3] "Distinctions and Definitions in Ethics," *Philosophy and Phenomenological Research*, XII (1951), 74.

2. A second type of sentence offered as equivalent of "X is good" consists of factual statements expressing the comparative strength or inclusiveness of affect or conation, for example:

X is more pleasant than Y

X satisfies interest A more completely (or more easily) than Y

X satisfies a wide range of interests, needs, or desires

X satisfies the widest possible range of interests, needs, or desires

X is object of strong, or of widespread, approval

The same objection applies here as to definitions of good of the first type. As stated it is clear that these propositions are not normative. Yet those who adopt definitions of value of this type often seem to assume that they are. A great deal of printer's ink has been expended, mostly in America, by those who hold to definitions of this type to refute the distinction between fact and value, and to show that value statements are verifiable because they are simply statements of a certain kind of fact. With definitions of value of this second type this matter of verifiability (at least in principle) should be so obvious as not to need argument—except insofar as unnecessary difficulties are created by arbitrary behavioristic criteria of meaning which make it difficult or impossible to refer to private feeling-states like pleasure and satisfaction. But writers adopting this second type of definition often assume that they are refuting those who, understanding value statements as normative, draw a distinction between fact and value. That could not be the case, however, unless statements of "better" and "worse," defined in terms of comparative measurements of pleasure or satisfaction of need or interest, are taken as statements of norms.

It is clear, however, that such statements do not, of themselves, involve the concept of a *norm*. They can only imply norms if coupled with a normative principle to the effect that that which produces the greater pleasure, or the greatest or most numerous satisfactions, ought to be preferred. It is the fact that some such principle is very widely assumed that gives plausibility to the assumption that definitions of this second type have a normative content. But the acknowledged difficulty of justifying the assertion of any such principle, either as an ethical intuition or on empirical grounds, should lead to the recognition that definitions of our second type do not do justice to the normative associations of the idea of "good."

3. A third set of suggested equivalents of "X is good" consists of factual statements asserting the comparative reliability or reason-

ableness of the judgments upon which attitudes of approval rest, for example:

X is a reliable object of approval

X is a reasonable object of a favorable attitude

I shall pass over this third type of definition for the present, for it is one of these which I wish to defend.

4. A fourth group consists of normative statements in which the character of being normative is directly predicated of X, for example:

X ought to exist

The existence of X is better than the nonexistence of X[4]

The concept of "good" as "ought to exist" or "ought to be" is widely held. It is offered by G. E. Moore in *Principia Ethica,* as a synonym but not an analysis of "good." This use of "ought," however, is not its primary or basic sense. In its primary sense "ought" refers to responsible human actions. It is only by metonymy that it is transferred to objectives with which such actions are concerned. To say that health "ought to exist" is merely a figurative way of saying that people ought to promote and care for health. When this metaphorical "ought" is incorporated into the concept "good," that term becomes, as Moore finds, an indefinable nonnatural predicate; and those who insist upon finding referents and giving precision to meaning find it meaningless. If "ought to exist," or "ought to be" is to be rendered intelligible, therefore, it must be translated into a statement that someone, in some circumstances, ought to prefer, appreciate, promote, or otherwise favor the existence of that which it is said "ought to exist."

5. Statements in which a certain attitude toward X is predicated as normative, for example:

X is a fitting object of a pro attitude

X is an object which ought to be approved

In this fifth type we have a definition of good in the terms last suggested. The difficulty with this type of definition, however, is with the meaning of "ought." A. C. Ewing,[5] discussing the definition, "X is good" = "X ought to be the object of a pro attitude," points out that "ought" cannot here have the sense of "obligation." For instance, it would not be self-contradictory to assert that a certain innocent

---

[4] E. T. Mitchell, *A System of Ethics* (New York, 1950). "Better than" is offered as a "primitive term" in ethics but is evidently meant as normative, for "X is good and X is possible" is offered as equivalent of "X ought to exist."

[5] *The Definition of Good* (New York, 1947, and London, 1948), p. 150.

but not very elevated pleasure is good and at the same time deny that there is any obligation to adopt a favorable attitude toward it. Ewing therefore distinguishes a sense of "ought" which does not entail moral obligation, but which is vaguely described (following Broad) as a certain unique kind of "fittingness." An action that "ought to be done," in this sense of "ought," is one that has a certain relation to its environment such that it is "fitting, appropriate, suitable"[6] or "preferable, rational, desirable."[7] To indicate the use of "ought" in this sense Ewing selects as synonym the term "fitting" and defines "good" as "fitting object of a pro attitude." The peculiar kind of normativeness thus vaguely indicated by the word "fitting" is something we are supposed to be able to intuit with confidence, and we are also supposed to be able to intuit its distinction from obligation and a synthetic a priori connection between it and obligation.

We may agree with Ewing that if "ought" is used in the sense of "obligation" we cannot say that "X is to me a good" entails "X is an object toward which I ought to adopt a pro attitude." For there are many things which we may appreciate as goods but certainly not regard ourselves as under obligation to cultivate. Further when we say that something morally ought to be made the object of a pro attitude we may give as a reason for this that the object is good, without feeling that in doing so we are merely uttering a tautology. It is clear therefore that "good" does not entail the idea of obligation.

The allegedly normative concept of "fittingness" is, however, so vague as to be useless. The synonyms offered, with one exception, do not help. "Preferable," by Ewing's own admission, involves a vicious circle. The same is true of "desirable." "Appropriate" and "suitable" are as vague as "fitting." The one term that casts a little light is "rational." If Ewing had chosen to define "good" as "rational object of a pro attitude," we should have been inclined to agree with him. But then it must be admitted that the definition does not entail any concept that is normative.

6. Sentences expressing certain attitudes and demands concerning X without asserting anything factual or normative, for example:

I approve of X

I demand that you approve of X

I approve of X and demand that you do so also

[6] *Ibid.*, p. 132.
[7] *Ibid.*, p. 151.

We shall confine our attention to C. L. Stevenson's exposition in *Ethics and Language*.[8] Here we find a clear recognition that the term "good," in its ethical sense, somehow carries implications of something more than factual statements of the first two types that we have considered. But this "something more," it is argued, is not the assertion of a norm. It is the making of a demand. Stevenson, indeed, speaks of ethical terms as "normative," and refuses to recognize any significant difference between "good" and "right." But the only sense in which he will admit that ethical terms express norms is that in using such terms each person expresses his present personal demand that those to whom he is speaking adopt the same attitudes of approval and disapproval as those that he is expressing.

The emotive theory thus recognizes that "good" somehow sets up a norm, but the only naturalistic interpretation it can find for a norm is that of a personal demand. This, however, is entirely inadequate. It is true that social and legal norms are established by agreement to join in supporting certain demands. But it is generally recognized that a norm so established may be ethically *wrong*. The mere fact of multiple approval does not make it right. But if any person gave, as his reason for saying such a norm is wrong, nothing more than the fact that he disapproved of it and demanded that others do so also, he would be regarded as simply ludicrous. Yet, when a person expresses an attitude of *ethical* approval or disapproval he is expected to have *reasons* for his attitude. His hearers, if they disagree, are likely to challenge him to give his reasons. If he has none they regard him as having uttered nonsense. This indicates that when a person expresses an *ethical* attitude he is understood as doing *more* than expressing personal approval or disapproval and a demand for agreement by others. He is also understood as *claiming* that his attitude is *reasonable*. That is why he is regarded as talking nonsense if he can give no reasons.

Now Stevenson and other emotive theorists point out that, when people disagree in their ethical judgments, they do not merely continue to vociferate their approvals and demands; they usually proceed, instead, to give reasons for their ethical utterances which they hope will persuade the other person to change his mind. And Stevenson rightly interprets this as a giving of reasons for the attitude of approval

[8] New Haven, Conn., 1944.

expressed in saying something is "good" in the hope that these reasons will induce a similar attitude of approval in the other person. This clearly indicates that when a person, speaking in earnest, says "X is good" he not only expresses his own approval of X but also *believes* that his approval is one for which good reasons can be found. And it is also clear that the other person *understands* him to be, not only *expressing* approval, but *claiming that approval is reasonable.* But this means that "good" has a *cognitive* or *logical* as well as an emotive meaning. It asserts that *approval is reasonable.*

This brings us to the definition to which we have previously referred. "X is good" = "X is a reasonable object of a favorable attitude." But it must at once be recognized that there is nothing normative in this definition. It simply says that the sort of enlightened understanding of all the relevant factors in the situation which can be obtained by the exercise of reason will tend to induce a favorable attitude to X. It does not say that one *ought* to have a favorable attitude to X, in the sense that one is under obligation to do so, or that such an attitude is *morally right,* but only that it is reasonable, that is, that it is the sort of attitude which reason, or understanding, tends to induce.

This definition of "good," therefore, cannot be applied to *right.* It is not equivalent to "ought to exist." The distinction between "good" and "right," which the emotivists have ignored, must be restored. The term "good" does not, of itself, entail a normative concept. However, by reason of a generally recognized assumption coupled with the idea of "good," the term comes to have a normative implication. This is the assumption that one ought to be reasonable. Thus we have the implicit syllogism:

Whatever is a reasonable object of a favorable attitude ought to be made the object of a favorable attitude.

X is good, that is, is a reasonable object of a favorable attitude. Therefore,

X ought to be made the object of a favorable attitude.

The "ought" in this syllogism is the "ought" of moral obligation. And it is by reason of the assumption that there is an obligation upon everyone to shape his attitudes by the use of his intelligence (that is, to be reasonable) that the term "good" acquires its normative implication. At the same time, the fact that "good" does not of itself entail "ought" (in the sense of "obligation") allows for the exceptions pointed out by Ewing. For strict application the major premise of our syllogism, though generally held to be true in general, requires some qualification. The obligation attaches only to such attitudes, and such aspects of attitude, as are within voluntary control, not to feeling elements beyond our control. And perhaps an exception should be made of one's own pleasure, especially trivial and nonelevating (though innocent) pleasures, which may be good though not obligatory. Our non-normative definition of "good," therefore, together with the assumption that one ought to be reasonable, fits the common usage of the term with such exactitude as to justify the claim that it analyzes the essential features of what people have in mind when they use the term with mutual understanding.

It remains to make some comment on the meaning of "ought" in the assumption that one ought to be reasonable. We have defined the term "reasonable" in our definition of "good" as follows: "By saying that an attitude is reasonable we mean that the attitude is such as would arise from enlightened understanding of the object and of oneself and of the relation of the object to oneself." So to say that one ought to be reasonable is to say that one ought to maintain such attitudes. The "ought," of course, implies something in the nature of a requirement, a demand. But the requirement or demand here implied does not come from any external source. It comes from within the personality. It is true that a man does not always shape his attitudes by the use of his intelligence, but insofar as he fails to do so the purposive structure of his life suffers from inner conflict and disorder. His personality loses in integrity. In reflection he must recognize such conduct as folly. The constraint of the ought that operates here is therefore an inner constraint, the demand of the personality for its own integrity as a purposive and intelligent structure. It involves no intuition of an essence, but simply the recognition of a psychological fact which becomes clear to the individual when he calmly and unemotionally reflects on his conduct. It is just as natural, and "naturalistic," as the operations of feeling and intellect that are referred to by the non-normative term "good."

This obligation to be reasonable does not, of course, explain the whole of our sense of obligation. It is simply a duty one owes to oneself. There are also duties one owes to other people. But whether these, too, can be explained as arising from the requirements of personal integrity is a question that would take us into an inquiry

into the structure of personality which cannot be pursued here. For
our purpose of justifying a naturalistic and non-normative definition
of "good," which nevertheless explains the common assumption that
it has normative implications, a naturalistic explanation of the obligation to be reasonable, as here given, is quite sufficient.[9]

[9] For the Comments and Response which relate to this paper see pp. 303-9,
366-69, and 383, 384-86, below.

THE JUDGMENTAL FUNCTIONS
OF MORAL LANGUAGE

HERBERT FINGARETTE

I

THERE ARE three functions of ethical terms which are fundamental, intimately related to each other, and, as yet, inadequately studied. Consideration of these three functions throws light upon perennial problems of the first importance in ethical theory. It also serves to show, in a systematic way, the increasing convergence of the main streams of empirical ethical theory today.

The three functions of ethical terms in question are: (a) to elicit the act of rational choice, (b) to express a certain phase of the act of rational choice, and (c) to refer to an act of rational choice. So far as these functions are concerned, there is no basis for distinguishing among individual ethical terms such as "right" and "good." I am proposing that *all* ethical terms, whatever their differences from one another in some respects, frequently function judgmentally and are therefore alike in this respect.

For handy reference to the view just indicated, I shall use the phrase, "the judgmental functions of ethical terms," or, more briefly yet, "the judgmental analysis," or, again, "the judgmental functions."[1]

Of course I shall discuss shortly such terms as "elicit," "express," and "rational choice." However, I would like to emphasize here that I am concerned primarily with types of functions of ethical terms rather than with the definitions of the latter. This, I believe, is the more fundamental way of approaching the analysis of "typically moral" use of ethical terms.

---

[1] "*Judgment* ... the decision or conclusion reached, as after consideration or deliberation." Funk & Wagnalls, *New College Standard Dictionary* (New York and London, 1947), p. 646. This word is simply the closest approximation I have found in a single English word for the central conception (rational choice) in the theory here presented. See Section III of this paper, where the concept of rational choice is more fully explicated.

While the judgmental analysis is presumed to show how ethical terms frequently do function, it is not to be taken to imply that this is the *only* way ethical terms function. I believe that ethical terms have a number of "typically ethical" functions in addition to the ones just mentioned. It seems to me that the current proliferation of analyses of ethical terms is most profitably interpreted as evidence of the discovery of these varied functions. It has at times been interpreted, however, as a symptom of the difficulty of recognizing the "one true" meaning or function of ethical terms.

Rather than present the remainder of a more formal discussion of the meaning and antecedents of this analysis, I shall proceed to an application of it to a few characteristic problems in ethical theory (Section II). Then, following this, it will be appropriate to return to explicit and direct clarification of the analysis itself (Section III). Finally, I shall consider its relationships to a variety of contemporary, empirical ethical analyses (Section IV).

II

1. I shall turn rather abruptly, therefore, to one of the persistent problems in modern ethical theory. This may be expressed by the following paradox: (a) No statement about the nature of the good or the definition of "good" seems to be free from a sensible challenge. (b) Yet, so frequently, these challenges seem simultaneously to be like playing a childish game instead of sensibly dealing in mature fashion with a serious moral issue.

The philosopher who in the doctor's office accepts the moral justness of the command to take medicine, and so to remain alive, may in his academic office question that rightness. Each action, in its context, seems to have a certain appropriateness. But questioning the morality of the command in the doctor's office would very likely make even the philosopher feel foolish for talking words but saying nonsense.

A number of philosophers—for example Charner Perry, Carnap, Ayer, and G. E. Moore—have, in the critical portions of their analyses of ethical terms, in one way or another emphasized the challengeability of any proposed definition of such terms. They have argued, and I here only very roughly summarize the relevant aspects of their arguments, that such definitions are logically arbitrary, contradictable with consistency, and/or significantly questionable by virtue of our intuitive, though not necessarily analyzed, perception of the proper significance of the term in its typically moral usage. In short, they have gone a long way toward showing that ethical terms, in typical moral usage, are indeterminate in reference. (Although, as is well known, Moore did not go this far until recently, nevertheless, his *critical* arguments pointed in this direction.)

On the other hand, there are ethical philosophers who, in one way or another, have emphasized the sense of moral conclusiveness of the ethical judgment. The "conclusiveness" in question is not felt to be one of dogmatic or arbitrary decision or merely "personal" whim or attitude, but rather of *objectively justifiable, moral* conclusiveness.

Prichard, Moore, Carritt, Ewing, Ross, Broad, and others have concentrated upon the characteristically objective, moral aspect of situations as *intuited*. They have, however, made explicit the importance of such intuition being "preceded and informed by the fullest reflection we can bestow on the act in all its bearings."[2] Others—for example Dewey, G. H. Mead, and Lepley—have argued for the objectivity of moral judgment, with special emphasis upon the reflective, experimental phases of such judgment. These writers, in turn however, make explicit the fundamental importance of the intuited aspect of the moral. Both groups, in effect, emphasize the "objective determinateness" of moral judgment, a judgment requiring both reflection, inquiry, and sensitive intuition.

The paradox mentioned at the beginning of this section may now be restated as follows: On the one hand there is an emphasis upon the indeterminate reference of the moral term when used correctly and normatively. On the other hand, there is an emphasis upon the objectively justified determinateness of reference of the moral term.

Just such an outcome is consistent with, indeed predictable from, the judgmental analysis of moral terms. According to this analysis, one of the functions of such terms is to elicit rational choice. A second function is to express a rational choice, that is, to be a characteristic verbal aspect of the very act of so choosing.

Now if we think of the moral term as elicitative of choice, we sense the essential element of indeterminateness in it; for to use it in this way is not to settle on something but to start the process going which, perhaps, will result in something being chosen at some future

---

[2] W. D. Ross, *The Right and the Good* (London, 1930), quoted from W. Sellars and J. Hospers (eds.), *Readings in Ethical Theory* (New York, 1952), p. 193.

moment. For example, when I say to a young man hesitant about fighting in wars, "It is right to fight in defense of your country," I am not merely announcing a "fact" of some kind. In this typical usage, I am *proposing* to him a question for consideration and urging him to make a rational choice in the matter. The fact that I do suggest what I hope the outcome of his choice will be has led to undue emphasis upon the emotive function of such a statement. There is no doubt that I am expressing some feeling of mine which is favorable to fighting for one's country. Yet there have been many students of the moral process who have felt that the so-called emotivist analysis of ethical terms was lacking and left the usage with a more arbitrary flavor than was actually the case. The judgmental functions, especially the elicitative function, supply the lack. Serious moral discourse involves not merely expressing one's own attitudes, but also proposing an issue upon which the audience may itself make a rational choice.

If, on the other hand, we concentrate our attention not upon the use of the moral term as elicitative of choice but rather upon the *kind* of choice elicited, we sense at once the objective determinateness which use of the moral term elicits. The choice in question must be *rational*. Finally, when we recall the expressive function of moral terms, we can see why one can often have the feeling that a moral term typically does have a determinate reference. For at the moment of choice we express our choice and emphasize its rationality with the help of moral terms. All that anyone need do, however, to revert to the other side of the fence is to take the moral term so uttered as elicitative rather than as expressive. At once it becomes indeterminate in reference.

Thus, from a formal standpoint—that is, according to the customary rules of use—the use of moral terms establishes a situation of choice, and, in this sense, of *indeterminateness*. Yet, in an appropriate way, the use of a moral term has "reference to" (elicits) and eventually expresses, a *determinate*, objectively (rationally) justified object of choice. This is precisely what we previously referred to as the paradoxical outcome of the two opposing types of analysis of ethical terms. But it is now seen to follow, without paradox, from the judgmental analysis.

There remains a further question to be considered in connection with this issue. Is not the burden of the argument of such writers as

Ayer, and others, that there is no logical basis for making choices?

According to the judgmental analysis, that which moral terms are concerned with is *rational* choice. The term "rational" is used here expressly because it is more inclusive and vaguer than "deductive and/or inductive reasoning," or "logical." "Rational" is also more a term of common language than are the latter phrases, since the latter have taken on too much of the technical precision of the post-analytic concept. "Rational" may have its technical meanings in some contexts, but it also retains a good hold in the popular speech. With this fact in mind, there remain two mutually compatible, alternative ways of meeting the criticisms mentioned just previously:

(a) We may suppose that in interpreting "rational" to mean "deductive and/or inductive reasoning" or "logical," the actual sense of "rational" is unwarrantedly narrowed and distorted. We may suppose that there are other modes of reasoning besides inductive and deductive reasoning as these are traditionally interpreted. This alternative has in fact been presented more and more persuasively in the past few years and is gaining increasing acceptance among moral philosophers.[3] I would hold that this alternative is a correct one and a most important one. I shall discuss it in subsequent sections of this paper.

(b) We may suppose that some persons have taken "rational" to mean "deductive and/or inductive reasoning" and that, further, they have supposed it is possible to establish moral judgments by logic alone, or by logic, using as premises only statements of fact. If there are such persons, and if the critical arguments are sound, these persons have been mistaken in their suppositions. This, however, is quite compatible with the judgmental analysis. For it is quite conceivable that a person might *try* to elicit such a rational choice, or *suppose* that he is making one or reporting on one already made, and yet be mistaken in supposing that such a thing is possible. This kind of use would in important respects be like saying, as many people did and still do, that Mr. So-and-So has been bewitched. To be bewitched implies that contact has been made with spirits or "supernatural" forces. But if there happen to be no such, then the belief that there can be any bewitching is mistaken. Nevertheless, it makes perfect sense to say someone is bewitched, and even today, more

---

[3] See Section IV of this paper.

people on this earth do say it or something substantially like it than do not.

A philosophic example pertinent to this second alternative is Kant's moral theory. Kant saw correctly that rationality is essential to morality. It is rationality which distinguishes moral choice from choice based on mere personal taste or coercive force. But Kant supposed that one could discover what is the right thing to do simply by use of the principle of contradiction after having universalized the motive of an act. That is, he took "rational" in a philosophically traditional sense as meaning strictly demonstrative. It is quite widely agreed today that one could not arrive at the choices which Kant did by the use of such a logical test alone. If everyone were to lie or be a misanthrope, it does seem as if life would be difficult, but there is no logical contradiction in supposing that these things could be. Yet this does not prevent Kant from *supposing* he had actually settled upon the right by pure logic, nor does it prevent others from seeing what he is trying to do, and often enough supposing that they themselves have done it. If it cannot in fact be done, then here is simply an important case of people trying to do, and thinking they have done, what is in fact impossible.

I believe there are relatively few persons, except for Western philosophers, whose usage of moral terms is to be interpreted in the light of this second alternative—if only because there are relatively few persons who have any sufficiently precise usage of "rational" such that it is restricted to meaning deductive and inductive reasoning.

In summary, then, moral terms are at once (a) essentially indeterminate in reference (that is, depending for their final reference upon a choice not yet made) and (b) yet justifiably determinate in reference (that is, elicitative and/or expressive of the choice of a particular alternative in a particular situation and of such a choice as is at least believed to be the outcome of rational deliberation). Further, this analysis can hold whether or not rational choice is in fact possible.

2. Another major problem in ethical theory upon which the judgmental analysis throws some light is the problem of identifying the impelling force behind moral behavior when this force is considered to be somehow a "rational" one. Even if we grant a determinate reference to words like "good," we can still ask, "Why bother about what is good?" Whence comes the "rational impulse" to do right?

For example, Schlick grants for the sake of argument the existence of absolute values—values independent of our feelings. He then asks, "How does it concern us? ... The absolutist answers, 'In setting up your goals of action you should prefer the higher to the lower.' If I then ask, 'Why?' the absolutist simply cannot give any answer."[4]

But various moral philosophers have given at least one very interesting answer to Schlick's rhetorical question: they have said, in effect, that to ask this question is to reveal that one has not properly understood or recognized what it is to perceive a moral characteristic. A moral term refers to something which as Bishop Butler said about conscience "carries its own authority with it."[5] Prichard, for example, argued that the sense of obligation is self-evidently authoritative—it is a motive to action, and a motive whose authority is evident to reflection. Its authority cannot be "proven."[6]

How can the judgmental analysis account for these differing, yet quite plausible views? We need here to recall again two at least of the different functions of moral terms mentioned in the judgmental analysis: the elicitative and the expressive.

Suppose Mr. A to have been engaged in moral deliberation and to be in the very act of making what he is convinced is a rational choice in the matter at hand. When he says "This is the right thing to do," he is *expressing* his decision, contemporary with his utterance, to engage in that act as the outcome of rational inquiry. Thus with regard to A's statement, it is senseless to ask, "But why should you do it even if it is right? Suppose you don't desire it?" To ask this is to miss the point of what is going on. He is not at this point arguing, questioning, or persuading himself or anyone else. He is beyond the stage of wondering what to do, or of being concerned with what his audience (if any) will or could do. He is in the very act of firmly committing himself to it, or of actually doing it. Thus the use of moral terms here typically *expresses* an actual motivation, present and already active. Thus A could well say that his judgment carries with it its own authority joined to impulse to act.

Yet with respect to Mr B, who may happen to be present when

[4] M. Schlick, *Problems of Ethics,* trans. by David Rynin (New York, 1939), pp. 116-17. By permission of Prentice-Hall, Inc., publishers.

[5] J. Butler, *The Analogy of Religion and Sermons* (London, 1856), Sermon III, p. 411.

[6] H. A. Prichard, "Does Moral Philosophy Rest on a Mistake?" quoted in A. I. Melden (ed.), *Ethical Theories* (New York, 1950), p. 331.

Mr. A utters his statement expressive of his choice, the moral terms may function differently. Mr. B, if he be at all prone to question the rationality of the decision, may take the moral term in its elicitative function. That is, it may elicit in him the process of reflective choice. This he may make evident by himself using a moral term (elicitatively) in a question à la Schlick: "But why should I or you do this action which you say is right?" This is a proper response so far as the elicitative function of the moral term is concerned. He is not convinced that Mr. A has made a rational choice, or that A's choice would be rational for him, B. Further he is setting about to reflect upon and choose in this matter. He may even be trying to elicit from Mr. A further deliberation and a new act of choice.

III

Now that I have indicated at least two of the typical problems and disputes which the judgmental analysis helps to clarify, it is appropriate to return to a more formal analysis of its key terms. This will allow for a more rigorous examination of its application to the previously mentioned problems and for application of the theory to still other problems. Of course, some of our previous discussion has already pointed the way toward the more precisely formulated analysis to follow.

The term which, perhaps, is likely to raise the most immediate questions is "rational." I have already indicated that this term is to be taken in its ordinary, common sense meaning, and that it is not to be restricted to what, in philosophy, have come to be known as deductive reasoning and inductive reasoning. I am assuming, then, that its ordinary meaning is other than, or more inclusive than, merely one or both of these kinds of reasoning. (It is perhaps worth repeating that even if I am wrong in this, the judgmental analysis would still make sense, and the implications of it, if true, would be that moral statements have made perfect sense but that people have been quite mistaken or misguided in every case of their use.[7] But I do not think that people have been mistaken in this manner.)

I think people have used the term "rational" (or other, roughly synonymous terms) much more broadly than many philosophers and

---

[7] R. Robinson, "The Emotive Theory of Ethics," in Aristotelian Society for the Systematic Study of Philosophy, *Logical Positivism and Ethics*, Supplementary Vol. XXII (London, 1948), pp. 101-3.

logicians have been prone to use it. It is true that observation of common usage makes it evident that most persons would consider appropriately used deductive demonstration or inductive inference as rational or as characteristic of the rational.

In the case of moral questions, however, I believe we have to do with a kind of rationality which may include the previous in some way but is not restricted to them. What is the structure of reasoning in moral matters?

I do not propose to give a complete analysis of rationality in the context of choice. It is part of the point of this paper that it is precisely this problem which we should concentrate upon analyzing from now on because of its central importance and because of its obscurity. Nevertheless, I do have a few comments by way of indicating that my use of "rational" need not be left entirely in the dark, and that its use in analyzing moral terms does not involve circularity. I shall try to show that there is no need to suppose that in analyzing the term "rational" we need, in turn, to use the concept of the moral in any of its variants. That is, we need not suppose that "choose rationally" is a disguised way of saying "use the morally appropriate method of choosing."

I should say that an essential characteristic of a rational choice is that it is a choice for which there is at least one reason. This is the single characteristic which I find universally required as a condition of the actual use of moral terms, and it is, I believe, at times the *only* one which the user of moral terms has at all clearly in mind insofar as this can be determined by the evidence. Even so, knowledge of this single requirement throws additional light on some perennially puzzling problems. I shall indicate how this is so shortly.

But, first, what is the meaning of "reason" in this context of common usage of moral terms?

A reason is a statement (expression of a fact or a norm)[8] such that: (a) It is granted, and, by itself or taken together with other statements granted, it implies that the alternatives to choice are, or are

---

[8] At times, "reason" refers to the state of affairs to which the statement refers, but this does not materially change the analysis. Here, and in what follows, I have tried to avoid using terminology which begs the question regarding such issues as: Are norms facts? Are norms true? Thus I speak of granting statements which, in turn, express facts or norms, and which have implications. I think the meaning of what I say is sufficiently clear for the purposes at hand.

likely to be, either more alike or more different in some respect than they could be shown to be, on the same evidence, if the statement in question were not granted; and (b) the respect in which the alternatives are more alike or more different is itself an object of interest[9] to a person concerned with making the choice.

Here are a few examples which will illustrate this point and make evident some of the reasons for it. In each case, the results of applying the previous criteria coincide with the results of good common sense usage.

Suppose I am trying to decide whether to travel comfortably to meet a friend or to travel by an uncomfortable mode of transportation where the latter is quicker than the former. I now look for reasons why I should choose one or the other.

Statement 1. "I will be late if I travel comfortably but not if I take the other route." This is a reason according to the criteria above. It asserts that something is true of one alternative but not true of the other. Further, I am interested in that characteristic in respect of which they are different—that is, in being on time. If, however, I were not to grant the statement as offered that one will make me late and the other not, then, on the evidence, although it still remains *possible* that they differ as described, it cannot be shown to be so.

Statement 2. "Traveling comfortably usually costs more money than traveling uncomfortably." This is a reason because taken together with facts granted about my present alternatives, it implies that the comfortable one will *more likely* cost more than the other. It thus asserts a difference between the two which, on the basis of the evidence, might not exist if it were not granted that one costs more than the other. Further, I am interested in the cost of travel.

Statement 3. "Only if you take the slower route, will you pass by Myrtle Street." There is implied a difference between the alternatives which might not hold, so far as the evidence goes, if the statement were not granted. However, it happens that I am *not* interested in whether or not I do pass Myrtle Street. Thus I would consider this as irrelevant, that is, *not* a reason.

Statement 4. "Elizabeth is Queen of England." Even if I do have an interest in what is expressed by this statement, it still remains that, so far as I can see, granting it would in no way show any

[9] "Object of interest" is here used very broadly. Anything which a person favors or disfavors, either in attitude, disposition to act, or action, is an object of interest.

increase or decrease of the differences between the alternatives I now face. Consequently it is irrelevant—not a reason; and this, too, accords with ordinary good judgment.

Statement 5. "It is wrong to be late." Here a norm is expressed. Taken in conjunction with Statement 1, it implies that, with respect to being wrong, the alternatives are more different than they could be shown to be on the evidence available if Statement 5 were not granted. In addition, I am interested in statements about whether or not what I do is wrong. Statement 5 is therefore a reason.

It is perhaps worth noting here that treating Statement 5 as a reason is entirely compatible with the judgmental analysis of moral terms and illustrates the complexity of these functions. The term "wrong" functions here in a sentence in which a previous rational choice (or set of them) is reported (it functions referentially). Further, the statement serves to elicit a new rational choice in this situation, itself providing, by means of its report of the prior rational choices, reasons relevant to my present choice. Finally, it expresses my present, new rational-decision-in-the-making that I will now avoid a means of travel which will make me late. It therefore functions to *express* rational choice and thus has the characteristic "feel" of a normative statement. It will be evident from the foregoing that statements in the "indicative" mode and containing moral terms can (but need not) have all three judgmental functions simultaneously. Such statements can, however, function in still other ways: they may, regardless of reason, influence someone to make the choice I have made. This is indeed another, much discussed function of moral terms. However, I should say it is not the *right* way for them to function. (I am, in this last sentence, attempting to elicit from the reader a choice, based upon reasons, with regard to the use by him or others of moral terms to influence others' choices without regard to reasons.)

In summary of the discussion of what constitutes a reason, I shall simply note that the proposed criteria consistently enable us to distinguish between reasons and non-reasons as these are distinguished by common sense usage and intuition.

Of course, I have not distinguished between poor reasons and good reasons, strong reasons and weak reasons. Nor have I discussed how a person properly weighs or organizes reasons so as to make a final choice. I do not propose to do so here since, as I have indicated, I believe that this is a complex and largely untapped field for analysis in contemporary ethical theory. I believe I have done this much, however: I have shown what are the necessary and sufficient conditions for being a reason for rational choice, and have thereby shown that one of the necessary conditions of rational choice—that is, having reasons—can be explained independently of ethical terms.

Since I have not shown it to be otherwise, it remains possible that some of the other conditions necessary for rational choice may require in their analysis ethical terms. I know that some persons who might admit that the analysis of what is a reason in ethical decisions requires no peculiar, irreducible moral concept, yet would hold that when it comes to *evaluating* reasons in morals, we must refer to a unique moral quality or relationship which some reasons possess and others do not. Since, as I have said, I present no conclusive evidence against this, I should criticize such a belief by asking on what grounds this belief is held. The answers to this latter question appear these days to fall into two categories.

Some might hold that there is an irreducibly moral element required in evaluating reasons on the ground that all analyses not containing an irreducible moral element can significantly be challenged from the standpoint of moral practice and theory. Now this question has already been partially examined in Section II, Subsection 1 of this paper. The challengeability of moral analyses can be explained as resting upon the elicitative function of moral terms. Moral terms have as *a* proper function that of eliciting a new act of choice, and since it is always possible to choose anew, to this extent a challenge always is significant. The challenge, then, need not be significant because of some "moral" characteristic which one has in mind.

But the judgmental analysis accounts for such challenge in still an additional very important way which we are now prepared to consider. All we need do is recall that an essential of rational choice is having one or more *reasons*. It then becomes clear that *any* proposal about morality, whether of how a moral term is to be analyzed or of what method is to be used in acting morally, may be meaningfully challenged. For in each case one may be seeking one or more reasons for accepting the decision proposed. Thus, if one is presented with a correct analysis of how a certain moral term such as "right" has been used, one might ask meaningfully, "But why is it right to do X?" (where X is the kind of act which "right" refers to according to the proposed analysis). This question is a demand for reasons, additional to those already given, for doing what is urged or for accepting the proposed analysis. At times it is a demand for a reason for evaluating a previously given reason in a certain way, or for using a certain method in collecting and organizing one's reasons for a choice. If rationality in morals were like deductive reasoning, such a request would, of course, be inappropriate when an actual demonstration of the conclusion has been presented. But moral reasoning is not deductive argument pure and simple, and experience shows that there is no comparably conclusive type of argument in morals. One must always be prepared, therefore, for a meaningful (even if unwise) request for still additional reasons.

Even a request such as "Why is it moral for my choices to be rational?" is actually understood as a request for *reasons for choosing the policy* of making *rational* choices. Therefore "moral" in the quoted question *does* function to elicit a new choice based on (new) reasons.

The second type of answer to the question as to why one should hold that "moral reasoning" has a unique, irreducible moral character is that observation of experience reveals this to be so. Introspection reveals this qualitatively unique, this moral aspect of some relationships or situations. The test is sensitive observation of one's experience.

There is clearly some substance in this thesis. However, it should provoke no surprise in the area of morals, since it is well known that, in other areas, long and practiced exercise of a complex set of abilities leads to largely automatic execution and "simplicity" of perception. There is, for example, an immediate sense of "rightness" when we see a picture hung straight upon a wall. It is the result of a long and elaborate learning process. We learn to relate the edges of the frame to the nearest edges of the wall and, at times, to other lines, points, or objects in a room. At last we do it automatically. When hanging or adjusting pictures, we often rely upon the unique and immediate perceptual quality which the situation has. I do not argue that the intuited quality of "rightness" in this case can be identified with or "reduced to" relations among edges and points. Still it is easy to see that these are the conditions which generally produce the quality, and these are the conditions under which it originally arose. Further, it is not difficult to see that the quality may arise under peculiar circumstances, that is, where these usually concomitant relationships do not exist. We are then "deceived." It then often becomes appropriate to concentrate directly upon the edge, point, object relationships and to pronounce the quality "deceptive." Of course, we may, and sometimes do, choose the alternative. We seek the immediate perceptual quality rather than the original conditions under which this quality arose and of which it generally is a sign. We would rather have the picture "look" straight and yet "be" crooked, than the other way around.

Similarly, in ethics, it seems evident to me that there is a unique moral quality to some aspects of some of our experiences. Yet it makes sense to question in any case whether the quality is a sign of the conditions under which it arose and which it generally represents, or whether, due to personal or environmental causes, it is not. Some persons argue (whatever they may do in their practice) that the *quality* is of "final" importance whenever discrepancy arises. It is the purport of the judgmental analysis, however, that this quality is not final: that is, it may sensibly be questioned as the criterion of any particular choice, and when so questioned, is being tested by reference to the objective test of whether or not it is the product of a rational choice. The judgmental analysis thereby explains what experience tells us is the fact—that sensible people can, with sense, question the moral finality of a perceived quality. We perceive something as good, but we wonder whether it is *really* good. In short, we want reasons for choosing what appears in perception to be "good."[10]

[10] I do not wish to introduce unnecessary complications, but it is worth noting that I am not arguing that the *only* conditions generally productive of a unique "moral" quality in perception are the conditions of rational choice. There are, perhaps, several such unique, "moral" qualities. Or we might prefer to say that there is a variety of "shadings" of this quality. To mention only one, I think that the mere automatic operation of conscience resulting from the responses built up in earlier experiences is accompanied by a unique, recognizable quality. For some persons—the "conscience-oriented" type—this characteristic "voice of conscience" perceptual quality is perhaps more frequently associated with the use of moral terms than are the conditions of rational choice. This is consistent with what I indicated earlier. The judgmental analysis is not, as I see it, the only correct analysis of the functioning of ethical terms but rather a correct analysis of one set of fundamental uses of ethical terms. Yet I think the judgmental analysis marks the more general use in the following sense. It is logically possible in terms of the judgmental analysis to question the morality of some act without reference to conscience, but it is *not* possible to use conscience as the criterion for moral judgment and yet avoid

In summary, I have shown that there are inadequate grounds for urging that somewhere in the process of rational choice an essential, irreducible moral element will be found. The principal types of evidence offered can be accounted for within the judgmental analysis, and without going beyond those aspects of the analysis already shown not to suppose the existence of some necessary, irreducible moral elements in experience. Therefore there is good reason to suppose, especially since part of the job has already been done, that moral terms may be analyzed as functioning judgmentally, and that the latter term, in turn, may be understood without reference to un-analyzable moral elements. In the present section of this Essay, I have been carrying out such an analysis with respect to the term "rational," a crucial term in the judgmental analysis.

I shall now attempt more briefly to clarify the meanings of the other key terms in the statement of the judgmental analysis. The first term I shall consider is "choice."

"Choice" is simply the best of a group of possible terms, none of which is entirely satisfactory for the purposes at hand. The central notion at which I am directing attention is the selection of one alternative from among others. "Choice," however, emphasizes the overt behavioral aspect of this process. Yet often we do not follow up our moral probings with overt action. It is possible to settle upon a disposition as well as an immediate course of overt behavior. Thus we might speak of "decision" among alternatives. Given a decision, a person need do nothing except be *ready* to act in certain ways. While "decision" probably covers choice, I have rejected "decision" for general use here for one major reason. We speak of deciding that an arithmetic problem was done correctly or of deciding what the nature of a chemical precipitate is. In these cases, "decision" may mean something different from what takes place in moral "decision." I do not wish to raise here the issue as to whether a choice in moral matters is necessarily the same kind of thing as a decision in arithmetic or chemistry.

Two other terms requiring some elucidation are "elicit" and "express" as used in the statement of the judgmental analysis. To say that moral terms are properly used to elicit rational choice is to

---

the judgmental functions of moral terms. For to use conscience as the basis of moral decision is to use *one special kind of reason* upon which to base one's choice.

say that it is appropriate when addressed in moral terms to attempt to formulate a rational choice about the alternatives mentioned explicitly or indicated indirectly in the particular life context where the moral terms are used. It is "appropriate" in the same general way that it is appropriate for you to answer a question, to obey a command, to ponder a suggestion, or to attend to the meaning of what is being reported to you. In these types of instances and in the use of moral terms, you may in fact not do what I have called the "appropriate" thing. There is clearly no purely logical or purely legal or purely grammatical rule which provides what your response shall be. Nevertheless, the type of appropriateness in question is very familiar. It is in this sense that the use of moral terms in certain situations appropriately calls forth from the party addressed (often the speaker himself) an attempt at making a rational choice.

To *express* a rational choice by the use of moral terms is to be at that stage of the process of rational choice which we may roughly delimit by saying that one is in the very act of making up one's mind. The preliminary weighing and reasoning having been substantially finished, moral terms are used as an integral, integrating and learned part of that final phase. The language involving the moral terms is organized in certain customary ways correlative to the nature and direction of choice. Here we have nothing more mysterious than is the case of a person suffering a sudden pain and crying, "Ouch!" As a result of learning, the sound "Ouch!" is used. It is not an instinctive (that is, innate) aspect of the response to pain. Perhaps the most we could say is that it is instinctive to respond to sharp pain with vocalization, but it is not instinctive to respond with "Ouch!" This is a sound which is learned and is customarily associated with intense pain only when the English language is used. "Ouch!" can indeed be used to *mean* pain or "I am in pain," as when one says "Ouch!" to the dentist in order to inform him that he is drilling too near the nerve. But in the type of situation of which I speak, it is not functioning *in order to* inform anyone. It is an automatic, learned linguistic aspect of the total pain response. It expresses pain, in the sense of "expression" which I have in mind when saying that moral terms at times express the act of rational choice.

It should be added that, while it is not used *in order to* inform, "Ouch!" probably does in fact function to organize and focus the pain response, specifically to highlight localized pain as distinguished from generalized anxiety or discomfort. Similarly, moral terms, when used expressively, do not quite function to inform, or report upon a rational choice, but they may and probably do function to further organize activity and to focus attention on the activity as one of rational choice.

IV

It is relevant to indicate at least briefly some of the ways in which the judgmental analysis is like or unlike certain other views in contemporary theory. It is clear that it is not entirely novel. In fact, I believe that a number of different aspects of it have been proposed in isolation from the rest by various writers. The analysis as a whole is contained, in other language, in at least one contemporary theory as a small but important part of that theory. As I see it what I have done may be interpreted in either of several ways.

(a) One might say that I have drawn together into more systematic form a number of ideas which have been brewing, and that I have added a bit myself, and that, as a result of all this, I have slightly shifted the perspective in which one may view these ideas. I refer in this connection mainly but not solely to recent developments in positivist and analytic philosophy.

(b) Alternatively, one might say that I have abstracted from a larger and more complex theory one aspect of that theory and that I have set this forth in different, less "school-bound," language. I refer here to pragmatist ethical theory.

(c) Finally, the present thesis may be considered as an attempt to suggest, in reasonably neutral language, how the positivist and analytic trends in ethical philosophy seem to be developing, in their own way, toward a position which is in a number of important respects the position held in substance by the pragmatists. I think the trend has been obvious to all, but I also think that the attempts to formulate plainly and correctly the growing similarity have failed in one important respect or another.

In connection with Alternative (a), perhaps the element which is easiest to discover elsewhere is the notion of choice as central. Charner M. Perry in 1933 stated in his well-known paper that "the purpose of judgments of value is not to describe but to make a selection among possible courses of action."[11] Further, Perry holds that "the problem of value is to find reasons for choice."[12] Perry thus connects the concept of reason with that of moral choice. However, Perry makes one of the serious mistakes I have earlier pointed out: he uses "rational" or "reason" to refer to the process of deductive and inductive reasoning alone. The result is naturally a peculiar mixture of rationality in morals with "the arbitrary as basis." Perry also omits the specific kinds of functions which moral terms have in choice: the elicitative, the expressive, and the informative.

K. R. Popper in 1945 argued that norms which we adopt are decisions which we make.[13] Margaret MacDonald, arguing later in a very similar vein, and with more elaborate explanation, states that ethical assertions are expression of decisions. She also says they are "more like records of decisions than propositions."[14] Further she says that "to assert that 'Freedom is better than slavery' . . . is not to state a fact but to *choose a side*."[15] MacDonald also notes that we can make *intelligent* choices. We cannot prove them correct by evidence, but we do support and defend our decisions. The method of support is not simple demonstration or induction. It is in some ways analogous to that of the lawyer or critic of art—it involves, for example, appeal to previous decisions in similar cases.

Popper and MacDonald argue that value utterances express decisions. I have argued that they express, in their judgmental function, *rational* choice (or decision). It is one thing to hold that a value utterance is merely an expression of a choice, but that in various instances it may be supported; it is quite another to hold that a value utterance expresses a rational choice. If someone were merely expressing a purely personal, non-reasoned and non-reasonable decision, most people, knowing this, would deny that he could properly use moral terms for expressing it—even though they might be hard put to specify just what reasons would definitely justify using moral terms. Most people would hold that he was "merely expressing his

[11] Charner M. Perry, "The Arbitrary As Basis for Rational Morality," *The International Journal of Ethics*, XLIII (1932-33), 133.

[12] *Ibid.*, p. 133.

[13] K. R. Popper, *The Open Society and Its Enemies* (London, 1949), I, 52.

[14] M. MacDonald, "Natural Rights" in *Proceedings of the Aristotelian Society*, New Series, XLVII (1946-47), 243-34.

[15] *Ibid.*, p. 244.

attitude or opinion." We *do* differentiate in serious practice between a "personal decision" and "a morally justified decision," and I think this matter is subject to empirical test.

It should be noted, however, that MacDonald attempts briefly to clarify the nature of the support for a decision which we give. She thereby attacks the problem of how we reason in making moral choices but does not explicitly state the general point: that the analysis of rational method in ethics is a central problem of theory. This is perhaps a natural consequence of omitting rationality from the essence of moral judgment and treating it as a possible, but not necessary, characteristic of moral utterances.

Nor does the Popper-MacDonald statement clarify the different functions of ethical terms as fully as is done in the judgmental analysis. Failure to focus attention upon the elicitative function of ethical terms leaves the sensibleness of questioning a moral utterance open to question. For, on the Popper-MacDonald view, how could one sensibly *question* the expression of a person's decision? One would not, presumably, be questioning the fact that the decision was made. Nor would one be necessarily expressing one's own different decision, for it is possible to agree in choice, but still question the morality of the choice. Nor need one be subtly trying to cause the person to decide otherwise than he has. The judgmental analysis provides a sensible answer: one questions an ethical utterance in order to elicit from either the utterer of the original statement or from oneself a new act of choice based on reasons for and against some alternative(s). And this always makes sense in a formal way, and makes practical sense if one takes it to be the case that the reasoning behind the choice is not as sound as it could be, even though at times the alternative chosen earlier is finally rechosen.

There are today an increasing number of writers who are emphasizing and studying the broader kind of rationality associated with choice and decision. Hampshire, for example, says that "the typical moral problem is ... a problem of practical choice and decision."[16] Further, he says in connection with rationality:

If the procedure of practical deliberation does not conform either in its intermediate steps or in the form of its conclusions, with any forms of

---

[16] S. Hampshire, "Fallacies in Moral Philosophy," *Mind,* LVIII (1949), 468. Excerpts from this article are reprinted in the present Essay by permission of the editor of *Mind.*

argument acknowledged as respectable in logical text-books, this is a deficiency of the logical text-books. Or rather it is a mistake in the *interpretation* of text books of logic to assume that they provide, or that they are intended to provide, patterns of all forms of reasoning or argument which can properly be described as rational argument. Arguments may be, in the ordinary and wider sense, rational, without being included among the types of argument which are ordinarily studied by logicians, since logicians are generally concerned exclusively with the types of argument which are characteristic of the *a priori* and empirical sciences. There are other patterns of argument habitually used outside the sciences, which may be described as more or less rational in the sense that they are more or less strictly governed by recognized (though not necessarily formulated) rules of relevance.[17]

We do not need here to beg the question as to whether or not the pattern of rationality in question in morality is substantially different from that used in the empirical sciences. The issue is moot, but there is agreement, I believe, on the thesis that rationality in choice, if there be such a thing at all, is not the same as what is ordinarily classified as either deductive or inductive logic.

Hampshire, however, argues that the meaning of a moral term is revealed by the kind of reason offered for the moral judgment in much the same way that we know what a man means by "intelligent" when we discover the decisive reasons for his applying the word in any case. Thus, it would follow that if people give different types of reasons in support of their moral judgment, they use moral terms with different meanings. This differs in an important respect from the judgmental analysis. For, on the judgmental analysis, there is a common core of meaning in *all* use of moral terms: that there do exist reasons of some kind or other for the choice (or moral judgment) in question.

The following seems to me to describe nicely the actual facts of the case and to be implied by the judgmental analysis: (a) *people are correct in supposing that they use moral terms in some fundamentally similar way*, since they all mean to base their judgment upon reasons and not mere hazard, yet (b) they argue about the precise application of moral terms in practice because they are often not settled in their own minds as to how to determine *which* reasons are *weightier* than others, or which are decisive. Hampshire's for-

[17] *Ibid.*, pp. 470-71.

mulation is consistent, however, with the denial of (a)—a point of great practical importance, if true.

Hampshire's position may be further distinguished for the sake of clarity, from the judgmental analysis in that the latter specifies the various functions of ethical *terms* in the context of rational choice, whereas Hampshire discusses primarily the *process* of choosing rationally rather than the precise functions of ethical terms insofar as they have to do with that process.

I shall conclude with a brief consideration of pragmatist ethical theory. While pragmatist ethical theory is far broader and more complex than the judgmental analysis, I believe that the substance of the judgmental analysis is contained as a part of pragmatist theory as the latter is exemplified, for example, by Dewey. Rather than develop this thesis in detail, I shall simply present a brief and highly schematized interpretation of some important pragmatist theses. Brief study should then make apparent at least the plausibility of my view that the judgmental analysis is, in substance, a systematic statement, in nonpragmatist terminology, of certain fundamental features of pragmatist ethical theory.

Dewey may be read as saying the following: The raising of a moral question (linguistic behavior) is normally evidence of the existence of a problem of selecting among preferences in a particular situation; raising the (linguistic) question is a device for provoking and roughly focusing systematic, rational, reflection and experiment (inquiry), resulting, if the process is successful, in a value judgment. A value judgment is the conclusive phase of the rational reconstruction of the problem-situation, and the linguistic aspect of such a settlement or judgment is a moral statement expressive of the judgment; past judgments may, in turn, be reported in linguistic form, and this need not occur in the context of inquiry.[18]

If the preceding suggestive resumé is essentially correct (so far as it goes), then I think one can already recognize in it the thesis that moral terms function to elicit rational inquiry leading to a choice yet to be made, to express that choice as the result of a rational inquiry, and to report such choices as may already have been consummated. I shall restrict further comment to noting the following:

While pragmatist theory covers topics and includes details not here

---

[18] See, for example, J. Dewey, "Theory of Valuation," in *International Encyclopedia of Unified Science* (Chicago, 1939), Vol. II, No. 4.

mentioned, there is one further point of prime importance which needs mentioning. In this paper, I have left the analysis of "rational" unfinished. I have indicated an essential condition of rationality but no set of sufficient conditions. Dewey, however, has written at great length on the structure of the rationality involved. He has concluded that it is the same, in essence, as that of empirical science. It is well known that many students of the problem disagree with Dewey on this issue. I have purposely attempted to formulate the judgmental analysis in such a way as to take maximum advantage of the growing common ground, without requiring a decision on this, as yet controversial, issue. It is fair to note, however, that the controversy seems to be shifting to the study of the structure of rationality in morals as against the debate about whether there is, fundamentally, any rationality in morals.[19]

[19] For the Comments and Response which relate to this paper see pp. 310-16, 369-70, and 384, below.

SOME PUZZLES FOR
ATTITUDE THEORIES OF VALUE

RICHARD B. BRANDT

THE MOST important question theories of value language[1] have to answer is: What kind of query are we putting to ourselves when we ask whether something is desirable, right, or obligatory? Or, in other words, what must be the case in order for us to be able to say correctly, "That is a desirable thing," or "That is right"?

The possibility of giving a simple straightforward answer to these questions is affected by the fact that value language—and hence these questions and statements—is in some sense vague. That it is vague is shown by the fact that philosophers are still arguing, for instance, whether "duty" has only one ethical sense, or at least three. And by the fact that nonphilosophers are staggered by a request for a definition of value terms, or by a request for an opinion how value statements may be confirmed. In fact, one justification for the existence of ethical (or value) theory is that conceivably it may clarify these questions, so that nonphilosophers may not confuse different issues, and may proceed more intelligently to the solution of practical problems.

This vagueness of value language means that the theorist, in the course of discussing the above questions, must aim at once at two targets. On the one hand he must seek a definition or (if this is impossible because, for example, emotive meaning is an essential part of ethical terms) a characterization of ethical terms which adheres to or is sensitive to ordinary meanings, adequate to the questions people

---

[1] I shall use "value language" and "ethical language" as synonyms. Later I shall have more to say about their denotation, but the class denoted is to include statements of ethical evaluation in the narrower sense of "ethical" (for example, statements about what conduct is right, obligatory, or blameworthy) as well as statements that are ethical only in a broader sense (for instance, "It is a desirable thing that . . ."). It seems to me that the important problems are the same throughout this area.

put to themselves when they use value language. And on the other hand, since the commitment to explicit formulation inevitably involves the sharpening of ordinary meanings, he must point out in what direction sharpened meanings must go, if we are to avoid paradox or inconsistency in ethical thinking. This latter job, of course, requires deliberate departure from pure reflection of ordinary usages. The goal of the theorist in this area, then, is an explication of value terms which mirrors ordinary language as closely as is compatible with precision, explicitness, and the avoidance of inconsistency and paradox.

The notion of "adherence to" or "adequacy to" ordinary meanings needs explanation. Adherence to ordinary meanings does not necessarily require that a proposed explication is to be rejected just because it does not strike us as synonymous with the analysandum in just the way in which "eligible unmarried male" strikes us as being synonymous with "bachelor." There is a good deal of agreement now that, in drawing his conclusions about ordinary usage, a philosopher should consider carefully (a) the class of things to which an individual (whose usage is being studied) applies the value term in question, and what he believes about those things, (b) the reasons he may offer in defense of his applications of value terms, or which he finds compelling grounds for accepting a certain value statement, and (c) his behavior when he is trying to decide whether a statement containing the value term is acceptable—what typically runs through his mind, what tests he is disposed to make. A great deal needs to be said about the precise way in which evidence of these sorts should be used, for which there is here no space; but it is clear that the theorist's conclusions about the kind of analysis which adheres to ordinary meanings will have the epistemological status of an empirical hypothesis, and no more. Of course, we may anticipate that, if the philosopher's proposal is a good one, the individual being analyzed, on reviewing his own procedures in settling value questions, will agree that the analyst has succeeded in formulating explicitly what in practice he himself was groping for.

Some philosophers believe that an explication of value terms which is adequate to ordinary meanings can be framed in an empiricist language. More exactly, they think that adequate synonyms for value terms can be given in a language in which the primitive predicates are observation predicates including ones designating qualities observable only by introspection, and the logical apparatus is that used in *Principia Mathematica* plus symbols for strict and counterfactual implication. Correspondingly, these philosophers hold that value statements have an epistemological status essentially identical with that of many statements of empirical science, and are in principle confirmable by observation, in the manner in which this is possible in empirical science. Let us call this view the *Cognitivist Theory*. (I am deliberately ignoring rationalist, non-naturalist theories; but such theorists can, I think, agree with almost all I have to say.) It should be noted that a cognitivist need not deny that value language is especially effective as a means of stirring to action, or that we may draw inferences about a person's probable value attitudes from the value statements he makes. A cognitivist, furthermore, can even consistently allow that value language has what I have elsewhere called Blind Emotive Meaning (Stevenson's independent emotive meaning) —as long as he does not think this fact renders it impossible to claim that value statements can be reformulated in an empirical language in a way that does justice to their essential point. Nor is there any reason why he should deny that saying to ourselves, "That would be wrong," sometimes operates to direct behavior. Finally, it should be added—since apparently there has been much misunderstanding on the point—that a cognitivist need not hold that value statements give *information* in the way in which many statements do. Thus a cognitivist need not say that to assert that Mr. A's behavior is reprehensible is to give information about it in the way one does if one says that Mr. A lied, or broke such-and-such a clause of his contract with his company. How this is the case is quite clear if we can construe —as I think we may—the statement that Mr. A's act is reprehensible as roughly the statement that an informed and impartial person would disapprove of Mr. A for doing it.

Other philosophers disagree with the cognitivists. They hold that no satisfactory definition of value terms can be framed in an empiricist language without serious misconception, and this for the reason that value language is essentially imperative language, a language of recommendation, expressive of attitudes, or freighted with emotive meaning. (They do not, of course, hold that value language is the especial servant of the speaker's *personal* interests.) Correspondingly, they hold that value issues are in principle *not* decidable by observation in the manner in which this is possible in empirical science, and that value statements do *not* enjoy an epistemological status in any way comparable to that of the statements of science. Let us call this general view *Noncognitivism*.[2]

In the past few years a great many arguments have been put forward, intended to show that one or the other of these types of explication, or at least some important form of them, is essentially disqualified as an adequate reflection of the ordinary meanings of ethical terms. As a result, various forms of these types of view have been definitely eliminated from the field of contending theories; but there are forms of each main type of theory which have not yet been eliminated.

In the central part of this paper I shall pose three objections to Noncognitivism which I think have not received sufficient consideration.

In order to make clear the precise bearing of the facts to be described, I shall first formulate a specific type of Noncognitivism which I shall call the *Attitude Theory*. I shall discuss my objections particularly in relation to it. I have selected this particular form of Noncognitivism partly because it has been defended by very able philosophers, and partly because in my opinion it is a theory with serious attractions. Philosophers who are more convinced by other forms of Noncognitivism will I hope be able to see, from the treatment of the Attitude Theory, whether the difficulties to be raised pose problems for the forms of Noncognitivism of interest to them. I am inclined to think that the facts to be described are incompatible with all forms of Noncognitivism except some which are so weak as to be indistinguishable from some forms of Cognitive Theory, except in point of terminology.

I. The Attitude Theory

Let us begin, then, by formulating the Attitude Theory. I shall

[2] Notice the points which Stevenson says are *central* to his conception of ethics: "(1) The emotive meaning of the ethical terms must not be neglected . . .; (2) an ethical issue involves (at least in part) a disagreement in attitude . . .; (3) a disagreement in attitude can be settled by reasoning and inquiry only if it is rooted in a disagreement in belief, as it may or may not be . . .; (4) the reasons that are relevant-I to ethical judgments have a special sort of variety and complexity in their subject matter." These are also the points, he says, which distinguish ethics from a descriptive science. "Brandt's Questions about Emotive Ethics," *The Philosophical Review*, LIX (1950), 533. The excerpts from *The Philosophical Review* are reprinted in the present Essay by permission of the editors.

say that a person accepts the Attitude Theory if he accepts both the following theses.

1. Differences of opinion about the value of something ultimately involve differences of attitude toward that thing. More exactly, the necessary and sufficient condition of there being an ethical difference about something (difference of opinion about its value) is a difference of *corresponding*[3] attitude toward it—either difference of sign, or noticeable difference in intensity. Let us call this the *Difference in Attitude Thesis*.

2. Value statements do not make assertions and hence are neither true nor false in the scientific sense. But they can be correctly or incorrectly used; and the necessary and sufficient condition of its being correct for a person to use a certain value statement is his having a corresponding attitude. For example, the necessary and sufficient condition of its being correct to say, in a normative sense, "Dishonesty is a bad thing" is the speaker's disapproving of dishonesty. Let us put this in the terminology of a causal theory of meaning. The foregoing statement about the conditions of correct use, then, may be construed as shorthand for the following two statements. First, speakers, as a consequence of their familiarity with a language, will not

---

[3] A person may simultaneously have different attitudes to the same thing. For instance, he may think it a good thing—although not really a moral obligation—that he should arise at 6:30 A.M. daily, and at the same time strongly dislike the idea of doing so. Obviously, two persons may have opposed personal preferences about something, while being in agreement about what is obligatory or desirable from an impersonal point of view; conversely, they may agree in their personal preferences, but disagree about whether they have a right to do it. I suppose these points are obvious, but they are sometimes overlooked. A fully developed Attitude Theory must in my opinion formulate descriptions of types of attitude corresponding to different types of value statement.

What I mean by "attitude" is a *disposition* to respond behaviorally (in emotion, motivation) as a consequence of a certain type of judgment. Thus a person can have an attitude toward something without having any feelings at the time.

It should be noticed that Stevenson distinguishes difference in attitude from disagreement in attitude. He says two persons *disagree* in attitude only if, in addition to differing in attitude in the above sense, "at least one of them has a motive for altering or calling into question the attitude of the other" (*Ethics and Language* [New Haven, Conn., 1944], p. 3) or "neither is content to let the other's interest remain unchanged" (*Mind* XLVI [1937], 27). This difference is important for the logic of his view (see *Ethics and Language*, pp. 4-5, and *Mind* XLVII [1938], 336).

In the present Essay the excerpts from *Ethics and Language* are reprinted by permission of Yale University Press, publishers; those from *Mind* are quoted by permission of its editor.

use value statements in that language unless they have corresponding attitudes, except with intent to mislead. Second, auditors who hear a value statement in a language they understand will, on account of their familiarity with the language, take the speaker to have a corresponding attitude unless they suppose he is attempting to mislead. Let us call this the *Expressive Thesis,* the thesis that value statements express the speaker's attitudes—in just the same way, I suppose, as that in which, in the sentence "The king is dead," the indicative form and the falling inflection express the speaker's *belief* that the king is dead—for he would not use this form honestly unless he did so believe, and auditors would take him so to believe, on this basis, if they understood the language. In the same way, use of the imperative mood and a certain tone of voice may express a desire of the speaker; and in a sentence like "Would you please close the door?" the mood, word order, rise in inflection, and the term "please" serve jointly to express a wish on the part of the speaker.[4]

These two theses are closely related. In fact, the second entails the first—as is clear as soon as we ask how to decide when two persons have *differing opinions* about the *value* of something, which of course we have to do before we can test the truth of the Difference in Attitude Thesis. For, if we ask for a nonquestion-begging criterion for there being difference of opinion about values, we shall see that the only available one is a *verbal* one—whether two persons can correctly make verbally contradictory value statements. That is, it seems the only available criterion will commit us to saying that A and B differ in opinion about values (or ethically) if and only if A is of a state of mind correctly expressed by, say, "X is wrong" used in a normative sense, and B of a state of mind correctly expressed by "X is *not* wrong." (How to identify a normative or value statement will be discussed below.) Similarly, if each can say "X is wrong," we have to say there is *no* ethical difference (difference of opinion about values) between them, about X. Now obviously, if this is how we are

---

[4] Of course, more is done too. By expressing a wish, the speaker may present the auditor with the dilemma of compliance or of appearing rude, etc.

Some philosophers probably would urge that any verbal form which expressed a certain state of the speaker, in this sense, would necessarily be *asserting* that he was in that state of mind. Whether this is the case, however, depends on one's definition of "designation." This would not be the case, given the definition of "designation" I should want to accept. (See *Mind* LXI [1952], 467). Of course, the same expression *could* both designate and express the speaker's state of mind.

to identify differences of opinion about values, then it follows, from the Expressive Thesis, that whenever there is such a difference about an object X, there will be a corresponding difference in attitude toward X. Given a verbal criterion for ethical differences, then, the Expressive Thesis entails that ethical differences are or include differences in attitude. The Difference in Attitude Thesis does not, however, entail the Expressive Thesis.[5]

There are many philosophers who in substance either now subscribe to the Attitude Theory, or at one time did so. Among them are A. J. Ayer, Bertrand Russell, A. I. Melden, J. E. Ledden, Hans Reichenbach, D. H. Parker, and probably W. F. R. Hardie and John Ladd. C. L. Stevenson, I believe, accepts it in substance, although he would prefer to say that ethical statements at least in some contexts can be properly said to express beliefs as well as attitudes.[6] R. M. Hare is

[5] It might seem simpler, in view of the logical relation, to define the Attitude Theory simply in terms of the Expressive Thesis. But it is useful to separate the two points, since we shall want to know whether some of our objections, which seem serious for Thesis 2, are equally problems for the weaker Thesis 1.

[6] It would be a great mistake to overlook Stevenson's substantial agreement with the Attitude Theory, because of some disagreements. (1) Notice that, on his view, people use ethical terms in correspondence with their attitudes. The reason for this is that ethical terms are emotively charged, and can be used for redirecting attitudes (*Ethics and Language*, p. 17). As he puts it, " 'good' has ... a laudatory emotive meaning which permits it to express the speaker's approval." (*Ethics and Language*, p. 207). This is true even on what he calls "second pattern" uses of the terms which have a more complex descriptive meaning. As he says, "The issue centers about disagreement in attitude, which, regardless of divergent descriptive senses, will be indicated by emotive meaning" (*Ethics and Language*, p. 236); "the use of 'good' and 'not good,' whatever descriptive meaning they might have, indicated that one man was in favor of O and the other was not" (*Ethics and Language*, p. 232); "the emotive effects of 'good' and 'not good' are indicative of a disagreement in attitude" (*Ethics and Language*, p. 233). There is no reason for supposing that the necessary and sufficient condition, on his view, for correctly applying an ethical term to something, is not having a corresponding attitude toward it. The essential point of statements using ethical terms is persuasion or expression of attitude, not information or assertion of descriptive content. (2) Correspondingly, Stevenson holds that the reasons which will naturally be adduced to support an ethical statement are ones that support the attitude it expresses (*Ethics and Language*, pp. 154-55, 27-28). This is true even of "second pattern" uses (*Ethics and Language*, pp. 232-33). (3) Therefore, despite the fact that Stevenson argues that ethical terms may in specific contexts be ascribed descriptive meaning, we cannot count on using this fact to settle ethical disagreements. "Rational methods can resolve ethical disagreement if and only if it is rooted in disagreement in belief" (*Ethics and Language*, p. 237). The descriptive meanings of ethical terms do not firmly secure us corresponding analytic statements including them. "No analytic judgment of the form 'N is good' can be held up as an in-

concerned to explicate value statements as a species of imperative, but his approximate acceptance of the Expressive Thesis is manifest in what he has to say about what it is to *assent* to an ethical statement. For Hare insists that if someone says, "You ought to do X," and I assent to it—that is, say honestly, "Yes, I ought"—then I am also assenting to the command, "Let me do X," which according to him I cannot do unless I actually resolve to do X. To assent to a moral statement, then, for him, is to make a resolve, to be ready to act; and of course this is very different from assent to a descriptive statement.[7] Now compare this view with the Expressive Thesis. According to the latter, if someone responds to "You ought to do X" with an assenting "Yes, I ought," he is thereby expressing an agreeing moral attitude and in so far is resolved to act in a corresponding way. Therefore this Thesis, very like Mr. Hare, holds that there is a connection between resolution or motivation and assent to a moral statement, quite different from the case of assent to a descriptive statement.

The Attitude Theory, of course, does not encompass all the positive theses emphasized by critics of Cognitive theories. Some writers, for instance, would feel that it does not take adequate note of the incitiveness of ethical language—although of course it is quite consistent with such an emphasis. But in defense of the importance of the Attitude Theory it may be said that it is questionable whether it has been shown that ethical language has inherent incitive powers beyond what is derivative from the fact that it expresses the speaker's attitudes. Again, it might be said that the theory fails to take account of the fact that the purpose, aim, or function of value statements is practical, although again the theory could say this without inconsistency. But it is hardly to the point to include such matters in an

---

controvertible axiom, for one can always disagree in attitude with the persuasive definition that *makes* it analytic" (*Ethics and Language,* p. 272). Analytic propositions in ethics cannot be defended by "appeal to what people commonly mean"; they have to be defended by persuasion, by leading people to accept the attitudes which one's definitions express or evoke. (*The Philosophical Review,* LIX [1950], 529.) "The difference between the two patterns, here as elsewhere, is only of linguistic interest. It has no bearing on the nature of ethical disagreement or on the extent to which it can be resolved" (*Ethics and Language,* p. 240). Hence we can understand why he says it would not be a serious error to attribute no descriptive meaning at all to ethical terms. (*Ethics and Language,* p. 96; *The Philosophical Review,* LIX [1950], 301-2.)

[7] See *The Language of Morals* (London, 1952), pp. 19, 168-69.

account of value language any more than it is in an account of assertive language; and in any case no one has shown that value statements have any distinctive aim or function.[8]

II. The Attitude Theory is empirically testable

Since the theses of the Attitude Theory state or imply general statements about the conditions in which value statements are made, it seems natural to suppose that they have empirical commitments, and that important counterinstances would be fatal for them. I believe that this is in fact the case.

It seems wise, however, to digress briefly to consider an alternative proposal to the effect that they are analytically true. In particular, a philosopher might say that any attempt to discover counterinstances presupposes a method for deciding when value language has been used, which does not imply the truth of these theses. But value language, he might say, does not carry any distinctive mark; you cannot identify it by the words used, for value words all have non-normative uses. And the only feasible procedure for picking out value language is the specification that it is language used to express an attitude— which seems to make the Attitude Theory analytically true.

Duncan-Jones, in providing instructions for picking out an *ethical* judgment, specifies as follows: "A man who makes a *moral* judgment about lying and stealing must have an attitude of some kind to those types of action; and the attitude must include a tendency to favour and promote, or else a tendency to condemn and oppose, that kind of action."[9] And R. M. Hare, discussing why we must suppose normative judgments to entail imperatives, says:

I propose to get over this difficulty in the only possible way, by making it a matter of definition. I propose to say that the test, whether someone is using the judgment "I ought to do X" as a value judgment or not is, "Does he or does he not recognize that if he assents to the judgment, he must also assent to the command, 'Let me do X'?"[10]

---

[8] See E. Gilman, "The Distinctive Purpose of Moral Judgments," *Mind,* LXI (1952), 307-16.

[9] A. Duncan-Jones, *Butler's Moral Philosophy* (Hammondsworth, England, 1952), p. 170.

[10] *The Language of Morals,* pp. 169-70; by permission of the Clarendon Press, publishers. H. D. Aiken has sometimes made rather similar suggestions: "I shall define 'judgment of obligation' to mean any judgment, in whatever form or language it may be expressed, and whatever may be its subject-matter, which functions

Some philosophers are, I think, inclined to this view by the fact that it seems natural to ask, "Does the ethical language of the Navaho raise the same analytic problems as English?" They feel that the sensibility of this question suggests that there is a way of picking out the value language of a people before we know anything about whether it contains terms cognitively synonymous with English terms, or indeed anything about their vocabulary—presumably for the reason that we mean by "value language" whatever language they use to express certain attitudes.

Is questioning the Attitude Theory on empirical grounds, then, inconsistent with the only criterion we have for deciding when we have a value or ethical statement before us?

I do not think we need to make this concession, for two reasons.

First, the argument has weight only if we agree that we cannot proceed to criticize until we have a general definition of "value language." But we need not agree to this. The reason we need not is that we are able to pick out many statements which are prime examples of ethical language, in fact are examples we should use to test the adequacy of a definition of "ethical language." And if we can make a telling point by appeal to such samples, we shall have been successful even though we have no general definition of "value language."

But second, we can do very well with the formulation of a definition of "ethical language" without making any assumptions which involve the truth of the Attitude Theory. A definition can I think be formulated approximately as follows. Let us first see if we can distinguish the ethical-value-normative senses of a single term, "duty." Webster's Dictionary distinguishes eight senses of this word, three of them technical senses not in common use, and two of them obsolete. This leaves three ordinary senses: the ethical-normative sense, the sense in which a duty is a tax or custom's charge, and the sense in which a

---

normatively, i.e., which functions as a determinant of attitude in the broad sense"
(from "Evaluation and Obligation," *The Journal of Philosophy*, XLVII [1950], 16–
17; by permission of the editors). See too *Philosophy and Phenomenological
Research*, XII (1952), 513. Stevenson also seems to hold that, no matter what
people *say*, we should not regard them as really ethically disagreed, if there is no
clash of attitude. See *Ethics and Language, p. 16*; and "The Emotive Meaning of
Ethical Terms," *Mind*, XLVI (1937), 27. Also see D. H. Parker's essay in R. Lepley
(ed.), *Value: A Cooperative Inquiry* (New York, 1949), p. 239.

duty is a customary responsibility of an office, say, "The duties of a dean." Now we can easily give a criterion for picking out the ethical one among these ordinary senses of "duty." For we can propose that this term is being used in its value sense whenever it is used assertively in a context of appraisal of conduct, and would be said by speaker and hearers to be roughly synonymous with "moral obligation." If this is correct, we have a way of identifying those sentences in which "duty" has occurred in its value or ethical sense. Now I think we can formulate criteria of a similar sort, which will enable us to pick out the normative senses of some other key terms, including "obligatory," "blameworthy," "praiseworthy," and "desirable." Having done this, we may then propose, as a general definition, that a value (ethical) statement is either one which uses one of the listed terms in its normative sense, or else one which would *ordinarily be said to imply* a statement of the already specified class. Why is this not a satisfactory definition of the term "value statement"?

The reader may feel at first that this proposal is somewhat artificial. But I think he will find that those and only those statements which he would wish to include in the class "value statement" will meet this test. And I think further he will find that, in case a novel example is put to him, with the query whether it raises a value question, he instinctively appeals to this test for a decision. (If we omit the term "desirable," I think we have a criterion for "ethical statement" in the narrower sense of "ethical.")

On both these counts, then, it is unproved that the only feasible procedure for identifying value language is one which somehow presupposes that the Attitude Theory is analytically true. There may, of course, be other grounds for supposing this theory to be analytically true, but until they have been stated we are justified in assuming the theory to have empirical commitments subject to empirical testing.

III. First Puzzle: Value statements do not always correspond with attitudes; ethical disagreements do not always reflect a clash of attitudes

Various objections to the Attitude Theory have a good deal of force. For instance, the fact that value statements do *seem* like assertions, as is attested by the fact that no one thought to question their assertive character until recently. And there is the puzzling status of statements like "Everyone ought to do his duty" which seems an analytic truth but must be quite peculiar if the Attitude Theory is correct. There is also the fact that ethical doubt at least often seems like theoretical doubt; if someone finds an inconsistency in my theory of punishment, I shall be dismayed just as I should have been if he had found an inconsistency in my epistemology.

But I wish to concentrate on three difficulties in the theory which I think need more discussion and which, despite persistent doubts about them, incline me rather strongly to reject the Attitude Theory, in favor of some kind of Cognitive Theory.

The first objection is this. I think people sometimes properly say, "That is wrong" ("undesirable") when they do not have corresponding attitudes, and know they do not. Further, I think sometimes people differ or agree about values, out of line with any corresponding difference or agreement in their attitudes. And if so, I do not see how the Attitude Theory can be correct. The difficulty is parallel to the one which is the standard method of refuting Cognitive theories: for instance, by pointing out to a person who holds that "X is wrong" means "All informed people disapprove of X," that a person may well assert that "X is wrong" when he is quite aware that many well-informed people do *not* disapprove—a point which of course really does dispose of the theory in question.

In considering this question we must obviously be reasonably definite about the designation of "value attitude." If we do not make this term reasonably sharp, we shall not know how to decide when there is a value attitude toward something—with the consequence that we cannot conceivably answer our question. (Attitude theorists also have no business claiming there *is* a correlation of value opinion and value attitude until they have made up their minds definitely how to identify a value attitude.) There is not space here to discuss a general definition, and I shall merely propose rather dogmatically a definition of one type of value attitude. I propose that we say a person has an *unfavorable ethical attitude* toward something (for example, racial discrimination) if and only if he has some inclination to refrain, and a decided disposition to feel obligated to refrain from performing acts of discrimination himself, a disposition to feel guilt or remorse about any act of his in the past which condoned such behavior, to feel indignant with those who perform or condone such acts (except in special circumstances of blamelessness which we need not discuss), and so on. In short we might say that an ethical attitude is a disposition for certain affective events to occur in a person when he considers courses of action for the future or reflects upon such courses of action in the past. Ordinarily I think further that we should not want to call an attitude ethical unless it were causally independent of one's personal interests; but let us ignore this point.

Now are there situations in which people can or do correctly say, "That is wrong" in the absence of an unfavorable ethical attitude in the foregoing sense? (In other words, can we think of cases which are more simply construed by viewing ethical statements as expressing intellectual beliefs rather than attitudes?) I think there are. One hears, for instance, that there are Southerners who have disapproving attitudes, in the above sense, toward racial equality, particularly to white and colored children attending the same grade school. Now—while agreeing that we here need detailed factual evidence—I think it fair to suppose that sometimes such Southerners are convinced by elaborate discussion that such an attitude is unjustified, and agree that it is wrong to require colored children to attend separate schools. And it seems fair to suppose further, considering the difficulty of extinguishing emotional attitudes, that sometimes such intellectual admissions are made long before the original ethical attitude is changed. (Many of us will have noticed that we are not able to get over feeling guilty about performing a certain act, even when we no longer think there is anything wrong about it.) Now, if our Southerner says, "It is wrong to have separate schools," I do not see any ground for supposing that he is speaking incorrectly, as long as he thinks his lingering disapproving attitude cannot be justified. It looks, then, as if one can *believe* something is wrong, and correctly *say* it is wrong, even if one does not have a corresponding attitude. And I see no reason for supposing that this Southerner cannot correctly be said to differ in ethical opinion on this point with some other Southerner who has not been convinced, even though their attitudes are in large measure similar.[11]

---

[11] Similarly, I should be surprised if there are not people who have been convinced by the utilitarian arguments about retributive punishment, or at least are in doubt whether these arguments are not decisive, who cannot help approving of some cases of retributive punishment even when they believe intellectually that it could not be justified—for instance, when the crime has been particularly vicious and cold-blooded. (See F. C. Sharp and M. C. Otto, "Retribution and Deterrence in the Moral Judgments of Common-sense," *The International Journal of Ethics*, XX [1909-10], 438-53.)

It might be objected that this example is plausible only because of failure to make an important distinction, which might be called the distinction between *real* and *quasi*-ethical attitudes. Such an objector might agree that our Southerner may be subject to occasional irrepressible feelings of disapproval about mixed schools, even when he has come to the opinion that they are right. But he might affirm that such feelings must be distinguished from the ones he would have in more serious moments when taking a wider view of the situation—when he is bearing in mind those very points which made him decide that it is indefensible to have separate schools. These latter must be regarded as constitutive of his *real* ethical attitudes. Moreover, it may be added, it is these reactions which take over at times of serious decision; for we shall expect a person to show corresponding motivation at times of decision, if he can honestly say he thinks separate schools are wrong.

This objection is not without weight. It points to facts the precise nature of which needs further description. But, even if we grant the objection, we may at least ask for a further specification of the Attitude Theory—an account of that precise sense of "ethical attitude" in which ethical attitudes are to be regarded as correlated with ethical opinions. This has never been given. And it is at least very odd and misleading to say that ethical terms function to express actual attitudes, if it is admitted that a person can properly say something is wrong when at least half of him feels no disapproval. A serious complication in the theory is called for, at the least; and we may well wonder whether, when this has been introduced, the theory may not seem less plausible, and turn out to require endless patching.

Another point has often been mentioned, which supports the view that ethical opinions must be distinguished from ethical attitudes. This is the fact that sometimes a disapproving attitude seemingly *gets produced* in us by the thought that something is wrong. That is, we are apt to develop dispositions to feel shocked, be indignant, and so on, seemingly as the result of having come to believe that some-

---

Nor, I think, is it difficult to find parallel cases for statements containing "desirable," although here we need a somewhat different definition of "value attitude." Suppose that in the course of a faculty discussion of curricular matters a professor of French eventually is convinced that it is desirable as an educational policy not to require proficiency in a language as a requirement for graduation. What will this tell us about his attitudes?

thing is wrong. Similarly, of course, we sometimes seem to get over a disapproving attitude toward something, as a result of having come to the conclusion that there is nothing wrong about it. How will the Attitude Theory take care of such facts? How can an ethical belief influence our attitudes, if having a belief is construed as just the same thing as having a corresponding attitude?

Hence, there is reason for thinking that ethical *beliefs* should be distinguished from ethical *attitudes*, and for thinking that the connection between difference in value attitude and difference in opinion about values is more complex than the Disagreement in Attitude Theory suggests.

IV. Second Puzzle: The explication of "ethical relevance"

It would be widely agreed that people sometimes say correctly, of a statement offered in justification of an ethical view, "That is a relevant (good, valid) point." At other times, it would be agreed, they say correctly, "That is not a relevant (good, valid) point." There is a further wide consensus of opinion about the obligation of ethical theories to give a plausible characterization or explication of these statements, compatibly with their respective views about ethical terms and their respective arguments to support their views about the analysis of ethical terms. The cognitivists, for instance, would regard "relevance" as meaning, in ethical contexts, what it does in scientific ones: a statement S is relevant to an ethical statement E if and only if the truth of S tends to confirm or disconfirm E.

In order to justify believing, as I am inclined to do, that the problem of analyzing "ethical relevance" is a point against the Attitude Theory, we have to show (a) that some conclusions about this problem would tend to disconfirm the Attitude Theory, and (b) that there is evidence for such a conclusion which makes it more probable than not. Both of these matters raise complex issues, and I shall be satisfied if in the available space I am able to state the problem accurately.

First of all, what are the basic facts relevant to the issue? Not, of course, what "relevant" means in ethical contexts, for this is the point in dispute. The basic fact, I think, is rather what it is correct to say, in some particular situations. In order to be convinced that it is sometimes correct to say that a statement is relevant or irrelevant, let us look at some examples of ethical disputes, drawn from Stevenson.

A: "You are much too hard on your employees."

B: "But you, certainly, are not the one to say so. Your own factory
would bear investigation far less easily than mine."

I think we may take as a fact that any person who knew English, had
had an ordinary amount of experience and general knowledge, and
was—like a good lawyer or journalist—reasonably skilled at detecting
the difference between reasons and pressures would, at least if he
reflected with some care, agree that B's argument might show that
his opponent is well advised to stop his criticizing, but that it has no
relevance whatever to the content of A's statement. I think we may
further say that such a view of its relevance is correct.

A: "You ought to give the speech, as you promised."

B: "That is unfortunately beyond my power. My health will not
permit it."

I think we may suppose that all competent persons would think B's
point relevant to A's statement; and that they would be correct.

We may then take as a basic fact that some *nonethical* statements,
which might well be made in the course of an ethical (value) argument,
can correctly be said to be relevant; others irrelevant. Further, it is
plausible to assume that there are some such statements about the
relevance of which competent persons would not agree. Nobody has
ever produced a satisfactory classification of types of reason which
would universally be admitted as relevant by competent persons; but
we could mention several examples.

We can now state what a satisfactory account of "ethical relevance"
has to do. It has to explicate or characterize this term, so as to make
clear how it is correct to say, in some cases, that a statement is
relevant (or irrelevant), and how there can reasonably be difference
of opinion among competent persons in other cases. For instance, a
Cognitive Theory, analyzing relevance in terms of "confirms or dis-
confirms," would do this by showing that, given its analysis of ethical
predicates, in the one group of cases the factual statement is decidedly
either relevant or irrelevant, while in the other group of cases there
are complications or obscurities which make difference of opinion
intelligible—as can happen in science.

What kind of proposal must the Attitude Theory make on this point?
Unfortunately we cannot appeal here to any accepted standard view.
We can say, of course, that no analysis can be acceptable to this theory
which either by itself or taken with verifiable statements denies the
Expressive Thesis or the Disagreement in Attitude Thesis; nor can

any individual writer accept a view inconsistent with the reasons he offers for adopting an Attitude Theory in ethics.

There are obviously two courses an Attitude Theorist may take: (a) he may regard "ethically relevant" as itself expressive of an attitude, not having descriptive meaning; or (b) he may adopt some form of cognitive analysis of "ethically relevant." Both these lines have actually been proposed.

Let us begin with the second possible view.

The attitude theorist must tread warily in proposing a cognitive analysis of "ethically relevant," for two reasons. The first is that such a step renders it an empirically decidable question whether a certain fact is a point *pro* or *con* a given ethical statement, at least as used by a given individual; and it is questionable whether this is compatible with the attitude point that ethical issues are not empirically decidable. In the second place, by giving a criterion of relevance which distinguishes a class of relevant arguments, the analysis is a standing invitation to naturalists to devise an analysis of ethical terms such that, given the cognitive view of "relevance," it can be explained why this particular class of reasons is relevant—so that the admittedly delimited class of relevant arguments constitutes some evidence in favor of a naturalistic theory of ethical terms. It is not surprising that Stevenson inclines to a noncognitive analysis of relevance.[12]

An attitude theorist might avoid such consequences by saying that his analysis is an analysis of the way in which people actually use "relevant" in ethical contexts, adding that this has no necessary bearing on the analysis of ethical terms because it just so happens that people may well be mistaken in thinking factual points *are* relevant to ethical statements in this sense. But this counter would not be plausible; and it would be inconsistent with our decision above, which seems tenable, that statements of relevance in cases like the examples cited are in some sense correct.

There are some arguments which attitude theorists often use to support their view of ethical terms, which they must further take care not to contradict in their analysis of "ethical relevance." (a) The reasons that are relevant to ethical judgments have a special sort of variety in their subject matter—a point Stevenson has used for criticism

---

[12] See *The Philosophical Review*, LIX (1950), pp. 528-30. On the importance of the exception in favor of "second pattern" uses see footnote 6, p. 159, above.

of most types of naturalist analysis, which he regards as too restrictive.[13] Any cognitive analysis of "relevant" must not so restrict the variety of relevant reasons as to render this argument nugatory. (b) Ethical deliberation is not an attempt to *find out* something, but to resolve the conflict in one's attitudes. (c) The analysis of ethical terms must make it possible for verbally contradictory ethical statements to be construed as disagreements—a point which has been used to disparage the adequacy of some attitudinal analyses of "good," such as "approved by me." This argument must not be weakened. Moreover, I think attitude theorists would want an analysis of "relevance" which left open the possibility that people can sensibly disagree about whether a factual statement is relevant to an ethical one.

What are the chances of getting a cognitive analysis of "relevant" which an attitude theorist could use, without falling into any of these traps? Several possibilities might well be considered, but space permits me to discuss only one; and I shall of course take up the one which strikes me as the most plausible. This most plausible analysis is as follows: "S is relevant to E" (where E is a value statement) is the same as to say, "If I came to believe S in place of non-S (or in place of having no opinion about S), then my corresponding impersonal value attitudes toward the subject O (the subject matter of the value statement E) would be *immediately* modified."[14]

Use of this analysis by an attitude theorist cannot, I think, be shown to land him in any serious inconsistency. Point (c) above perhaps comes closest to being a difficulty, but in my opinion no serious problem is raised. The serious objections to this analysis rather arise from the fact it is inadequate as an account of the actual meaning of "relevance" as used in ethical contexts.

The objections to this proposal are all really variations on a common theme: the theme that after all whether it is correct for a person to

---

[13] *The Philosophical Review*, LIX (1950), 296-98.

[14] This is a modification of a proposal by Jonathan Harrison: "A fact is a relevant fact if it actually has a tendency to show that some action or state of affairs is of a sort which I approve or disapprove" (from "Can Ethics Do Without Propositions?" *Mind*, LIX [1950], 368).

For reasons which will occur to the reader, it is useful (a) not to restrict the kind of fact mentioned by S, (b) to make the truth of statements of relevance dependent on the attitudes of the speaker, (c) to restrict the changes in attitude involved to corresponding value attitudes (thereby eliminating changes in personal preference), and (d) to restrict the relevant changes to immediate ones, as contrasted with long-term conditionings.

say S is relevant is *not* dependent just on whether coming to believe S would affect his attitudes. Suppose, for instance, someone were so constituted that the first example posed on page 168 *did* affect his ethical attitudes, and the second one did *not*. Would we in fact suppose him to be speaking correctly if he expressed these facts by corresponding statements about relevance? Decidedly not. (Nor does it help to reply that this only means *we* should say something verbally contradictory; for we should think such a person incompetent and intellectually confused.) Or again, suppose someone's attitudes are modified by believing S, but we happen to know that they would *not* have been, had he been better informed, or had he not been anxious or angry, or had he been consistent in his ethical attitudes. In this case, should we not think his judgment of relevance at least doubtful? I think we should. Or again, suppose we happen to know that of a group of persons better placed to know the facts and to be impartial, every one has come to a conclusion opposite to that expressed in E. Now if the speaker was quite unmoved by hearing of this fact—or by learning of the facts mentioned previously, that he would have judged differently if he had been better informed (and so forth)—and consequently by the analysis could properly say this was an irrelevant point, should we agree that he had spoken correctly? I think we should not.

Furthermore, if we try to patch up the proposed analysis to meet these points, we shall find that we cannot do so without falling into serious inconsistency with other points of the Attitude Theory.

Therefore I am doubtful whether there is any cognitive analysis of "ethical relevance" which will do the trick needed by the Attitude Theory.

Let us turn now to the alternative noncognitive proposal, which is a rough extension of the theses of the Attitude Theory from ethical terms themselves to the term "relevance" when used in ethical contexts. This view is obviously consistent with the Attitude Theory.

It is profitable to distinguish two types of this theory. (a) The simpler view is to say that "That's relevant" is an expression of the moving appeal of the reason denoted by "that," of the felt increased inclination or disinclination to express an attitude toward something on account of thinking of the reason. (b) Or one may regard statements of relevance as themselves expressions of attitudes (dispositions) toward certain kinds of transformations of attitudes, or as inclinations to moralize about the ways of moralists.[15] This second type (b) has some difficulties with the kind of attitude intended. For obviously "That's a relevant point" does not express an *ethical* attitude in the narrow sense. (We do, of course, sometimes disapprove of a person for urging or even being influenced by an irrelevant point, depending on how deliberate the act is, and how unadmirable a character is manifested. On the other hand, we also sometimes approve of a person being influenced by irrelevant propaganda, if we think this the only way in which he will ever acquire desirable attitudes.) For we have here to do with appraisals of *arguments* or *reasons,* not with the appraisal of *using* an irrelevant argument for a certain end. (Sometimes attitude theorists do not distinguish as clearly as they should the morality of the *use* of irrelevant propaganda from the question whether a statement *is* irrelevant propaganda.) Nor is "That's relevant" plausibly regarded as the expression of a preference, or liking, for an argument or reason. In fact, we can often wish an argument were relevant, or irrelevant, when we can see that it is not. In general, it is not easy to point out the occurrent manifestations in terms of which an attitude of the kind required can be defined. The most plausible suggestion I can make is to say that "That's irrelevant" gives expression, in the Attitude Theory sense, to a disposition not to be influenced by others' use of an argument like that, not to use such an argument myself except when it serves some important end, to feel particularly annoyed at people if they use such arguments to promote ends I do not care for, and so on. (Of course, it must be assumed that these reactions would tend to occur independently of any judgment about relevance.)

Does this kind of proposal have any serious defects? Well, on the basis of introspection I should say that the impression of the irrelevance of an ethical reason does not differ from the impression of the irrelevance of a reason in the context of science. Therefore, in order to justify giving up a cognitive view for either form of noncognitivist analysis we ought to have some positive reason for distinguishing the two cases. As far as I know, none has been given, beyond whatever ground there is for supposing that ethical statements do not make assertions. (It is true that to say a certain statement is relevant to an

[15] See J. Ladd in J. Wild (ed.), *The Return to Reason* (Chicago, 1953), p. 255; and Stevenson, *Ethics and Language,* Chap. VII, Section 2, and in *The Philosophical Review,* LIX (1950), 528-30.

ethical issue may be construed in some contexts as a recommendation; but this is true for *all* terms of logical appraisal.) However, there are various reasons for doubting the adequacy of these noncognitive analyses. Clearly we judge arguments to be relevant or irrelevant when we have no noticeable feelings about them at all, in familiar types of cases. Nor is it impossible that there should be a cynic who could distinguish relevant from irrelevant arguments, but was moved himself only by considerations of a personal kind, would use an irrelevant argument as quickly as a relevant one where it served his purpose—in short, who had no attitude of the kind described, to be expressed. Moreover, if this is all a person is doing when he says a reason is relevant to a given point, we can express disagreement with him, express our contrary feeling or attitude, but we cannot regard his statement as *mistaken*—a consequence inconsistent with a view plausible for the examples we considered. And—what seems definitely the most important matter—all the objections raised to the specimen cognitive analysis on page 171 could be repeated with suitable modifications in the present context.

Noncognitivist characterizations of "relevance," then, seem to be as unpromising for the Attitude Theory as are the cognitive analyses. The Attitude Theory cannot, I think, give an adequate explication of "relevance" consistent with itself and the arguments used to support it.

V. Third Puzzle: The effectiveness of some ethical reasons

A theory of ethical language is unsatisfactory if it implies that a certain ethical reason will not influence ethical convictions causally when it is known to do so in fact. One reason for doubting the adequacy of the Attitude Theory is of just this sort. For there are certain reasons which are *immediately convincing*, that is, are reasons which we at once recognize as rendering our ethical view untenable unless we can rebut them; and the Attitude Theory has no room for this fact. (Such immediate convincingness is to be distinguished from a capacity to alter attitudes over a period of time—perhaps unconsciously by serving as rewards, in the manner suggested by psychologists like Clark Hull. Immediately convincing reasons are ones which, as soon as they are grasped, have an effect on our value convictions; and they are consciously recognized as serious or decisive points.)

Let us begin by noting that, according to the Attitude Theory, what it means for a reason to be effective (with a possible exception to be noted at the end) is for it to change the relevant ethical attitude. Thus, for a statement to be immediately convincing is for it to have an immediate effect upon an attitude. Therefore, if we are to see how far the Attitude Theory provides for immediately convincing reasons, we have to examine the theory of how reasons can have an immediate influence on attitudes.

What proposals have been offered by way of a theory of the effects of statements on attitudes, of this immediate sort? I know of only two. First, it is a natural extension of the stimulus-generalization mechanism in the area of behavioral "habits" to suppose that an attitude toward things of the kind K will be extended to new objects recognized as very similar to it. Thus any reason which functioned to cause a new type of object to be recognized as very similar to a type of object already connected with an ethical attitude would have the function of extending the ethical attitude to the novel type of object. Second, alterations in the conception of something's means-end relation to something which is wanted or disliked will be followed by corresponding changes in the desire or aversion for the former (and related affects). Reasons will therefore be effective when they disclose means-end relations to other objects already of interest. Let us assume for the moment that psychology recognizes no other ways in which reasons can alter attitudes.

Now the difficulty with the Attitude Theory is this. There are some reasons in ethics which are immediately convincing, the effectiveness of which cannot be fitted into this framework. Therefore they can not work by modifying attitudes, and the Attitude Theory must be too simple.

In considering this argument, we must be careful not to lose our perspective. We must recognize that we do not know what further psychological investigation will bring to light, what further relevant laws or mechanisms will be discovered. Therefore the argument should be taken merely as a challenge to show why we should not be doubtful of the Attitude Theory, given plain lacunae in its psychological account; the argument cannot claim to be conclusive. On the other hand, it must not be underestimated. It cannot reasonably be passed off with the explanation that, since the Attitude Theory is obviously correct, there must *be* some explanation how these reasons can affect attitudes immediately, even though we do not know what it is. This view would be unreasonable, because the Attitude Theory is one of several competing hypotheses about what is going on in ethical discourse, deliberation, and controversy; and, as such, its truth must be assessed on the basis of its capacity to handle the total evidence available. The ability of the theory to account for the immediate convincingness of certain reasons is part of the reason for accepting or rejecting it. If at present the theory cannot account for this fact plausibly, that is a point against it.

But are there in fact any immediately convincing reasons, the effectiveness of which the Attitude Theory cannot explain? In order to extract an example of such, let us consider the following typical ethical dialogue.

A: "The prohibition of abortion for other than medical reasons is unjustified. It is stupid not to use known methods to prevent the birth of unwanted children in families that are poverty stricken, and in which another child must face life with dim prospects for happiness."

B: "I don't agree. From the moment of conception human life is present. There is no difference between abortion and infanticide or murder. Surely you do not think infanticide is justified?"

A: "Abortion and infanticide are by no means the same. The unborn child has no personality. It is personality, not simply life, that justifies the right to live. You must recognize this yourself; for you believe animals may be used as a means to human survival, and the only difference which can justify your distinction is the lack of personality."

B: "Human life is different. Surely we cannot claim that a human being loses his right to life if he lacks personality or mental development. In these respects an imbecile is hardly superior to some animals. Yet you would hardly agree they have no right to life."

This dialogue is instructive. Both parties agree that one thing, infanticide, cannot be wrong, and another, abortion, right unless there is some difference between the two. Moreover, they agree that this difference cannot be just *any* difference; for there is always *some* difference between two acts. I think it fair to say they would agree that the difference must be one which makes a difference in general. Thus if personality is what enables us to distinguish morally between infanticide and abortion, it must make a difference of a similar sort wherever it is involved—hence with respect to the treatment of animals and the mentally defective.

My example of an immediately convincing reason, then, is this. If a person is making opposite appraisals of two things, but is shown there is no difference of this sort between the things, he at once is convinced that at least one of his appraisals is untenable. We might call this an Argument from the Identity of Justifying Grounds. Or, with this meaning in mind, we might call it an Argument from Ethical Inconsistency.

Now how will the Attitude Theory construe the immediate convincingness of this argument?

We must not of course overlook the possibility of future developments. But as of the present the most plausible explanation with which I am acquainted is the following. (a) People in our moral community are taught an unfavorable attitude toward Ethical Inconsistency in this sense. (b) This attitude is engaged by a disclosure of inconsistency with the result of felt dissatisfaction with the situation, and a willingness to withdraw one or the other of the ethical statements.

This proposal seems to me unsatisfactory. First, although we may concede that an unfavorable attitude toward inconsistency will manifest itself as dissatisfaction when we find ourselves being inconsistent, I do not see that all this explains our clear view that one or the other of two such opinions must be mistaken. Second, the explanation does not make clear why our ethical attitudes (as distinct from our willingness to argue something further publicly) should suddenly become weaker—assuming this is what happens when ethical doubt arises. There is no psychological law to the effect that when one emotional attitude becomes directed at another, the latter automatically disappears; in fact, I believe that some emotional tendencies in ourselves which we deplore may last for years.

There are other types of reason which anyone who understands ethical language would I think find decisive, the effect of which the Attitude Theory is similarly incompetent to explain.

The Attitude Theory might, however, take an entirely different line. It might hold that ethical language is properly used only to express ethical attitudes, and then proceed to say that an attitude is not an *ethical* attitude unless it is consistent with one's other ethical attitudes. It might then construe the Argument from the Identity of

Justifying Grounds as showing a person that he had used ethical language improperly because he had no corresponding *ethical* attitude. Whether this alternative approach is more satisfactory, or whether, if so, it differs other than terminologically from a Cognitive Theory, are questions I shall leave with the reader.[16]

[16] For the Comments and Response which relate to this paper see pp. 317-25, 358-59, and 386-88, below.

THE MEANING OF
"INTRINSIC VALUE"

HAROLD N. LEE

I

WHEN I was a student writing my doctoral dissertation, I went to Professor Whitehead one day with what I would now recognize to be a semantic problem. I was puzzled as to what words would best communicate the conceptual system I had worked out. After some thought, he said, "When you have a new concept, and consider by what name you want to call it, you can do either of two things: you can use an old word which you redefine, but if you do, you will be always misunderstood; or you can invent a new word, but if you do, you will be never understood. Take your choice."

Professor Whitehead gave a nice statement of the semantic dilemma facing every philosopher. If the philosopher's language is strictly in the common idiom, his theory will probably be no more precise or clear than common sense: the common idiom is not overly sensitive to precision or clarity. Yet if he uses words in ways that are too strange or contrary to their common usage, not only is he making communication difficult, but it may be questioned that he is adequately performing the task of philosophy.

When philosophy deals with subject matter which is close to our ordinary experience (and surely, value theory falls here), its theoretic conclusions must be clearly and unequivocally applicable to experience; else it is not performing its task. A strange or unusual vocabulary makes application difficult, to say the least, and sometimes defeats it altogether, even for the author of the theory. Philosophic theory sometimes invents its own world to live in and has only an oblique reference to the common world. Perhaps this is desirable in pure mathematics or logic, but it is objectionable in value theory.

Because values are so close to the core of our life and conduct, value theory should have application that is neither obscure or oblique, nor equivocal. Hence, the present Essay will neither reject the common idiom nor revise it gratuitously. In particular, it will avoid the solution of the semantic dilemma that leads to the rejection of such expressions as "the sunset is beautiful," "the conduct is good," "the tool is useful," or "the book is valuable" as either meaningless, incorrect or figurative.[1]

"Beauty" is the common name for aesthetic value; "goodness" (when used in a specifically moral sense) for moral value; and "utility" for use or practical value. When most persons who speak English say that anything is beautiful, they mean that it has beauty —aesthetic value. When they say that it is good, they mean that it has moral value. When they say that it is useful, they mean that it has practical value. In short, when they say that anything is valuable, they mean that it has value. The present Essay does not hold such expressions to be either meaningless or figures of speech. Thus, in the semantic usage of the present paper, "value" will designate something that something can have. This statement is not intended to have exclusive metaphysical implications; I am simply calling attention to the way that most persons who speak English use the words in question, and am pointing out that the present Essay will use them in the same way.

Of course, I am not going to stay slavishly within the common idiom. It was not devised for the purposes of philosophy. The semantic reference of most of its words is vague. The reference must be sharpened and made precise to fulfill the purposes of philosophy; and this requires definition uncommon to the common idiom. The definitions, however, need not do violence to ordinary language in their departure from it, and the present paper will attempt to hold such departures to a minimum.

Definitions in philosophy are not arbitrary, but must be controlled in accordance with two factors: 1) the linguistic habits of the persons who use the word defined; 2) the adequacy of the definition in

---

[1] "It is convenient to speak of things as *having* value, but it must not be forgotten that this is only a *façon de parler;* things do not really have value" (D. H. Parker, *Human Values* [New York, 1931], p. 21). "No thing (object) in the universe *has* values. The proposition 'z has value,' if z designates an object, is, in its literal sense, a meaningless proposition in our axiological system" (A. L. Hilliard, *The Forms of Value* [New York, 1950], p. 47). See also P. B. Rice's discussion on p. 281 of R. Lepley (ed.), *Value: A Cooperative Inquiry* (New York, 1949); and my discussion on p. 155 of the same work.

reducing to order the subject matter within which the word is intended to apply. As long as words are to be used for the purposes of communication, the first consideration can not be disregarded; as long as they are to be used for the purposes of philosophy, the second cannot be disregarded. If one invents a new word for the new concept, he may be operating within the demands of the second consideration, but not be communicating well. In the words of Professor Whitehead, he may never be understood. If he uses an old word in a *completely* new way, however, it is really a new sign spelled and pronounced just like the old one. Nothing could be better designed to cause confusion.

II

At the very outset of a theory of value, an important semantic question arises in the consideration of whether the meaning of "value" is to be derived from its noun (or in oldfashioned language, its substantive) sense, or from its verb (actional) sense. On the one hand, "value" may designate a property or characteristic of an object; this is what I call the noun sense. On the other hand, "value" may designate an act; this is what I call the verb sense. The common idiom uses the word in either way, but a choice must be made by theory. I am sure that sometimes the authors of different value theories argue at cross purposes because "value" means to one of them a property and to the other an act.

The semantic problem here is not a question of when value is used as a noun and when as a verb in the syntax of a sentence. Such a question is one of grammar, not of semantics. The present problem is one of designation: if the word in its most general sense—that upon which all specific meanings and derivatives depend—designates an act, then the verb sense is semantically prior; but if the word most generally designates a property or characteristic, and every other meaning depends on this, then the noun sense is semantically prior. This is regardless of what part of speech the word happens to be in the syntax of any particular sentence.

To Dewey, for example, the verb sense seems to be basic. He holds the meaning of "value" to be closely connected with some or several of the following words: prizing, desiring, holding dear, or liking, taking interest in, enjoying, or appraising.[2] Dewey prefers

[2] See *Value: A Cooperative Inquiry,* pp. 6 and 68.

to call the general theory the theory of valuation rather than of value.[3] Nevertheless, that he does not clearly envisage the semantic problem I am pointing out is shown by his insistence that value is adjectival, and by his mention of possible terms such as "valuity" or "valueness."[4] Toward the end of his essay in *Value: A Cooperative Inquiry*, he calls the theory the "general theory of valuings-values," apparently attempting to amalgamate the two senses of the word.

I suggest that some of the differences between Pepper and me displayed in my Comment on his Essay in *Value: A Cooperative Inquiry* and in his Rejoinder are due to his taking "value" in the verb sense and my taking it in the noun sense.[5] The place he puts his own *value* on his chart shows that he takes "value" in the verb sense.[6] His chart indicates that Perry uses the word primarily in the noun sense; and that Lewis uses "immediate (intrinsic) value" in the verb sense but "inherent value" in the noun sense. I agree with these judgments (though I may have read them into Pepper's chart rather than out of it); but whether they are correct is neither here nor there for the purposes of the present illustration. They illustrate that the two senses of the word "value" are quite different. Theory of value should be clear about the distinction. Is the designatum of "value" an act or is it a property?

Inasmuch as I have said that the present Essay will take "value" to mean something that something can have, it is apparent that I am using the word in the noun sense. Value is a property or characteristic of an object. When I use the verb "to value," the syntax will show it. My reference then is to the act of valuing, or, alternately, valuation. The noun meaning of the word is still primary, however, for when I value an object, I am finding value in it or ascribing value to it. The value is something that the object has. This is only a semantic statement. I am stipulating how I shall use the word, and it remains to be seen if the question "What does an object have when we say 'it has value?'" can be answered.

Before going any farther, I had better make explicit my use of the word "object." Whatever is an object is so by virtue of its being

[3] Note his title, "Theory of Valuation," in *International Encyclopedia of Unified Science* (Chicago, 1939), Vol. II, No. 4.
[4] See *Value: A Cooperative Inquiry*, p. 66.
[5] See *ibid.*, pp. 373-74.
[6] *Ibid.*, p. 378.

capable of having an action directed toward it. In the special use I shall make of the word, anything is an object that can have the act of attention directed toward it—that is, an object is whatever can be attended to either concretely or in abstraction. I do not confer any special ontological status on whatever I am talking about by calling it an object. Thus, by "object," I do not necessarily mean a physical object. A thing, an event, a situation, a state, an action, a feeling, a condition or set of conditions, a class, the defining characteristics of a class—these may all be objects in suitable contexts. A physical object is whatever has physical characteristics toward which attention can be directed. A valuable object is whatever has value toward which attention can be directed. A valuable physical object is whatever has both kinds of characteristics. This usage seems both clear and close enough to ordinary language to serve the purposes of communication.

The expressions "such and such *is* value" and "such and such *has* value" are never equipollent in the semantic usage here advocated. It is correct to say "beauty is value (aesthetic value)," but never "beauty has value." Similarly, it is correct to say "the sunset is beautiful (valuable aesthetically or having aesthetic value)," but never "the sunset is beauty." If one says "*x* has value," the term "value" refers to a characteristic or property of the object *x*. This statement also is semantic. It gives the designatum of "value" and says nothing about its ontological status. As far as we have gone, the designatum may be an empty class, an illusion, or what have you.[7]

To sum up: "value," a noun, is the name of a characteristic or property of an object. The adjective form "valuable" asserts that an object has or possesses the property. Even as I say that an object possesses redness (noun form) and is red (adjective form), so I say that an object possesses value (noun form) and is valuable (adjective form). Nouns for special kinds of value with their adjective equivalents are: "beauty—beautiful," "goodness—good," "utility—useful," "holiness—holy," "justice—just," and so on.

III

The semantic usage advocated in Section II is easily compatible

---

[7] See C. Morris, "Foundations of the Theory of Signs," in *International Encyclopedia of Unified Science* (Chicago, 1938), Vol. I, No. 2, p. 5.

with either a realistic or a relational theory of value, but it is not easily compatible with a subjective theory or one that is purely affective such as classic hedonism. Such a circumstance might have been expected, for semantic usage can not be completely divorced from the logical structure of theory in the field where it is to apply. One of the questions asked in the survey preliminary to the present cooperative study was, "Can and should semiotic be developed prior to axiology, or can (or must) the two be of mutual assistance?" I take "axiology" here to mean the general theory of value, and my answer to the question is that neither the semantics nor the theory can be developed without the other. Theory uses signs and is expressed in some sort of language, else there is no theory. Signs have meanings; else they are not signs. Some meanings imply others or may be said to contain others; unless they did, there would be no such thing as analytical propositions. This interconnection of meanings (or intensions) forms a logical structure. Such logic is applied, not pure logic, but here we are considering the logic of a general theory of value, and this, in any case, would be applied logic.

The upshot of the whole argument is that the semantic scheme and the logical scheme of theory are the obverse and reverse of the same medal. The meanings of the signs are bound up with each other in the logical scheme of the theory; and the meanings, in so far as they are general, are inexpressible and incommunicable except in the signs. The conclusion then, is that the semantics of axiology and the logical structure of axiology are inseparable. We may elaborate the semantics in great detail, but if the meanings of the words do not fit into the logical scheme, we do not have even good semantics.

The study of semantics by itself solves only semantic problems; it solves no theoretic problems except in the pure theory of semantics. There, we are interested in the use of language about the use of language, but in the semantics of axiology, we are interested in the use of language about values. Good semantic usage is a necessary but not a sufficient condition of good theory. The semantics of axiology must be a tool adequate to deal with all the varieties and complexities of actual experiences of values, and must enable the theorist to make fruitful generalizations about values. Its purpose is to enable one to find his way around in the value situation, and it cannot be developed in abstraction from that situation.

IV

All theory is constructed from generalizations; thus, many of the words of axiology will be general terms. A general term does not denote a fact; facts are specific. Behind the generalizations of axiology, however, lie facts. A particular value experience is a fact, and in the semantic usage of the present paper, the specific value in that experience will be called a fact too. Instead of contrasting values with facts, this Essay holds that a value is a special kind of fact: a fact whose existence lies in a peculiar contextual situation.

A fact, in the usage of the present paper, is whatever has a locus in space and time. (Perhaps I should say "space-time," as I would hold that they are necessary to each other. They can vary independently, and hence, can be abstracted from each other, but they "go together.") The contextual situation in which any particular value lies has a locus in space and time, hence, is a (complex) fact.[8] The value is part of that situation, and thus can be located spatially and temporally. Note that I am speaking of a particular value—and more than that, of what will be called later an actual value. If I speak of the beauty of a Bach chorale, that is a generalization of the specific beauties of the various renditions of the chorale, and it has no meaning otherwise. (That the rendition may be imaginative to one who can read the score fluently alters the case no whit.) To speak of the chorale apart from the renditions is an abstraction. The score is not the music. Music is sound or the imagery of sound, and it is the music, not the score, that is beautiful.

We do not have separate signs for facts unless their individuality is of sufficient importance for us to give them proper names, such as the Battle of Bunker Hill. Specific values are no exception to this rule, but are referred to by a gesture, a demonstrative pronoun or a descriptive phrase, such as "this value" or "that value" or "the beauty of this sunset" or "the justice of the decision rendered by the Supreme Court of the United States on April 23, 1945, in the case Cramer v. United States." Nevertheless, the whole theory of value rests upon the existence of specific values whether or not we have separate signs for them.

Any object with a locus in space and time, thus any fact, exists in

---

[8] I doubt that there are any simple, or "atomic," facts, but that is not the problem of the present Essay.

a context. When considered in relation to its context, it has properties which it does not have in isolation. Many of the words of ordinary language designate such contextual properties. For example, suppose that John is five feet tall. Put into the context where all his companions are Lilliputians, he is big: his bigness is a fact. Put into the context of the champion basketball team, however, he is not big: his smallness is a fact. "Bigness" and "smallness" designate contextual or relative properties. Such properties are factual when they are parts of actual contexts and the contexts are factual. In order to justify this usage, however, we must be able to identify the context that is necessary and sufficient to the existence of value.

V

A contexture common to all value experiences can be pointed out. If there are values that are not experienced, their consideration must be laid aside here, for we are seeking to generalize from actual contexts. One component in the value contexture is an object (not necessarily a physical object, as previously noted). Another component is the sort of conative-affective sensitivity of an organism that can be generally characterized as an attitude. It is conative-affective in that it reacts to an object both with a tendency toward or away from it and with a feeling. A third component of the contexture is an actual transaction between the object and the conative-affective sensitivity; that is, actual contact is made and the sensitivity reacts by a pleasant expansive tendency or by an unpleasant shrinking tendency. The third component depends on the first two, but it is something in addition to them as it is an actual interaction between them. A fourth component is a contextual property dependent upon the first three. This fourth component, the contextual property, is the designatum of "value" in the present Essay. These four components are very general, and apply to much if not all experience. This is to say that much within our experience is valued, and anything may be valued.

Value may be called objective, because it is the property of an object. It is not independent, however, of whatever subjective elements there are in the conative-affective attitude. Conation can be treated, perhaps, behavioristically, and thus may be supposed to be objective, but I do not see how affection can be so treated in spite of Dewey's strictures on page 14 of his *Theory of Valuation.*[9]

I call the attitude conative-affective because what is involved in the contexture of the value experience is anterior to the distinction between conation and affection. Cognition, conation, and affection are not here regarded as atomistic faculties which interact with each other to make up psychological activity. Instead, they are regarded as factors which are analyzed out of psychological activity taken as the original whole. The analysis is legitimate because they vary independently of each other and thus can always be distinguished. There are ways in which conation and affection are more like each other than either is like cognition, and these ways are peculiarly relevant to the value situation. Striving is both doing and feeling; so is desiring; so is liking; and so on. It is true that in special cases of striving, desiring or liking, doing and feeling may vary independently, and so the distinction can still be made and is well made It is the contention of the present Essay, however, that the description of the second component in the value contexture should not make the distinction.

It is perhaps unfortunate that psychology has no general name for conation-affection as distinguished from cognition. "Preference" comes close to being such a name, but if it emphasizes actual choice, it stresses conation at the expense of affection. Perry uses "interest," but this also stresses conation. Rice uses "joy," but this stresses affection. Parker uses "satisfaction," but its meaning in ordinary language also stresses affection. In my own attempt to give an account of aesthetic value, I tended to emphasize conation, but I defined the aesthetic attitude first of all ostensively.[10] I now hold the nature of the general attitude to be anterior to the distinction between conation and affection.

So far, I have used "value" to designate a property in an actual contexture. If there are reasons to hold that there are unrealized values (and I think there are), the designation of the word must be expanded. If the property designated by "value" could be shown to be independent of a contexture in which an organic sensibility is a

[9] *International Encyclopedia of Unified Science* (Chicago, 1939), Vol. II, No. 4. In this connection, see my criticism of Dewey's behaviorism on pp. 148-53 of *Value: A Cooperative Inquiry.* I hold that "affective" *does* refer to private feelings.

[10] *Perception and Aesthetic Value* (New York, 1938), Chap. II.

part, there would be no special problem of unrealized values. I do not think that it has been so shown. In addition, attempts to develop such a theory must have some special way of finding the independent value, such as G. E. Moore's moral intuition, for which I do not think there is any direct evidence. It is a hypothesis to explain what does not need to be explained except in terms of Moore's theory. Some kinds of moral rationalism also offer to explain how we find this independent value, but whereas they can be made to fit (with some Procrustean violence) moral value, I do not see how they can be made to fit aesthetic value. An axiology that takes its point of departure from moral value and treats aesthetic value casually or not at all is manifestly inadequate.

The best way to treat the problem of unrealized values is to develop a concept of potential value. This entails explicating a clear meaning for "potential" which will fit the meaning of "value" in such a way that the combination has its own special meaning. I shall take up this problem after considering the meaning of "intrinsic value," which can best be approached from the standpoint of the actual value experience and again, later, be expanded to include potential values.

VI

The difference in degree of intensity of values is part of the data of experience only after we compare one value with another. Difference in degree is a matter of comparison. If one experience of value existed in absolute isolation, there would be no question of degree; but of course, none does so exist. As long as there are memory and foresight, there is comparison of values.

Comparison of values involves judgment. Although judgment is not one of the necessary components in a value contexture, we may make judgments about values. The word "evaluation" will be used in the present paper to designate comparative judgments of value which involve (explicitly or implicitly) either more or less. To measure different intensities of value, we must find the factor underlying the judgment of more or less. This will be called the "evaluating factor," and it will be maintained that it is the degree of pleasantness-unpleasantness of the conative-affective component of the value contexture.[11] Perhaps a better name for this evaluating factor, lying closer to the common idiom is "satisfaction-dissatisfaction."

In choosing the affective element in the conative-affective attitude as the evaluating factor, I am not implying any concrete separation between conation and affection. I should suppose that *in concreto* the connection between them is indissoluble. I am saying that the conative-affective component in the value contexture determines the intensity of the value. The feeling of pleasantness or satisfaction (or their negatives) is the *measure in consciousness* of the conative-affective component. Therefore, the feeling of pleasantness or satisfaction (or their negatives) offers a measure of the intensity of the value.

Those persons who approach the theory of value with the assumption, either explicit or implicit, that moral value is *the* value *par excellence* usually overemphasize the conative element in the value contexture, though even here, hedonism has always been an exception. Moral values involve choices, and choices are conative, but if choices and the results of choices did not also have an affective aspect, hedonism could never have been even proposed.

In contrast to theories that overemphasize conation, classic hedonism takes the affective factor in the value context to be the whole value, neglecting everything else in the contexture. As the opponents of hedonism have always felt, this is too simple. The affective component, being the evaluating factor, is important, but it is not everything.

The emotive theory of value is a recent aberration that also overemphasizes the affective factor in the contexture. Always to call the affective factor an emotion involves a peculiarly imprecise use of the term "emotion." Psychology does not call any affective state an emotion, but reserves the term for those more carefully delimited affective states in which characteristic stimuli and reactions are identified. The emotive theory is guilty not only of this semantic error, but also of the graver error of identifying the whole with a part. Synecdoche is a legitimate figure of speech, but philosophic theory should be more than a figure of speech.

To sum up: The value in any contexture depends in part upon the

---

[11] I avoid the word "pleasure" as having irrelevant connotations. "Pain" is the name of a sensation, which is usually though not always unpleasant. For this use of "pleasantness-unpleasantness" see *Perception and Aesthetic Value*, Chap. V.

conative-affective component of the contexture. The affective factor, the positive pole of which I have called pleasantness or satisfaction, is the measure of the intensity and direction of the conative-affective component, and thus it is the measure of the intensity and direction of the value. (By the direction of the value, I mean whether positive or negative.) For this reason, I have called it the evaluating factor.

VII

Up to the present time, I have limited my analysis to the contexture of the actual value experience. The pleasantness or unpleasantness is actually present in the transaction between the object and the attitude in the value contexture. This is the meaning of the rather loose but ordinary definition of intrinsic value—that the object is valued for its own sake. Thus, without explicitly calling attention to it, I have been analyzing the experience of intrinsic value. An object has positive intrinsic value when the positive evaluating factor is part of the actual transaction of the value contexture.

An object may sometimes be judged to have positive value, however, even when the actual transaction is unpleasant or unsatisfactory. This is the case when the present object is judged to be a cause or necessary condition of a pleasant or satisfactory transaction in the future. Here we have instrumental value. The object in a value contexture has positive instrumental value if it is judged to be the cause or necessary condition of a positive intrinsic value. This is the meaning of the ordinary definition that the object having instrumental value is valued for the sake of that for which it is the instrument.

Such an analysis makes no reference to absolute ends, and thus avoids Dewey's attack on the concept of intrinsic value. An intrinsic value, in the semantic usage of the present Essay, is not an end-in-itself. It is not something to be striven after, as Dewey would seem to have it, for its own sake. If there were any such thing as an end-in-itself, it would *have* intrinsic value, it would not *be* intrinsic value. We strive after objects (an analytical statement in the semantics of the present paper); objects have value. We do not strive after values. Values can be obtained only by obtaining objects that are valuable. We may strive after objects *because* they have value, but this raises the question of motivation, a proper subject of investigation for psychology, and not under discussion in the present Essay.

Dewey objects to the concept of intrinsic value because he holds it to be absolutistic.[12] If intrinsic value is defined by reference to the locus of the evaluating factor, however, this objection does not hold. Any object may have both intrinsic and instrumental value at the same time but in different respects. A noxious medicine may have negative intrinsic value and positive instrumental value both at the same time. The medicine is unpleasant, but is instrumental to a more pleasant transaction in the future. In a contrasting vein, imbibing intoxicating liquor may have great positive intrinsic value for a confirmed alcoholic, but at the same time have negative instrumental values which outweigh the intrinsic in the unpleasantness or misery caused. It may be that *every* object having intrinsic value also has instrumental value, but even so, this offers no reason for refusing to distinguish between the two. The object *is not* the value; it *has* the value; and any object may have many values according to the various contextures of which it may be a part.

It has already been noted that the primary experience of value is not cognitive—none of the components of the value contexture is a judgment. Now, however, this scheme must be extended for instrumental values, because here a judgment is necessary. In addition to the object, the attitude and the transaction, a judgment of causal efficacy or necessary conditionality enters into the contexture wherein instrumental value becomes a property of the object.

Dewey's position that cognition or appraisal enters into all valuations[13] is bound up with his rejection of the concept of intrinsic value. Instrumental value involves cognition, and as all values are instrumental, at least in part, to Dewey, it follows that all involve cognition. If, however, the value experience is analyzed as it has been in the present Essay, cognition is involved in the attribution of instrumental value but not in the primary experience of intrinsic value. Instrumental value depends on intrinsic value because the evaluating factor is referred to a future experience of intrinsic value.

Aesthetic value best illustrates the present definition of intrinsic value. Insofar as moral values involve choice, they involve comparison, and hence, judgment. Characteristically moral choices look to results, and results depend on causal efficacy or conditionality. Thus,

---

[12] "So called relational theories often retain an attenuated relic of absolutistic theories in the use of the word 'intrinsic'" (*Value: A Cooperative Inquiry*, p. 69).
[13] See *Value: A Cooperative Inquiry*, pp. 7, 68, and 74.

moral values are usually if not always instrumental.[14] One can easily be in error in his judgments of instrumentality. Hence, he is often in error in what he takes to be morally valuable. When the immediate context is actually pleasant or satisfying (or their negatives), it does not appear how one could be in error in apprehending value.

Immediacy cannot be in error; only judgment can be in error. What *seems* to be *is* when only the immediate experience is taken into account. Insofar as one feels pleasantness or satisfaction in an experience, it is pleasant or satisfactory. When, however, one makes judgments concerning future pleasures or satisfactions, he may well be in error. Moral values usually refer to a larger context than that immediately present; and to a person who takes moral values to be paradigmatic for axiology, the statement that the experience of (intrinsic) value cannot be in error will always appear perverse.[15]

The present usage of "intrinsic" in "intrinsic value" is to be contrasted with those usages that define it by reference to the intrinsic nature or intrinsic properties of an object.[16] If value is always to be found in a contexture, then it is obvious that it is never found in the intrinsic nature or intrinsic properties of an object, that is, in the nature or properties of the object outside of the contexture. G. E. Moore's usage is part and parcel of his theory of value. This is an example of the contention in Section III of the present paper that semantics and the logical structure of theory are bound up with each other, at least in the case of axiology. One cannot use the expression "intrinsic value" at all in the present theory if he defines it as does Moore.

VIII

It remains to be seen whether the present analysis of "value" and "intrinsic value" can take account of unrealized values, for evaluations indicate that we must take account of them. We can recognize the conditions of the value experience and make choices in the light of contexts larger than the immediate one. Such choices often refer to

[14] It might be argued (though to do so here would take us afield) that the intrinsic value toward which moral values point is aesthetic.

[15] I suggest that this consideration is at the bottom of the dispute between Ayres and me in *Value: A Cooperative Inquiry*. See Ayres's criticism of my Essay, and my Rejoinder, *ibid.*, pp. 302-11.

[16] See G. E. Moore, *Philosophical Studies* (London and New York, 1922), p. 260, "The Conception of Intrinsic Value."

unrealized values. We make errors in judgments of value, but many of the errors would be difficult to account for if there were no unrealized values. Moral ideals are formed in the light of values to be realized in circumstances other than those which obtain. In art criticism, we make reference to unrealized values which sometimes are judged to be greater than those realized. All of these judgments are judgments of potentiality.

The concept of possibility is, at bottom, a negative concept. A logical possibility is marked by the absence of any logical incompatibility. A physical possibility is marked by the absence of factors incompatible with actual physical conditions. It is not physically possible for me to jump one hundred feet into the air. That means that such a jump is incompatible with my frame and musculature and the conditions of terrestrial gravitation. A practical possibility is marked by the absence of conditions incompatible with practice. It is not practically possible for me to solve mathematical problems involving integral calculus. I do not know the principles and procedures of integral calculus.

The concept of potentiality, on the other hand, is a positive concept: it is more than possibility. It involves not only the absence of incompatibility, but in addition is marked by the presence of conditions such that the imposition of other compatible conditions will produce a specific result. For example, a fresh flashlight cell will produce light if the connections and switch function and if the filament of the bulb is unbroken. The cell possesses potential energy. Where we have potential x, some of the conditions necessary and sufficient to the actual existence of x are present and some are absent. The absent conditions may be actual, but the two sets are not compresent. If and when they become compresent, x becomes actual in contradistinction to potential. Potentiality may be said to be due to a broken contexture.

To say that conditions necessary to whatever is potential are actually present is to say that they are facts. The potentiality can be located where these actual conditions are located. Thus a potentiality is a fact under the semantic stipulations herein advocated. It has a locus in space and time. It is a fact that the flashlight cell I now hold in my hand is a "live" cell. That is, it contains potential energy. The potential energy is here-now.

What a potentiality *is* must not be confused with how we know it.

Potentialities are known by inference, and inferences yield probability estimates. The potentiality, however, is not a probability estimate; only my knowledge of it is. The potentiality is either there or it is not; it is what the probability estimate is *about*. We know many kinds of fact other than potentialities only by inference; for example, that there is another side to the moon. Such knowledge is only probable, but if there is another side to the moon, it is none the less a fact. Potentialities are inferred from past and present actualities. My flashlight gave out a strong light a moment ago. This, with my knowledge of the general principles of electricity, yields a high probability estimate that the cell has potential energy; that is, the conditions are present such that if a contact is made, the cell will discharge kinetic energy. The knowledge of this situation is factual knowledge.

If the concept of potentiality means any more or any different, metaphysically or otherwise, than the foregoing, the present usage is not concerned with it. There is potential value when objective conditions similar to those which have entered into past experiences of value are actual, but the transaction with an organic sensitivity is not taking place. Given the missing conditions, the potential value becomes actual value.

We can attribute potential value to an object only as the result of a judgment. Although the contexture of the primary experience of value contains no cognitive component, here again, as is the case in the attribution of instrumental value, a cognitive component must be added. In addition to the object, the attitude, and the transaction, there is the judgment of potentiality here. We have potential intrinsic value when the evaluating factor is judged to be a part of the actual contexture in case it is realized. When we have potential instrumental value, the evaluating factor is judged to be dependent on the instrumentality of the object in the contexture in case it is realized. The judgment of potential instrumental value is doubly fallible: the judgment of potentiality may be incorrect, or the judgment of instrumentality may be incorrect or both. This is one of the things that makes it so hard to solve moral problems.

IX

The present semantic scheme gives an evaluative hedonism, not a definitive hedonism. Classic hedonism, in defining value as pleasure, confuses the value with the evaluating factor. Evaluative hedonism offers a much simpler semantics for axiology than does definitive hedonism.

Take the semantic scheme of A. L. Hilliard's *The Forms of Value,* for example.[17] This is definitive hedonism. For Hilliard, value cannot be the property of an object, for value is affectivity.[18] Beauty, however, and good and utility are characters predicable of objects.[19] With these definitions, beauty, goodness, and utility cannot be species of value except in some Pickwickian sense. The semantic scheme would be simpler if value were also defined as a property or characteristic of an object; hundreds of quotation marks around "has" could thus be deleted. Hilliard finds it convenient to speak of objects "having" value,[20] but as they cannot really *have* value, he uses the quotation marks to show that he does not literally mean what he says. Why not define value so that objects can have it if this is the best way of speaking? The pleasantness can be adequately taken care of as the evaluating factor.

The semantic usage advocated in the present Essay would also render unnecessary Hilliard's Postulate 2.[21] This would be a theoretic simplification as well as a semantic one. Psychological hedonism is, at best, a principle of doubtful validity, and in addition, it brings up the question of motivation, which is an unnecessary complication. It cannot be verified, but must be taken as a postulate in the sense of modern logic—a basic assumption. I choose not to take it because although purportedly about experience, it is empirically unverifiable, and because it is unnecessary if we take the pleasantness to be the evaluating factor.[22]

C. I. Lewis, in *An Analysis of Knowledge and Valuation,*[23] calls pleasantness or satisfaction intrinsic value, and calls what the present

[17] New York, 1950.

[18] *Ibid.,* p. 21.

[19] *Ibid.,* pp. 45, 207, and 275.

[20] Sometimes as often as a dozen times a page. See *ibid.,* p. 54, for instance.

[21] *Ibid.,* p. 13. This postulate is what is ordinarily called psychological hedonism.

[22] It may be pointed out in addition that an evaluative hedonism avoids what G. E. Moore calls the "naturalistic fallacy." It seems to me that the only thing fallacious in what Moore inveighs against is the reductionism of definitive hedonism. Evaluative hedonism avoids the reductionism.

[23] LaSalle, Ill., 1947.

Essay names intrinsic value inherent value. This is a doubtfully desirable semantic usage because "value" is not used univocally in the two expressions. In his "intrinsic value," it is used in what I have called the verb sense: intrinsic value is a way of feeling about something. In "inherent value," on the other hand, it is used in the noun sense: it is the property of an object. His usage also gets him into a long and partly unnecessary argument about the usage of "objective" and "subjective" in value theory.[24]

Instead of saying that intrinsic value is satisfaction, it would be better to say that it is the satisfactoriness of an object. Aside from the awkwardness of the word, however, there is a further semantic objection to its use (harking back to the semantic dilemma of Section I). In the common idiom, "satisfaction" is used to designate only feeling; but if "satisfactoriness" were to be equated with "value," the word would have to be understood to designate a *fulfillment* of the conative-affective sensibility. This would not be an unreasonable requirement for the meaning of the word, but it would offer fertile ground for misunderstanding.

Lewis says that he has no quarrel with those who insist on reserving "intrinsic value" for use such as the present paper advocates.[25] He indicates that the choice is terminological. I think it is more than terminological. It is semantic in the way that semantics and theory are inseparable.[26] Nevertheless, I reciprocate the tolerance of Lewis's statement: the theory of value indicated in the present Essay agrees very largely with his. The essential difference is the way that the feeling of pleasantness or satisfaction is fitted in. This is indicated in my use of the expression "evaluating factor." I hold the affective factor to be as important as he holds it to be. It seems to me to be both semantically and theoretically simpler to fit it in as the evaluating factor.

Value, in the broadest sense, is a potentiality in an object (including those potentialities that become actual). If it is a potentiality in which pleasantness or satisfaction is located in the transaction of the value contexture, the value is intrinsic. If it is a potentiality in which the conditions of other transactions in other value contextures which will themselves (somewhere along the line) be pleasant or satisfying

[24] *Ibid.*, pp. 406-24.
[25] *Ibid.*, p. 390.
[26] See p. 183, above.

is produced, the value is instrumental. In any case, however, the value is a value only by virtue of the possibility of the actual value contexture being formed. Potentialities are what they are only in the light of actualities. Actual intrinsic value is the property of an object whereby it affords pleasantness or satisfaction in a complete contexture such as has been described.[27]

[27] For the Comments and Response which relate to this paper see pp. 326-32, 364-65, and 388-89, below.

VALUE PROPOSITIONS

ROBERT S. HARTMAN

I. Value Terms

THE PRESENT PAPER regards value language as the result of logical abstraction: depending on how we classify a thing it is either good or bad. A good house, to speak with Spinoza, is a bad ruin, and a good ruin is a bad house. Words like "good," "bad," and the like will be called axiological or value terms. Value terms may be either axiological predicates or axiological relations. Propositions containing such predicates or relations will be called axiological or value propositions.

The subject of a value proposition is in all cases a term referring to an empirical thing. By an empirical thing we shall understand, with G. E. Moore, anything "that has existed, does exist, or will exist in time." The concept of such a thing is an empirical concept in the Kantian sense, which may be defined analytically. A nonempirical thing, on the other hand, is one which is referred to by a synthetic definition, in the Kantian sense, or a nominal or stipulative definition in the modern sense. Such a thing will be called a *systemic* or *logical* thing. As such, it is not in time, even though it may inhere in a temporal thing. If x is a systemic thing and belongs to class C, and any member of C by definition has the properties α and β, then x is not a member of C unless x has α and β. A class consisting of systemic or logical things will be called a *systemic* or *logical class*. Its concept *defines* the class; the definition exhausts the concept.

With empirical things, on the other hand, the definition does not exhaust the concept. Rather, to follow Kant again, the definition of an empirical thing is only the most complete and most concise statement of its concept. This definition arises through abstraction from experience. The process of abstraction from the less to the more defined concept is called by Kant *exposition*, and the same word serves for signifying a concept not yet defined. Since the minimum properties *defining* a thing must be a genus and a differentia, the *exposition* of a thing theoretically may contain any number of properties larger than two. The exact line where an exposition becomes a definition is not ascertainable, precisely for the reason that the thing is an empirical and not a systemic one. Exposition and definition, however, are easily discernible in practice. Thus, to use G. E. Moore's example, the expression "hoofed quadruped of the genus equus" is the analytic definiens of the concept "horse." The *exposition* of "horse," on the other hand, as found in a scientific dictionary like Funk and Wagnalls, is "a solid-hoofed and odd-toed quadruped (*Equus caballus*), varying much in size, color, speed, and so forth, having horny patches or chestnuts on the inner side of both pairs of legs (above the knee and below the hock), a mane and tail of long coarse hair (which distinguish it from other species of the *Equidae*, as the asses and zebras), and . . .," in all fifty properties, as against the three of the definition.

If x is an empirical thing and belongs to the class C, the question whether x is a C is not so easily answered as in the case of a systemic thing. Suppose the *definition* of C to be α and β, and the *exposition*, γ, δ, and ε. Then, if x has α, β, γ, δ, and ε, x will be a C according both to exposition and to definition. But if x has only α and β it will be a C only according to definition and not to exposition; and if x has only γ, δ, ε, or any of these, it will not be a C according to definition but only to exposition. Thus, if x is hoofed, quadrupedal, and of genus Equus it is a horse, even if it lacks a mane, a tail, and all its teeth. It is, in this case, "not much of" a horse—it is a horse by definition but not by exposition. If, on the other hand, it is neither hoofed nor of genus Equus it is not a horse, even though it may have a mane, a tail, and all its teeth—it is, say, a lion.

There is, of course, a difference between a horse and a lion, and the difference between the *definitions* of "horse" and of "lion," respectively, takes care of that difference. But there is also a difference between a horse with a mane and a tail and teeth and one without. This difference is taken care of by the difference between *definition* and *exposition,* and the differences within the exposition. In everyday language these differences are obscured. By "horse" may be meant either the defined or the expounded horse. Language, therefore, had to develop words whose function it is to refer to the difference between definition and exposition, and within the exposition.

These words are the value terms.

Thus, *a good horse* is one which is a horse not only according to definition—this is given by the noun "horse"—but also according to exposition—this is given by the adjective "good." *x is a good horse* means that x is a *horse* in having the definitional properties of "horse" and that x is a *good* one in having the expositional properties of "horse." *x is a bad horse* means that x is still a horse, in having the definitional attributes a and β, but not a good one, in lacking some of the expositional attributes, γ, δ, or ε. On the other hand, *y is a good lion* does not, of course, mean that y is a horse, but that y is a lion; yet, *y is a good lion* has in common with x, which is a good horse, the *goodness*, even though y's goodness is leonine and x's goodness is equine. But both goodnesses are alike in being the possession of the respective expositional properties. In general, therefore, *x is a good C* means that *x has all the expositional properties of C,* or that *x fulfills the exposition of C.* Since we are usually not concerned with the C-ness of x but only with its goodness, hence not the definition of C but only its exposition, we may use "exposition" and "definition" interchangeably. Thus, whenever we deal with empirical things, and unless otherwise specified, by "definition" is meant "exposition." A class of empirical things, whose definition is an exposition, will be called an *empirical* or *existential class.*[1]

We are now ready to define the value terms in terms of the expositional or definitional properties of empirical things. But first, three things must be clearly understood.

(a) The "value" in question is not moral or ethical or any other specific kind of value but *value in general.* We do not deal with ethics, aesthetics, or economics, but with axiology. Axiology is a formal discipline which is *applicable to* ethics, aesthetics, economics, and other philosophical and social disciplines, but which *is* not any of these disciplines—just as geometry is applicable to but *is* not physics. However, certain rules of application or interpretation determine— and in a way produce—these philosophical and social disciplines,

[1] For details on this application of Kantian logic to value theory see the writer's "The Analytic, the Synthetic, and the Good: Kant and the Paradoxes of G. E. Moore," *Kant-Studien,* XLV (1953-54), 67-82, and XLVI (1954-55), 3-18. See also "The Analytic and the Synthetic as Categories of Inquiry," in Department of Philosophy, Ohio State University, *Perspectives in Philosophy* (Columbus, Ohio, 1953), pp. 55-78; and "Group Membership and Class Membership," *Philosophy and Phenomenological Research,* XIII (1953), 353-70.

just as the application of say, Riemannian geometry to certain events determines—and in a way produces—relativity physics. These philosophical and social disciplines become, by the application of axiology, systematic fields of knowledge.[2]

(b) Systemic things are excluded from valuation, for the reason that they have no expositions. Electrons, numbers, circles, and triangles cannot *as such* be either good or bad. The same applies to the philosophical and social disciplines once they have become systems. Their terms then are systemic terms. Thus, if "virtue" is such a term, propositions like "virtue is good" will be as meaningless as, say, "circles are good"—unless goodness is to virtue what roundness is to circle. But in this case goodness would be moral and not axiological goodness. A similar thing is true of "God is good." Here "good" is a theological and not an axiological term.

(c) Each empirical thing may be considered in two aspects, either as resembling other things or as being unique. In the former case it is a member of a class C which has other members besides it, and the value of the thing is comparable with the values of those other things. This I have elsewhere[3] called *extrinsic* value. In the latter case, the class C has no other member but this thing, and the value of the thing is not comparable with any other value. This kind of value was called *intrinsic*. In this paper only extrinsic value will be discussed.

To define the value terms we must first cast a glance at the axiological proposition itself. Its simple form disguises a certain complexity. When I say "x is a good C," I am saying that x has all the definitional and expositional properties of C. I am saying, in other words, three different things:

$$\text{I. x is a member of C}$$
$$\text{II. C contains } \alpha, \beta, \gamma, \delta, \varepsilon$$
$$\text{III. (1) x is } \alpha$$
$$\text{(2) x is } \beta$$
$$\text{(3) x is } \gamma$$
$$\text{(4) x is } \delta$$
$$\text{(5) x is } \varepsilon$$

---

[2] See the writer's "A Logical Definition of Value," *The Journal of Philosophy,* XLVIII (1951), 419 f.; and pp. 218 f., 338, 352 f., 356, 358 f., 374, below.

[3] "A Logical Definition of Value," *The Journal of Philosophy,* XLVIII (1951), 413-20; and "The Analytic, the Synthetic, and the Good: Kant and the Paradoxes of G. E. Moore," *Kant-Studien,* XLV (1953-54), 67-82, and XLVI (1954-55), 3-18.

This total pattern we shall call the *value pattern* of the proposition *x is a good C*. If and only if I mean this pattern do I mean that x is a good C.

The relation between I and II taken together and any of the propositions in III is that of entailment. This entailment, as again Kant has shown—in *Die falsche Spitzfindigkeit der vier syllogistischen Figuren* (which may well be translated as The Synthetic Subtlety of the Four Syllogistic Figures, in both the early Kantian and the modern sense of "synthetic" as "artificial")—represents the original and natural function of the human mind, expressed by the rule *nota notae rei ipsius nota*. If x is a C and C is *α, β, γ, δ, ε*, then the propositions under III are all analytic propositions following from the premise that x is a C, and they are all the analytic propositions possible. For the moment we shall not make a distinction between definitional and expositional analyticity, that is, between propositions concerning the properties contained in the *definition* of C—*α* and *β*—and propositions concerning the properties contained in the *exposition* of C. Both kinds of properties are "contained in" C, and the propositions in question are therefore analytic. The value pattern, therefore, is a pattern of "analytic entailments."[4]

The axiological proposition *x is a good C*, then, stands for a totality of analytic entailments or a value pattern. Introducing the variable "*φ*" for expositional properties—*γ, δ, ε*, and so on—the pattern simply is I: x is a member of C; II: C contains *φ*; III: x is *φ*. In I we have class-membership, in II conceptual analysis, in III predication. The pattern combines the extensional and the intensional view of a class. In I we have class extension, signified by "x *ε* C"; in II we have class intension, which we shall discuss presently; in III we have the combination of both, signified by "*φ* x," where "*φ*" is the intensional and "x" the extensional constituent.

The relationship between a concept and its analytic parts has not yet been systematically investigated. The concept as consisting of such parts is said to be "complex"[5] and to "contain" these parts. Let us

---

[4] About the difference between expositional and definitional analyticity and its significance for the value pattern see "The Analytic, the Synthetic, and the Good: Kant and the Paradoxes of G. E. Moore," *Kant-Studien*, XLV (1953-54), 67-82, and XLVI (1954-55), 3-18. See also K. Marc-Wogau, "Kants Lehre vom analytischen Urteil," *Theoria*, XVII (1951), 140 ff.

[5] G. E. Moore, *Principia Ethica* (London and New York, 1922), pp. 7 ff. On the relation between Moore's "complex" and the Kantian "containment," see the articles

symbolize the relation "is contained in," in the Kant-Moorean sense, by some sign, say "ω." "$\varphi \; \omega \; C$" then means that any or all of the values of φ are contained in C. "$\varphi \; \omega \; C$" then corresponds on the intensional side to "$x \; \varepsilon \; C$" on the extensional side. Just as "$x \; \varepsilon \; C$" through either quantification or specification of "x" can become an extensional proposition, so "$\varphi \; \omega \; C$," through quantification or specification of "φ," can become an intensional proposition. Thus, "$(\varphi) \; \varphi \; \omega \; C$" signifies that all values of φ—γ, δ, ε, and so on—are contained in C, "$\gamma \; \omega \; C$" means that the specific value γ, say "rational," is contained in C, which latter may stand for "man," and so on. Through quantification and specification of "φ" the concept C can thus be used in whole or in part intensionally, just as through quantification and specification of "x" it can so be used extensionally. The two roles of the concept, the extensional and the intensional, are different, since in the former role the concept determines a set of *similar* elements—this man, that man, any man—while in the latter, the intensional role, it determines a set of *dissimilar* elements—"rational," "animal," etc. In the former role it acts as a class concept, in the latter role as a determinable in the sense of W. E. Johnson. This view, of course, involves a host of problems which cannot be discussed here. It is clear, however, that *any* concept may be regarded as a determinable; that if it is so regarded the determinates are "contained" in it in the Kantian sense; and that the relation ω is to determinable and determinate as the relation ε is to class and class-member.

The axiological pattern, then, stands for the sequence of the functions I: $x \; \varepsilon \; C$; II: $\varphi \; \omega \; C$ (or $\varphi \; \omega \; \Phi$, if by "$\Phi$" we designate the determinable aspect of the class concept C); and III: φx, which latter is entailed by the conjunction of I and II. If this entailment is quantified with respect to "x" we shall call it logically quantified and if it is quantified with respect to "φ" we shall call it axiologically quantified. If it is universally axiologically quantified it means that x being a member of C has all the properties φ contained in C (or Φ), that is, that all the analytic entailments possible with x as a C are true. In this case x is a good member of C. This is our final definition of "good."

---

mentioned in footnote 3, above. It must be noted that containment in this sense is different from entailment. A subject-predicate proposition S-P *entails* another such proposition S-Q if P *contains* Q.

The definitions of the other value terms follow logically. If x has some of the values φ of C, then x is a *fair* or a *so-so* member of C. If there are some of the values of φ that x does not possess, then x is a *bad* member of C.[6] And if x has none of the values of C and none of the analytic entailments are true, then x is a *no good* member of C. At this point, however, we must make the distinction between expositional and definitional entailments. For, if x does not have the *definitional* properties of C, then x is not a C. Whereas, when x has none of the *expositional* properties but *does* have the definitional properties, then x is a C but a no good one. Thus, whenever we speak of the values of φ, we mean the expositional properties in this narrow sense. For, loss of the definitional properties would mean not loss of goodness but of C-ness, and we could not speak any more of x as a C, whether a good or a bad one. The same distinction applies in the case of "fair" and in that of "bad." For here, too, none of the definitional properties of C must be missing. Thus, if x is to be a fair C, among the properties x has must be α and β. And if x is to be a

---

[6] The question is, whether "bad" means that a subject partly fulfills or partly does not fulfill its definition. The answer must be the latter. The emphasis must be on nonfulfillment. On the one hand, partial fulfillment has a positive emphasis and therefore means "fair," and the like. On the other hand, "bad" is a negative term, "not bad" a positive one. The difference is well illustrated by this little dialogue. *Obstetrician:* "Mrs. Jones, I have very good news for you." *Patient:* "I am not Mrs. Jones, I am Miss Jones." *Obstetrician:* "Miss Jones, I have very bad news for you." A term x is "good for" another term y if x partly fulfills the definition (exposition) of y. A child is "good for" Mrs. Jones but "bad for" Miss Jones—it partly fulfills the exposition of Mrs. Jones but does not fulfill the exposition of Miss Jones. This means that "bad" means partial nonfulfillment (not having some properties of C) rather than partial fulfillment (having some properties of C). To *have* a husband and child fulfills the exposition of Mrs. Jones, to *lack* husband and child fulfills the exposition of Miss Jones. Not to lack a child is partial nonfulfillment of Miss Jones's exposition, whereas to lack a husband is partial fulfillment of her exposition. The comparison between Miss Jones and Mrs. Jones shows that what actually is *bad* is the *transposition* of fulfillments and nonfulfillments (see "A Logical Definition of Value," *The Journal of Philosophy*, XLVIII [1951], 413-20.) In having no husband and a child Miss Jones partly fulfills her exposition and partly that of Mrs. Jones, or, she partly fulfills (having a child) and partly does not fulfill (having no husband) the exposition of Mrs. Jones. According to our definition of "good for," insofar as Miss Jones partly fulfills the exposition of Mrs. Jones, Miss Jones is good for Mrs. Jones. That is, having the baby is good for her future marriage, for the baby's father may marry her. But insofar as Miss Jones partly does not fulfill the exposition of Mrs. Jones, Miss Jones is not good for Mrs. Jones. Having no husband, yet a baby, is not good for her future marriage to another man. (Both men, for argument's sake, have the name "Jones.")

bad C, among the properties it lacks must not be α or β. Only in the case of "good" does the distinction not *have* to be made, because in that case x does have α and β anyway. Thus, in *all* cases the definitional properties must be present, and valuation is exclusively a matter of the expositional properties. Therefore the class defined by the exposition, which we called the empirical or existential class, may also be called the *axiological class*; while the class defined by the definition is a logical class in the sense defined above. The logical class is always a systemic class, even if the thing in question in other respects is empirical. The logical or systemic part of an empirical thing is what Kant calls the schema.[7] Systemic class, logical class, and schematic class are therefore one and the same, and so are empirical, existential, and axiological class.

Classes, whether systemic or existential, are combinations of the extension and the intension of a concept in the sense that without intension extension is not possible and without extension we should not speak of intension. For this reason, concepts without either extension ("null classes") or intension (undefined or of contradictory attributes) are not classes in our sense. "Extension" means logical or schematic existence for systemic class-members and actual or empirical existence for existential class-members. There is a systemic but no empirical class of unicorns or proconsuls of France, but there is no class of native aliens. There is both a systemic and an empirical class of horses. There is a *systemic* class of horses if (a) there is a definitional concept "horse," and (b) there are (at least two) things which have the properties of the definition of "horse." (Unless there were at least two such things no *abstraction* of *common* horse properties would be possible). What is considered in these (two) things, however, is not their individual, total character but merely their common character, the logical schema "horse" inherent in them, the set of minimum characteristics of horseyness. There is an *empirical* class of horses if (a) there is an expositional concept "horse," and (b) there are (at least two) things which have the properties of the exposition of "horse." These (two) things, again, are not considered in their individuality but in the character they have in common, which is that of empirical horses, having maximum common characteristics of horseyness. They

---

[7] Considering both the First and the Third Critique. See G. Schrader, "The Status of Teleological Judgment in the Critical Philosophy," *Kant-Studien*, XLV (1953-54), 204 ff.

are more concrete than the schemata of "horse" but less concrete than an individual horse, say, Brownie.[8]

Whereas the systemic class can exist without the empirical class, the empirical class cannot exist without the systemic class; all actual horses necessarily contain the schema "horse," but the schema "horse" does not necessitate the empirical existence of horses (otherwise St. Anselm would have been right and, as Kant showed, we would all be millionaires). The two kinds of horse must not be confused; in particular, it must not be held that a horse whose hoofs, say, have been amputated, is no horse anymore because it has lost its definitional attributes. These attributes belong to the schema "horse," not the empirical horse. They can be omitted in thought from the schema, but not "amputated" from a horse. The hoofless horse is still an ungulate; even though it has lost its hoofs it has not lost its "ungues" which inhere in the schema. And the latter is still with the amputee, just as the blueprint is still with the roofless house. Thus, axiological and logical classification must be strictly distinguished. Any axiological proposition must be analyzed both logically and axiologically. There is, for example, both logical and axiological quantification. *All x are good members of C* is logically as well as axiologically universal; it means that all x have all the properties of C. *All x are bad members of C* is logically universal and axiologically particular; *Some x are good members of C* is logically particular and axiologically universal; and so on. What is true of quantification is true of qualification. "Good" and "fair" have positive quality, "bad" and "no good" have negative quality. *No x are good*, therefore, is logically universal and negative, and axiologically universal and positive; *Some x are bad* is logically particular and affirmative, and axiologically particular and negative; and so on.

While "good," "fair," "bad," and "no good" are the basic value terms, there are a great number of equivalents which are to them as the various linguistic quantifiers—"few," "only," and so forth—are to the four basic quantifiers. Such linguistic axiological quantifiers are "excellent," "perfect," "fine," and so on for *good*; "so-so," "not bad," "o.k.," and so forth for *fair*; "poor," "not good," "inferior," "deficient," and so forth for *bad*; "rotten," "lousy," "miserable," and so on for *no good*.

---

[8] There may be an additional requirement for an empirical class in our sense, namely (c) an agent who calls what has the expositional properties of "horse," "a horse."

Sometimes expressions identical with, or similar to, logical quantifiers are used as axiological quantifiers, for instance, "some . . .," as in "some boy!", "quite a . . .," "quite the . . .," "not much of a . . .," and so on.[9] Sometimes axiological quantifiers are used as logical quantifiers, for example, "lousy with . . .," or the French "n'importe . . ." for "some."

All these expressions are axiological predicates. There are also axiological relations. *x is a better C than y* means that x has more expositional properties of C than y and is therefore "more of" a C than y. "Better than," in other words, relates two members of the same empirical class, the first of which has more of the expositional class properties than the second. The converse axiological relation, that between y and x, is the relation "worse than"; *y is worse than x* means that y has fewer expositional class properties than x. *x is good for y* means, as we have seen,[10] that x and y are in different definitional classes but have overlapping expositions such that the exposition of x is part of that of y. *Hay is good for horses* means that "hay" and "horse" are in different definitional classes but that the exposition of "hay" is part of that of "horse"; the digestive part of horses has an affinity to something that is in hay. *x is bad for y* means that x is contrary to some part of the exposition of y. *Arsenic is not good for horses* means that arsenic is contrary to something which is good for horses. *y is better for x than z* means that x is in a different definitional class from both y and z, but that the expositions of x and y overlap while those of x and z either do not overlap or do not overlap in the same degree. *Hay is better for horses than arsenic* may mean either that the exposition of "arsenic" does not at all overlap with that of "horse" or that it does so very much less than that of "hay"; in a very specific case horses may be given very small doses of arsenic as medicine. The converse relation, that between z, x, and y, is *Is worse for . . . than*; *Arsenic is worse for horses than hay*. *It is good that*

---

[9] See "Group Membership and Class Membership," *Philosophy and Phenomenological Research*, XIII (1953), 353-70. Note that "no good" is the contrary and "not good" or "bad" the contradictory of "good." Similarly, "not-bad" is the contrary rather than the contradictory of "bad." The axiological square of oppositions shows "good" and "no good" as contraries, "fair" and "bad" as subcontraries, "good" and "fair," and "no good" and "bad" as subalterns, and "good" and "bad," and "no good" and "fair" as contradictories. For a similar "square of oppositions" see William Kneale, "Objectivity in Morals," *Philosophy*, XXV (1950), 149-66; reprinted in W. Sellars and J. Hospers (eds.), *Readings in Ethical Theory* (New York, 1952), pp. 681-97. Kneale's terms are "obligatory" and "wrong" as contraries, and "right" and "non-obligatory" as subcontraries.

[10] Footnote 6, p. 203, above.

xRy means that the relation R is part of the exposition of one or all of its terms. *It is good that John reads "Ivanhoe"* means that reading *Ivanhoe* is good for John or that such reading belongs to the nature or exposition ("disposition"?) of John. *It is good that John loves Betty* means that love is good for either John or Betty or both. The relation *It is better that ... than that ...* has two forms. *It is better that xRy than that xRz* (or *It is better for x-to-Ry than for x-to-Rz*) means that the relation R is part of the exposition of x and y, but either not at all or not in the same degree of the exposition of z. *It is better that John reads "Ivanhoe" than that he reads "Lady Killer Comics"* means that reading *Ivanhoe* does but reading *Lady Killer Comics* does not or does not in the same degree belong to John's exposition. *It is better for John to date Betty than Lou* means that John's and Betty's dispositions are more compatible than John's and Lou's. The converse relation is *It is worse that xRz than that xRy.* The second form of the relation in question is *It is better that xRy than that xSy.* This means that the relation R but not, or not in the same degree, the relation S is part of the exposition of either or both x and y. *It is better that John love Betty than that he beat her* means that it is better for John and/or Betty and/or both that he love rather than beat her. Predicates may here be regarded as monadic relations. *It is better that John studies than that he loafs* means that studying does, or does to a higher degree, fulfill his exposition rather than loafing. Since for anything to be good means fulfilling its definition, *It is better for x to be good than to be bad* is always true. The converse relation is *It is worse that xRy than that xSy.* *It is worse for x to be bad than to be good* is always true.

In summary, *"better" and "worse" are axiological relations between members of the same class; "good for" and "bad for" and "better for" and "worse for" are axiological relations between members of different classes; and "it is good that" and "it is bad that," and "it is better that" and "it is worse that" are axiological relations for relations.* What is missing, then, is an axiological relation between a member and its class.

This relation, the *axiological copula,* is the relation "ought."

"Ought" does not relate two things, such as x and y. To say that x ought to be y is meaningless, since it says that one thing ought to be another. Rather, "ought" relates things to concepts or relations. *x ought to be a C* or *x ought to be φ* means that either x is a member of C and is or is not deficient in its C-ness, or that x is not a member of C but, say, of B, and that it would be "better for x to be" a C.

"Ought" thus is equivalent to the relation "It is better that." *x ought to be φ* is equivalent to *It is better for x to be φ* and *x ought to be a C* is equivalent to *It is better for x to be a C.*[11] *x ought to . . .* thus is an elliptic expression for *It is better that xRy than that xRz* or *It is better that xRy than that xSy.* In both cases the "than that . . ." part is suppressed. Thus, *John ought to read "Ivanhoe"* is equivalent to either of the two forms of *It is better that,* namely, (1) *It is better for John to read "Ivanhoe" than to read something else, say, "Lady Killer Comics,"* and/or (2) *It is better for John to read "Ivanhoe" than not to read it (or to burn it, or eat it, or the like).* *John ought to love Betty* may mean (1) *It is better for John to love Betty than to love Lou,* and/or (2) *It is better for John to love Betty than to beat her* (or *not to love her, and so on*). Again, *x ought to be good* is always true; for it is equivalent to *It is better for x to be good than to be bad,* which we found to be always true. Since this is a monadic relation there is only one form of it. Since "ought" is equivalent to "It is better that," *x ought to be . . .* means *It is better for x to be . . .* In other words, what x ought to be is what is better for x to be. What is better for x to be is what better fulfills x's exposition. Thus, if x's exposition is γ, δ, ε, what x ought to be must add to this exposition some properties which make x better. Hence, what x ought to be is better than what x is. Conversely, what x ought not to be is worse than what x is. "Ought" thus relates the worseness of a thing to its betterness, and "ought not" relates the betterness of a thing to its worseness.

Besides axiological predicates and relations there are axiological terms which are combinations of predicates and relations, such as, for example, "best" and "worst." *x is the best C* means that x is the one and only C that has the maximum of expositional properties of C, and *x is the worst C* means that x is the one and only C that has the minimum of expositional properties of C—which does not have to mean that x is no good. The worst C may be a fair one.

A great deal could be said about all the axiological relations, but we shall confine ourselves to only one of them, the axiological copula "ought" which then, for us, is *the* axiological relation. "Ought," as all axiological relations, has what we shall call a *positive* and a *negative sense.* The positive sense is the direction toward fulfillment of the exposition and the negative sense is the direction toward nonfulfill-

---

[11] Cf. the forms *x better be C* and *x better had be C,* which are strong forms of "ought."

ment of the exposition, of one of the terms of the proposition, either the predicate or, if the predicate refers—positively or negatively—to the exposition of the subject, the latter. Thus, *x ought to be good* uses "ought" in the positive sense: the predicate refers to the subject and goodness means fulfillment of the subject's exposition. On the other hand, *x ought to be bad* uses "ought" in the negative sense: the predicate refers again to the subject, but badness means nonfulfillment of the subject's exposition. *These houses ought to be roofed, Bachelors ought not to marry* are also positive uses of "ought," for "roofed" and "not to marry" refer to the expositions of the subjects, and in a positive way, for houses that are roofed and bachelors that do not marry fulfill their respective expositions, or even definitions. On the other hand, *These houses ought not to be roofed, Bachelors ought to marry* are negative uses of "ought." Examples where not the exposition of the subject but that of the predicate is in question are propositions of the type *x ought to be a C, x ought not to be a not-C*, which are both positive uses of "ought," and *x ought not to be a C, x ought to be a not-C*, which are negative uses of "ought." Here the predicate does not refer, positively or negatively, to the exposition of the subject. All *axiological* predicates—"good," "bad," and so forth—refer to the exposition of the subject, and therefore the positive or negative sense of "ought" in the case of all axiological propositions with axiological predicate depends on the exposition of the subject; whereas the sense of "ought" in the case of axiological propositions with *non-axiological* predicate—"C"—depends on the nature of the predicate. In the former case, the logical *and* the axiological quality of the proposition determines the sense of "ought"; in the latter case only the logical quality does, for there is no axiological quality.

Let us call any predicate other than an axiological predicate a *logical* predicate. Then *x ought to be a C* is an axiological proposition with a logical predicate whereas *x ought to be good* is an axiological proposition with an axiological predicate. Both are simple value propositions. Conjunctions of both or compound axiological propositions would be *x ought to be good and a C, x ought to be good as a C, x ought to be a good C,* and the like. In the following, we shall deal only with simple value propositions.

II. VALUE PROPOSITIONS

Value propositions now fall into four categories: propositions with logical predicate, propositions with axiological predicate, propositions with logical copula, and propositions with axiological copula—the logical copula being, of course, "is," the axiological copula "ought." Value propositions with logical copula will be called *logical value propositions,* value propositions with axiological copula *axiological value propositions,* or *axiological propositions proper.* Logical value propositions with logical predicate will be called *pure logical* value propositions and logical value propositions with axiological predicate *mixed logical* value propositions. Axiological value propositions with axiological predicate will be called *pure axiological* value propositions and axiological value propositions with logical predicate *mixed axiological* value propositions.

Since all our propositions, unless otherwise specified, are value propositions, we may omit the word "value."

The *subjects* of all simple value propositions are logical, not axiological terms. Thus, *x is a C* is a pure logical, *x is good* is a mixed logical, *x ought to be good* a pure axiological, and *x ought to be a C* a mixed axiological proposition. An axiological term can be the subject of a value proposition only if the proposition is compound, for example, *The good x . . .* A subject such as *The Good . . .* is a highly complex term whose meaning can only be ascertained by an axiological analysis too extensive for this paper.

Value propositions are, as we have seen, subject to both logical and axiological quantification and qualification. Logical quantifiers and qualifiers sometimes are special words, sometimes are implicit. Thus, the word "no" is both a quantifier and a qualifier, and the affirmative qualifier is always implicit in the copula. Axiological quantification and qualification are always implicit in the value predicate. For analysis, the implicit quantifications and qualifications must be made explicit. One means, in logic, for this purpose is the use of the letters A, E, I, O. In axiology a similar means must be used. "Good" is the universal affirmative, "no good" the universal negative, "fair" the particular affirmative, and "bad" the particular negative quantifier and qualifier. Let us call axiologically universal and affirmative propositions G-propositions, axiologically universal and negative propositions T-propositions, axiologically particular and affirmative propositions B-propositions, and axiologically particular and negative propositions D-propositions.[12]

[12] From German "GuT" and English "BaD." The "u" in "gut" reminds of *u*niversal,

The combination of logical with axiological letters, then, gives us all the possible kinds of propositions with axiological predicates, that is, mixed logical and pure axiological propositions. Using "—" for the logical relation between subject and predicate and "→" for the axiological relation between them we have A—G (*All x are good*), A—T (*All x are no good*), A—B (*All x are fair* or *All x are not-bad*), A—D (*All x are bad*), and correspondingly E—G, E—T, E—B, E—D; I—G, I—T, I—B, I—D; O—G, O—T, O—B, O—D. The forms of the pure axiological propositions are A→G (*All x ought to be good*), A→T (*All x ought to be no good*), A→B (*All x ought to be fair*), A→D (*All x ought to be bad*), and E→G, E→T, E→B, E→D; I→G, I→T, I→B, I→D; O→G, O→T, O→B, O→D.

Following this pattern we may symbolize the value propositions with logical predicate, that is, pure logical and mixed axiological propositions. The former are A—C (*All x are C*), E—C, I—C, O—C; the latter A→C (*All x ought to be C*), E→C, I→C, O→C.

Axiological value propositions, that is, propositions with the copula "ought," are called *positive* if the copula is used in the positive sense and *negative* if it is used in the negative sense. Thus, positive axiological propositions are A→G, E→T, A→B,[13] E→D, I→G, O→T, I→B, O→D; A→C, E→C̄, I→C, and O→C̄, where "C̄" means "non-C." Negative axiological propositions are A→T, E→B, A→D, E→G, I→T, O→B, I→D, O→G; A→C̄, E→C, I→C̄, and O→C.

It is obvious already at this point that some of these propositions are true and some are false. *All x ought to be no good* (A→T), for example, seems obviously false, for if no x ought to fulfill its exposition (E→G) then there ought to be no empirical class of x; and, since valuation is based on classification, this means that there ought to be no valuation. This, obviously, cannot be axiologically true. Again, *No x are good* (E—G) would mean that there is no empirical class of which x is a member since no x fulfills any exposition. Thus, again, valuation would be impossible and the proposition must be axiologically false. *All x are good* (A—G) seems false for a different reason. In this case all x would fulfill their exposition, but it is, precisely, the

the "a" in "bad" of particular. The "T" reminds of negate. The "D" is the weaker phonetic form of "T."

[13] Whether B-propositions are positive or negative depends on whether partial fulfillment of the exposition ("fair") is meant positively or negatively. We take it positively, as indicating fulfillment. See footnote 6, p. 203, above.

nature of exposition that some members fulfill it and others do not; for if all would fulfill it the members would be schematic or logical and not empirical, and thus again excluded from valuation. Other propositions seem obviously true, such as *Some x ought to be good* (I→G), *Some x ought to be bad* (I→D), *Some x are good* (I—G), *Some x are no good* (I—T). Thus emerges a pattern of axiological validity. It must, obviously, have a connection with the value pattern. Let us return to our "depth analysis" of axiological propositions.[14]

As we have seen, an axiological proposition of the form "x is a good C" has a complex pattern which includes three types of what we now call pure logical propositions, namely, I: x is a member of C; II: C contains φ; III: x is φ. Depending on the quantification of φ, x is a good, fair, bad, or no good C. The proposition *x is a good C* is what we now call a compound axiological proposition, namely, the conjunction of the pure logical proposition *x is a C* and the mixed logical proposition *x is good*.

We shall now extend our analysis of this compound axiological proposition to all value propositions and say that all value propositions follow the value pattern. That is to say, no value proposition is ever merely what it seems to be, namely, the mere proposition, but each such proposition is more than it seems to be: it always means the whole pattern. The pattern consists exclusively of pure logical propositions.

These propositions are not *stated* in the value proposition but merely *assumed*. A value proposition is like a woman or an iceberg; it hides more than it shows. In order to understand the validity of value propositions we must examine the value pattern.

Since the pure logical propositions which form the value pattern underlying the value proposition are not expressed, we shall call them, again following the example of Kant, *judgments* rather than propositions. Judgment and proposition are, for Kant, "moments of thought," judgment a thought not yet clearly understood, where the relation between subject and predicate is still problematic, proposition the thought understood, and stated assertorily or apodictically. The dif-

---

[14] Even in the analysis of the validity of *logical* propositions the analysis of the horizontal propositional structure alone is insufficient and "depth analyses" have to be made, as in the assumption of existence of the subject's referent in particular propositions and its nonexistence in universal propositions, or the assumption of existence of the predicate's contradictory in the partial inverse, and the like. Here also belong the so-called "laws of thought."

ference between judgment and proposition thus lies in the modality of thought.[15]

Since the judgments underlying the axiological proposition are not expressed, more likely than not they are not clearly thought out. Their modality, therefore, plays a role and must also be of importance for the meaning of the axiological proposition itself. It must make a difference for that meaning whether the underlying judgment is thought assertorily, say, "x *is* a C," problematically, "x may (or may not) be a C," or apodictically, "x must be a C." We shall not make any distinction between assertory and apodictic modality, but instead add the modality of negatoriness, which is to negation and limitation as assertoriness is to affirmation. It is, in other words, negative assertoriness. By problematicness we shall mean both positive and negative problematicness; for if x may be C then it is doubtful that x *is* C, and this means that x may not be C. The three modalities of the first of the three kinds of judgment underlying an axiological proposition are then (a) the assertory, in which it is assumed that x *is* a C, that is, that the copula expresses an existing relation between subject and predicate; (b) the problematical, in which nothing specific is assumed concerning the relation between x and C, that is, it is assumed that x may or may not be a C; (c) the negatory, in which it is assumed that x is *not* a C, that is, that the copula expresses a nonexisting relation between x and C. In this case the judgment would be "x is not a C."

Not only the first pure logical judgment of the value pattern, "x is a C," has a modality but every single one of them may have a different kind of modality. This gives a great variety to the value pattern which, however, cannot be discussed in detail in the present context. The main lines of the pattern, however, and its significance for the validity of the value propositions will become clear.

We shall now classify the value propositions according to the modalities of the underlying pure logical judgments. If the modality of such a judgment is assertory, we shall call the corresponding value proposition axiologically *analytic*; if the underlying modality is problematical, we shall call the corresponding value proposition axiologically *hypothetical*; and if the underlying modality is negatory, we shall call the corresponding value proposition axiologically *synthetic*. Axiological analyticity, hypotheticity, and syntheticity will be called the *modes* or *moods* of value propositions.

---

[15] *Logic,* par. 30; *Critique of Pure Reason,* pp. B 100 ff.

Axiological analyticity, hypotheticity, and syntheticity must, of course, be distinguished from logical analyticity, hypotheticity, and syntheticity. There are definite and significant relations between the two kinds, but we cannot discuss them here. Suffice it to say that the main difference is that logical analyticity and so on are relations within the logical proposition itself, whereas axiological analyticity and so on are relations not of the value proposition itself but of its underlying logical judgments. In the following, whenever we speak of analyticity, hypotheticity, and syntheticity we mean the axiological moods.

The importance of these moods will appear at once. To take a compound axiological proposition, say *John is a good student*, we find that the proposition is axiologically *analytic* if the speaker assumes that I: John *is* a student (x *is* a C); and/or II: the concept "student" corresponds to what he says John is (C *is* φ); and/or III: John has all the properties which the speaker takes to be the properties of a student (x *is* φ). But the same axiological proposition is *hypothetical* if the speaker assumes that I: John may or may not be a student; and/or II: The concept "student" may or may not correspond to what he says John is; and/or III: John may or may not have any or all of the properties of a student. (In these cases the proposition will be stated *questioningly*; with the tone on "student" in cases I and II and on "good" in case III.) The same axiological proposition is *synthetic* if the speaker assumes that I: John is not a student; and/or II: The concept "student" does not correspond to what he says John is; and/or III: John does not have all of the properties of a student. (In these cases the proposition will be stated *ironically*, with the same emphasis as above.) A synthetic axiological proposition is not a *false* proposition.[16]

Let us now exchange the copula "is" in our example for the copula "ought" and discuss the proposition *John ought to be a good student*. This proposition is a compound axiological proposition of greater complexity. It may be composed of a variety of propositions, such as

---

[16] This is obvious, since the modalities are assumptions, not facts. We shall not deal with the validity of compound axiological propositions. However, from the rules of validity of simple axiological propositions it will become clear that truth and falsity of a compound axiological proposition of the above kind is itself compounded of logical and axiological truth and falsity, and that it therefore cannot simply be "false." Axiological falsity we shall find to be an entirely different thing from logical falsity.

the pure logical proposition *John is a student* and the pure axiological proposition *John ought to be good*; or of the mixed axiological proposition *John ought to be a student* and the mixed logical proposition *John is good*; or the mixed axiological proposition *John ought to be a student* and the pure axiological proposition *John ought to be good*. The exact composition makes, of course, a difference in the analysis of the compound propositions which here, however, does not need to concern us. Again, the proposition is *analytic* insofar as the underlying modalities are assertory. This refers, of course, to the modalities of the underlying pure logical judgments. Where the constituent parts of the compound axiological proposition are themselves axiological propositions, *their* underlying modalities must be analyzed. The iceberg of this kind of compound axiological proposition stretches into deeper layers than that of the previous kind. Insofar as the underlying modalities are problematical the proposition is *hypothetical,* and insofar as they are negatory the proposition is *synthetic*. (Here the different moods do not have to be indicated by tone of voice, though they may be. But the shadings are lighter; "ought" itself takes over the role of attitude indicator.)

In the first case——if the proposition is analytic—the "ought" is an *analytic ought*. It does not say anything new, it only confirms what is assumed as true anyway: that John is a student, that a student studies, that therefore John is studious—hence that he ought to be a good student. The proposition therefore is true; it is not different in this respect from the proposition *Circles ought to be round,*[17] which is equally true, for it simply means that *Circles ought to be circles,* which is an axiological truism, based on the logical truism *Circles are circles.*

Circles ought to be round is an analytic mixed axiological proposition; *John ought to be a good student* is a compound value proposition, composed of value propositions at least one of which is analytic. Other analytic mixed axiological propositions are *Kings ought to be regal, Justices ought to be just, Students ought to be studious, Teachers ought to be pedagogues, You ought to be yourself,* and so forth.

But *John ought to be a good student* can also be hypothetical. In

---

[17] Note that this is not a systemic and hence axiologically false proposition. The systemetic prohibition of value predication (p. 200, above) only refers to value *predicates,* not to value relations. *Circles ought to be good* or *Circles are good* would be axiologically false; "good" here is used systemically, for circles either are good (circles) or else no circles.

this case nothing is assumed about John's being a student or his study habits. He may be a student or he may not be one, he may be studious or he may not be. But if he is a student, or, depending on the speaker's imagination concerning John's being a student, if he is to graduate, or if he is what his parents think he is, or if the college is a bad one, and so on—then *John ought to be a good student.* The truth value of such a proposition is not so easy to ascertain as that of the corresponding analytic proposition.

Finally, the proposition may be a synthetic one, if namely, I assume that John is *not* a student or not studious. In this case *John ought to be a good student* adds something new to my assumption: John will have to change. Whether he will change or not nobody knows—hence the truth-value of synthetic value propositions is indeterminate. On the one hand, the present exposition or nature of John, if fulfilled, would not make him a good student—although it would make him, of course, a good John. On the other hand, what I assume John's exposition or nature to be may not be so at all. I assume what John is *not,* I do not assume what John is. The negatory modality corresponds to both negation and limitation.

If we denote hypothetical and synthetic "ought" by "$\leftrightarrow$" and "$\leftarrow$," respectively, then the three models of the proposition *All students ought to be honor students*—denoting "honor student" by "CG" to signify the compound logical-axiological character of the predicate— would be, respectively, A$\rightarrow$CG, A$\leftrightarrow$CG, and A$\leftarrow$CG, for the analytic, the hypothetical, and the synthetic mood.

The classification of the axiological *propositions* according to moods corresponds to the classification of axiological *terms.* The latter were defined by their reference to the expositional properties. "Good" meant the subject's possession of all these properties, "fair" and "bad" meant the partial possession or nonpossession of these properties, and "no good" meant their nonpossession. As we saw, a difference had to be made between the definitional and the expositional properties. The definitional properties must in all cases be fulfilled; the value differentiations adhere to the expositional properties exclusively. This means, however, that the definitional properties must always be asserted, whereas the expositional properties must not. In other words, any value judgment *asserts* that the thing is a member of the logical class of which it is said to be a member, for there is no qualification to the logical membership. But it does not in the same sense assert that the thing is a member of the expositional class, for the possession of the expositional properties, and hence the belonging to the expositional class, and the kind of this belonging are, precisely, what is in question. Therefore the belonging to the expositional class is *problematical.* The thing may or may not, fully or partially, belong to this class. The problematicness of this belonging is, precisely, what makes the judgment a value judgment. For if that belonging were not problematical, the class in question would be systemic and the proposition concerning membership in it a logical and not an axiological one. In this case, the value character of the proposition would be *negated.* Thus, *All circles are good* (circles), if it means the circles of geometry, is a logical proposition—since "good" here is not an axiological but a systemic predicate—and the proposition, as we have seen, is axiologically false. The relation between definition and exposition is thus similar to that between proposition and judgment—as also becomes clear in Kant's own analysis:[18] it is a relation of modality.

Valuation, then, comes about through the "modalities" of exposition; that is, the unexpressed status of the relation between subject and predicate. When that modality is *assertory,* that is, it is assumed that x has all the expositional properties of C, then x is said to be a *good* C. If, however, the modality is *problematical,* that is, it is assumed that x may or may not have some or all the expositional properties of C, then x is said to be a *fair,* a *so-so,* a *poor,* or a *bad* C. And if the modality is *negatory,* that is, it is assumed that x has none of the expositional properties of C, then x is said to be a *no good* C. Valuation, in this sense, is the modalization of class-membership. Axiological quantification and qualification, then, represent a certain kind of modality.

We have, thus, a relationship between the modes of axiological propositions and the axiological terms, which themselves express modifications of the class-membership relation. Analytic propositions correspond in logical nature to the predicate "good"; just as "good" means fulfillment, by the subject, of the exposition of the predicate, so the analytic axiological proposition assumes a definite relation between subject and predicate of the underlying logical judgments.

---

[18] See "The Analytic, the Synthetic, and the Good: Kant and the Paradoxes of G. E. Moore," *Kant-Studien,* XLV (1953-54), 67-82, and XLIV (1954-55), 3-18; and "The Analytic and the Synthetic as Categories of Inquiry," in Department of Philosophy, Ohio State University, *Perspectives in Philosophy,* pp. 55-78.

Hypothetical propositions correspond in logical nature to the predicates "fair" and "bad"; just as these predicates are indeterminate as
to fulfillment, by the subject, of the exposition of the predicate, so
the hypothetical axiological proposition assumes an indeterminate
relationship between subject and predicate of some or all of the
underlying judgments. Synthetic propositions correspond in logical
nature to the predicate "no good"; just as "no good" means nonfulfillment, by the subject, of the exposition of the predicate, so the
synthetic axiological proposition assumes no relation between the
subject and predicate of some or all of the underlying logical judgments.

We can now assign the three propositional modes, the analytic,
hypothetical, and synthetic, to the four kinds of value propositions.

1. It might seem that *pure logical propositions*, of the form *x is C*,
can have no *axiological* analyticity, hypotheticity, or syntheticity, but
only logical analyticity and syntheticity. Actually, however, pure
logical propositions *can* have the axiological modes, that is, they can
have underlying logical judgments whose unexpressed modalities
influence the meaning of the pure logical propositions. In this direction may lie answers to the questions about the logical nature of
contrary-to-fact conditionals, interrogatory, imperative, and nonsensical
propositions—a subject which, again, we must pass by, but which we
touched upon on 214 above. We have, here, axiological relationships
as significant for logical propositions. Conversely, logical propositions
may be significant for axiological relations and propositions. Just as
an axiological proposition assumes unexpressed logical judgments, so
expressed logical propositions may assume an unexpressed axiological
judgment—when, namely, the logical proposition is part of a value
pattern the axiological proposition of which is not expressed. Such
pure logical propositions are, so to speak, *enthymemic axiological
propositions*. Another axiological meaning of a logical proposition is
given in those cases in which the logical predicate implies an axiological predicate, as in the case of the "honor student" mentioned
above.[19] Here we had a compound axiological proposition. Other
such cases are the predicates which although not purely axiological
are what we called *applied axiological terms*, that is, terms which do
not belong to pure axiology, the formal science of value, as do "good,"
"fair," and so forth, but to one of the specific value sciences, such as

---

[19] Here belong all terms with both fact and value meaning, such as epithets; per-
jorative, euphemistic, metaphorical, parabolic terms; and the like.

ethics, aesthetics, economics, religion, and so on. Such applied (or interpreted) axiological terms are "honest" (ethics), "beautiful" (aesthetics), "expensive" (economics), "holy" (religion), and so on. These applied axiological terms are to the pure axiological terms as physical are to geometrical terms, for example, the path of a ray of light in a homogeneous medium is to a straight line. Thus, "beautiful" (aesthetic "good") is, in this sense, an aesthetic interpretation of axiological "good," and moral "good" is an ethical such interpretation. All these are applied axiological predicates. There are also applied axiological relations, such as *All men follow their conscience, John is true to himself,*[20] *Rita likes ice skating*, and the like. Such applied axiological relations are interpretations of pure axiological relations. Applied axiological propositions, whether with applied axiological predicates or with applied axiological relations, have the form of pure logical propositions but follow the rules of mixed logical or mixed axiological propositions. They have, therefore, again all three axiological modes. However, these axiological modes of pure logical propositions need not concern us in the following.

2. *Mixed logical propositions,* of the form *x is good,* mean that x has all the properties x has; thus the values of x can never be mere things or events as such but only things and events having properties. They may be designated by proper names, by descriptions, or by expositional class names. Strictly speaking, it is never a thing x as such that is good but always a thing as having some properties; just as in the form *x is a good (member of) C* it was presupposed that C contains φ and therefore x is φ, so here it is presupposed that x has a set of properties and that by virtue of having them x is good. Thus "x" here is not a thing variable in the usual sense.[21] But neither is *x is good* a compound axiological proposition as was *x is a good C.* The latter presupposed the underlying judgment "x is a C" and all the entailments thereof. *x is good,* on the other hand, simply means *x is good as x, x is good being x, x is a good x,* or the like. The underlying assumption here is simply "x is x." But this assumption is not the same as the identical-looking assumption—often called a law

---

[20] For the pure axiological forms of these relations see "A Logical Definition of Value," *The Journal of Philosophy,* XLVIII (1951), 413-20.
[21] Eventually a different symbol must be used here; the more so as what we are dealing with is the logical form of intrinsic rather than extrinsic value. See above p. 200 and "A Logical Definition of Value," *The Journal of Philosophy,* XLVII (1951), 413-20.

of thought— underlying the logical proposition *x is a C*. This proposition, too, may be said to presuppose the assumption "x is x." But whereas in the latter case "x is x" is a mere tautology and "x" *is* a mere thing variable, in the former, the axiological case, "x is x" is not a mere tautology for "x" is not a mere thing variable. The assumption "x is x" in this latter case guarantees that x, whatever its properties, will always be x; that is, it guarantees the identity of x throughout the whole range of its definition and exposition: it is a kind of substantial guarantee of x, a guarantee of x as substance in the old sense of the word, but without the metaphysical connotation. x is a "continuant" in the sense of W. E. Johnson:[22] it remains the same though its set of properties may change. For *x is good* is only one of many mixed logical propositions about x, others being *x is fair, x is bad, x is no good,* and so forth. In all these cases the assumption is that x is x, no matter whether x is good, bad, or indifferent, and that the x which in one value proposition is said to be good is the same which in another value proposition is said to be bad. Unless it is assumed that x is one and the same throughout the whole range of its expositional determinations, and that this x is the same as the definitional x, the x of each expositional value might be thought of as being different from that of every other expositional value, and all of these different from the x which has the *definitional* properties.[23] The axiological assumption "x is x" thus guarantees that the expositional "modalities"—the value terms—can be applied. In other words, the modality of the value pattern—the assumption "x is x"—guarantees the expositional modality. The only modality of the value pattern, however, which is applicable for this purpose is assertoriness, namely that x *is* x; and therefore mixed logical propositions are *analytic*.

3. *Pure axiological propositions*, of the form *x ought to be good*, have two underlying assumptions. One is, as above, that x is x, in which case the pure axiological proposition, like the mixed logical, is *analytic*. The assumption "x is x," we said, meant more than merely a relation of identity: it meant the guarantee of x's identity *throughout its exposition and definition*. But if this is so, then x cannot merely be x, that is, a thing or event, because things or events as such have no

[22] *Logic* (Cambridge, England), I (1921), 199, and III (1924), Chap. VII. This points to the determinable rather than the class character of the "good" here in question.
[23] This is the kind of problem that troubled the Korzybskians.

exposition and definition. Exposition and definition are matters of *concepts.* Hence the "x" which has exposition and definition must be a concept, namely, the concept of x, say, "X." There are thus two kinds of x—x as thing or event, that is, as "x," and x as concept of that thing or event, and of that thing or event exclusively, that is, as "X." In other words, there is no thing without its concept—again something of a Kantian tenet. Indeed, if this were not so, *x ought to be good* would be meaningless. For, we remember, "ought" is a relation exclusively between thing and concept. Thus, if *x ought to be good* is to have any meaning, it must mean *x ought to be a good X.* The assumption underlying *x ought to be good* is not merely "x is x," as in the case of the mixed logical proposition *x is good,* but "x is X"—and this is not an identity but a class-membership relation, where x is the only member of X. It spells out the curious identity of "x is x" which we discussed above and did not regard as a tautology. We cannot go into the details of this matter, which defines intrinsic as against extrinsic value.[24] The assumption "x is X" is again assertory. For unless x *is* X, *x ought to be good* is meaningless. Hence, pure axiological propositions are analytic, just as are mixed logical propositions.

But there is another side to the matter. In order for *x ought to be good* to be valid I must assume that x is X. But do I necessarily have to assume that which makes what I say valid? It seems much more natural to assume that x is x than to assume that x is X. It may well be assumed that everybody assumes that x is x. But only a sophisticated mind assumes assertorily that x is X. There is, after all, a difference between x and X. Indeed, just a sophisticated mind may well doubt that x is X; x may be X and again, x may not be X. That in the first case the proposition x *ought to be good* may be valid and in the second invalid is an entirely different matter. My assumptions are one thing and the validity of what I say another. Thus, we cannot exclude the assumption of x either being X or not being X, that is, the problematic modality.

While *x ought to be good* thus leaves room for the problematic modality, it does not seem to leave room for the negatory modality, that x is not x, or X not X, or x not X. For if x ought to be good,

---

[24] For details see "A Logical Definition of Value," *The Journal of Philosophy,* XLVIII (1951), 413-20; and "The Analytic, the Synthetic, and the Good: Kant and the Paradoxes of G. E. Moore," *Kant-Studien,* XLV (1953-54), 67-82, and XLVI (1954-55), 3-18.

certainly there must be x, and that x must be x, and at least *may* be X; it cannot be assumed that it is not X; for this would mean that there is no definition and exposition of x. Doubt of x's being X may be permitted but not the assumption of its not being X. Thus, we must say that pure axiological propositions may also be *hypothetical* but not that they are synthetic. Our reasoning has brought out a close connection between the axiological mode and axiological validity.

4. *Mixed axiological propositions,* of the form *x ought to be C,* may have all the three axiological moods, for the underlying modalities may be either assertory, problematical, or negatory. When I say "x ought to be C," then, as we have seen before, I can assume that x *is* C, in which case the mixed axiological proposition is *analytic;* or I may assume that x may or may not be C, in which case the axiological proposition is *hypothetical;* or I may assume that x is *not* C, in which case the mixed axiological proposition is *synthetic.*

Since in all value propositions the underlying logical judgment contains the subject and the, explicit or implicit, predicate of the value proposition itself, axiological *analyticity* means that there is assumed a connection between the subject and the predicate of the value proposition; axiological *hypotheticity* means that nothing is assumed about such a connection; and axiological *syntheticity* means that there is assumed not to be such a connection. In the first case, the subject is assumed to be a member of the class of, or referred to by, the predicate; in the second case nothing about such a membership is assumed; and in the third case there is assumed not to be such a membership. In the first case the exposition of the predicate class is normative for the subject, in the second case it may or may not be normative, and in the third case it is not normative.

Depending on the mode of the value proposition, the "ought" in it is either analytic, hypothetical, or synthetic. In analytic propositions, *analytic* or *logical* "ought" merely confirms an existing logical relationship, namely the one assumed in the assertory modality. In *hypothetical* propositions "ought" has two functions. Since the assumed logical relation is in the problematical mood and is assumed as possibly existing and as possibly nonexisting, "ought" may confirm one of these possibilities and "ought not" the other. Both senses of ought thus confirm *something.* Depending on which sense is used, we shall call hypothetical "ought" either *existential* or *statistical* (the reason for the choice of terms will appear later). In *synthetic* propositions, synthetic "ought" appears in three varieties. The underlying assumption is in the negatory modality, "x is not C." If the proposition itself is positive, *x ought to be C*, the relation between x and C, which is assumed not to exist, is to be constituted. This we shall call *constitutive* or *constructive* "ought." Constitutive or constructive propositions are, for example, *All governments ought to merge into world government, All airplanes ought to be jet-planes, Latvia ought to be free.* If the proposition is negative, *x ought not to be C,* two cases must be distinguished: the connection between subject and predicate is to be *abolished* or it is to be *prevented.* In both cases it is assumed that this connection does not exist, in the first case partially, in the second case wholly. If the connection between subject and predicate is to be abolished, that is, if x ought not to be C, then, since "ought not" relates the betterness of a thing to its worseness,[25] x as something else, say B, is better than x as C: x is not a good C; which means that x does not fulfill the exposition of C. This not being the case, x may "just as well" not be a C at all: it is "better for" x not to be a C. This kind of logically negative synthetic axiological proposition we shall call *destructive.* The second kind, where x is assumed to be no C at all, we shall call *obstructive.* The assumption, thus, that the subject does *not* belong to the class of the predicate is common to all synthetic axiological propositions. In the case of constructive and obstructive propositions it refers to total not-belonging: the subject does wholly not belong to the predicate. In the case of destructive propositions it refers to partial not-belonging: the subject partially does not belong to the predicate. Destructive and obstructive propositions can be regarded as obversions of one another when they agree in subject and predicate: *Betty ought-not to steal* is destructive "ought," meaning that Betty is not by nature made to be a thief, although she steals; *Betty ought not-to-steal* is obstructive "ought," meaning that Betty ought not to do what she is assumed not to be doing.

The classifications of value propositions are summarized on page 224.

25 P. 208, above.

VALUE PROPOSITIONS			
Logical Propositions (Copula *Is*)		Axiological Propositions (Copula *Ought*)	
Pure Logical (Logical Predicate)	Mixed Logical (Axiological Predicate)	Pure Axiological (Axiological Predicate)	Mixed Axiological (Logical Predicate)
Logically Analytic or Synthetic and Axiologically Analytic, Hypothetical, and Synthetic	Analytic	Analytic or Hypothetical (Existential or Statistical)	Analytic or Hypothetical (Existential or Statistical) or Synthetic (Constructive, Obstructive, or Destructive)

III. Truth-Values of Value Propositions

We can now pull the threads together and determine the truth-values of value propositions. In logical propositions we distinguish between truth and validity, meaning by truth in this sense truth in terms of reference to reality and by validity truth in terms of the systemic pattern of logic. Logical propositions, in the first sense, appear against a background of empirical reality. Logic, in the second sense, has so constructed its rules that in sound reasoning, that is, reasoning from sound premises, empirical truth and falsity and systemic truth and falsity coincide. It is this co-incidence, this *sym-ballein*, by which symbols enable us to deal with the world.

The same reflection will now lead us to the truth-values of axiological propositions. These propositions, also, appear against a background of empirical reality, even though that reality is, as it were, not quite so empirical as that against which the logical propositions appear. But it is reality, nevertheless, and it is empirical, even though of a more subjective kind. The background against which value propositions are presented, that is, pro-posited, *vor-gesetzt,* is the value-pattern—the pattern of assumptions and modalities which we have discussed.

Thus we are now led to the concepts of axiological truth and axiological validity. An axiological proposition is true if it corresponds to the underlying value pattern and it is false if it does not; just as a logical proposition is true if it corresponds to the "facts," that is, the pattern of reality to which it refers, and is false if it does not. The difference between logical and axiological propositions, in this respect, is only that logical propositions semantically *refer to* their background —or foreground?—and axiological propositions pragmatically *arise from* it.

But, just as logical propositions *as such* can have nothing to do with this kind of truth and falsity, neither can axiological propositions. Indeed, they can even less, for their correspondence with the underlying pattern is generally much more vague—and less testable—than the correspondence of logical propositions with their empirical reference. Thus, the truth and falsity of value propositions *as such* must be based on the system of axiology, just as that of the logical propositions *as such* on the system of logic; it must be based on rules of validity and invalidity. These rules must be so constructed that, as in the case of logical propositions, a sound psyche, that is, in the case of valuation, not merely sound reasoning but sound reasoning on the basis of sound assumptions, will lead to correct results both empirically and axiologically. In other words, in the case of valuation on sound assumptions, truth and validity of value propositions must coincide.

This being understood, the formulation of the rules of axiological validity is simple and follows naturally and logically from our analysis of value propositions.

Value propositions are either axiologically true, axiologically false, or axiologically indeterminate ("a-true," "a-false," "a-indeterminate").[26] Axiological truth (T), axiological falsity (F), axiological indeterminacy (I) are the *axiological truth-values* or the *truth-values of value propositions*.

Depending on the nature of "ought," axiological value propositions having the truth-value Truth may be logically (analytically), existentially, or statistically a-true. If they have the truth-value Falsity, they may be logically (analytically) or existentially a-false.

1. Propositions are axiologically *true* if they conform to the rules of axiology and *false* if they do not so conform. They do not conform if they contradict these rules (a) implicitly, (b) explicitly. The latter is the case if they are excluded from the range of these rules by an axiological rule itself. They are *indeterminate* if (c) they are

---

[26] Unless otherwise specified, by "true," "false," "indeterminate" we shall in the following understand "a-true," "a-false," "a-indeterminate."

not axiological in nature, that is, neither have an axiological copula nor an axiological predicate, or if (d) there is assumed to be no relation between subject and predicate.

2. *Pure Logical Propositions*
   Pure logical propositions are indeterminate.

Pure logical propositions are not axiological in nature (1c).[27] Their truth is not axiological truth but logical truth.

3. *Mixed Logical Propositions*
   Mixed logical propositions are true if logically particular and false if logically universal.

Mixed logical propositions are axiologically analytic. This means that it is a-false that all members of a class C—that is, all those that have existed, do exist, or will exist in time[28]—are good. For in this case they would all fulfill both exposition and definition, we would have a systemic class, and value predication would be impossible. Hence it is false that all members of a class are good (1a or 1b).[29] If all members of a class are less than good or no member of a class is good, then no member fulfills the exposition and there would be no empirical class; for such a class presupposes that at least two members fulfill the exposition.[30] But if there is no expositional class, valuation is again impossible, since valuation depends on the existence of the empirical class (1a or 1b). Hence it is false that all members of a class are less than good or that no member of the class is good. If it

---

[27] Insofar as they *are* axiological in nature, the rule is different. But this, we said on p. 219, is not part of our present concern. Insofar as they *seem* to be axiological but are not, they are false. See footnote 17, above.

[28] See p. 197, above.

[29] A question arises in the case of propositions with qualified subjects, such as *All my children are good,* which, according to this rule, must be axiologically false. That this actually is the case is easily seen. "Good" refers back to the subject, which is "my children." Thus, as the proposition stands, it means "All my children are good (my children)"—my children fulfill the exposition of "my children." This exposition states merely the fact of my parenthood or the "mineness" of my children. "Good my children" then merely means that my children *are* really my children—and mineness allows of no degrees, hence the proposition is systemic. In other words, the qualification of the subject excludes the subject's exposition, and hence the intended meaning of "good," which of course is intended to refer to "children" and not to "my children." The proposition, then, is elliptic for "Some children are good, among them my own" or "My own children are the kind of children that are good" or "My own children are good children." These are compound axiological propositions, and they may be true.

[30] See pp. 336 and 340 f., below.

is both false that all members of a class are good and that all members of a class are less than good, then it must be true, if there is to be an empirical class at all, that some members of the class are good and some are less than good. This means that logically universal mixed logical propositions are false and logically particular mixed logical propositions are true.

Mixed logical propositions are all logical propositions with axiological predicate, such as the true propositions *Some men are good* (men), *Some automobiles are good* (automobiles), *Some things are no good* (things), and the false propositions *All men are good* (men), *No automobiles are good* (automobiles), *All things are no good* (things). All these propositions demonstrate the rule that generalization in axiologically analytic propositions is a-false. Violations of this rule may be called the *Fallacy of Illicit Generalization*. This rule, which in logic proper has no systemic status, is a theorem in axiology, following from the axiological distinction between systemic and empirical propositions and the consequent value exemption of systemic propositions. Any class all of whose members are good or fulfill both exposition and definition, is a systemic class.[31]

4. *Pure Axiological Propositions*

Analytic pure axiological propositions are true if positive and false if negative.

Hypothetical pure axiological propositions are true if positive; if negative they are true if logically particular and false if logically universal.

Analytic pure axiological propositions are logically a-true and a-false.

---

[31] To give a hint at applications of axiology, this goes for the class of angels and for the class of God, as well as for the class of the world, insofar as the latter necessarily proceeds from God. Therefore, Spinoza's world is a systemic class. From this follows, in accordance with our rules, that value predication can only be applied by a mind which is in error about the nature of the world. A mind which knows the world as what it is, is beyond using the value predicates, "good," "bad," and the like, in their usual meaning. For the world as logical system is exempt from valuation. A mind that understands the world in this way becomes itself systemic. Leibniz's world, on the other hand, as the best possible, is the one which, according to our definition of "best," alone fulfills the exposition of "world"—in, say, the Creator's mind. Such a world would be a world with the maximum of good things, that is, of things with maximum expositions, which means, with maximum interrelations; for the larger the expositions, the larger their interrelations. This is, indeed, Leibniz's interpretation of the best possible world. As many things as possible are to mirror as fully as possible as many as possible other things, each a complete microcosm.

Hypothetical pure axiological propositions, if positive, are existentially a-true; if negative, they are statistically a-true when logically particular, and existentially a-false when logically universal.

(a) In analytic propositions it is assumed that the subject *is* a member of its class, hence the copula "ought," used in its positive sense, merely confirms what is assumed to be the case. Positive analytic pure axiological propositions are therefore true. "Ought" used in the negative sense, on the other hand, contradicts what is assumed, and the proposition is therefore false.

(b) In hypothetical pure axiological propositions it is indeterminate whether the subject belongs to its class or fulfills the exposition. Hence the copula "ought," used in the positive sense, confirms what may be the case, and the proposition is existentially true. "Ought" used in the negative sense confirms as negative what may *not* be the case; the proposition is therefore statistically[32] true. This, however, can apply only to logically particular propositions; for, while it may be assumed that some members of a class may be bad it cannot be assumed that all of them are bad, and hence do not fulfill the exposition. This assumption would contradict the possibility of the empirical class itself. It may be assumed, however, that all members of the class may be good, for this assumption does not contradict the *possibility* of the empirical class—even though, if all *were* in fact good, the class would *actually* be a systemic one. But this class would be more than, and include, the expositional one. Therefore, if positive, *all* hypothetical pure axiological propositions are true, whether logically universal or particular. But if negative, only logically particular propositions are true, while logically universal ones are false.

Examples of true propositions of this kind are *All teachers* (being teachers) *ought to be good* (teachers) (A→G: logically or analytically a-true; *All teachers* (if they are teachers, that is, belong to the expositional class "teacher") *ought to be good* (teachers) (A↔G: existentially true); *Some teachers* (teachers being what they are, either fulfilling or not fulfilling the exposition of "teacher") *ought to be bad* (teachers) I↔D: statistically true).

Examples of false propositions of this kind are *All teachers* (being teachers) *ought to be no good* (teachers) (A→T: logically a-false); *All*

---

[32] Because to the axiological *rule* that in an existential class there *must* be some members which do not fulfill the exposition there corresponds the statistical *fact* that there usually *are* such members.

teachers (if they are teachers) *ought to be no good* (teachers) (A↔T: existentially a-false); *Some teachers* (being teachers) *ought to be no good* (teachers) (I→T: logically a-false).

5. *Mixed Axiological Propositions*

Analytic mixed axiological propositions are true if positive and false if negative.

Hypothetical mixed axiological propositions are true if positive; if negative, they are true if logically particular and false if logically universal.

Synthetic mixed axiological propositions are indeterminate.

Analytic and hypothetical mixed axiological propositions are a-true and a-false following the pattern of pure axiological propositions.

(a) In analytic mixed axiological propositions it is assumed that the subject *is* a member of the class of the predicate. Such propositions use the copula "ought" logically, and the same argument applies as for analytic pure axiological propositions.

(b) In hypothetical mixed axiological propositions it is indeterminate whether the subject belongs to the class, or fulfills the exposition of, the predicate. The copula "ought" is used hypothetically, and the same argument applies as for hypothetical pure axiological propositions.

(c) In synthetic mixed axiological propositions it is assumed that no relationship exists between subject and predicate. Such propositions are, therefore, indeterminate (1d), for there is no exposition which can serve as norm for the subject. These propositions use "ought" either constructively, obstructively, or destructively, depending on the positive or negative sense of "ought."

True propositions of this kind are *All promises ought to be kept* (A→C: analytically a-true if it is part of a promise to be kept); *All promises* (if they are promises) *ought to be kept* (A↔C: existentially true); *Some promises* (promises being what they are, for example, some of them foolish) *ought not to be kept* (O↔C: statistically true); *Your duty in this situation* (whether or not it can be done) *ought to be done* (A↔C: existentially true); *Your duty* (defined as what ought to be done) *always ought to be done* (A→C: logically true); *Your duty* (duties being what they are, that is, at times conflicting with each other) *sometimes ought not to be done* (O↔C: statistically true); *No bachelors ought to marry* (E→C̄: analytically true).

False propositions of this kind are *No promises ought to be kept* (E→C or E↔C: logically or existentially a-false); *Some promises ought not to be kept* (O→C: logically false if "to be kept" is part of the definition or exposition of promise); *Your duty in this situation* (whether or not it can be done) *never ought to be done* (E←→C: existentially false); *Your duty* (defined as what ought to be done) *sometimes ought not to be done* (O→C, I→C̄: logically a-false).

Indeterminate propositions of this kind are *Promises ought to be kept* (A←C, I←C—if there is supposed to be no connection between promises and keeping them); *Promises ought not to be kept* (E←C, O←C—under the same Machiavellian presupposition); *Duties ought to be done* (A←C, I←C—if there is supposed to be no relation between duties and doing them); *There ought to be craters on the other side of the moon* (I←C—I know nothing of the other side of the moon and assume there are no craters, but I infer from what I know of this side that there should be craters: constructive or constitutive "ought"[33]); *You ought not (never) to become a doctor* (A←C̄: obstructive "ought"); *You ought not to be a doctor* (E←C: destructive "ought"); *You ought to close the door* (A←C: constructive "ought").[34]

6. Summary: See the table which follows, on page 231.[35]

---

[33] This kind of constitutive "ought" most closely resembles the "ought" of hypothesis. Some historical such propositions are: *The earth ought to revolve around the sun, There ought to be a sea lane to India, There ought to be the ruins of Troy, There ought to be a law to Balmer's numbers, The atom ought to be split(able).* This constitutive "ought" refers to the spatially or the timelessly (cf. the law of Balmer's numbers) existing but to the human mind as yet unknown, except by intuition (cf. Gauss's remark: "The result I have, if only I knew how to get there.") It does not refer to the potential which has yet to be created, such as *The Thirteen Colonies ought to be free, Europe ought to be united.* This is a different kind of constitutive "ought." For the epistemological idealist there is not much difference between the two kinds.

[34] But *You* (being the janitor) *ought to close the door* is an analytic mixed axiological proposition and hence a-true (A→C). The difference appears well when the equivalent is used: *It is better for you to close the door.* In the case of the janitor this means *You better . . . (or else),* in the case of anybody else it means it is better for your health, and the like. There is no reason why imperatives should not be interpreted as "ought"-propositions and thus subsumed under our rules. Also, see p. 218, above.

[35] For the Comments and Response which relate to this paper see pp. 333-42, 374, and 389-90, below.

TRUTH-VALUES OF VALUE PROPOSITIONS

	Pure Logical	Mixed Logical — Logical Universal	Mixed Logical — Logical Particular	Pure Axiological — Positive		Pure Axiological — Negative		Mixed Axiological — Positive		Mixed Axiological — Negative		
Propositions	A—C E—C I—C O—C	A—G A—T A—B A—D E—G E—T E—B E—D	I—G I—T I—B I—D O—G O—T O—B O—D	A→G E→T A→B E→D I→G O→T I→B O→D	A↔G E↔T A↔B E↔D I↔G O↔T I↔B O↔D	A→T E→B A→D E→G I→T O→B I→D O→G	A↔T E↔B A↔D E↔G I↔T O↔B I↔D O↔G	A→C E→C̄ I→C O→C̄	A↔C E↔C̄ I↔C O↔C̄	A→C̄ E→C I→C̄ O→C	A↔C̄ E↔C I↔C O↔C	A←C̄ E←C I←C̄ O←C I↔C̄ O↔C̄
Is	I	F	T									
Analytic Ought				T		F		T		F		
Hypothetical Ought (Existential)					T		F		T		F	
Hypothetical Ought (Statistical)							T					T
Synthetic Ought									I			I

A SECOND SEQUEL ON VALUE

RAY LEPLEY

IN MUCH recent discussion of value, attention has focused especially
upon the nature of the signs or language forms and functions
which characterize what are commonly called valuative terms,
sentences, and judgments, as contrasted with factual terms, sentences,
and judgments. On the one hand, the position has been taken that
value terms are essentially expressions of attitude, desire, or feeling
rather than assertions, that they have emotive meaning but little or
no theoretical or cognitive meaning.[1] On the other hand, it has been
held that there is no difference, except possibly in subject matter or
language form, between valuative judgments, sentences, or terms and
factual judgments, sentences, or terms.[2] Dewey countered the view
that value terms and sentences are merely ejaculations or expressions
of feeling or wish, with the contention that there are "distinctive
valuation-propositions."[3] There have appeared several variants of
the idea that there are two kinds of value judgments, distinguished,
for example, as the descriptive and the operational;[4] the designative
and the appraisive;[5] judgments *about* value and judgments *of* value.[6]

---

[1] See, for example, A. J. Ayer, *Language, Truth and Logic* (London, 1936, and
rev. ed., 1946); R. Carnap, *Philosophy and Logical Syntax* (London, 1935), and
"Empiricism, Semantics, and Ontology," *Revue Internationale de Philosophie*, IV
(1950), 20-40; A. Kaplan, "Are Moral Judgments Assertions?" *The Philosophical
Review*, LI (1942), 280-303; C. L. Stevenson, "The Emotive Meaning of Ethical
Terms," *Mind*, XLVI (1937), 14-31, and *Ethics and Language* (New Haven, Conn.,
1944).

Excerpts from *Ethics and Language* are printed in the present Essay by permission of Yale University Press, publishers. Those from *Mind* are by permission
of its editor.

[2] See, for example, the positions held by J. Dewey, S. C. Pepper, and some of the
other contributors to *Value: A Cooperative Inquiry* (New York, 1949).

[3] J. Dewey, "Theory of Valuation," in *International Encyclopedia of Unified
Science* (Chicago, 1939), Vol. II, No. 4.

[4] B. M. Jessup, in *Value: a Cooperative Inquiry*, p. 139 f.

[5] C. Morris, in *Value: A Cooperative Inquiry*, pp. 217-19, 394-95.

[6] D. H. Parker, in *Value: A Cooperative Inquiry*, p. 238 *et passim*.

These and many other analyses have led increasingly into semantic or semiotic issues in value theory.[7]

The present paper is an attempt to develop further, with reference to some of these issues, the general point of view expressed by the author in his "Sequel on Value" and the other parts which he contributed to the volume *Value: A Cooperative Inquiry*. The questions considered in this second sequel are those listed in the Summary of Issues, which appears on page 4, above. As the reader may recognize, the terminology employed is from many sources. The aim has not been to adhere to any one of the current terminologies—which obviously has not been done—but to achieve or work toward a synthesis which may for the present problems be in some respects more adequate than any one special semantic or semiotic vocabulary.

I

Some studies of value from the linguistic standpoint have sought to analyze what are commonly accepted as valuative terms ("good," "right," "better," "best," "ought," "should," "beautiful," and so forth, and their opposites) or valuative sentences ("X is good," and so on). Other analyses have attempted to discern what, in the nature of meaning as experience or response, or what in the references and/or other functions of the terms or sentences differentiates valuative from nonvaluative signs or sign-occurrences. Still other semantic or semiotic treatments have endeavored to clarify these differences by analysis of the total situations in which signs rise as a part of the behaviors or activities by which organisms—especially humans—seek to make life adjustments.

Such analyses, whether directed primarily to the nature of signs

---

[7] See, for example, E. M. Adams, "Word-Magic and Logical Analysis in the Field of Ethics," *The Journal of Philosophy*, XLVII (1950), 313-19; H. Fingarette, "How Normativeness Can Be Cognitive But Not Descriptive in Dewey's Theory of Valuation," *The Journal of Philosophy*, XLVIII (1951), 625-35; E. W. Hall, *What is Value?* (London and New York, 1952); P. Kecskemeti, *Meaning, Communication, and Value* (Chicago, 1952); J. Ladd, "Value Judgments, Emotive Meanings, and Attitudes," *The Journal of Philosophy*, XLVI (1949), 119-28; H. S. Leonard, "Ethical Predicates," *The Journal of Philosophy*, XLVI (1949), 601-7; C. I. Lewis, *An Analysis of Knowledge and Valuation* (La Salle, Ill., 1947); R. M. Millard, "Types of Value and Value Terms," *The Journal of Philosophy*, XLVI (1949), 129-33; C. Morris, "Signs about Signs about Signs," *Philosophy and Phenomenological Research*, IX (1948-49), 115-33; and V. Tomas, "Ethical Disagreement and the Emotive Theory of Values," *Mind*, LX (1951), 205-22. See also the writings cited in the Appendix, pp. 395-401, below.

or language, to the nature of the meanings involved, or to the kinds of activities which occur in or as adjustment, have all served to emphasize what to some extent was already clear from grammatical distinctions made between nouns, verbs, adjectives, adverbs, and other parts of speech; between declarative, interrogative, exclamatory, and imperative sentences; and between indicative, subjunctive, and imperative moods—namely, that signs perform a variety of different functions and that in different contexts the same term may 'function,' 'mean,' 'mediate,' or operate for or as adjustment in slightly or widely different ways.[8]

As Richards, Stevenson, Parker, Kaplan, and others have stressed, value terms and sentences perform in marked degree such dynamic, or emotive, functions as may be called expression (of attitude, wish, or feeling), making commitment, or motivation. Although, as Tomas has seen,[9] these same emotive functions are performed in some degree or in some instances by factual, descriptive, or cognitive signs, it may well be that more characteristically or more frequently or in larger degree such terms as "good," "right," "ought," "beautiful," and their opposites perform 'dynamic functions' or have 'emotive meanings.' Also, organisms are, as correctly emphasized by Morris[10] and

[8] In some contexts or under exceptional scrutiny the meaning of almost any sign may of course appear "fuzzy" or uncertain. Words and phrases enclosed in single quotation marks which are not within double quotation marks are felt by the present writer to be particularly in need of clarification. Double quotation marks indicate quotations or words as words. As may be noted, the term "function," whether as noun or as verb, is used in this paper in a very broad sense to signify any sign event in either its significative or its nonsignificative role, or both. The term "occur" is also employed in this broad, neutral sense. Perhaps all words by which we recognize and discuss sign phenomena—such words as "sign," "reference," "meaning," "signify," "use," "cognitive," "emotive," "designate," "appraisive," "express," and so forth—may occur or function in either extended or restricted ways. One aim of semantic or semiotic analysis is of course to make clear or clearer the different ways in which various words, phrases, and sentences do or can mediate or assist in personal or social 'adjustment.' The meanings of some 'terms' (words or phrases) are considered at appropriate points in the text.
[9] V. Tomas, "Ethical Disagreements and the Emotive Theory of Values," *Mind*, LX (1951), 205-22.
[10] C. Morris, *Signs, Language, and Behavior*, New York, 1946. I find particularly helpful Morris's analysis of the modes of signifying and the use of signs, and have in the present paper employed much of his terminology (for example, the modes as including the "designative," "appraisive," "prescriptive," and "formative," and the uses as including the "informative," "valuative," "incitive," and "systematic"). I am inclined, however, to question a sharp distinction between mode and use and to feel that "expressive" may need to be added both to the modes and to the uses,

Bales,[11] confronted by an environment which must (for survival and prosperous adjustment) be rightly interpreted; objects and acts[12] must be given proper preference in relation to one another; effective means must be used in effective ways. Some signs and sign complexes (ascriptors) thus rise and come to function characteristically or commonly to designate (recognize, interpret, anticipate) what *is* —the objects and states of affairs in or of the physical or social environment or in or of the organism itself; other signs and sign complexes rise and function to give objects, processes, acts, and so forth, an order of priority or preference—as good or bad, better or worse; other sign mediations or activities occur to contrive or specify ways of behavior which effect the organism's needed or desired adjustments; and still other signs rise to help organize the complex activities (linguistic and nonlinguistic) which occur in the total adjustment process. Here again it is evident that, although often the same signs may in different contexts of situation, intent, or sign complex perform any or all of these several functions, some signs and complexes have come to serve, characteristically or most frequently, one main function (expressive, designative, appraisive, prescriptive, formative, incitive) rather than another.

Now, although it has become increasingly clear that markedly different functions are performed by signs, that signs rise to perform particular functions, and that particular signs do characteristically perform one or more functions, the complexities and flexibilities of

---

and "incitive" added to the modes (as well as being one of the uses). Also, I am inclined to think that the two sets of terms (the modes and the uses) could be employed about as well interchangeably and that by assigning one set to modes and the other to uses there is danger of overemphasizing the sharpness of the distinction and of making it appear that the various categories of one set are quite different and distinct from those of the other set. I am aware, however, that my feelings and thoughts about these matters result from my own reflective analysis of instances, in view of the writings of Dewey, Richards, Stevenson, Morris, and others. Until more extensive and crucial studies are made, in larger part by methods such as reported in Morris's present Essay (pp. 61-76) and Response (p. 280), I can only invite other students of these problems to indicate the reasons for their agreements or disagreements with the views suggested in the present paper.

[11] R. F. Bales, *Interaction Process Analysis: A Method for the Study of Small Groups* (Cambridge, Mass.), 1950.

[12] When used singly in this paper the word "object" (or "objects") signifies any and every thing, event, relation, act, state of affairs, and so forth, which might be pointed to or conceived. When used in series, such as "objects and acts," "objects" includes every thing other than what is specifically mentioned ("acts" in this case), to which special attention is called.

the total situation, especially in its language aspects, are such that it does not necessarily follow that the way in which any particular sign or sign complex 'signifies' or otherwise functions is determined by the sign's characteristic or common 'use' apart from the context of intent or interpretation in which the sign occurs. A distinction can usually be made, and for clarity may need to be made, between the mode in which the sign 'signifies' and the 'use' made of the sign. But if and when this distinction is made, it should not be permitted to conceal the fact that the mode of signifying, the kind of behavior produced or 'prepared' by the sign, is determined by the kind of 'interpretation' (conscious or not) which is made in the particular instance in which the sign occurs. The way in which a sign characteristically functions will of course tend to determine its 'use' in the particular case, but the flexibilities are such that a sign may in some contexts rise and function in ways other than the 'normal' (average), usual, or characteristic. For example, as Morris has recognized[13] the sentence "The table is good" may in one context be a designative ascriptor, or sign complex, and in other context be an appraisive ascriptor.

Whether or not a distinction should be made between the modes in which signs signify and the uses which signs serve is perhaps to be decided, for general usage or in individual cases, in view of the consequences of making or not making it. If the distinction is made universally,[14] we are in danger of forgetting that signs do not have an inherent or intrinsic meaning or mode, that they do not signify in any particular mode per se, or within themselves, apart from the interpretation (a use?) made of them. From the standpoint that modes are or involve interpretation and that interpretation is always affected by the purpose(s) of the interpreter, it is perhaps not possible, without distorting or misrepresenting the actual situation, to make a distinction which excludes "interpretation" from "use." On the other hand, if the term "use" is employed in so broad a sense as to include the interpretation or cognitive response made to the sign as well as the other purposes for which it may be employed as a means—say, to get or make a commitment or to motivate oneself or another to

13 C. Morris, in *Value: A Cooperative Inquiry,* p. 217 f.
14 That is, if modes and uses are conceived as being two classes of processes, relations, and/or states which never overlap nor have members common to both classes, or as being entirely distinct or separate (except possibly for abstraction) within any particular instance of semiosis.

some particular kind of attitude or act—we may neglect, or appear to neglect, the fact that signs do have (because of habits in the respondents) potentialities for eliciting characteristic meanings, significations, or other reactions.

Perhaps here, as at many other points, the difficulties may be avoided or reduced by distinguishing between a broad and a narrow meaning of "use," or by the semantic device of numbering—employing, say, "use$_1$" as a term the reference of which may include the interpretations or cognitive significations of signs as well as their employment as means to ends, and "use$_2$" as a term which may signify the employment of signs as means to ends, as distinguished from their interpretation or cognitive signification. Of course more important than the system of notation are the facts to be kept in mind: "use" in a more restricted sense (use$_2$) marks a contrast between the cognitive 'meanings' occasioned by or with signs and the purposes (expressive, informative, valuative, incitive, systemic) for which the signs may be employed, and signifies only the latter; "use" in the broader sense (use$_1$) emphasizes the point that no sign has meaning or even stimulus effect without the occurrence of some level of signification or interpretation.[15]

II

The bifurcation between fact and value which has become increasingly sharp and pervasive since the rise of modern science and technology has, if anything, been accentuated by linguistic or semantic analyses. These analyses have commonly assumed a basic difference between fact and value and then sought to discover and depict the nature of the difference. The analyses themselves have generally been regarded as confirming the view that there is an essential or ultimate difference, at least between value facts and nonvalue facts. Even those who have recognized that every thing

---

[15] Throughout the present Essay, except as specifically noted, the term "meaning" is employed in a somewhat restricted sense (which at a later point is called "meaning$_2$"). The term signifies cognitive and/or emotive awarenesses as distinguished from total sign responses within or along with which the awarenesses occur: cognitive and emotive meanings are distinguished from, for example, expressive, designative, appraisive, prescriptive, and incitive modes of response. "Emotive meaning" is thus used in a less inclusive sense than by Ayer, Richards, Stevenson, and others, as indicated in footnote 28, p. 242, below.

can be both signified and of significance,[16] or that every thing in the whole gamut of things can be an object of both factual and valuative judgments,[17] usually refuse or fail to consider the possibility that facts and values may be more intimately related or more extensively identical than is commonly recognized when value facts are contrasted (as facts) with nonvalue facts.

Few will deny that for the purpose of common-sense interpretation and clarification it is often helpful to make a distinction between, say, physical facts, on the one hand, and human values, on the other. And with a little examination of the matter even beginning students of value theory can usually be brought to recognize that any and every experienced or experienceable object can be an object of interest as well as an object of cognition, a value as well as a nonvalue fact. Regardless of what the ultimate relation of fact and value may be—a matter to which we shall return briefly in Section IV of this paper, it seems clear that they stand over against each other in marked contrast both as one range of phenomena or subject matter different from another (which we shall call the "contrast relation" of facts and values) and as two different ways of experiencing and referring to every possible object in the whole gamut of objects (which we shall call the "parallel relation" of facts and values).[18]

But thus to recognize the necessity, or at least the convenience, of distinguishing between facts and values as widely contrasting subject matters and as parallel modes of relation or experience, and even as two sets of terms and sentence forms which have become somewhat differentiated from each other, does not necessarily answer the question "Are the modes of sign response (possibly the interpretants) different in the valuative as compared with those in the factual; and

[16] See, for example, C. Morris, pp. 69-70, above.

[17] See E. W. Hall, *What is Value?*

[18] These distinctions are discussed more fully in "Three Relations of Facts and Values," *The Philosophical Review*, LII (1943), 499-504. The terms "facts and values as subject matters," "as parallel modes," "as two sets of terms and sentence forms," and the like, which occur at a number of points in the remainder of the present Essay are employed because they are convenient elliptical phrases. The "as" does not signify a simple identity between fact (or value) and, say, subject matter. A more complete rendering would be "facts and values as distinguished from each other because of experienced contrasts of subject matters," and so on. I am grateful to E. S. Robinson for calling my attention to possible ambiguities at these points and at others indicated in footnote 30, below.

if there are differences in mode, are they differences of kind or of degree?" The differences may result wholly or largely from differences of subject matter, not from differences in the nature of the problem solvings, the judgments, or the modes of sign response which occur in experiencing or adjusting to or as the valuative as compared with those which occur in experiencing or adjusting to or as the factual. It appears probable that the same general pattern of problem solving, described for example by Dewey, Wallas, and others, occurs or can occur in dealing with valuative as with factual matters.[19] But the elements of subject matter and of psychological-social-semiotic processes within the general pattern may differ widely in valuative as compared with factual problems.

That differences of subject matter bulk very large in producing experiences of difference between facts and values in the contrast relation is obvious. But in the parallel relation, where the same object is or may be experienced, referred to, 'expressed,' or judged either as a fact (say, an existent) or as a value (say, an object of interest), the effect of subject matter may appear to be eliminated or at least reduced. For example, the difference between "This is a table" and "Beauty is intrinsically good" (an instance of the contrast relation) seems much greater, because of wide difference of subject matter, than does the difference between "This is a table" or "This is a good table" or between "Beauty is enjoyed perception" and "Beauty is intrinsically good" (instances of the parallel relation). Still it is evident that even in the examples of the parallel relation there are differences of subject matter. Though the referent of both "This is a table" and "This is a good table" may at first glance appear to be an actual or imagined table a moment's consideration makes clear that in "This is a good table" the referent is not solely the table but is more essentially the table as sustaining or able to sustain a certain relation with an interest of a subject—say, with his need for a surface on which to write or place tools or parcels, and with the sentence which affirms the relation. Or if we examine what may appear to be a closer parallel relation, such as "This is a table" and "'Table' is a good (or correct) designation for this object," and also if we recognize that even in the case of "This is a table" the referent is not merely the table as an independent existent but essentially is a triadic relation which the object sustains with an interest of a subject and with the

[19] See *Verifiability of Value* (New York, 1944), Chap. II.

sentence which affirms the relation, it may still be true that in or with these two sentences there are two different interests and therefore two different referents. As long as this is the case it follows that even in the parallel relation of facts and values there remains a difference of subject matter which may cause or be a factor in causing any apparent or actual differences between the problem solvings, judgments, or sign responses in valuative as compared with factual adjustments.

Consideration of instances of facts and values in the parallel relation, especially in the closer parallels where differences of subject matter reduce to a minimum or appear to result only from difference of interests involved in the triadic relations of object, subject, and language, may suggest that the essential differences between fact and value—if indeed there are such differences—result from the nature of the interests and/or the nature or functions of the language, the meanings, or the sign responses which occur in transactions with even the 'same' or closely related objects.

The possibility that the essential difference between facts and values may be one of interest recalls Dewey's position that

there is nothing whatever that methodologically (qua judgment) marks off "value-judgments" from conclusions reached in astronomical, chemical, or biological inquiries.[20] The genuinely important difference resides in the fact of the greater *importance with respect to the conduct of life-behavior* possessed by the special subject matter of so-called value-judgments.[21]

The possibility that the difference may be due to the nature or function of the language, meanings, or sign responses involved may recall the view held by Ayer, Richards, Stevenson, and others, that valuative terms and sentences have dynamic as contrasted with descriptive use and emotive as distinguished from descriptive meaning:

On the one hand we use words (as in science) to record, clarify, and communicate *beliefs*. On the other hand we use words to give vent to our feelings (interjections), or to create moods (poetry), or to incite people to actions or attitudes (oratory). The first use of words I shall call "descriptive"; the second, "dynamic."[22]

[20] J. Dewey, in *Value: A Cooperative Inquiry*, p. 77.
[21] J. Dewey, *Problems of Men* (New York, 1946), pp. 258-59.
[22] C. L. Stevenson, "The Emotive Meaning of Ethical Terms," *Mind*, XLVI (1937), quoted in W. Sellars and J. Hospers (eds.), *Readings in Ethical Theory* (New York, 1952), p. 421.

It is clear, then, ... that emotive words are fitted both to express the feelings of the speaker and to evoke the feelings of the hearer, and that they derive their fitness from the habits that have been formed throughout the course of their use in emotional situations.[23] ... Emotive meaning is a meaning in which the response (from the hearer's point of view) or the stimulus (from the speaker's point of view) is a range of emotions[24] ... descriptive meaning is the disposition of a sign to affect cognition. ... Thus the distinction between descriptive and emotive meaning depends largely on the kind of psychological disposition that a sign, in its turn, is disposed to evoke.[25]

And the possibility that the difference between fact and value may coincide with or result from a basic difference in the modes in which signs signify, or 'prepare' behavior, may recall Morris's position that:

An appraisive sign signifies the position of something within a series of objects or acts ordered in terms of the interpreter's preferential behavior; it therefore disposes its interpreter to preferential behavior toward what is signified. A designative sign does not regularly evoke a disposition to preferential behavior; it signifies properties of objects which are causally efficacious upon sense-organs or other instruments of discrimination.[26] ... If evaluation is limited—as we have limited it—to inquiries eventuating in appraisive signs, then evaluative language and descriptive language are different in important respects, that is, the interpretant of one is a disposition to preferential behavior, while the interpretant of the second is a disposition to expect objects with certain causally efficacious properties.[27]

When the realm of physical fact is contrasted with that of human value, it may seem that an obvious difference between the two is that the latter is characterized by greater importance with respect to the conduct of life. And in the less close parallel relations, such as "This is a table" and "This is a good table," the latter sentence may appear to relate more closely to, and possibly to be more important for, the conduct of life. The closer the parallels of fact and value become, however, the less apparent it is that the one is more important for the conduct of life than is the other. Indeed, "This is a table" may under some circumstances be more important than "'Table' is a good term by which to designate this object" or

[23] C. L. Stevenson, *Ethics and Language*, p. 41.
[24] *Ibid.*, p. 59.
[25] *Ibid.*, p. 67.
[26] C. Morris, in *Value: A Cooperative Inquiry*, p. 217.
[27] *Ibid.*, p. 218.

more important than even "This is a good table"; and in fact the most impersonal formulations of the physical sciences and technologies would appear in many instances to have at least as great importance for the conduct of life as have formulations which deal with or express human interests, goals, or means more directly or conspicuously. But as long as fact and value are different, even in the closest parallel relations, there is doubtless a difference of interest. On the one hand, the interest is usually one of signifying what the object is or is correlated with; on the other hand, the interest is one of expressing, signifying, or appraising something as "good," "right," "beautiful," and so forth, either 'in itself,' for the sake of experience as such, or as a means to some end. In the expression or statement of the former interest all reference to interest is commonly omitted; in the expression or statement of the latter interest reference to interest is made explicit or is more or less evidently assumed.

Similarly, when viewed in the frame of reference of the contrast of physical facts and human values and the everyday language common to this contrast, it may be concluded that such terms as "good," "ought," "beautiful," "excellent," and their opposites and derivatives, have or produce meanings or sign responses which are essentially different in kind from those had or produced by such terms as "true," "cause of," "correlated with," "exists," "dissolves," and so forth. It may appear that the former, 'valuative,' terms have emotive meanings —that they express attitude, make commitment, or motivate action, or that they cause the respondent to give or to be ready to give the designated thing, attitude, or act a preferential rank in relation to other actual or possible things, attitudes, or acts;[28] whereas the latter, 'factual,' terms affirm or deny the existence of some thing, event, or relation, or cause the respondent to expect or not to expect some thing, event, or relation with certain designated or suggested properties. But these appearances and this conclusion may result from unrepresentative sampling and from failure to recognize that in

[28] "Emotive meaning" as used here includes roughly what it appears to signify for Ayer, Richards, Stevenson, and many others, and also what Morris calls the appraisive mode of signifying. In an attempt to avoid duplication between Morris's analysis and that of the emotivists on this point, the present paper recognizes expressive, appraisive, and incitive modes of response; and, in order to call particular attention to the distinctive awarenesses which so commonly occur in or with such responses, retains the term "emotive meaning" but limits its extension as indicated in footnote 15, p. 237, above.

different contexts both groups perform various functions and have various sorts of meanings and other effects. For it is clear that in some instances, especially in exclamations and commands, the terms "true," "cause of," "dissolve," and so forth are used$_2$ or occur mainly to express, to make commitment, to give preferential status, or to motivate; and that in some instances, as for example in reporting or giving directions, "good," "ought," "beautiful," and so on are used$_1$ (occur) to affirm some relation or effect or to cause the respondent to expect some thing, event, or relation with specified properties.

In short, it is easy, especially from the standpoint of the contrast of physical facts and human values, to select the extremes of scientific statement and description, on the one hand, and of moral judgment or aesthetic expression, on the other, and to regard the terms and sentences which occur in these as typical or characteristic of fact and value in general. There may then be failure to see that even in the contrast relation the same terms, whether commonly called factual or valuative, perform several different functions and have or give rise to different sorts of meaning and sign response. For example, "good" occurs not only to express attitude, to give preferential status, or to incite a desired line of action, but also to designate something as an effective means or as an end deemed worthy to be 'in itself'; and "cause of" occurs not only to affirm causal relations, but also, in some contexts, to express praise or blame ("He is the cause of this!"), to affect preference ("Be a cause of justice, not of injustice!"), and so forth.

That the same sorts of sign response (say, designative or appraisive) and of meaning (cognitive or emotive) are effected by either 'factual' or 'valuative' terms or sentences is more apparent from examination of representative instances in the whole range of the parallel relation of facts and values, and especially in the closer parallels. For example, in some occurrences of "Sulfuric acid dissolves iron" and "Sulfuric acid is a good solvent for iron" or "Sulfuric acid is an effective substance for dissolving iron," it seems clear that the term "good" *may* carry the same kind of meaning and produce the same kind of sign response as the term "effective" and that both of the sentences which contain these terms may occur with meanings or sign responses very similar to (but if the relation of fact and value is here a parallel one, never actually the same as) the meaning of and response to "Sulfuric acid dissolves iron." The meaning of "good" as well as of "effective" and of the entire sentences of which they are parts may be predominantly cognitive rather than emotive and the interpretants or other sign responses elicited by these terms or ascriptors may be predominantly designative rather than appraisive or prescriptive. And somewhere near the other end of the scale of parallel relations, it seems equally evident that in some instances of the occurrence of, say, "This painting is beautiful" and "I enjoy this painting" or "This painting is one which elicits in me (or us or any 'sufficiently endowed' person) the experience, judgment, and expression that it is beautiful," the term "enjoy" *may* carry the same kind of meaning and produce the same kind of sign response as the term "the experience, judgment, and expression that it is beautiful" and that the sentences which contain these terms may occur with meanings and sign responses very similar to (but if the relation of fact and value is here a parallel one, never exactly the same as) the meaning of and response to "This painting is beautiful." The meaning of these terms and sentences *may* be predominantly emotive and the sign responses *may* be predominantly appraisive rather than designative.

It will be noted that in citing these examples emphasis has been placed upon the point that the kind of meaning of or sign response to factual and valuative terms or sentences *may* be the same. Whether or not they *are* the same appears to depend upon the context of situation (including the intent) in which they occur. The matter is complicated by the fact that apparently any term or sentence may occur with different meanings and modes of response in different contexts. "Sulfuric acid dissolves iron" will perhaps in most situations produce or prepare behavior in a designative mode and 'carry' or 'have' mainly cognitive meaning. But it is possible to imagine situations in which this sentence may produce or prepare behavior in an appraisive mode and have chiefly emotive meaning.[29] If terms or sentences when in designative mode be numbered "(1)" and those in appraisive mode numbered "(2)", then in some contexts "Sulfuric acid is a good solvent for iron (1)" will cause the respondent

---

[29] The original discovery that "Sulfuric acid dissolves iron" no doubt expressed some excitement on the part of the discoverer, and any student who observes for himself the effect of sulfuric acid on iron may voice somewhat similar feeling. The sentence may also prepare behavior appraisively and emotively in situations where an effective solvent of iron is sought—say, in a manufacturing or chemical process.

to expect sulfuric acid to dissolve iron and will have the same kind of meaning and produce the same kind of response as does "Sulfuric acid dissolves iron (1)." But if employed with the intent to give sulfuric acid a preferential status among substances which might be used or tried in order to dissolve iron, "Sulfuric acid is a good solvent for iron (2)" would not have the same kind of meaning or response effect as "Sulfuric acid dissolves iron (1)," but would have the same kind of meaning and response effect as "Sulfuric acid dissolves iron (2)." The same will hold true, *mutatis mutandis*, of the relation of "This picture is beautiful" and "I enjoy this painting," and so forth, except that here the more usual meaning may be the emotive, the more usual mode the appraisive.

That the same term or sentence, whether commonly called factual or valuative, may produce or prepare behavior in either designative or appraisive mode and have either cognitive or emotive meaning is perhaps most apparent in instances which are somewhere near midway between the extremes along the entire gamut of parallel relations. For example, "This is a good (or better) table" may occur either to designate that, say, this table will bear such and such weights, or to appraise it as, say, an object to be given preference over certain other tables. And a closely parallel sentence, "This table supports weights in excess of those supported by the other tables," may likewise either designate the properties of the table or appraise it as an object to be selected in preference to other tables. In the context of one sort of situation or intent each sentence has predominantly cognitive meaning and designative effect and in another context has predominantly emotive meaning and appraisive effect. Hence "This is a better table (1)" will have the same kind of meaning and effect as "This table supports weights in excess of those supported by the other tables (1)," but not the same as "This table supports ... (2)," and so on.

But despite the extreme flexibilities of language which make it possible for perhaps any sign to occur with either cognitive or emotive meaning and with either designative or appraisive effect, it may well be that some terms and sentences occur most frequently with one sort of meaning or effect and other terms and sentences with another sort of meaning or effect. Or the position may be taken that a term or sentence—any term or sentence—is a factual one only if and when and to the extent that it has or produces cognitive meaning or

designative effect, and is a valuative term or sentence only if and
when and to the extent that it produces emotive meaning or appraisive
effect.

It thus becomes apparent that in the occurrence of the terms "fact"
and "value," "factual" and "valuative," one or more of several different referents may be assumed; and it also becomes apparent that
the answer to the question "Are the modes of sign response (possibly
the interpretants) different in the valuative as compared with those
in the factual, and if there are differences of mode, are they differences of kind or of degree?" will vary according to the referent
assumed. If it is assumed that the difference between fact and value,
factual and valuative,[30] is one of subject matter or of the relation of
different interests—the contrast of the nonhuman and the human or
the parallel relation of the knowings and the valuings or valuations
which occur with reference to each object in the whole gamut of
experienced or experienceable objects—the answer is that the general
pattern of adjustment or problem solving is probably the same, but
that in even the closest parallel relations the constituent processes
of, say, sensory, cognitive, affective, conative, and motor elements
of experience or response may differ in presence or proportion: more
conative, affective, preferential, or appraisive elements usually being
present or dominant in the valuative, more perceptual, cognitive,
descriptive, or designative elements usually present or dominant in
the factual. If it be assumed, however, that the difference between
fact and value, factual and valuative, is basically a matter of language
differentiation which has taken place in the occurrence, meaning, and
effect of one set of terms and sentences (such as "is," "exists," "cause
of," "correlated with") as contrasted with another set (such as "good,"
"right," "ought," "beautiful"), it is evident that for this frame of
reference the modes of meaning and sign response do not differ in
kind; for any of the terms, whether called factual or valuative, may
'have' or produce either cognitive or emotive meanings and either
designative or appraisive effects; but the modes probably differ in

[30] The expression "fact and value, factual and valuative" used here and at some
subsequent points in this paper does not signify that "factual and valuative" is in
apposition with "fact and value." The phrase is used as a convenient elliptical
expression the meaning of which will, I trust, be sufficiently clear from the
preceding discussion and the immediate context. For the origin of this use of
"factual and valuative" see the second group of questions in the "Summary of
Issues," p. 4, above.

frequency of occurrence: the valuative terms more frequently having emotive meaning and appraisive effect, the factual more frequently having cognitive meaning and designative effect. And, of course, if it be assumed that the difference between fact and value, the factual and the valuative, is basically a matter of the mode of meaning or response occasioned by the sign(s) involved in a particular adjustment or reaction, it is obvious that in consequence of this assumption (or "by definition")[31] the modes in the valuative do differ in kind or degree from those in the factual: terms and sentences are factual if, when, and to the extent that the meaning is cognitive, the effect designative; and are valuative if, when, and to the extent that the meaning is emotive, the effect appraisive.

That the modes are indeed different in kind may seem clear from analysis of the functions which signs occur to effect. As noted above, they assist in expressing attitudes, feelings, or wants, interpreting objects, giving objects preferential ranks, taking steps effective for attaining goals, organizing the relations of signs, motivating behaviors, and so forth. The roles of cognitive and emotive, of expressive, designative, appraisive, prescriptive, formative, and incitive signs (or modes of response 'to' and experience 'of' signs) may appear in this perspective to be sharply different. Each *is*, or may seem to be in, a distinct, unique dimension of being and having. Yet, from another standpoint, the difference appears less sharp, less certain; for although the sentence "This is a good table," for example, may cause the hearer to buy the table or to be disposed toward buying it, he may ask, "What do you *mean* by "good"?" and the salesman may say (correctly or not), "I *mean* that the table will stand up under hard use" (or "that I like its design," or "that I wish to persuade you to buy this table," or something else). Hence, it may be held that an ascriptor, or sign complex, can have appraisive or emotive *effect*, but only designative or cognitive *meaning* (say, meaning$_3$). Signs may be used (use$_2$) or responded to in several different ways, but can 'mean' or 'signify' in an emotive or appraisive way if "meaning" and "signifying" are employed in a sense sufficiently broad (meaning$_1$, signify-

---

[31] Of course whatever assumption is made with regard to the basis of the signification of any term determines "by definition," or by the nature of the assumption itself, what the term shall signify. Insofar as the definition rises from or on the basis of the facts disclosed by careful and continuing inquiry, the assumption need not be unduly arbitrary or prejudiced.

ing$_1$) to include the rank-giving conditioned responses made to "good" and to other terms which evoke rank-giving reactions, whether or not they are attended by awareness (cognitive and/or emotive awareness —meaning$_2$; or cognitive awareness only—meaning$_3$).[32] Not all the responses to 'signs'[33] are significations or meanings in a 'strict' sense (signification$_2$, meaning$_3$). In other words, there are different modes of signifying (and of meaning) only if "signifying" is used in a broad sense (signifying$_1$) to include noncognitive and nondesignative, as well as cognitive and designative sign responses and experiences. If "signifying" is limited to but includes all cognition and designation, the appraisive, prescriptive, formative, and other nondesignative and noncognitive modes of response and experience are not modes of signifying$_2$, but are modes of conditioned response, or signifying$_1$. In short, differences of mode may result from differences of use$_2$, not from differences of signifying$_2$ or of meaning$_3$.

Although analysis of the relation of fact and value, the factual and the valuative, may thus appear to have progressed from gross, crude comparisons within the contrast and parallel relations through comparison of terms and sentences commonly called "valuative" with those called "factual" to the recognition of different semiotic functions which seem to coincide closely with, and to some extent to clarify the distinction between, the factual and the valuative, even these functions may be subjected to further analysis; and it appears also that recognition of the contrast and parallel relations, as well as further analysis of the sign functions themselves, may counteract a tendency for more strictly or narrowly semantic or semiotic analyses to fall into the assumption (from which they seem unable to escape) that there is a sharp, basic difference of kind between fact and value, the factual and the valuative. And recognition that the same terms, whether those called factual or those called valuative, can and often

---

[32] The relation of the cognitive and the emotive is considered in Section III, pp. 249-54, below.

[33] "Sign" may of course be limited (sign$_2$) to include only stimuli which produce responses involving awareness, or may be employed in a broader sense (sign$_1$) to include all or some proportion of stimuli which produce nonconscious conditioned responses. It will be clear that in the sentence to which this note relates the term occurs in the sense of sign$_1$. A distinction should perhaps be made between sign and sign-vehicle, as Morris emphasizes, p. 391, below; as he sees, I have at some points used "sign" in a sense synonymous with "sign-vehicle," a fact which might have been made more explicit by designating this sense as, say, "sign$_3$" or by using the term "sign-vehicle" itself.

do perform either appraisive or designative functions and have either emotive or cognitive meanings may warn against taking too seriously such analyses of terms or sentences as proceed in isolation from the larger linguistic, psychological, and social contexts from which they are abstracted.

III

The questions in the third group may from one standpoint appear to be somewhat elliptical. If terms and sentences, whether factual or valuative, are conceived as, say, marks on a sheet or on a blackboard, it may be that they do not and cannot in themselves possess emotive elements.[34] Feeling, emotion, desire, interest, attitude may occur only in or as the activities and experiences of organisms. From this standpoint the questions should, therefore, be restated somewhat as follows: "Are emotive elements always present in the activities and experiences which occasion or result from valuative terms, sentences, judgments, but not in the activities and experiences which occasion or result from factual terms, sentences, or judgments? And why and how are emotive elements present or absent? Are emotive factors *basic* in the activities or experiences which occasion or result from valuative terms, sentences, judgments, but not in the activities or experiences which occasion or result from factual terms, sentences, judgments?" If the position is taken, however, that even written or printed marks become terms or sentences only when and as interpreted by the writer or by a reader, there may appear to be no impropriety in the original form of the questions. In fact, from this point of view the questions in the original form may be seen to have precisely the same meaning which they have in the revised form suggested here.

As noted above,[35] emotive elements (conations, feelings, expressions of attitude, and the like) are probably more prevalent in valuative than in factual adjustments, judgments, sentences, and terms, whether

---

[34] "Emotive elements" and "emotive factors" as employed here and at various other points in this Essay include unconscious or subconscious aspects of affective, conative, appraisive responses as well as emotive meanings (awarenesses). Similarly, "cognitive elements" and "cognitive factors" include unconscious or subconscious aspects of sensory, perceptual, conceptual, designative responses as well as cognitive meanings (awarenesses).

[35] Pages 246-47.

the contrast of the factual and the valuative is assumed to rest upon a contrast of subject matters, a linguistic differentiation, or a difference in the modes of meaning or response occasioned by a particular sign or ascriptor. But even upon the last of these bases it is held only that terms and sentences are factual "if, when, and to the extent" that the meaning is cognitive, the effect appraisive. On this view, emotive elements are always present in (or in the activities which accompany) factual terms; and this does not necessarily signify that there are not also always or to some extent emotive elements in or with factual terms, cognitive elements in or with valuative terms.

Indeed, it seems probable that both cognitive and emotive factors are pervasively present in or with all sorts of responses which involve any degree of awareness. This may result in part from the fact that feeling is to some extent a function of the intensity of neural activity. An unusually intense response is apt to be attended by marked emotion or feeling; experimental studies show a positive correlation between the intensity of neural response and the strength of affective experience.[36] Any level of awareness may be a product of a corresponding level of intensity in neural response. The simplest sensory experiences are perhaps undifferentiated affective-cognitive events, and even the most complex processes of problem solving and judgment clearly involve both feelings and cognitions (here also for most part inextricably woven together in or as the flashes and flows of awareness) of agreement and disagreement, similarity and difference, completeness and incompleteness, and so on. Every response has some intensity which, insofar as it becomes conscious, is both felt and cognized.

The pervasive intermixture of emotive and cognitive factors appears to result also from differentiations within the nervous system which make possible some considerable measure of differentiation between such 'purely' intellectual pursuits, judgments, statements, and terms as those of the sciences, on the one hand, and such 'purely' creative activities, appraisals, sentences, and terms as those of the fine and applied arts, on the other. The central nervous system has developed primarily to take account of, and help make adjustments to, the external environment; the autonomic nervous system has developed to help integrate and regulate the more vegetative, bio-

---

[36] See "Fact, Value, and Meaning," *The Philosophical Review*, LIV (1945), 121 ff., especially footnotes 13, 14, and 15.

chemical processes and conditions within the organism itself. The cerebral cortex has become specialized to carry on the more strictly sensory, perceptual, conceptual, intellectual processes; the midbrain has become the special center for connections between the central and the autonomic nervous systems, and the thalamus the special center for distinctly emotional and affective behaviors and experiences. But even the most distinctively expressive and emotive activities (sign activities included) clearly operate through and are affected by sensory and cognitive 'channels' as well as through the more emotive centers; and the most distinctively intellectual or scientific activities operate by aid of drives and feelings which are in some measure centered in the thalamus and the autonomic nervous system. By their physiological and psychological conditions, the emotive and the cognitive are thus inseparably wed (except for abstraction) in their most highly developed and differentiated expressions as well as in their minimal occurrences.

In view of these considerations it seems probable that both emotive and cognitive elements are always present in the activities and experiences which occasion or result from both factual and valuative terms, sentences, judgments, adjustments—though the degree to which the emotive and the cognitive are present, and their proportion to each other, vary widely with the level of awareness and with the nature of the goals operative in the particular situation and at the particular time. At one extreme, signs occur almost wholly as expressions of feeling ("Ouch!" "Hurrah!" "Hail, hail, the gang's all here!"), and at the other extreme to state, designate, describe, predict cognitions ("It is water," "It is cold," "Water is H_2O," "The eclipse will start here at 2 : 31 P.M. on July 7, 1955"). And in dealing with any particular problem or situation—whether in, say, family life, artistic creation, or scientific investigation—the proportion in which emotive and cognitive elements are present varies widely from person to person and in the responses of even the same person at different times: in one person or in one instance the responses may be predominantly emotive and in another person or another instance predominantly cognitive. Moreover, it is possible, within limits, to develop such habits as will increase the degree to which situations are met by predominantly cognitive or predominantly emotive responses. But no matter how predominant one or the other may become, both are probably present in some manner and degree in even the most highly intellectual and the most deeply affective sign experiences.

Yet, must it be concluded that the physiological and the psychological mechanisms or processes through which facts and values are experienced necessarily enter into or affect the facts or values themselves or the terms and sentences by which they are designated or expressed? Is it not clear that with regard to the factual we can and frequently do strive to reduce—indeed to eliminate—all emotive elements from the reference of our terms and sentences? And if perchance we cannot or do not entirely eliminate the emotive from the statements and the processes by which we know objects, do not the successes of the sciences, technologies, and arts justify us in proceeding upon at least the hypothesis that the references and the referents themselves are not determined constituitively or essentially by emotive or other noetic processes or elements and that our formulations can be freed wholly or in increasing degree from any distorting effects which may result from the presence of such factors? Must we not, then, for clear and correct grasp of the situation, make a sharp distinction between the psychological and epistemological processes through or by which we know and the existential and logical relations to which our factual terms and sentences refer? On the other hand, is it not equally clear that in or with value judgments, sentences, and terms the emotive is always a determining factor, not only as an element within the processes of valuing and evaluating but also as a part—possibly the most basic and ultimate part—of the subject matter or referent which is expressed, assessed, and accepted as the final arbiter of choices among both ends and means? And is not this actually the situation with regard to all values, even though it be recognized that at least in the case of instrumental values the objects or relations involved are in some cases as existentially and logically independent of emotive factors as are any non-value facts and that at some phases of inquiry into and choice of values—even of the most ultimate ends—we can and sometimes do strive to be strictly objective, to discern actual causal continuities and to choose "objectively," "impartially," "in light of the actual conditions and probable consequences"?

An affirmative answer to the last two of these questions would appear, however, to presuppose that fulfillment of desire, pleasure, satisfaction, or the like is necessarily the final test or criterion of value, and, further, that any particular occurrence or moment of pleasure or satisfaction is final and cannot be 'tested' or 'corrected' by or in relation to other factors within a continuing experimental process of individual and social experience. That pleasure, satisfaction, or fulfillment is the essence or final measure of value may of course be questioned. Achievement, development, or the furtherance of cosmic purposes may be, or be conceived as, the basic and final determinant of value. When contribution, say, to public health or education or to scientific, philosophic, artistic, or technological creativity, is accepted as the yardstick of value, emotive elements may operate only *within* the processes of valuing and valuation, not as a part of the subject matter or referent of valuative terms and sentences. And whether fulfillment, pleasure, or satisfaction, on the one hand, or some nonemotive criterion, on the other, is accepted as the final basis of value and valuation, one must be peculiarly blind not to recognize that satisfaction (or whatever) does not, or at least need not, occur in isolation from a continuing life process in which factors of foresight and hindsight, and comparison of alternatives viewed and felt in long-run perspective as well as in their immediate appeals, can be utilized as test and corrective in the achievement of a maximum of critically examined and approved satisfactions or contributions.

But is not the 'acceptance' of any criterion or standard—even if it be social achievement or contribution to a cosmic purpose—an expression of wish, anticipated enjoyment, or attitude, in short, of an emotive factor or factors? Are not all valuations therefore unavoidably infected with and prejudiced by affection or volition, whereas factual formulation is able to escape from the effects of such factors? To answer affirmatively is, again, to overlook important considerations. For the acceptance of a criterion can result from a process of inquiry and interpretation which is primarily cognitive in aim and method. An interpretation as to what determines value (whether the factors are judged to be psychological, social, or/and cosmic) may or may not be correct, just as any judgment of fact, and especially a formulation of wide applicability, may be true *or* false—wholly or in some degree. But as long as the formulation is treated as hypothetical and held subject to change in the light of further evidence, its acceptance need not be more the result of emotive elements than is the acceptance of a formulation called "scientific hypothesis," "scientific theory," "scientific attitude," "scientific standard," or the like. Moreover, the acceptance (however firmly or tentatively, correctly or incorrectly) of the more general interpretations made in science does not prevent experimental making and testing of more limited formulations; and judgments of limited scope with regard to or *of* value are not necessarily dependent upon which criterion or standard is accepted nor upon its correctness. For example, in physics a bar of copper can be weighed, and the correctness of the weight for many practical purposes tested, regardless of the correctness or incorrectness of Newton's or Einstein's theories of gravitation. Similarly, the moral values (positive or negative) of stealing in a particular instance or the aesthetic values of a particular work of art may be considered and 'tested,' and the conclusions reached in the limited instance may be the same or much the same, whether the general criterion accepted is maximum satisfaction for self or others, contribution to social achievement, or furtherance of a cosmic purpose for, say, the development of some particular kind of personality.

So brief a discussion of the relations of emotive, cognitive, and other elements in knowing and valuing-valuation of course leaves much to be desired in both clarity and completeness. But to direct attention to the considerations mentioned is certainly more important than to present a supposedly "clear" analysis which concludes or assumes (prematurely) that value judgments, terms, and sentences are inescapably infected with distortive attitude or preference and are therefore essentially different in nature and ontological or logical status from factual judgments, terms, and sentences—an analysis which then acts as a mental block to prevent recognition of the actual and potential continuities between factual and valuative formulation and acceptance, or which serves as justification (rationalization) for not giving attention to the steps needed in order to develop and extend a more experimental point of view and procedure in dealing with problems of human goals and means.[37]

IV

When the distinction between the factual and the valuative is regarded as deriving from the contrast relation of facts and values,[38]

[37] The conditions for such development and extension are considered in *Verifiability of Value*, Chap. XII.
[38] See pp. 238-39, above.

it is clear that valuative terms and sentences are never translatable into or interchangeable with factual terms or sentences. In this relation of facts and values the referent of any valuative term or sentence is obviously different from the referent of any factual term or sentence. Apparently, the same factual referent can be designated by different factual terms or sentences, which can, when employed with the same designative intent, be mutually translated or interchanged; and the same valuative referent may be designated or expressed by different valuative terms or sentences, which can, when they occur with the same designative and appraisive intent, be mutually translated or interchanged. But a term or sentence (for example, "Water is H_2O") which is regarded as factual because it refers to or states, say, a physical fact, on the one hand, and a term or sentence (for example, "Beauty is good") which is regarded as valuative because it refers to, states, or expresses, say, a human value, on the other, are not by any stretch of the imagination mutually translatable, interchangeable, or equivalent.

When facts and values are viewed in the parallel relation and some terms and sentences are regarded as being factual and others valuative because of a differentiation which has taken place within language itself, the situation is less clear. Any object in the whole gamut of experienceable objects may be the referent of both factual and valuative terms or sentences. As noted before,[39] in the less close parallel relations, for example, "This is a table" and "This is a good table," the referents are evidently not the same. Even though the "object" referred to by each of the sentences is in a loose sense the same (the table), actually the referents are two different triadic relations among the table, the subject, and the sentences which occur; each sentence 'has' or is involved in one of the objects (one of the triadic relations). Apparently, each object may, when intents are the same, be designated by mutually translatable or interchangeable terms or sentences; one object, for example, "This is a table" and "This is called a table"; and the other by "This is a good table" and "This table serves well my purpose." In the closer parallels, however, it is often difficult or impossible to tell whether different terms or sentences—factual or valuative or both—have the same or different objects, the same or different intents and references. In some cases "This is a good table" and "This table supports weights

[39] P. 239 f.

up to 2,000 pounds" may be mutually and (for some purposes) fully translatable or equivalent, but with other intents not translatable or equivalent. When the intents, significative or/and nonsignificative, are the same, or insofar as they are the same, the referents of any two terms or sentences, whether factual or valuative or both, are identical and the terms or sentences are interchangeable, or equivalent. And since both factual and valuative terms or sentences can be used (use$_1$) or occur with reference to any and all objects, it appears from this standpoint that facts and values are identical as actual or potential referents, but different as language forms.

From the point of view that terms, sentences, judgments, and so forth are factual, only if, when, and to the extent that they have or produce cognitive meaning or designative response, and valuative, only if, when, and to the extent that they have or produce emotive meaning or appraisive (or prescriptive) response, it appears that by definition or by the nature of the distinction valuative terms or sentences cannot be translated into or interchanged with factual ones. The factual and the valuative are, so to speak, at right angles to each other—each is going or lies in a different direction, in a different dimension of signification$_1$, or experience and response. "This is a table" produces or accompanies a cognition or an expectation of certain sensory-perceptual responses if one, say, looks or feels in the right place or if a camera is set up under certain conditions and the film is properly developed and scrutinized. On the other hand, "This is a good table" produces or assists the expression of an attitude or commitment, produces or prepares a tendency or readiness to give this table a preferential status—that is, to accept it as effective for some purpose or to choose it rather than other tables.

But if, as seems patent, the difference of dimension in the meanings and the response effects of valuative as compared with factual terms and sentences should be fully recognized, it is equally important to make a clear distinction between the evidence by which we may determine or judge whether the mode of meaning and effect is cognitive-designative or emotive-appraisive and the evidence by which we determine or judge whether sentences such as "This is a table" and "This is a good table" are true, false, or in some degree probable. The mode of meaning and effect is determined by the kind of reactions which occur with or from the sign or sign complex:

the mode is cognitive-designative if the subject does expect an object with the properties designated or suggested by the signs; the mode is emotive-appraisive if the subject does give, or gets prepared to give, a preferential rank to the designated object. The truth or correctness of the signs is, however, quite a different matter, one upon which mode of signifying need have no bearing or effect. Whether this is a table, or is a good one, a student who needs financial assistance, or one to whom financial assistance should be given (or one to whom it is good to give financial assistance), is a matter to be determined—so far as it may be—by experimental operations which do or do not lead to anticipated effects. The testing of appraisive as well as of designative ascriptors is thus a continuing process which is or can be as essentially or basically cognitive as it is emotive in nature. In consequence, the logical and the ontological status of values is perhaps not different from the status of facts—whatever the status may be.[40]

---

[40] My views on the logical and ontological status of facts and values are indicated more fully in *Verifiability of Value*, Chaps. III, IV, X, and XI.

For the Comments and Response which relate to this paper see pp. 343-51, 359-61, and 391, below.

PART II: COMMENTS AND RESPONSES

COMMENTS BY ADAMS

Moore rightly contends, I think, that the structures embodied in language are "the skeletal character of the gross experience whence language evolved" and, therefore, that study of the language of values, indeed of any kind of language, must "penetrate beyond the stratum of mere rhetoric to the level of ... [its] nonverbal referent."[1] However, I disagree with what seems to be an underlying assumption to the effect that we can reflect upon and study the referent value situation independently of and unbiased by language. Although language structures reflect the structure of experience, the structure of the particular language employed determines the structure of experience upon which attention is focused.

Following the guideposts of value language, our author finds that the referent value situations are those in which an organism has an affective involvement with an object. Thus value subject matter consists of likes and dislikes, approvals and disapprovals, acceptances and rejections. His attention is then focused upon this subject matter through scientific descriptions and he concludes that there can be a science of it. The all-important question is the relationship of such a science to the value disciplines.

Moore assumes that "I like X" or "Most people like X," and so on, are value sentences since likes and dislikes, and so on, are the nonverbal value situations referred to by value sentences.[2] But this, I think, is not the case. I agree that the same element of experience may be a common referent for "I like X" and an appropriately worded value sentence, but this is not sufficient to warrant replacement of the value sentence with "I like X" or for considering "I like X" to be a value sentence. When we examine the common referent through "I like X," we find something different from what we do when we examine it through the "equivalent" value sentence. The language employed places it in a different relationship and attention is focused upon different aspects of the common referent.

I take this to be the valid point involved in the so-called "natural-

---

[1] Pages 9, 13. [2] P. 10.

istic fallacy" charge against such theories as Moore espouses. However, I disagree with the usual interpretation of the naturalistic fallacy as consisting of defining value terms in such a way that value sentences become descriptive in an ordinary sense and thus empirically testable for truth-value. My account of value sentences recognizes a distinctively axiological element which renders reduction of value disciplines to science wrong headed and yet permits empirical testing of value sentences for truth-value. This is, in a sense, naturalism without the reductionistic fallacy.

Moore seems to identify descriptive, empirically testable, and scientific sentences. On this I beg to disagree. I have, im my Essay above, distinguished between descriptive-explanatory and descriptive-justificatory sentences and tried to show that scientific sentences are the former and value sentences the latter, with both being equally descriptive and empirically testable.

Now for several finer points.

1. Throughout the Essay, Moore assumes that *approval* and *liking* are the same or at least very similar. In one place he writes, "when a person expresses linguistically his approval of an apple he is eating by saying 'I like it,' ..."[3] I think that approval differs in kind from liking and that failure to recognize the difference inevitably results in false analysis of several types of value statements, especially the ethical. Liking is simply a pro-affective response to an object because of what the object is perceived or believed to be. Approval involves a radically different factor, namely, a judgment to the effect that the object as perceived or believed to be measures up to or meets some standard of excellence and thereby is acceptable. It may or may not involve a pro-affective response. In fact, an object that is liked may be disapproved and one that is disliked approved. Approval, as thus conceived, involves as a constituent element a complex value judgment and, therefore, cannot be taken as primitive value data in the sense in which likes and dislikes may be so taken.

2. All moral valuing seems to me to be a matter of approval or disapproval and, if our analysis of approval is correct, it follows, contrary to our author, that moral valuing is not liking and disliking causally influenced by social pressure of the likes and dislikes of others of the society.

Furthermore, the characterization of a *moral* situation as one "in

[3] P. 10.

which the individual is being persuaded through his desire to live in accord with the desires and expectations of others"[4] does not do justice to ordinary usage according to which we say that certain persons who seek to alter the customary desires and expectations of the people of their society are *morally* motivated. Indeed, Moore seems to grant as much when he says "in broad outlines what is or has been in regard to human valuings may be a justified set of guiding principles."[5] Here he seems to be appealing to a norm that transcends the patterns of group valuings in terms of which such valuings are appraised and found *justified*.

3. "From the perspective of the participating organism," Moore says, ". . . the value situation seems a sort of polar arrangement with the organism and the gross sensory object as the two extremes of a continuous, though momentary, organic strand."[6] The so-called language of science describes "a focal node near the object end of the axis" and reflects the relationship of the object with other objects. "Value language," he contends, "is descriptive of what appears at a node near the subject end of the same polar line." Value phenomena seem to exist at the node between colors and tastes and the experiencing subject. Yet he clearly identifies value phenomena as likes and dislikes, approvals and disapprovals, and acceptances and rejections. It is difficult to see how acceptances and rejections fit into this account. They seem to be entities of quite a different order. Indeed approvals and disapprovals fit only if they are identified with likes and dislikes.

Moore speaks as though all phenomena at the node between colors and tastes and the experiencing subject were value phenomena. But there are such phenomena as tickles, pains and pleasures at this node which he does not mention and gives no indication that he considers them to be value phenomena. Are they value phenomena? And if not, by what criterion are value phenomena distinguished from them?

4. According to Moore, the referent of "I like X," or of any value expression, is a private, subjective element open to inspection only by the experiencing subject. A consequence of this is, as Moore recognizes, that "we are compelled to assume the perspective of the participating organism for descriptive detail." However, he maintains that it "may, through ordinary analogical procedures, be divested of a portion of its initial privacy and relativity."[7] Further-

[4] P. 20.   [5] P. 25.   [6] P. 11.   [7] P. 11.

more, in spite of this subjective interpretation of the referents of value sentences, our author maintains that value sentences are not only descriptive but scientific.

I must content myself with merely raising several questions: (a) Can there be a language in terms of which we can describe a purely private subjective element of experience? (b) If there could be such a language, would it not be a private language usable only for purely private purposes, for (1) how could we teach it to others or learn it from them, and (2) how could we communicate anything to others with a purely private language? (c) Could there be a criterion or test of correct private use? (d) If no test, then no correct use, and if no correct use, would there be a language? (e) Even if there could be a private language, would description of private data in terms of it be scientific, for do not scientific statements have to be publicly testable? (f) How can my private data be divested of its privacy by ordinary analogical procedures when there is no possible way to test the analogies involved?

5. According to Moore, "ought" is a verb and its referent is "a sort of field of force in which a person is subject to the structuring tendencies of a social norm."[8] And, although at a higher level it is persuasive and has a push and pull function, at its first level of functioning it is "factual, informative, descriptive, and scientific."[9]

It seems to me that ordinary grammatical classifications such as nouns, adjectives, verbs and so on are inadequate. We need the techniques and distinctions of logical analysis. "Ought" is a modal term like "is," "may," and "must." To classify "is" as a verb is not very enlightening for the purposes of logical analysis. There are several kinds of "is": (a) the copulative "is," which expresses class-inclusion, class membership, or identity; (b) the existential "is," as in "There *is* an X such that X is a man"; and (c) what I call the factual "is," as in "It *is* the case that snow is white." (b) and (c) are quite similar, differing only in that (b) concerns the *existence* of an individual and (c) the *being* of a fact. These terms certainly do not have referents like ordinary nouns, verbs, and adjectives. "Ought" seems to me to be akin to the factual "is," but of course quite different in certain respects. It occupies the same syntactical position in sentences. For example: "It *is* the case that Johnny is eating his spinach," and "It *ought* to be the case that Johnny is eating his

8 P. 23.   9 *Ibid.*

spinach." It expresses a contextual requirement or necessity that may go wanting, rather than simply factuality. Logical necessity is requirement for the logical objective of consistency; moral necessity, expressed by the moral "ought," is requirement for the moral objective, and so on. But it is not descriptive of a felt pressure or set of tensions so that if a person does not feel the pressure, an ought statement about his behavior is false. The moral or any other kind of requirement or necessity may obtain without being felt or recognized by anyone.

In conclusion, let me say that, although I have disagreed in general and in detail with his Essay, I think that Moore has made a considerable contribution to value theory by working out so carefully and stating so clearly the details and implications of an important point of view in the field so that we all, whether we see it his way or not, may better understand the position.

RESPONSE BY MOORE

Adams's first critical comment is to the effect that I seem to assume "that we can reflect upon and study the referent value situation independently of and unbiased by language."[10] I do hold both that value situations exist and that we may confront and, however crudely, study them *without benefit of any language use whatever*. Were this not so man could neither get started in this project of describing the value experience nor subsequently correct the errors that admittedly infect his descriptions. Adams's contention that "the structure of the particular language employed determines the structure of experience upon which attention is focused,"[11] conjoined with his apparent rejection of the possibility of studying a situation without the use of language, constitutes a linguistic determinism which, if it allowed any describing activity at all, would insure an incurable bias in any description, including his own. My view does not preclude the observation that linguistic descriptions once constructed may become frozen into habits of expectation which thenceforth tend to prejudice even the perceptions of their constructors. The corrective technique with regard to error so incorporated in our descriptions and habits is the checking of the description, and of its competitors, against the concrete situation of which it is supposedly a symbolic rendition.

[10] P. 261, above.   [11] *Ibid.*

Adams properly contends that scientific discourse is more than empirical description. My point was that a science is possible whenever data lends itself to such description; but, of course, the resulting description, even when verified, constitutes only the first storey of the scientific structure. I agree that this primitive data must be systematically organized and correlated with logical schema before we can call it a science in the full sense of the term. We are as yet, for the most part, only at the first level of science, and scarcely that, in the area of values.

Adams seems dubious about the possibility of even a language of subjective elements. I cannot argue the matter fully here but will simply say that in some sense we certainly do have a language of the so-called "private" elements of experience, even at the level of common sense. We are forever conversing with others about our aches and pains, our pleasures and hopes, all of which are as "private" as the affective component of the value experience. And, I maintain that for the other man's discourse about his toothache to have the sort of meaning the term would have for me I must think analogically. There is no test which can give absolute certainty with regard to such statements, I admit; but is there such a test for any empirical proposition?

Adams's basic disagreement with my account of the value experience is as to the character of the primitive value element. I say it is an affective response to an object, that is, as objectively described, a rejection or acceptance, subjectively rendered, a disliking or a liking of something. He believes that the term is properly applied only to an experience involving "a judgment ... that the object ... measures up to or meets some standard of excellence and is thereby acceptable."[12] Now I suppose that it matters little what we call these primitive affective responses as long as their existence is recognized and we have some theory as to their connection with the more sophisticated level of value experience with which Adams prefers to begin. I too recognize this more complex situation involving judgments of comparative worth and "standards of excellence." I recognize the operation of such standards of excellence as indicative of the moral component in a value situation, something over and above and logically independent of the purely affective factor. He, in turn, recognizes an affective factor in this more com-

[12] P. 262, above.

plex structure when he says that an object so judged may be thereby found *acceptable*. Adams tends to place overwhelming weight on this judgmental factor partly because his primary interest is in *moral* situations, which always contain such, and partly because in it he senses a component which can be shown to yield to a sort of cognitive treatment. Our differences here are more verbal than real.

I believe that a proper analysis of the moral situation will show that these "standards of excellence" have a natural origin. I admit that my original explanation of them in terms of "the desires and expectations of others" is too crude; but I maintain that it is these with which we may begin such an explanation. Ultimately, as I indicated in my paper, these standards may be shown to derive of the very structure of nature and of man as a part of it. This is as far as a science of such standards can go; but there is nothing in my theory to prevent a supernaturalist from attributing these structures of nature to the creative power of a Deity, immanent or external to nature.

Adams's criticism of my treatment of the verb "ought" is in part well taken. In spite of his little lecture on logic I still think I am going beyond grammar into the logic of the functioning of "ought"; but he does point out a weak spot in my treatment of the actual operation of the moral factor. I suggest that a situation is not moral except the person subjected to the ought factor *feel* coercion.[13] This is, of course, not the case. Adams is right in contending that a moral situation "may obtain without being felt or recognized by anyone."[14] I should have said that the "ought" symbolizes a situation which the speaker believes to be *potentially* coercive, and actually is so under certain specifiable circumstances. I cannot agree further, however, that the "ought" functions in a manner comparable to that of the "is" of existence. Such a position would seem to interpret the *oughts* of experience as unanalyzable primitive givens. I think that both my study and that of Adams show them not to be so.

[13] P. 17, above.   [14] P. 265, above.

COMMENTS BY MORRIS

THE PROBLEM of the interrelation between signs and values, and hence the relation of the study of signs and the study of values, is a growing concern among contemporary thinkers. One of the merits of Robinson's careful and rewarding analysis is that it forces attention upon the most fundamental aspect of this problem.

One can perhaps go farther: it seems to me that Robinson has indicated the correct relation of the two studies. On his view "value theory in general ... has its semiotical, its speculative, and its systematic aspects, and even its value-judgmental aspects ... It is concerned with the study of value-theoretical terms, with description of the things they stand for (whatever these may conceivably be), with speculation as to how these are related to each other and to anything else which the theorist may see fit to consider in the same context ... Moreover, as a body of theory, value theory includes many 'theories of values' or 'theories about value,' which may take any of these forms, singly or in combination."[1] Further, the theory of signs (semiotic) includes the study of signs in the theory of value, and this phase of semiotic he calls "semiotical value theory," "that portion of semiotic which is concerned with value-theoretical terms."[2] So conceived, axiology and semiotic are distinguishable studies (one a theory of values and the other a theory of signs), but overlapping (since the study of signs about values can equally well be regarded as part of axiology or part of semiotic), and mutually supporting (since the development of each would benefit the other). This position seems to me, in its larger outline, clear, straightforward, and defensible. Why then does Robinson terminate his paper with the statement that "the relations of value theory and sign theory are still in a tangle"?

This conclusion arises from a conviction that at detailed points both his procedures and mine are unsatisfactory. Now this may very well be, and certainly his arguments to show this deserve serious attention. But even if sound, they do not seem to me to negate the over-all relation of axiology and semiotic which has been outlined, and which

[1] Pages 39-40, above.   [2] P. 46.

Robinson and I apparently share. Where then do the specific difficulties arise, and why have they led him to the view that the general
situation is still confused?

Robinson is well aware of some of the weaknesses (as well as some
of the advantages) of starting ostensively with a list of value-theoretical
terms. But the main trouble with this procedure is that it provides no
criterion for determining whether a term does or does not belong to
the set. And it follows that the identification of the field of value
theory has whatever arbitrariness that the list of terms has. We might
of course say that a theory of value is any theory in which terms from
this list appear (perhaps adding that the theory is nonsemiotical if
the terms are used and semiotical if they are mentioned). Robinson
seems at times to take this tack. But in other places he makes it clear
that most, if not all, of the terms in his list are not always value-
theoretical terms, in which case the criterion for a theory of value
cannot be given by reference to the set of listed terms.

This indicates, it would seem, that Robinson is not simply basing
his analysis upon the list of value-theoretical terms, but is using in
addition a set of terms whose formal relation to each other is not made
explicit. To be specific, the relations of the terms "value-theoretical
term," "value theory," "value judgment," "theory of value," "theory
about value" to each other are not clear, yet at crucial points his
arguments rests on the relations of these terms, and not simply on the
set of ostensively exhibited terms. And since all of these expressions
involve the terms "value" or "theory" or both, it is these two terms,
in their unanalyzed state, that may be the ultimate source of his un-
certainties. Thus Robinson seems to have overlaid an apparently
ostensive approach with an implicit and undeveloped level of formative
axiological discourse. Perhaps his doubt as to whether his own discourse is primarily designative or formative reflects this situation.
The result, at any rate, is that in the "official" argument no demarcation
of the subject matter of axiology is given, and consequently the
relation of axiology to semiotic seems more nebulous than I think
his over-all "unofficial" position requires.

The point can be made clearer by considering his main objection
to my own analysis. Here the central point seems to be that semiotic,
at least as I have handled it, cannot make fundamental contributions
to the theory of value since it "presupposes" a theory of value in its
analysis of value terms. Now this argument would be clear if Robin-

son simply meant that any theory in which occurred terms from his list of value-theoretical terms is by that fact alone a theory of value. At times this does seem to underlie his contentions. Thus he says, "the important point is that in order to develop the theory of the appraisive and prescriptive modes, which is a contribution to pure semiotic, Morris has apparently taken for granted a naïve descriptive semantics of certain value-theoretical terms, which might well be considered a portion of second-level value theory, even if it is of a very rudimentary sort."[3] But that the issue is not so simple is brought out by the fact that Robinson himself distinguishes between the use and mention of value-theoretical terms; and while he does not say that the mention of such terms is essential to a theory of value (though a "convenient rule of thumb" to distinguish value theories and value judgments), it would seem that such mention is, on his approach, essential to second-level value theory since this involves names or descriptions of value-theoretical terms. But if this is so, the fact that I have used certain terms from Robinson's list can hardly be said to presuppose a "naïve descriptive semantics" of these terms, for this would require a mention of the terms. And since, as has been said, Robinson does not at the formative level of his discourse strictly define a theory of value as simply any theory which uses terms from his list, it is not clear that I have in any significant sense presupposed a theory of value (at any level) in my attempted analysis of appraisive and prescriptive modes of signification.

As far as I can see, the relation of semiotic to axiology is no different than its relation to any other study. Thus a semiotic analysis of certain terms in physics will certainly use (without mention) some other terms which occur in writings on physics, but this does not presuppose in any important sense the acceptance of a semantics of these terms nor the acceptance of any particular theory of physics. Mach's analysis of certain terms in classical physics did not dispense with all terms in physics, nor did it involve an acceptance of classical physics. And although his analysis was in turn relevant to the further development of physics it did not in itself supply a physical theory. The relation of the semiotical analysis of certain terms in existing value theory to the possible further development of value theory seems to me precisely analogous.

[3] P. 50; see also p. 53.

Response by Robinson

Morris has put his finger on what I hope are the most serious flaws of my Essay. When I wrote the preliminary version I thought I could show that his treatment of semiotic did "presuppose value theory" in an important way and that this was something of a scandal. His own earlier comments led me to refine this position, but not enough.

It is true that many terms in my list have senses which I do not want to call "value-theoretical," so that even if the presence of value-theoretical terms were sufficient to show the presence of value theory, the mere presence of terms from my list would not be sufficient. It is also true that even if Morris were using these terms in unmistakably value-theoretical senses, this would not *prove* that he is employing a descriptive semantics of them on the second level of value theory unless he is mentioning them by their names.

I still feel, however, that his usage of such expressions as "needs," "in order to satisfy," "preferential status," "requiredness," "purpose," "motivates," and so forth, is good *indirect* evidence that he is tacitly employing some definitional conventions for the use of these terms which could be made explicit without mentioning them. So it does not seem far-fetched to say that while he is not *providing* a descriptive semantics for them, he is still *presupposing* it, both in the sense that he is assuming these conventions and in the sense that they require a more penetrating analysis than they have as yet received. I also feel that he is using most and perhaps all of these terms in senses which I like to call "value-theoretical," and that their definitions thus have a place on what I have called "the second level of value theory." I have not succeeded in showing *precisely* why I want to describe them this way; but even if this is only my own idiosyncrasy in using the term "value theory," it still reflects a considered opinion as to what kinds of problems belong together.

I am not quite sure what Morris has in mind in distinguishing between my "official" and my "unofficial" positions, for I had supposed that my attempts to show how I use such expressions as "value theory" and "value judgment" were just as "official" as my ostensive definitions of "value-theoretical term," "valuative term," and so on. The ostensive definitions perhaps look more impressive because I have presented them more systematically. But in both cases I am presumably operating on what Morris calls "an implicit and undeveloped level of formative axiological discourse," just as I think he is doing, and none of my definitions is more than a partial approximation. At any rate I have taken pains to give examples of some things which I would *not* want to call "value theories" or "value judgments,"[4] while in my ostensive classification I have used only positive examples.

Morris is distressed to find that after describing the relations between sign theory and value theory in a way he is so generous as to defend, I still wind up with the complaint that these relations are in a tangle. I feel, however, that there is no inconsistency in accepting the "larger outline" of which he approves, and being dissatisfied with its details. In this case my "larger outline" certainly shares the murkiness of the expressions which occur in it, such as "value-judgmental aspects," "value-theoretical terms," and "theories of value." But of course the vagueness of these expressions need not indicate that sign theory and value theory are in any way intertangled. On the other hand, I think one finds a real entanglement when one considers the *languages* of sign theory and value theory and asks how they are related. This question can hardly be given a final answer until both languages have been formalized; and even then the answer would still be an artefact of whatever conventions of formalization have been adopted, and would have to be revised for each alternative set. Now Morris has sketched out a definitional system for sign theory without trying to formalize it, and I have proposed an even less ambitious classification for some of the terms of value theory. I have gone far enough, however, to show that some of the defined semiotical terms of his system seem to include nonsemiotical value-theoretical terms in their *definientia*. This suggests that either value theory and sign theory (as presented by Morris) share certain primitives, or that at least some of the primitives of Morris's sign theory are definable in value theory. In the absence of proper formalization, however, we cannot tell which is the case. And while I now see that when I claimed to find a tangle in the relations between sign theory and value theory, most of the reasons I cited were strictly irrelevant to that issue, however relevant they might be to others, I still feel that this entanglement of language is important enough to justify my claim.

But is this a scandal? At first I thought it was; for I was bemused by Morris's own early suggestion that semiotic might turn out to be an "essential organon" for philosophy and the sciences, and I took

[4] See p. 37, above.

for granted that it must accordingly be independent of them both in its assumptions and in its basic vocabulary. By the time I had finished the present version of my Essay, this sense of scandal had diminished, but it was still with me. I now think I was mistaken. I not only recognize that every science is in part a semiotical science, but I doubt whether any *pure* semiotic can be developed at all adequately without including conceptions from other sciences, especially psychology and perhaps even value theory itself; I doubt whether any organon for the sciences could be useful if it should preserve such rigid independence as I at first envisaged; and I like the things Morris says about physics at the end of his Comments.

On the other hand, I feel that the relations between sign theory and value theory are still problematic in ways which neither I nor any of the contributors to this volume has adequately faced. What, for instance, can we expect *pure* semiotic to contribute to value theory? It can of course remind us that there may be important psychological and sociological causes for our choosing the symbols we choose and combining them as we combine them; it can warn us to be sure that we know what our symbols mean to ourselves and what they are likely to mean to others; it can make us more careful to distinguish between tautologies, empirical generalizations, expressions of personal preference, and simple nonsense; it can provide us with methods for formalized system-building; it can help us to remember that what is undefined or unproved in one system may well be definable or provable in another; it may eventually enable us to classify different kinds of value-theoretical language in useful ways. This is a good deal, and value theory might be in a sounder and less interesting condition today if these things had been given more attention. But is this all that semiotic can do for value theory? And what can value theory do for semiotic? I have shown that it may contribute part of the basic vocabulary for at least one semiotical system; but will this be equally basic for *all* such systems? And can it perform other services which I have overlooked? Here the relations between sign theory and value theory may not be in a tangle, but I think they are still obscure.

COMMENTS BY McGREAL

With Morris's contention that one can find out "by objective methods the signification which a sign has for an individual or a group of individuals," I thoroughly agree. The method he specifies is in every important respect similar to one I have suggested in "The Third Man," and his analysis of the signification of the word "good" is in substantial agreement with my own.

Although I am not convinced that the kind of investigation Morris undertakes is necessary if the problem is that of determining the signification of a word as common as "good," I believe that his attempt to make philosophy more responsible scientifically may turn out to be an important contribution to contemporary philosophical method. With some care the experimental method might be used for the resolution of many perplexing semantic problems involving words somewhat less common than "good."

My main objection to Morris's Essay, then, has nothing to do with his method in general, or with his hypothesis concerning the signification of "good" in particular, but concerns the particular experimental situation he has constructed in the attempt to discover the signification of "good."

Morris's procedure was to show colored reproductions of paintings to various subjects and to ask them to indicate how much they liked each picture and to rank the pictures numerically. These ratings were called "P-ratings (preference-ratings)." "The subjects were told explicitly that they were *not* to judge a picture *as a work of art*."[1] Then the subjects were asked to appraise twenty of the pictures "as works of art" by the use of such phrases as "It is very good" and "It is somewhat bad." Such ratings were called "A-ratings (appraisal-ratings)."

Morris hoped by this procedure to find out "the relative strength within a group of persons of the preferences and appraisals of various items" and to compare "the consistency or discrepancy of preferences and appraisals in individuals and in groups."

[1] P. 61: italics added.

I suggest that to compare P-ratings to A-ratings, it would be necessary to have the subjects make P-ratings of a certain set of entities *considered in a certain respect* under controlled circumstances, and then to have the subjects make A-ratings of the same set of entities, under the same circumstances and *in the same respect.*

Morris's experiment, however, seems to nullify itself by controlling the situation in such a way as to guarantee a change of factors which makes comparison impossible! The subjects were told to indicate preferences but *not* to judge the paintings as works of art, but then told to appraise the paintings *as works of art.* It is not surprising, then, that Morris found that those subjects who made appraisals by adopting a subjective criterion achieved a correlation of .67, while those who appraised the paintings by objective criteria achieved only .43. If I were asked to rank paintings on the basis of which appealed to me quite apart from any consideration of the possible effect of the paintings on others, and then asked to appraise the paintings, I should expect a high correlation if I appraised them on the basis of their appeal to me quite apart from any consideration of the possible effect of the paintings on others, and a low correlation if I appraised them on the basis of which would be most likely to appeal to others.

Had the P-ratings and A-ratings been made concerning the same set of objects considered in the same respect, there would have been no problem of attempting to explain "both the positive correlation between the A- and P-ratings and why the correlation is not higher." As Morris established the experimental situation, the correlation was as high as it was because the subjects were indicating their preferences for paintings *present to them* and were therefore not likely to have been mistaken in supposing the paintings *capable of sustaining a preference*—which is what I suggest (with Morris) is what is implied by the word "good." *The correlation of P-ratings and A-ratings increases as ignorance of factors preferred decreases.* That is, as a person comes to know more and more about the features relevant to his preferences, he is less likely to be mistaken in asserting that the object having the preferred features is good, on account of those features, to him.

Another reason the positive correlation was as high as it was is that many of the subjects acquainted with the paintings appraised on the same basis they preferred; it was not higher because not all the subjects appraised the paintings in the same respect they preferred them.

I agree, then, with Morris's account explaining why the correlation was not higher, namely, that "the need which is involved in a preference-rating of an object may not be the same need, or the only need, which is controlling the appraisal-rating of that object."[2] But I do not agree that this is a *result* of the experiment; rather, it is a *description* of the circumstances under which the experiment was conducted. According to Morris's report, the directions to the subjects were such that the subjects were not required to appraise in the same respect they preferred, but rather encouraged to rate the paintings on the basis of preferences not determined by a consideration of the paintings as works of art, and then to rate the paintings on the basis of appraisals determined by a consideration of the paintings as works of art. Only if one were inclined to judge paintings as works of art on a subjective basis, then, could a positive correlation result.

Morris's statement that "the correlation was positive because to like an object is to find it satisfying"[3] should be amended to read that "the correlation was positive because to like an object *when acquainted with the features relevant to one's liking* is to find it satisfying" *or* "the correlation was positive because to like an object is to *regard* it as satisfying." And the statement that "objects which have this property [that of satisfying] are in general appraised positively"[4] should be amended to read that "objects which satisfy are in general appraised positively *provided* that the appraisal is made on the basis of the capacity of the object to satisfy, that is, to sustain a preference." In other words, if a subject appraises objects on the same basis which leads him to prefer some to others, he will appraise positively those he prefers. I should think that ordinary experience offers ample evidence to support this inductive generalization, but I have no objection to adding to the confirmatory evidence by experimentation.

The difficulty with experimenting to determine the signification of "good," however, is that it would be embarrassing to ask subjects to make P-ratings of objects not known to them, or known only in respects *not* relevant to their preferences. The experimental situation might alter the language habits of the subjects, either by distracting them or by forcing them into the kind of reflection that does not always accompany their use of the word "good." Yet unless one can compare the correlation of P- and A-ratings when relevant features of the objects rated are *not* known with P- and A-ratings when the relevant

[2] Pages 68-69.   [3] P. 68.   [4] *Ibid.*

features *are* known, one cannot show that P-ratings are not A-ratings, or that P-ratings do not always have a high positive correlation with A-ratings when both ratings are made on the same basis. Persons in *nonexperimental* situations often prefer certain objects to others and appraise them positively only to discover, as knowledge increases, that the objects capable of arousing and sustaining a liking are not always those initially preferred. P-ratings, made in ignorance of relevant features, *stand*; if an object is liked, it is true that it was liked even though it may turn out that the object was bad at the time of the liking. Yet A-ratings *fall* if an object once liked turns out to be incapable of sustaining that liking, that is, if the original preference was based upon the belief that an object had a character it did not have.

Morris's conclusion that "there is a tendency for persons to prefer and to appraise positively paintings which symbolize a situation that would satisfy their constitutional needs, that is, which portray a situation of a sort that is congenial to themselves," seems to me to be in effect a statement meaning that persons tend to like what they like. If it means more than this, it means that Morris is prepared to show a relationship between certain constitutional types and features of objects which persons of those types prefer. This is an interesting and useful result of his inquiry, although I am not sure that it is philosophically relevant to the problem of determining the signification of "good."

It would be interesting to me if Morris were to conduct a similar series of experiments to show the bearing of knowledge of factors relevant to preferences upon P-ratings and A-ratings. I believe that he could justify a probability generalization that not all expressions of liking or of value signify value, but P-ratings of objects known in the respect preferred have a very high degree of positive correlation with A-ratings of objects known in the respect appraised, provided that the P-ratings and A-ratings are made of the same set of objects considered in the same respect. The correlation of P-ratings of objects *only partially known* in respects relevant to the preferences with A-ratings of objects *known* in respects relevant to the appraisals would probably be low.

RESPONSE BY MORRIS

I would first like to add a few words amplifying my own report.

The correlation of .50 between the P-ratings and the A-ratings was obtained by simply correlating the items of one set with the corresponding items in the other set. This is not the favored statistical procedure. When the correlation between the two sets of ratings is computed for each individual separately, and these results are then averaged in the way appropriate to correlations, the correlation for the original group of subjects turns out to be .59 instead of .50. Similar procedures for two other groups gave correlations of .65 and .64. The average for the three groups is .63. This, then, is the figure to be explained.

Further, my paper raised a doubt in several readers whether the A-ratings were not in fact just another set of P-ratings, the difference being due simply to experimental error. However, an analysis of the mean differences in P-ratings given by the same subjects at two different times proves to be statistically significant (at the .01 level) from the mean differences between the A- and the P-ratings themselves. The variations from the mean differences (that is, the standard deviations) in the two cases are appreciably different (.11 in the first case and .36 in the latter). Hence the indications are that the two sets of ratings, from a statistical point of view, are genuinely different.

The implication of McGreal's Comment seems to be that this difference, and the order of magnitude of the correlation between the two sets of ratings, can be explained in terms of the experimental setup itself, so that they are not so much results of the study as descriptions of the experimental conditions under which the study was made. He then suggests another set of conditions under which the correlation of A- and P-ratings would be expected to be very high. The issues thus raised are of methodological importance. For while of course one expects differences of results under different experimental conditions, if one can predict the results of any particular experiment solely on the basis of the experimental setup itself (whether the one I followed or the one McGreal says I ought to have followed), then the experiment in question is scientifically worthless. I do not believe that either of the procedures in question is of this nature, nor that McGreal's procedure is the one which it is "necessary" to adopt.

McGreal's basic criticism is that my instructions to the subjects forced them to consider the paintings *in different respects*: in one case as works of art in the other case not as works of art. This he believes insured that the two set of ratings could not have a very high positive correlation. Hence I should have forced the subjects to P-ratings and A-ratings of the same objects "considered in the same respects."

I am not sure that I fully grasp what is intended by "consideration in the same respects," and so I may fail to do full justice to McGreal's position. But suppose the procedure recommended to be something of this sort: the subjects are first asked to indicate how much pleasure they get in looking at each picture (or how much pleasure they would get if they looked at each picture as long and as often as they wished). They are then asked, with respect to the results of the above consideration alone, to give two sets of ratings of the pictures, one indicating how much they like a picture, and one indicating how good it is. In this modified procedure both ratings are made solely with respect to the pleasures obtained in looking at the pictures.

What results are to be expected? McGreal presumably believes that a high positive correlation would be obtained. This may well be the case. But the result could not be predicted solely from the experimental setup. For it might be found that for some persons (some Kantians and Buddhists perhaps) the correlation was negative, that is, degree of liking might be linked with amount of pleasure, but capacity to stimulate pleasure be taken as a sign of badness rather than goodness. Or some persons (some Aristotelians perhaps) might be found who rated paintings which gave a moderate pleasure as very good, but rated paintings which gave either very much or very little pleasure as bad. In terms of our general knowledge of persons we might not expect such results very often, but the expectation is not based on the experimental setup alone.

Similarly, I fail to see how the results I found were prejudged by the form of the experiment itself. Some persons did in fact appraise the paintings as works of art solely in terms of how much they liked them, and it is conceivable that all the persons studied might have done this. But some did not, and to varying degrees. Such possibilities could not be ruled out in advance. They depended on the persons and not on the procedures. It seems to me, for these reasons, that the results of my study need "explanation", and that such explanation cannot be given simply, or even primarily, in terms of the experimental design.

As I see it, both my procedure and McGreal's suggested procedure are methodologically respectable. But I do not see why it is "necessary" to adopt his method, and I see good reasons for not ruling out mine. In science measures of objects based on one criterion are frequently found to be correlated with measures based on another criterion. It may be the case that the two criteria in question require consideration of different aspects of the objects being measured. To insist that only the same aspects be used might make impossible the very application of the two criteria as these normally are applied. I do not see why this possibility should be ruled out a priori in the study of the relation of liking to appraising.

All of this is not to say that the procedure actually used is the only one or that it might not be improved. On these points McGreal's suggestions for controlling the knowledge factor are valuable, and I hope that future workers in this field will take them into account. Also I quite agree with him that the use of scientific method in semiotical studies (including the semiotic of appraisals and prescriptions) may be more valuable for other problems than for the investigation of the generic signification of the term "good." In this connection I would like to call attention to the important experimental procedures of the psychologist Charles E. Osgood, first outlined in his paper "The Nature and Measurement of Meaning."[5] They seem to me to open wide the door of experimental semiotic.

[5] *The Psychological Bulletin*, XLIX (1952), 197-237.

COMMENTS BY LAFLEUR[1]

1. Pepper draws a clear distinction between quality of value and quantity, and asserts the priority of quality. As a matter of logic, this is no doubt true: a quality must exist before there can be more or less of it. However, as an empirical distinction, its practicality is less obvious; and, in many cases at least, it is difficult to imagine a definition of quality which would not strongly suggest a standard of quantity. It would not be easy to define "mass" so that we understand the meaning of that term, and yet would not know what would be meant by saying that one object was more "massive" than another; and even more difficult to define "height," without shedding light on the meaning of "higher." Much the same thing may be true, it seems to me, of value terms. Are there cases, however, in which this is not true? We might suggest "size," where the size of an object might be measured as its length, its volume, or its perimeter, and Pepper argues that this is true of pleasure, which may be measured in terms of its intensity, duration, or the number of individuals involved. Where such questions can arise, however, it appears more likely that the definition is defective, and that greater precision as to the quality meant would leave no doubt as to how the quantity was to be measured. There is an obvious lack of precision in saying that one object is large, without specifying whether we are talking about a linear dimension, area, or volume. Similarly, Bentham's early phrase, "the principle of the greatest happiness of the greatest number," was ambiguous; and he later made clear what he meant by this term and revised it accordingly to read "the greatest happiness principle."

Pepper maintains that "an indefinite number of standards can be applied to a defined field of values."[2] If "field of values" means something other than a specific value quality, then it may be that a "field of values" must be defined first, after that a value within this field, and only finally a standard of quantity. This analysis is exemplified in instances where we define ethics or aesthetics before we define "good" or "duty," "beauty" or "art"; but if the illustration of

[1] Laurence J. Lafleur, University of Akron.   [2] P. 79.

painting, used in the article with which we are concerned, is considered, it will be observed that the specific painting is an object rather than a field of values, and is not a proper illustration of the latter. No object can be measured until we determine what quality of it is to be treated quantitatively. To use Pepper's own terminology, the object asserted to be of value has "characters" and each one capable of being quantized leads to an intrinsic standard. This identification of object and value is misleading unless, in the case in question, the object has only one character, or if a large number of characters all have a perfect mutual correlation. But if there are several characters imperfectly correlated with each other, then the definition is ambiguous, and what is required for a proper definition is the isolation of a single character, or of an object which possesses no more than one independent character.

2. When Pepper's description of value, either in its original form or as it might be modified according to the suggestions already stated, is taken as a definition of value, it is unsatisfactory for at least one reason, and, if Pepper's own doubts are justified, possibly for two. Using Aristotle's description of definition, every definition should assert a genus which includes all the instances of the entity defined and differentia which exclude all entities which are not instances of it. Now I believe that the present definition specifies a genus correctly, in that it does include all instances of value, despite Pepper's own doubts as to whether there might not be instances of value which are purely qualitative. However, it fails completely as far as differentia are concerned, for it does include instances which are not values, and these in excessively great numbers. For any characteristic which is quantitative in nature fits the given definition, and by far the greater number of adjectives represent qualities of this sort. We conclude then that Pepper does a service in pointing out that value is always quantitative, but misses a most important point by failing to elucidate how we are to decide which of a number of quantitative items are values.

3. Pepper asks the question as to how a definition can be kept from being arbitrary and irresponsible. To this he offers a three-fold answer. First, a definition must be correct semiotically. Second, the definition must be descriptive, or indicative of fact. This excludes such definitions as a square circle, which can be excluded on a priori grounds, and those, such as pink elephants, which are empirically

discovered to lack a field of reference. Third, the definition must not be irrelevant. I think this third requirement is not itself basic, and that the fundamental rule is rather that the definition must not lead to confusion on the part of those using the term. Thus it is permissible to define in any way a term which has not been in use before; or an old term may be used in a sense which is not seriously modified from its previous usage. But when an old term is used in a totally new meaning, or even in a meaning which is in contrast to the original one, the definition is irrelevant in Pepper's sense, and an irrelevance is intolerable because it leads to confusion.

4. That control over definition is achieved by a field of reality is a *sine qua non* of true knowledge: for if we take the position of Protagoras, it necessarily follows that knowledge is impossible. So far I agree with Pepper; but I must add that this control need not be empirical in the more limited usage of that term. Intuition, revelation, and so forth would be equally satisfactory, and choice between these various methods by which the object may determine knowledge must be made in the light of considerations other than those pertinent to this article. As a consequence of the writer's limitation of control to empirical control, all his illustrations are of an extrinsic nature: this decision is good in reference to this terminal goal, or this technique advantageous for a man who wants to be president. But this treatment, suitable only to extrinsic values, leaves no answer available to the question whether terminal goals are good except on psychological or sociological grounds, and these can only affirm that such terminal goals do actually exist. The ethical question cannot be answered in this way. No doubt many terminal goals exist: our problem is to choose from the number of actually existing goals those which we maintain to be ethically good.

Response by Pepper

Let me comment on Lafleur's four criticisms of my treatment of evaluative procedure seriatim:

1. His first criticism seems to be an assertion of some lack of precision which arises in the clear-cut distinction I made between qualitative and quantitative criteria in discourse. There are some instances in which the definition of a term refers directly to a quantity and not to a quality—as, for instance, a definition of "height" or "size."

And this fact would be serious, he suggests, if value were intrinsically such a quantitative entity, as perhaps it is.[3]

First, I cannot see that this outcome would be a serious objection. The definition of a quantity, on the above assumption, would simply reveal a quantitative standard at once without the intermediate step of first demarcating a quality. And obviously the quantity would be an intrinsic standard, since this is all that is referred to in the definition.

But, second, I question if the definition of a quantity ever does avoid the quality out of which the quantity is generated. For in order to differentiate one quantity from another some qualitative difference must be specified. Granted that "height" is a quantity. This quantity has to be qualitatively distinguished in some way from "depth," for instance, or from "volume" or (to get out of space relationships) from "duration" or "brightness," or "loudness," or what you will. Whatever the qualitative differentiation which defines the distinction between "height" and these other qualitative terms, that would be, I should suppose, the qualitative criterion of differentiation, whereupon it would be immediately clear that what was differentiated was a quantity thus differentiated from other quantities. So, I do not see how a qualitative definitional criterion could ever be avoided in discourse even when the entity defined is itself a quantity.

But Lafleur goes further and suggests, if I follow him aright, that a precise definition of a quality would never yield more than one quantity. Thus the quality "size" might confusedly be thought to generate a number of intrinsic quantities such as "length," "volume," "perimeter." But when the term is precisely defined, "length" is one defined quality and "volume" another, and they are qualitatively(!) distinct quantities. And so, too, apparently with pleasure. Confusedly, a hedonist might think that pleasure generated two or more quantitative differences such as intensity and duration. But precisely discriminated and defined, pleasure intensity is one quantity and pleasure duration another and these are qualitatively(?) distinct. Analogously, he would have to say the same, I should think, of the intensity and duration of sound.

Such a complete qualitative atomism, of quantitative distinctions, if this is what Lafleur means, would constitute an hypothesis with difficulties of its own. But all I should want to say here is, that music, for instance, in fact builds up rhythms in which variations of intensities

[3] P. 281.

and duration are mutually essential to their patterns. The rhythmic patterns in fact depend upon both quantities interweaving. Even if the two quantities are qualitatively separated for sound, they cannot be separated for music. And so too for pleasure as it operates in patterns of human conduct. The intensities and durations of pleasure interpenetrate in human decisions, and are not separated as mutually insulated evaluations. When the hedonist defines value as pleasure, he defines a term which varies quantitatively in at least these two mutually interdependent ways—in degrees of intensity and degrees of duration such that men will in fact choose a less intense pleasure because it is more durable, but would acknowledge that a more intense pleasure that was also more durable would be even better. That is to say, the qualitative field within which these evaluations occur for the hedonist is one in which these *two* quantities operate in conjunction. To define the field even more narrowly might seem theoretically more precise (if indeed it is psychologically justifiable), but it would be false to the actual procedure of hedonic evaluation. And the same *mutatis mutandis* for any other quality defined as a value quality besides pleasure.

So, I do not think Lafleur's first criticism holds up.

2. His second criticism is to the effect that my "definition ... does include all instances of value [but] fails completely as far as differentiae are concerned, for it does include instances that are not values."[4] My reply is that I was not defining value at all, but only attempting to show an empirically responsible procedure for evaluating values. References to defined values were only illustrative.

3. Lafleur's third criticism takes exception to what he takes to be my requirement of a responsible definition of value that it "must not be irrelevant." This is a misunderstanding for which my verbal expressions may well be to blame. My demand of relevancy was in respect to the quantitative standards applied to objects defined as values through a qualitative definitional criterion. I did not intend to suggest that relevancy was a property of the definition itself.

Or is Lafleur here referring to my method for anchoring a definition in the tradition or usage for the term defined by employing a common sense definition as a test definition for the rough location of the field of application? But this device is only a convenience and not an intrinsic requirement of a definition.

4 P. 282.

4. The fourth criticism suggests that my use of "empirical" is unjustifiably limited. Lafleur invites me to admit "intuition, revelation, and so forth" as equally satisfactory methods to determine knowledge. He intimates that only extrinsic values come to light by my empirical limitations, and that intrinsic values are revealed only by such hyper-empirical cognition.

I am afraid I must be content with what he calls extrinsic values, then. For I have no confidence in unempirical conceptions of cognition. Moreover, I have great confidence in the empirical procedure and believe we shall find values and valuations in the end as open to empirical testing and verification as any complex field of human and cultural relations.

If, by chance, Lafleur means to imply that the empirical approach can yield only instrumental evaluations, and cannot yield evaluations of better or worse among ends, my answer is that such has not been my own empirical observation. I find selective systems operating in the consummatory field itself. Whenever a person adjusts a radio for the optimum reception of some music he enjoys, there is at work a selective system maximizing consummatory enjoyment. This is not a selection of a means fit to produce an end, it is a selection of a greater as against a lesser terminal satisfaction. If terminal satisfactions are intrinsic values, as usually asserted, my empirical method reveals these and evaluates them as easily as it does the extrinsic values.

COMMENTS BY FEIGL[1]

IN WHAT SENSE can value judgments be justifiably declared true (or false)?[2] Questions regarding the value of something arise more frequently and more importantly in the case of disagreements in *preference* rather than in the form of simple dichotomy between good and bad. "Better" or "worse" as dyadic, asymmetrical (and, as is often too complacently assumed, transitive and connexive) relations are to provide a rank-order of degrees of goodness. Certain comparable kinds of food, pieces of music, works of art, types of conduct, forms of government, and so forth, may thus be subjected to ordering on respective scales of preference.

The question of the truth or adequacy of such rank ordering can be settled responsibly only if we have some criterion, or a set of criteria, with respect to which the preferences can be consistently decided. The consistency may be purely subjective and short-lived; it may be communal and more permanent; it may be (humanly) universal and temporally unlimited. I submit that the criteria of factual truth (in the sense of high degree of confirmation), though neither universally accepted nor in any given case completely precise, are usually not called into question when a specific truth claim is disputed. "Is this really true?" is a question that is almost always concerned with the strength of the evidence for the proposition in question. It is thus directed toward further scrutiny of the evidence in the light of tacitly presupposed (and accepted) criteria of confirmation. When we reject a special hypothesis, for example, the Lamarckian doctrine of the inheritance of acquired properties, we do so without even giving a thought to the possibility that some day we might revise the very principles of induction and probability, and thus arrive at an entirely different estimate of the validity of the hypothesis under consideration. Such possibilities have, however, been envisaged

---

[1] Herbert Feigl, University of Minnesota.
[2] This central question is the primary concern of the present critical Comments on Adams's Essay. Some other related issues will be dealt with more briefly—because of limitations of space.

theoretically (as in the logic of induction)[3] and practically (as in the doubts raised by G. Spencer Brown)[4] regarding the statistical demonstrations of the reality of parapsychological phenomena. I mention these matters merely in order to avoid the air of dogmatism that so often surrounds the claim that the scientific method rests on a unique and precise set of criteria. I shall not pursue here the intriguing question, what sort of rational justification could be given for the preference of one set of criteria, or basic rules of inductive probability, over some other.

In any case, I do think that scientific disputes ordinarily concern questions of evidence, such as of adequate experimental controls, randomization, sampling, and so forth; and that these questions presuppose a (usually) tacitly and unquestioningly accepted frame of principles or criteria of validation. In striking contrast serious value disputes quite frequently call into question the very criteria of value. Here, then, we have just the opposite situation. The question "Is this really good (or better)?" frequently expresses uneasiness regarding the criteria or the definition of these value predicates. To be sure, if there is agreement on the criteria themselves, value disputes will reduce to purely factual issues. "Is democracy better than fascism?" is a decidable factual question, provided we mean by "better" some empirically confirmable aspect in the social consequences of one or the other form of government. This is clearly the case in all questions of purely instrumental values. But instrumental values presuppose terminal values—and disagreement regarding terminal values will invariably be reflected in disagreement regarding the norms of valuation. This is obviously the case where the terminal values are matters of taste. Now, I would be the first to insist that it is a mistake to assimilate disputes regarding the criteria of morality to disputes concerning tastes. Nevertheless, there are countless examples of moral disputes which involve fundamental disagreements in the very conceptions of justice, of kindness, of honesty, of self-realization, and so forth. The definition of these key-terms leaves a great deal of leeway for various emphases. By way of *persuasive definitions*[5] or

---

[3] See R. Carnap, *The Continuum of Inductive Methods* (Chicago, 1952).
[4] "Statistical Significance in Psychical Research," *Nature*, CLXXII (1953), 154-56. This reference to Brown's ideas does not necessarily express agreement with his critique of statistical method.
[5] C. L. Stevenson, *Ethics and Language* (New Haven, Conn., 1944), pp. 210 ff.

redefinitions we may change or shift the factual-empirical focus of these normative terms and thereby influence, direct or redirect attitudes or mold dispositions. The motivative function of language depends upon the emotive significance which can in principle be distinguished and by abstraction detached from the factual connotation of the terms in question. We use the expression-appeal function of language or the emotive significance of terms just as much in influencing others as ourselves. In those silent soliloquies in which our consciences (super-ego, ego-ideal, introjected parental or communal authorities) issue their approvals or disapprovals, encouragements or discouragements, we use language of the self-motivating kind, essentially akin to pledges, vows, or resolutions.

It is important to realize that not only clearly normative terms like "right," "wrong," "justice," and so forth, but also teleological terms such as "satisfaction," "happiness," "welfare," and so on, are open to persuasive definition. It is one of the prominent techniques of the practical moralist or the moral educator to advocate a certain type of conduct by the use of such phrases as "true satisfaction," "real happiness," "genuine welfare," and so forth.[6]

The definition suggested by Adams of the "ethical interest" in terms of the *good will*, that is, "an interest which has for its object the maximum net satisfaction of all relevant interests in any given situation," is open to a number of critical questions. As already suggested, the term "satisfaction" may be (persuasively) defined in a variety of ways: The satisfactions of the puritan are different from those of the cavalier; those of a Christian different from those of a Nietzschean, and so on. Similarly open to various persuasive definitions is the term "relevant." Presumably "relevant" in "relevant interests" connotes (possibly among other meanings) morally justifiable interests, interests to which those who have them are actually entitled by the facts of the situation and in the light of some

---

[1] Philosophers should realize that the definitions they give of their enterprise by such phrases as, "Philosophy really is . . .," "the true task of philosophy is . . .," and so forth, are also persuasive in that they use the time-honored word with its strong positive emotive appeal (though negative perhaps for hard-boiled practical people) in order to propagandize their own point of view. If this is done candidly and explicitly, confusion and false pretense can be avoided. Disagreements may then be returned to the proper arena of cognitive discussion—that is, inquiries can be made as to what consequences are entailed by this or that delimitation of the business of philosophy.

principle of justice. This may be denied by those who, possibly like Adams, believe that deontological (normative) judgments are completely reducible to teleological (purpose-interest, means-ends) judgments. I do not argue that such reduction is impossible, but I would insist that it can be achieved only if among the interests-to-be-satisfied we include such interests as those in the compliance with moral norms. To illustrate by an example: If in a joint enterprise it is agreed that the gains are to be distributed among the participants, it may be judged morally wrong if those who contributed more effort to the success of the enterprise received a smaller share than those who contributed less. The interests to be satisfied here are then not only those of the participants but also the over-individual interest in fairness or equity.

Now, it is obvious, the conceptions of justice, both distributive and retributive, vary tremendously from culture to culture. In order to apply such a term as "morally good" or "morally right" with any semblance of empirical meaning, it is indispensable first to specify that meaning to such a degree that utter vagueness is avoided. Nobody reasonably expects that these concepts could be so sharply defined that they could serve as criteria for the decision of every and any moral dispute or quandary. But one would expect—from value empiricists—a definition of (say) "better than" which achieves in the moral domain roughly what the ordinary definitions of "warmer than" or "heavier than" achieve in the physics of everyday life. The meaning of the relation "more just than" in an aristocratic ethics differs so sharply from the meaning of the same expression in a socialist ethics that definiteness can be achieved only if it is explicitly stated *which* conception of justice is used. If "warmer than" were to have a similar degree of vagueness or ambiguity as "more just than" it would have to be permissible and correct on occasion to say that ice is warmer than boiling water.

Concluding this part of my argument I submit that the neo-utilitarian criterion of morality formulated by Adams is doubly persuasive: it is open to a variety of factual interpretations, each of them capable of being motivationally proposed by applying one or the other empirical connotations of "satisfaction" and "relevance." But even if there were no vagueness at all in these terms, that is, even if there were complete agreement on their precise meaning (a truly utopian assumption!), then there would still be the motivative

appeal of the definiendum "morally good" which renders the definition inescapably persuasive. Can we convince people who do not
want or do not care to be morally good that they *ought to be* morally
good by purely cognitive (logico-empirical) arguments? We can call
them "morally insensitive," "morally irresponsible," "morally insane,"
and so forth, but we would be merely begging the question if we
thought we could thereby protect our own standard of morality
against external criticisms.

In short: if one means by "moral norm" any sort of (prescriptive)
rule of conduct, then one is free to speak of the moral norms of
cannibalism, Nazism, gangsterism just as much as of those of Con-
fucianism, Christianity, or Humanism. To do justice to the more
customary sense of "moral norm" it would seem advisable to restrict
its meaning to rules of benevolent and/or equitable conduct. And
by a further step of persuasive delimitation one will have to focus
more sharply the meaning of "benevolence" and "equity." In view
of the great variety of possibilities even in this last step, it is difficult
to be sanguine about *one* unique meaning of "morally good."

It has become the fashion at this point to turn the tables on the
logical empiricists by pointing out that the criteria of rational
knowledge are equally open to persuasive definition. What we call
"justified belief," "sufficient evidence," "highly confirmed," depends
(as already briefly hinted above) upon certain definitions of *inductive
probability*. Some have gone so far as to say that the choices which
in principle underlie the very frame of cognition are themselves
ethical in character, and that therefore science is really based upon
ethical decisions rather than the other way round. This way of
putting the matter seems to me, however, to be seriously misleading.
Knowledge in the sense of reliable foresight as a guide in life, is
needed equally by saint and sinner, by the decent citizen as well as
by the hardened criminal. The criteria of reliability are therefore
morally neutral. Moreover, all ethical judgments presuppose reliable
knowledge regarding the relations of attitudes to actions, and of
actions and their practical consequences. Nevertheless, I think it
should be admitted with equanimity that such key terms of cognitive
criticism, as "rational," "reliable," "justified expectation," "reasonably
sure," and so forth as well as their antonyms carry emotive appeals
in a way quite analogous to the emotive appeals of the terms of
moral criticism. Once this is realized, the whole issue of justification

appears in a new light. If by "justification" one means giving reasons
for the holding of certain attitudes or for the conforming to certain
rules of action, then indeed justification must at least implicitly
appeal to purposes (goals, aims, ends)—and this sort of justification
is what I label "vindication." The insane or feeble-minded, or even
the emotionally strongly biased sort of person cannot be convinced
by purely cognitive (logico-empirical) arguments to adopt different
standards of "reliable" belief, just as in the moral domain only
persuasion, reeducation, psychotherapy, and so forth may be effective
(if, indeed, anything can be effective at all) in changing deeply
entrenched attitudes.

The purely cognitive content of our empirical beliefs may therefore
be delimited in a more radical way than has been customary hitherto.
To the extent that beliefs (generalizations, hypotheses, inferences,
theories) depend on a criterion of confirmation which is only one in
a variety of alternative possibilities, the decision which criterion to
employ may well rest on value judgments. The content of empirical
knowledge may then be limited to observation protocols on the one
hand, and (analytic) statements regarding the degree of confirmation
bestowed upon inferential statements by their respective evidential
grounds and by virtue of (one or the other) definition of degree of
confirmation. To illustrate: whether it is rational to believe in the
existence of extraplanetary flying saucers, of psychokinesis, of a
designer-god (in the sense of the teleological argument), and so on
and so forth, may depend in principle upon a *decision* or a choice
between alternative conceptions of inductive probability. I say, "in
principle," because in practice there is a large measure of agreement
among scientifically oriented people regarding the goal of empirical
inquiry, and accordingly a high degree of unanimity as to the criteria
of reliability (that is, the definition of degree of confirmation or of
inductive probability). Also, it has been shown by Carnap that
alternative possibilities in the continuum of inductive methods, or
at least those which belong to the interval of "non-perverse" methods
lead in the long run (mathematically, in the limit) to equal appraisals
of probability.

It might be said that similarly in the ethical field the "normal,"
"sane," criteria of valuation are essentially agreed upon by all reasonable people. But, waiving the possibility that this is a flat tautology,
the reasons outlined before make it plausible that there is much

more room for alternative principles of morality even within the common "decent," "normal," "reasonable" frame than there is in the case of principles of inductive probability. To be sure, if for example, someone were to tell us that within *his* system of ethics it is entirely permissible to slaughter young babies in order to eat their delicate flesh, we would send either for the police or the psychiatrist. But there is a good deal of disagreement among "reasonable" people as to whether children should be given a religious education, as to whether euthanasia is permissible, about capital punishment, as to our obligations to the aged, the mentally insane, "outgroups" of various sorts, future generations, the dead, animals, and so forth.

To the one who holds certain moral ideals, these ideals may appear so self-evident that he considers anyone who disagrees seriously with him as immoral. Moral intuitions and convictions may, however, be no more than the precipitates of habits and customs. The socio-psychological fact of the plasticity of human nature, of the flexibility of our adjustments and the changeability of our goals and ideals, cannot be denied. Moral norms are dependent upon and in this sense relative to human needs and interests. Only when, owing to a high degree of social interdependence and cooperation in a certain group, the major goals and purposes have come to be fairly common to all concerned can we find moral principles which will be equally commonly accepted and effective.

I shall add only very briefly a few remarks on subsidiary points. While adhering to the empiricist criterion of meaningfulness, Adams thinks he can construe value judgments as empirical though not scientific, because scientific statements are descriptive-explanatory, and value judgments only descriptive. This seems to me to be irrelevant to the major issue as well as mistaken as an analysis of scientific statements. It is irrelevant because—as I have been at pains to point out in the preceding pages—the descriptive meaning of value predicates does not establish their typical valuational significance. And it is mistaken in that some branches of science may well be primarily descriptive, as, for example, physical geography, spherical astronomy, paleontology, and so forth. As long as the idiographic statements in these disciplines are ascertained by scrupulous scrutiny of the relevant evidence, we generally call them "scientific," although they are singular (not general) propositions or truth-functions of such singular propositions.

I am inclined to agree with Adams that the term "justification" means primarily and most customarily the process I called "vindication" or "pragmatic justification." By justification in the sense of validation I had in mind *proof*—deductive or inductive-verificative. Inasmuch as vindication involves deductive and/or inductive reasoning, it relies upon standards of validation. But vindication goes in any case beyond validation in that it depends upon reference to purposes. I contend that axiological truth is relative to the purposes which must be adduced when we vindicate any specification of the empirical meaning of value terms. The content of descriptive knowledge is *information*, no matter whether it concerns the location of a mountain, the birthrate of the U.S. in 1953, or the motivation of a moral reformer. The significance of a moral value judgment consists in *more* than its empirical content; the stamp of approval, the accent of endorsement, the force of encouragement, in short the motivative appeal is part of the life process itself, and while, as such, open to empirical study, is not by itself anything that could conceivably be true or false.[7]

RESPONSE BY ADAMS

The point of these remarks is to clarify my distinction between scientific and value statements, which Feigl has misunderstood. He says that I contend that "scientific statements are descriptive-explanatory, and value judgments only descriptive." This distinction, he argues, is irrelevant to the major issue because "the descriptive meaning of value-predicates does not establish their typical valuational significance." Furthermore, he says, it is "mistaken as an analysis of scientific statements ... in that some branches of science may well be primarily descriptive."

In the first place, instead of maintaining that value statements are only descriptive, I *explicitly state* that they are *descriptive-justificatory*. I stress the point that value and scientific statements differ not by the former's being nondescriptive and the latter descriptive, as is so often maintained, but rather in that the former are justificatory and the latter explanatory. Indeed I agree with Feigl that the typical valuational significance of value predicates is not to be found in their descriptive meaning, which can be expressed by

[7] For a fuller presentation on this point, see my article "Validation and Vindication," in W. Sellars and J. Hospers (eds.), *Readings in Ethical Theory* (New York, 1952).

"equivalent terms" (having the same referents) of the descriptive-explanatory language, but rather in their justificatory dimension. The same property may be selected and designated by terms in both the descriptive-justificatory and descriptive-explanatory languages. However, being designated by a term from one language places the property in a set of conceptual relationships different from that established by being designated by a term in the other. Therefore, there are statements (particularly ought-statements) entailed by some predicative value statements that are not entailed by "equivalent" statements of the scientific language; at least they are not recognized to be entailed by the statements of the scientific language, because the language employed indicates the pattern of conceptual relationships to be considered. This is why I emphasize the point that the primary difference between value and scientific language lies in the fact that one is justificatory and the other explanatory rather than with respect to the descriptive dimension.

Also the charge that I am mistaken in considering scientific statements to be descriptive-explanatory since some sciences are primarily descriptive seems to indicate that the point intended has not been made clear. Although some sciences may merely describe, we consider them to be relatively undeveloped while we consider the more explanatory-predicative ones to be more advanced *as sciences.* This, I think, supports my thesis that the objective of scientific inquiry as such is descriptive-explanatory knowledge. Furthermore, I maintain that governed by this descriptive-explanatory objective (at the common sense level as well as at the more advanced, refined levels of special disciplines), man develops a particular kind of language or set of concepts. Any statement formulated out of these concepts, although it may be completely lacking in the explanatory dimension and thus merely descriptive, is what I have called a "descriptive-explanatory" or scientific statement.

COMMENTS BY FINGARETTE

McGreal has attempted to make a marriage. The locale of the ceremony is the area of value theory. The bride and groom are, respectively, a representative monistic, "essentialist" account of how to determine the significance of a word, and a representative pluralistic, "semanticist" account. The marriage, I believe, is essentially sound and destined to last, although I suspect that Jean Monodogma's family may disown her. As arranged by McGreal, both parties retain, on the whole, their individual integrity along with their discovery of a basic compatibility. This much is a substantial and constructive achievement.

There remain, however, some unsolved difficulties for the newlyweds in their personal relationships, and it is these difficulties which give me the most concern.

In order to perform this marriage, McGreal has had to propose answers to three questions in such a way that both parties would be satisfied. I would like to consider, in turn, the three questions, the proposed answers, and the difficulties which remain. It will help to have the questions and answers before us in brief form at the start of our discussion.

1. *Question:* How is the significance of a word determined?
   Answer: This depends upon the interests of the "third man," that is, the person doing the study of the word's significance. There is not any one, essential significance for each word.
2. *Question:* What have most philosophers been interested in, then, when studying the significance of such words as "good," "real," and "beautiful"?
   Answer: They have been interested in discovering the "usual causal significance" of these words.
3. *Question:* What, as a result of inductive inquiry, does the "usual causal significance" of "good" turn out to be?

> *Answer:*   When "X is good" is uttered by a person A, it prob-
> ably signifies that X is such that if, under certain
> specifiable circumstances, A were to have knowledge
> of, or about, the entity X, he would favor it.

I shall first comment on the "third man" thesis, the thesis that
there is no one significance of a word but rather that its significance
depends in part upon the interest of the individual philosopher
studying the word.

From the logical standpoint, it is true that the student of symbols
may be interested in any relationships which the utterance of a word
may have to anything else. As a matter of historical fact, students
of symbols have had a variety of interests. But this thesis can be
very misleading unless it is pointed out—as McGreal does not—that
the interest of the philosopher in studying a word is neither arbitrary
nor ultimate.

I may say here that I think Jean Monodogma is untrue to her
heritage in admitting—indeed, volunteering—that the criterion of how
to determine the significance of "good" is the interest which anyone
happening to study the word happens to have. I am not a member of her family, but I would myself accuse her of giving up too
much.

There is no law, it is true, against being interested in stamp-
collecting or against being interested in, say, word-emotion relationships. Both are in the class of innocent hobbies. Interests in these
become philosophic, however, when the interest is related to some
larger purpose. The moral philosopher is interested primarily in
human, value problems. Only secondarily is he interested in the
technical questions which he hopes will help him to solve these
original problems.

If I am correct in supposing philosophy to be more than an innocent, if technical, hobby, then the basic criterion of how to determine
the significance of a word is not the interest of the philosopher. The
criterion is the instrumental efficacy of a particular analysis of
"significance" in achieving these larger purposes. The interest of the
philosopher, while relevant, is not final, and is itself instrumental.

I should, perhaps, make clear that I am taking the word "interest"
to refer to a wish or a desire. There is another usage in which we
speak of "what is to a person's interest." In this latter sense, I would

agree that the criterion of how to determine the significance of a word depends on what is *to* the philosopher's interest. In this case, however, the method of determination of the significance of a word is instrumental to the achievement of some larger, philosophic purpose, not to the satisfaction of a single or arbitrary wish.

McGreal's second thesis—that what philosophers have been for the most part interested in is the "usual causal significance" of the word "good"—is, I believe incorrect. I shall offer here only two considerations in support of my view. The first has to do with the words "causal significance" and the second with the word "usual."

I am inclined to think that most philosophers have been interested in the function of such words as "good" and "right," whether this be causal signification, incitement to action, elicitation of choice, expression of choice or wish, or anything else. Of course, should causal signification turn out to be a function relevant to some philosopher's inquiry, then the question of *what* is signified would become a prime question. However, I can think of one brief way to support my suggestion that causal signification by itself is not what philosophers have been primarily interested in. I would simply note that there is a long tradition in moral philosophy of holding that when we are talking about values, we are not merely describing what exists or what might exist. To put it positively, we are talking normatively. Now we need not here make pronouncements upon the correct analysis of "normative." It is enough to note the very existence and persistence of debate on this issue. This debate is evidence that McGreal is on uncertain ground in stating without weighty support that *most* philosophers have been primarily interested in causal significance when studying such normative words as "good." But, in addition, if one has to speculate, it seems to me much more plausible to suppose that most philosophers have, rightly or wrongly, felt strongly that the whole impulse behind normative language is the desire to deal with something which is other than, or more than, mere description. If this is so, then to say that most of them have been interested in causal significance is most implausible.

The second consideration which persuades me that McGreal's analysis is incorrect has to do with the word "usual." I am not at all sure that most philosophers have been looking for the *commonest* causal significance of the word. Philosophers have often been quite contemptuous of the common usage of such words. Indeed, what has largely spurred them on in their work has been their feeling that the common usage is inadequate.

A philosopher's asking "What does 'good' really mean?" is in some ways like an orator's asking "What does 'America' really mean?" The point of the question is that we are not interested in what the word most commonly is used to signify, whether this be the geographical area or the formal political institutions. We want to refine the usage and also to some extent *make it anew*. Philosophers' questions are aimed at a critical, creative treatment of usage, not an anthropological survey of usage. Needless to say, the latter can provide some data relevant to, but not decisive for, the philosopher's quest.

There remains for comment in the brief space remaining, the third question proposed by McGreal: What, finally, is it that is usually causally signified by the word "good"? While, as I have already indicated, I do not believe that this is what most philosophers have been primarily interested in, it is pertinent to ask whether McGreal has given us the correct answer to this question. I do not think he has.

Certainly many persons have at times used "good" to signify what, with or without qualifications, is favored by someone. Perhaps a smaller number of persons have held to the more restricted usage where "good" signifies what is favored by someone on the basis of knowledge. Yet, surely many, probably a strong majority, have used the word to signify not what is favored but rather what conscience or God demands. The demands of conscience, even when disregarded, *may* be interpreted as instances of favoring, but it is in no sense correct to say that God's demands are such. What biblical commandments and doctrinal rulings require of us is often not favored. In any case, the whole point is that whether or not one favors what they require of us, whether or not one even comprehends their justification, is irrelevant to the goodness of that which is required. Nor will an empiricist be much impressed with any verbal dialectics to the effect that God and conscience only demand of us what we ourselves would favor if we knew as much as God.

There are, of course, still other uses of "good," and I do not think that restricting the poll of usage to "confident" usage, as suggested by Jean Monodogma, would help matters much.

I am personally very much in sympathy with the sort of usage suggested by McGreal, and I think it is common enough. But it is not the most common usage, and even if it were, this would not have been what settled my sympathies.

If I have seemed to be the pessimistic uncle in this marriage, it is only because I feel that McGreal has done such a clear and genial job of matchmaking as to require no additional rooters to assist in bringing the two together. There is, indeed, in the Essay a good deal on which I have not commented. In most cases, it is because I find myself accepting and enjoying both the impulse and the execution.

RESPONSE BY McGREAL

In his Comments on my Essay, Fingarette responds to my thesis that the significance of a word is relative to the interests of a "third man," a student of signs and symbols, by maintaining that "this thesis can be very misleading unless it is pointed out—as McGreal does not—that the interest of the philosopher in studying a word is neither arbitrary nor ultimate." He claims that interest in some kind of significance becomes philosophic "when the interest is related to some larger purpose," that "the *moral* philosopher is interested primarily in human, value problems" (italics added), and that "only secondarily is he interested in the technical questions."

Since the major point of the Essay is to show that no one interest in signs has unqualified priority over other interests, I have certainly ruled out the idea that a philosopher's interest can be "ultimate." As to the suggestion that I have not ruled out the thesis that the philosopher's interest is arbitrary, I can only respond by saying that it seems to me that his interest *is* arbitrary in the sense that for any philosophic concern there are a number of equally legitimate philosophic concerns which might have been adopted instead.

I do not believe that a semantic problem need be related to some "larger purpose." The question "What does 'good' mean?" can be a philosophic question even if one does nothing with the answer. And I do not believe that the existence of a larger purpose makes a semantic problem philosophic. If what Fingarette desires is the use of the adjective "philosophic" to qualify "interest," he may have it, but he should use it himself to qualify "larger purpose." The engineer of applied philosophy is no more a philosopher by nature than any other moralist. His interest in a "larger purpose," even if the purpose is philosophic, is arbitrary in the sense that some other concern might have reigned instead.

When I had Jean say "I believe that I am interested in the kind of significance which interests most philosophers," I had Sam respond by saying "How rash of you to say so!" The contention that most philosophers have been interested in discovering the defining character of those entities usually denoted by a word was a rash contention because it is difficult to prove and because most philosophers have an unverified theory about the same matter. Nevertheless, I think that Socrates had this interest, that Morris has it, and a number of philosophers in between! Fortunately, Fingarette joins me in being rash. He notes that "there is a long tradition in *moral* philosophy of holding that when we are talking about values, we are not merely describing what exists ... we are talking normatively."[1] Fingarette seems to think that if we talk normatively we cannot be talking with words whose significance can be discovered by the kind of investigation Jean outlines.

It seems to me that what *moral* philosophers (that is, philosophers of morality) think or do is only partly relevant to a question about what most philosophers think or do. Furthermore, a long tradition in moral philosophy proves nothing but that traditions can be long. There is a sense, of course, in which we are never *merely* describing when we use value terms; we are always describing for a purpose. But we do not always talk normatively when we use value words unless "normatively" means "in a manner concerned with values." And even when we are talking normatively in the attempt to persuade others to adopt courses of action which do not yet exist, there is a sense in which we are describing: in using the word "ought" we are describing the situation as one in which something is not being done which is such that things would be better if it were done.

Fingarette maintains that most philosophers have not been looking for the "commonest" causal significance of words. On the contrary, most philosophers feel that "common usage is inadequate." Fingarette claims, therefore, that "philosophers' questions are aimed at a critical, creative treatment of usage."

I agree that philosophers have been interested in refining language, but to refine one must start with raw material, and the raw material of language is the language of common usage. An unqualified

[1] P. 298; italics added.

question such as "What is goodness?" makes sense because we suppose that the word "goodness" is related to "good" in its broadest and most common sense. If it is not, the question is meaningless (to me) and functions merely as a rhetorical prelude to somebody's construction of a new meaning for the word "good." Such artistic endeavors are not philosophical, although many persons have supposed them to be so.

Fingarette believes that my definition of the word "good," as that word is usually used, is not correct because "many, probably a strong majority, have used the word to signify not what is favored but rather what conscience or God demands." This is the third intrusion of moral matters into a problem having to do with the semantic analysis of "good." Perhaps there are circles of devout persons in which the word "good" is exclusively applied to such obscure matters as "what conscience or God demands," but in the world I have known in which the word "good" is applied to carpets, pies, beer, lustful activities, and so forth, what appears to be common to these varied things and activities, insofar as they are good in the common sense of "good," is their capacity to arouse and sustain a liking in somebody; they are such that if tried, they satisfy; if known, they are favored. If Fingarette does not like, approve *morally* (at least), what God demands, I cannot understand why he regards those demands as indicative of the good.

In effect, Fingarette criticizes my view concerning the relativity of significance, my contention as to the concern of most philosophers, and my definition of the common sense of "good" because I have not declared that *moral* efficacy is what justifies philosophic concern, that *moral* (normative) usage and not common usage has interested most philosophers, and that "*morally* good" (demanded by conscience or God) usually has the same significance as "good."

While eager to reassure everyone that I am not opposed to morality, provided it is philosophically disciplined, I must add that the problem of specifying semantic methods applicable to the analysis of value terms is *not* a moral problem, although some moral problems might finally be resolved because of the application of the results of semantic inquiry.

COMMENTS BY LEE

G ARNETT's Essay is a fine piece of work—clear, concise and well argued. It raises an important problem for ethics and for value theory; namely, the problem of the relation between the definition of value and the concept of obligation. It is not for me to disagree with Garnett's position that the definition of value is not to be given in terms of obligation. I would go even further and say that neither is *moral* value to be defined in terms of obligation. To suppose that it is would be to identify ethics with deontology. Ethics must take account of deontology, but I would not agree that it is to be identified with it. I have argued that moral value is not to be differentiated from other species of the genus value by reference merely to obligation, but that nevertheless a rational standard operates within the field of moral value.[1]

There may be a wide difference in semantic usage between Garnett's Essay and the present Comments. It is possible that what Garnett calls "ethics," I call "deontology"; and what he calls "value," I call "moral value." I do not see how he fits aesthetic value into his general scheme of value theory when "valuable" is equated with "good." It seems to me that the terms "reasonable" and "enlightened understanding" are not essential or definitive of aesthetic value. His definition, using these terms, is of something narrower than value in general.

Garnett's Essay raises in my mind some very fundamental questions the answers to which are not apparent; first, how much of what he says can be generalized to apply to all kinds of value; and second, what is the relation between the problem of obligation in ethics and the problem of standards in the general theory of value. The discussion of the second question depends upon that of the first.

---

[1] See "Ethics as Hypothesis," *The Philosophical Review*, LVI (1947), 645-55. See also "The Differentia of Moral Value," *The International Journal of Ethics*, XLI (1930-31), 222-29.

Although Garnett rejects so effectively the contention that obligation is the distinguishing and essential characteristic of value, he nevertheless seems (on a superficial reading, and in so far as "good" means "valuable") to leave the impression that ethics is the core of value theory. I do not think that it is. At least as good a case can be made out for the contrary contention that aesthetic value is the value *par excellence,* and that aesthetics is the core of value theory. My criticism here may be due, however, to my different semantic usage of "ethics."

Many of the papers in the present volume, as well as many of those in its predecessor *Value: A Cooperative Inquiry,* seem to make the implicit assumption that ethics is the center of value theory. In so far as this is the case, it offers the basis of my major criticism of both volumes. Much of Garnett's Essay in the present volume is directly concerned with what I would call ethics, as distinguished, for example, from aesthetics. If it cannot be generalized to apply to all kinds of value, then it is a study in ethics and not in the general theory of value.

In spite of my judgment that much of Garnett's Essay is concerned primarily with ethics, it must be noted that his own definition of good can (with only slight modification) apply to value in general; and furthermore, that most of the definitions in his first three types are stated in very general terms. The strictly ethical terms occur not in the definitions but in their discussion. Both the statements and discussions of the last three types are mostly in ethical terms. The reason for this is obvious: "obligation," "right," and "wrong" name peculiarly ethical concepts.

This brings me to the second of the fundamental questions posed in the third paragraph of the present Comments. It seems to me that the way that Garnett fits a standard of obligation into the moral scheme can be regarded as a special case of the way that standards in general can be fitted into the general scheme of values. We can define moral value, recognize and even attain it without obligation. Any ethics that defines the good in terms of pleasure or in terms of eudaemonia or in terms of harmony does so. But we may also recognize the obligatory nature of some sorts of conduct, and the fundamental obligation—the source of all moral obligation—to be reasonable, to control our action in accordance with enlightened understanding. As soon as we acknowledge the obligation of being reasonable, that very acknowledgment modifies and affects our recognition and attainment of moral values. Without reference to a standard such as the obligation to be reasonable sets up, there is no basis for preference of values except that given in the differences of intensity. With a standard, however, a more intense value that does not fit into a reasonable scheme is to be rejected in favor of a less intense one that does.

The interaction between intrinsic and instrumental values in the moral scheme is governed by the obligation to be reasonable. Moral obligation often demands that immediate values be sacrificed for instrumental ones; but such sacrifice cannot be made, much less demanded, except in the light of a rational knowledge of cause and effect. Instrumental values bulk larger in our day to day choices than intrinsic values. It has even been challenged that there are any intrinsic moral values, but maintained instead that all intrinsic values are aesthetic. Be this as it may (and I do not argue it), there is and can be no obligation to choose an act or object of instrumental value except in the light of a rational standard. The existence of the standard modifies all the values in the field. Whatever has a value might not have the kind of value it does except in the light of the standard; and the standard exists and is relevant even if any particular person does not recognize and acknowledge it. Choices of objects or acts which have some degree of positive value may nevertheless be evil if they (the choices) are made by persons who refuse to be or are not reasonable who are too unenlightened, stupid or perverse to know or care what is best for them in the long run.

On the other hand, although standards operate in our aesthetic valuations as they do in our moral valuations, they are of a different kind. The standard in our judgments of beauty is the reference to type. Judgments of type are not built up from a demand to be reasonable, but from habits of perception. There is nothing obligatory in habits of perception: they simply are the way that they are. Furthermore, all aesthetic values are intrinsic, and enlightened knowledge of cause and effect, although not wholly irrelevant, is not determinant. Complex standards of taste are built up, and strongly influence what we actually find beautiful in any specific case.[2]

Although aesthetic standards are neither composed nor do they operate as do moral standards, nevertheless, they fit into the theoretic

[2] See my *Perception and Aesthetic Value* (New York, 1938), Chap. VIII, Taste.

understanding of the experience in a parallel fashion. Thus, I hold that, although Garnett in his Essay is talking primarily about what I mean by ethics, what he says can be generalized to apply to the whole of value theory. His argument, thus, that the norm or standard is not to be included in the basic definition of the good can be generalized and find application in fields of value other than moral. The standard is never irrelevant, but enters into our understanding of the field as a further complication after the fundamental nature of the value is determined.

The problem of standards in any field of value is complex, and to attack it directly at the beginning of the investigation of the experience of value issues in no fruit except the fruit of confusion—philosophical poison. The nature of the value should first be tentatively determined. This value, however, is subject to the impact of the standard when that is determined. I am not suggesting that we first have an experience of some sort of pure value which subsequently is modified by our application to it of a standard. Of course not; but in our attempt to understand experience, we must be analytic, and our understanding is in terms of our analysis. There may be and probably is no adult *concrete experience* of values wherein reference to a standard does not explicitly or implicitly operate. I do not see how we could analyze from concrete experience the factor of standards unless it were there to be discovered. In our concrete experience of values, we find the nature of the value, the standard of judgment and the way that the standard impinges on the simple value in order to produce the concrete experience. This is the progression toward understanding the experience of values.

When Garnett, toward the end of his Essay, slips into the language of Ewing, and talks of "trivial and non-elevating (though innocent) pleasures, which may be good though not obligatory," he is calling attention to values that are not determined by the standard. The words "trivial," "non-elevating," "innocent" are question-begging, however, if there is no standard. Here we have values which, although they do not conflict with the standard, are nevertheless not beholden to it. Yet the very language in which they are described is language of the standard. This is an example of the complexity of the concrete value experience and an illustration of the principle that it is out of this concrete experience that we analyze the terms of our understanding.

RESPONSE BY GARNETT

I should agree with Immanuel Kant that the function of ethics is to answer the question "What ought I to do?" It may be defined as "the theory of obligation or duty." But, since our obligations are largely, if not entirely, concerned with values, ethics has also to answer a great many questions concerning what is good or bad, and its inquiries become involved in the general theory of value. I should insist that "moral value" cannot be defined without reference to obligations, although a decision as to the degree of moral value attaching to an act must take cognizance of other considerations besides the mere fulfillment or nonfulfillment of obligations, for example, the motives and the difficulty of the choices involved.

Lee raises the question as to how aesthetic value may be fitted into a scheme of value theory if "X is good" means "X is an object toward which enlightened understanding tends to develop a favorable attitude." The difficulty he finds is due to the fact that "the terms 'reasonable' and 'enlightened understanding' are not essential or definitive of aesthetic value." The definition therefore seems to him to refer to something narrower than value in general.

The reply to this objection is that, though these terms are not involved in the definition of "aesthetic" they (or synonyms) are involved in the definition of "good" and "value." "Good," as I have defined it, is a relational character which is no part of the definition of the things, or abstract qualities, or classes of things, which may be said to have this relational character. "Value," in the abstract sense, is equivalent to "goodness." In this sense value is the character of being an object such that enlightened understanding tends to develop a favorable attitude toward it. Aesthetic value is the character of being an object that does this by reason of its aesthetic character. Moral value is the character of being an object that does this by reason of its moral character. Hedonic value is the character of being an object which does this by reason of its hedonic character. And so forth.

Lee's second question concerns the relation between the problem of obligation in ethics and the problem of standards in general theory of value. My answer is that they are separate problems, though a solution of the second is usually required to provide data for the first, because the most basic principle of obligation is the requirement to

produce the greatest possible good. This requirement, which explicitly goes beyond the requirement to be reasonable, I have only
briefly referred to at the conclusion of my Essay. I have discussed
it more fully in *The Moral Nature of Man*.[3]

The standard of moral obligation, I believe, is set by the *general*
or *common* requirements for the complete development (in that
sense, the perfecting) of human personality. Psychological, social
and historical studies can, I believe, show that these requirements
are not identical with those for the development of the intelligent
egoist but include those principles of impartiality and good will
which have most generally commended themselves to the moral
consciousness of mankind. This standard of obligation is thus at
once naturalistic, perfectionist and absolutist, for the *general* or
common requirements of the complete development of personality
are set by the nature of man and the universe in which he dwells;
they are not relative to local conditions and individual desires. It
may be admitted that they are obscure, but there is a remarkable
consensus of moral genius endorsing as the basic principle that of
an impartial concern for the welfare of all.

The standards of value, of better and worse, among objects, are,
on the other hand, not absolute, but relative to every change in
conditions. No object can be said to be "an object toward which
enlightened understanding tends to develop a favorable attitude"
unless all its conditions and effects are taken into consideration.
Thus the good is relative, though the right is absolute. This radical
relativity of the good and absoluteness of the right shows that there
must be no question of looking for a "core" of value theory, or a
"highest good," or of putting "values," in the abstract, on a scale so
that we can say that one kind of value ought to have precedence.
To say that one ought to do right is a tautology; we do not have to
give a reason for doing right by saying that it is morally good and
moral goodness is the highest value. In considering which action is
right (that is, what we ought to do) we consider perhaps some
deontological grounds (such as W. D. Ross refers to), but, for the
most part, the value (good or bad) of the consequences. It is the
value of the consequences that is relevant to moral choice, not the
moral value of the act chosen. The moral value, as Scheler and

[3] New York, 1952.

Hartmann say, "rides on the back of the deed."[4] It is an incidental consequence of the rightness of choice and motive and the difficulty of the action.

The standard of value, then, as distinct from the standard of obligation, is decided by the answer to the question as to which of the objects under consideration is the one toward which enlightened understanding tends to develop the most favorable attitude. This then is the reasonable object of choice, if we must choose. To choose and act reasonably is a part of our obligation because unreasonable behavior is certainly not, in general, conducive to the perfecting of personality. The choice that would be reasonable from the purely egoistic point of view (of fulfilling the most and strongest of our desires) is not, however, always the most reasonable from the standpoint of the perfecting of personality. Moral choice therefore calls for penetrating insights far more profound than can be achieved by a superficial calculus of satisfactions.

Standards of value are, as Lee points out, relative to past judgments concerning the standard, for what people have thought in the past is often a perfectly relevant consideration in deciding which object it is reasonable to favor most. Standards of right action consisting of specific rules and laws are also relative; they must change with changes in the consequences, and in the value of the consequences, of conforming to the rules. Yet, if obligation is the requirement to fulfill the general conditions of complete development of personality, and if these are rooted in natural laws, we still have an ultimate and absolute standard (however difficult to find) for deciding what rules, under present conditions, should be adopted as our standard.

[4] M. F. Scheler, quoted in N. Hartmann, *Ethics*, trans. S. Coit (London, 1932), II, 31.

COMMENTS BY GARNETT

FINGARETTE'S Essay is an original attempt to build a bridge between some of the more recent positivist interpretations of ethical language and the pragmatism of John Dewey. He avoids the attempt to *define* ethical terms and seeks instead to clarify their significance by examining some of the functions which, in one way or another, they all have in common. With the positivists he agrees that their function is to *elicit* or *express* an attitude or action, rather than make an assertion. With Dewey he agrees that they are concerned with the process of inquiry, evaluation, or *rational* choice; and his analysis of the process of rational choosing is essentially Dewey's.

In defense of his analysis Fingarette claims that it eliminates a number of confusions in ethical thinking. The first example offered in support of this claim is the paradoxical fact that though philosophers find almost any ethical statement open to challenge yet the challenges often appear "like playing a childish game." For example, a philosopher might raise philosophical questions about the doctor's statement that he ought to take the medicine necessary to make him well, though as a man of common sense he agrees with it. This paradox, says Fingarette, is just what, on this theory, we should expect: if the function of ethical language is both to *elicit* and to *express* rational choice then we should expect it to have an indeterminate reference as well as a certain determinacy. The conflicting responses of the philosopher, as philosopher and as patient, to the doctor's instruction is therefore explained as due to different, but allied, functions of the ethical term.

The more usual explanation of this "paradox" (and, it seems to me, the correct one) is that the term "ought" is ambiguous. Taken merely as expressing a counsel of prudence with reference to health both doctor and patient agree on its use. Thinking of its other shades of meaning the philosopher raises questions about it. The use, or function, of the term depends on the fact that it *has* a meaning and it satisfactorily performs its function in communication only so far as its meaning is definite. The ambiguity the philosopher finds in the term is not due to the fact that it may be used both to *elicit* choice where choice is open and to *express* a choice already made, but to a more far-reaching ambiguity which can only be cleared up by an analysis of the different *meanings* of the term. The problem of *definition*, therefore, cannot be side-stepped by an examination of *use*, for use depends on meaning.

My disagreement with Fingarette begins at the point where he says, "So far as these functions (of ethical terms) are concerned, there is no basis for distinguishing among individual ethical terms such as 'right' and 'good.'"[1] As shown by my paper in the present volume I think this distinction vital and one which gives the two terms profoundly different functions, that of "right" being normative and that of "good" being non-normative. The function of "good" is simply to express a favorable attitude and to assert the conviction that full inquiry into all the facts relevant to such an attitude would tend to maintain it; that is, it claims that the favorable attitude is reasonable. "Right," on the other hand, asserts that the action or choice referred to is in accord with a certain standard—in the case of moral right this being the standard of existing moral obligations.

When the doctor tells the patient he ought to take a certain medicine he means that the medicine would be *good* for him, that from the standpoint of health it would be *prudent* to take it. Nothing is said as to whether taking the medicine would be morally right, or neglecting it morally wrong. That is another question which the patient (being a philosophical humbug) is, however, able to inject into the discussion by reason of the ambiguity of the word "ought," which sometimes expresses a counsel of prudence (like Kant's hypothetical imperative), or sometimes (like Kant's categorial imperative) asserts the existence of a duty.

This brings us to the most important point in the whole discussion of ethics—and the point which neither Fingarette's analysis nor Dewey's (as it seems to me) can adequately elucidate. It is the fact that ethical discussion, through all its history, has asserted the existence of duties that are not dependent upon (and even run counter to) counsels of prudence. The virtues of wisdom and temperance may usually be urged as counsels of prudence, but those of courage and justice have always been recognized as *not* dependent upon such considerations. At these points the moral judgments of every tribe

[1] P. 131.

and culture have asserted duties that a man is morally required to perform even if personal prudence should make him wish to avoid them. Some philosophers have said that such duties have no more basis than customary conventions or rules established by "the interest of the stronger." Others, for example, have said that they are requirements of "the health of the soul," or of "self-realization." The problem of the ground of these obligations is a profound and difficult one, but at least it should be clear that it is not merely that of individual prudence. It is not our problem here, fortunately, to explain the grounds of these obligations. We are concerned only to explicate what people mean when they use ethical terms, and it is sufficient to point out that terms which refer to ethical norms often have a meaning referring to a requirement other than what is prudent or "good for" the person on whom the requirement is laid.

Now Fingarette, while declining either to offer an analytical definition of any distinctively ethical term or to point to its referent, says that *all* ethical terms have in common three "fundamental" functions, that is, to *elicit* and *refer to* an act of rational choice and to *express* a phase of such an act. A "rational" choice, he says, is one "for which there is at least one reason," and a "reason" for a choice is a statement asserting some feature of the alternatives which "is itself an object of interest to *a person concerned with making the choice.*"[2] His examples show that he means quite definitely that a "rational choice" is always one made in the light of some consideration concerning the satisfaction of the interests or desires of the chooser. And to clinch the matter we are told that "This is the single characteristic which I find universally required as a condition of the actual use of moral terms, and it is, I believe, at times the only one which the user of moral terms has at all clearly in mind insofar as this can be determined by the evidence."

The inadequacy of this analysis of the use of the terms "right" and "ought" (in the sense referring to an obligation) may be seen in an example Fingarette himself uses—that of the young man seriously raising the question "Is it right to fight for my country?" Such a young man is very little concerned with the sort of question Fingarette's analysis would set before him: "Is it rational, in the sense of tending to fulfill my own desires and interests (including my interest in the welfare of other people as well as myself), to fight for my country?"

[2] P. 140; italics added.

He might decide that all these interests would be best served by fighting and yet remain convinced that it is wrong to take the life of another man even if it does promote all these interests. Obviously, the question of right and wrong means to him something other than the question of what is rational in the sense defined above. It is a question referring to a requirement or demand or standard which is not entirely (or chiefly) dependent upon the interests of the person upon whom the requirement to choose is laid.

Fingarette's analysis of ethical terms is inapplicable to the terms "right" and "obligation" and all cognate terms—that is, to terms referring to *norms*. It is, however, applicable to the term "good" and its cognates, for these terms, as I have argued in my Essay, are non-normative. "X is good" is equivalent to "X is a reasonable object of a favorable attitude," or in Fingarette's terminology, "a rational object of choice." Use of the term "good" and its cognates does therefore perform the three functions which he attributes to them. Analysis of the meaning of the terms need not, however, stop short with pointing out these uses or functions. "Good" functions as it does because it has a meaning which is logically analyzable in naturalistic terms referring to human intelligence, choices and attitudes. The confusion regarding the meaning of the term arises from the normative associations of the concept of the reasonable or rational which is involved in its connotation.

Dewey's analysis of judgments of value, of which Fingarette speaks with approval, has done for naturalistic ethics the service of distinguishing between valuing and evaluating (that is, between prizing or desiring, and judging these prizings and desires as better and worse). He has also shown how each person evaluates his valuings by inquiry into their relations to the further possibilities and probabilities of his interests. But Dewey leaves us with the assumption that, if a person has correctly decided what, in view of this calculation of his interests, is *best* for him to do, that this is what, as a *moral* being, he *ought* to do. The emotivists have performed the service for naturalistic ethics of recognizing that this assumption is not in accord with ordinary usage of ethical language, that is, that normative terms such as "ought" and "right" are used to set up requirements that are independent of such calculations of interest, though they have not yet developed a satisfactory explanation of how these norms or requirements are set up. The emotivists, however, have not recognized that the term "good," unlike "ought" and "right," does not set up a requirement or norm. It merely claims that a certain favorable attitude would be supported by intelligent inquiry into the factors relevant to it. If both pragmatists and positivists would recognize this non-normative character of "good," then they could probably agree as to its cognitive significance and the methods of testing statements of evaluation. This would clear the ground for examination of the question as to what requirements people have in mind when they assert that a person has duties and obligations which are not determined by a calculation of what from his own personal standpoint would be his most "rational choice."

Response by Fingarette

By way of preliminary, I should like to note briefly that in my example of the philosopher questioning the doctor's prescription to "take medicine, and so to remain alive," I meant to refer to the *entire* choice mentioned, that is, living as well as taking medicine. I am aware of the instrumental meaning of "ought" with regard to the taking of medicine. What I wished to emphasize was not the question where "ought" is used in a simple, instrumental sense, but rather the question as to why I ought to do that which will keep me alive.

The latter is the paradoxical question, usually so foolish in practical life, yet at times so puzzling in the philosophic study, which I was presenting. Garnett *says* that the philosopher is thinking of its shades of *meaning* other than the instrumental meaning when he raises questions about "ought." But in my detailed analysis, I tried to *show* that the puzzle arises because of a confusion about two different but allied *uses* of moral language.

I now turn to a central objection which Garnett makes to the thesis of my Essay.

Garnett argues that when we talk about what is right, we are not talking about what is prudent, nor are we talking about something which is entirely (or chiefly) dependent upon the interests of the person making a moral choice. He interprets me as saying something which is in conflict with this. While it may be true that we disagree on a basic issue connected with these assertions, I cannot say whether it is or not, for I do not think we disagree on the particular points mentioned by Garnett.

Garnett seems to feel that I have reduced the right to the prudent. The truth is that my analysis shows how, along with their distinctiveness, the prudent and the right also share certain fundamental traits. These traits are such as make them both fit within the framework of a naturalistic outlook wherein moral questions are properly dealt with rationally. The precise nature of the rationality in question I have stated only in part, that part which does not bear on the difference in role between the prudent and the right in moral reasoning.

Let us grant that an act may be prudent but not right. All that my thesis requires is that if a reason is urged for a course of action called right as against another course called prudent, that reason will have some connection, direct or indirect, with some interest(s) of the person making the choice. This is by no means the same as saying that the action called right is prudent.

As for "right" referring to something which is "entirely (or chiefly) dependent upon the interests" of the chooser, I have nowhere said that this is the case. A reason, I have said, in effect, is such because of its *connection* with the chooser's interest(s). The chain of circumstances and reasoning connecting it with the chooser's interest(s) may be long and complex. Clearly, something is a reason not solely because of the interest(s) of the chooser but also by virtue of all the other mediating facts and inferences.

What this means concretely is that a moral standard, which I include among reasons, may be of no direct interest to a person, but that it must be concerned, then, however indirectly, with features of the world in which the chooser does have interests. The same is true of any reason for choice.

This is a minimum, general requirement. However, unless Garnett holds that a moral standard can be a reason for choice even though it has no bearing on anything in which the chooser is interested, this minimum requirement at least provides us with a common ground. Upon such a common ground we can pursue further questions as to the distinctive characteristics of the prudent and the right and their relative priority in various types of moral reasoning.

In a good deal of ordinary moral thinking, moral standards function as decisive reasons for choice. We routinely do what is right. In such cases, the standard is a direct object of our dominating interest. It is thus a species of reason in the sense in which I have defined "reason." Our being interested in the standard is not, however, what justifies its being a standard. There are cases where our standards are questioned. "*Is* it right to kill for my country?" Here we are looking for the justification of our standards; we want *reasons* to justify acting in accordance with one or the other of two conflicting standards. The reasons offered must, if they are to be reasons at all, be connected with interests of ours in the manner formally outlined in my Essay. The gist of my point is that unless they are in *some* way so connected, we would feel that they are irrelevant, not reasons.

I do not know whether Garnett would go all the way with me here, but it seems to me clear that the particular reasons he offers in his Comments for disagreeing do not in truth imply any disagreement.

Should it appear, as a consequence of my attempt to show our basic agreement, that my thesis has been so modest as to be empty, I should like to note the following in connection with the issue raised by Garnett. I have shown in my Essay that both prudential considerations and moral standards, while distinguishable in important respects, can both be considered reasons for rational choice; that "reason," as used here, may be analyzed independently of the word "moral" or its synonyms; and that, in turn, all reasons can be criticized by asking for further reasons. In short, I have attempted to interpret the use of all moral language in a framework which is naturalistic and wherein moral questions are dealt with rationally.

COMMENTS BY STEVENSON[1]

I N THE FIRST HALF of his Essay Brandt argues that the Attitude Theory, in its attempt to clarify such terms as "good" and "wrong," must preserve a certain *adherence* or *adequacy* to our ordinary meanings. And in the second half he gives empirical examples that show, he thinks, that the theory fails to meet this requirement, and that it accordingly becomes untenable. Now for the purposes of argument, at least, I shall acknowledge that his examples, *if taken at their face value,* will do much to establish his case. But I shall claim that they need *not* be taken at their face value, and that the Attitude Theory can readily account for them.

In the course of stating his first objection (or "puzzle") Brandt asks us to consider the example of a Southerner who has suddenly become convinced that racial discrimination is wrong, and says so in *advance* of any change in his former approval of it.[2] The example seems to run counter to the Attitude Theory, since it involves no unfavorable attitude, on the Southerner's part, that the word "wrong" can be taken (in Attitude-Theory fashion) to express. Moreover the example, though fictitious, seems reasonably true to life, since a conviction that something is wrong is often found to come suddenly, whereas any full redirection of attitudes (though I worry a little, on Brandt's account, in thinking of sudden but highly emotional religious conversions) is normally found to be a slower process.

In my opinion this example can be reinterpreted, and without losing fidelity to any genuine empirical evidence that Brandt could be prepared to adduce, in a way that is entirely in accord with the Attitude Theory. It is altogether too much to suppose, to be sure, that the Southerner should suddenly undergo a *complete* change in all his attitudes toward racial discrimination; but it is not too much to suppose that, in any ethical case, his attitudes undergo a *partial* change. This partial change, under conditions of ordinary, uncontrolled observation, might be *mistaken* for no change at all. It would

---

[1] Charles L. Stevenson, University of Michigan.
[2] P. 165.

be odd, certainly, if our Southerner should say, "Yes, I am now con-
verted to the view that racial discrimination is wrong, but in no respect
whatsoever am I inclined to disfavor it any more than I have done in
the past." No one would say this without smiling, as though the
use of "wrong" had something fake about it. But if such a statement
were actually made with seriousness, would Brandt really be content,
preanalytically, to take "wrong" as being used in an *ethical* sense?
Or if so, wouldn't he begin to suspect that ethical analysis, in spite of
the fact that it must retain an adherence or adequacy to the usage
that occurs in *most* ethical situations (preanalytically indicated), can
readily be excused from doing so in *this* case? For unquestionably,
the practical import of the "conversion" would then be far less
extensive than a moralist is accustomed to hope for.

Now if the Southerner's conversion is attended by a *partial* disapproval of racial discrimination, we have a pretty clear case of what
Dewey and others have called a "conflict" of attitudes. And although
the term "conflict" is not easily defined, in this context it seems to me
to be intelligible from the examples to which it is commonly applied.
Thus when a man wants to buy a book, so far as owning it is concerned, but doesn't want to, so far as paying its high price is concerned,
we have a minor conflict, involving only ordinary wants or preferences.
And in the same way, there can be conflicts in which one or both
attitudes are peculiarly moral (or as Brandt puts it, are "value attitudes"), involving shame, remorse, indignation, and so on. We are
all of us familiar with such situations in ordinary life, and find them
portrayed in many plays and novels.

When Brandt's example is interpreted in this way, the only other
thing that a proponent of the Attitude Theory need do, in accounting
for it, is to maintain that the Southerner uses "wrong" to express his
newly formed disapproval, and does so in spite of the fact (or perhaps
I might even say, because of the fact) that this disapproval is in
conflict with his still continuing approval. And the point of insisting
on this, rather than taking it to be somewhat accidental to ethics, can
be explained (though I shall give only the outlines of an explanation)
by rounding out the Attitude Theory in this way:

The Southerner's use of "wrong" is not merely ephiphenomenal to
his change in attitudes; it has a more active role in helping him to
resolve his conflict. Even in an example like this one, where the man
is concerned with developing his own opinion, without yet attempting

to convince others, the quasi-imperative force of "wrong" requires careful attention. By verbally expressing his disapproval the man is encouraging himself in the development of it, and thus is taking steps to *make* it overcome his old disapproval, even though the steps are only first steps. That is to say, he is not simply *predicting* that this disapproval will win out, or even that it will win out in his more reflective moments; rather he is proceeding, having in the course of this sudden conversion attained a state of mind in which his disapproval is strong enough to begin a conflict with his approval, to talk in a way that will *help* it win out.

Certain *arguments,* we may assume, began the redirection of the man's attitudes, and were the principle causes of it; but the word "wrong" assists these arguments, and not only in the above way but in an indirect way. It may, for instance, by its cognitive *suggestions* (which are less closely tied up with it than its *meaning,* and which an Attitude Theory need in no way refuse to take account of) help the man to *remember* similarities between racial discrimination and other things that he has called "wrong," and direct his attitudes accordingly. And the word may remind him that other people may later ask him *why* he considers racial discrimination wrong, and this, in turn, may cause him to think over the arguments that led to his conversion, or to think of further arguments. In various ways, then, "wrong" becomes central to a process in which a conflict is in the course of being resolved. The process of resolving a conflict is not, certainly, a matter to be dismissed as of no importance. Nor is it to be confused with a *cognitive description of* such a process.

Let me now compare my remarks with Brandt's. I do not think that he will object to my explaining his example with reference to conflicts, for he comes very near to doing so himself. But he feels (and perhaps this is the central point of his objection) that it is "very odd and misleading to say that ethical terms function to express actual attitudes, if it is admitted that a person can properly say something is wrong when at least half of him feels no disapproval." This is odd, as I see it, only if one leaves out of account the role of "wrong" in a psychological process where the speaker is trying to *prevent* at least half of himself from feeling no disapproval. Once that is taken into account, I find it neither odd nor misleading.

Brandt's second objection is to the effect that the word "relevant," as applied to a factual reason advanced to support or attack an

ethical judgment, seems to him, intuitively, to designate a more *intimate* relation than any that the Attitude Theory can admit to be
possible; and he suggests by example that others talk as though they
share his intuition in this respect. I can regrettably say very little
about this, even though I should like to renew a discussion that
Brandt and I began some time ago.[3] But space so thoroughly forbids
a full treatment that I shall make only this suggestion:

When people talk as though they mean by "relevant" something
rather special, and foreign to anything that the Attitude Theory can
account for, it may be that their way of talking results simply from
an exceptional ambiguity of the term. Given any one definition of it
that accords with the Attitude Theory, then, it will always be possible,
in Brandt's fashion, to find some common-sense example that the
definition does not fit. But perhaps that is because the example
diverts the term to a *second* sense. And when the second sense is
suggested, without the mention of "something special," an example
can be found that diverts "relevant" to a third sense, and so forth.
So far as philosophical analysis has led me to examine what people
usually mean I am confident that our language repeatedly exemplifies
these "flexibilities," nor have the linguists that I have talked with
been in any way inclined to question my confidence. So I cannot be
convinced that the Attitude Theory is incapable of handling "relevance"
until this possibility has been explored much more thoroughly than
Brandt has explored it.

Quite apart from the above point, I should like to express my hope
that Brandt will discuss, on some future occasion, how his views on
"relevance" can be formulated to take account of what I have called
"the second pattern of analysis."[4] I have the impression that his
examples, *even if taken at their face value,* do not point uniquely
to a Cognitive Theory, as he thinks, but can equally well be taken
as showing that my second pattern of analysis, though tantamount to
my first (and hence tantamount to what Brandt calls the "Attitude
Theory") so far as the ultimate outcome of an ethical argument is
concerned, is for *some* contexts a little more faithful to the way in
which people actually speak. In particular the second pattern permits

[3] See our exchange of papers in *The Philosophical Review*, LIX (1950), 291-318
and 528-40.
[4] My remarks in this paragraph presuppose a familiarity with Chaps. IX and X of
my *Ethics and Language* (New Haven, Conn., 1944).

factual reasons to be *inductively or deductively relevant* to ethical judgments, and permits this to a quite complicated extent. And although the susceptibility of the ethical terms to persuasive definition, in my opinion, make these logically relevant reasons *less final* than those who defend ordinary Cognitive Theories have hoped for, this consideration does not prevent one from acknowledging that the reasons are genuinely logical ones, so long as a persuasive definition has not yet diverted the ethical judgment in question into a new (cognitive) sense. Now in what way do Brandt's examples, or any others that he may wish to adduce, show that we mean more by "relevant" than anything that an analysis of *this* sort cannot handle?

The third of Brandt's objections is essentially this: Certain reasons or arguments, such as those that reveal an "inconsistency" in a man's ethical position, lead him *immediately* to see that he must withdraw one of his judgments or the other. And the Attitude Theory, Brandt maintains, can explain this only by postulating an equally immediate effect on the man's attitudes, which in turn runs counter to our usual views of psychology. As in his first objection or "puzzle," Brandt is contrasting the *slow* change in *attitudes* with the relatively *quick* change of *beliefs,* and is suggesting that certain quick changes in value judgments accordingly point less in the direction of the Attitude Theory than in the direction of some form of a Cognitive Theory; but his argument here takes a somewhat different form, and requires a different sort of answer.

Let me say in passing that I find it difficult to understand just what Brandt means by "inconsistency," which he is pretty obviously using in some other sense than that current in logic. An "inconsistency," I take it, would be evidenced by the statement, "X is right and Y is wrong, and there is no difference between X and Y *that makes a difference in general*" (italics added). And I am afraid I may be misinterpreting this last clause—the one in italics, which I directly quote from his Essay.[5] But perhaps I can answer his objection in spite of this.

Let me assume, for the sake of argument, that there are reasons of *some* sort which immediately convince a man that he must withdraw one or the other of two judgments that he has just made. Now in my opinion the Attitude Theory (quite apart from any revised form of it that my second pattern of analysis may provide) can ade-

[5] P. 175.

quately take this into account; for the examples may all be of the sort
that follows:

Suppose that a man approves of X and disapproves of Y, but that
his attitudes are disturbed by a conflict. And suppose that these two
attitudes do not conflict directly with each other, but with some
third attitude that itself has attitudes as its object, and which directs
the man to organize the first two attitudes in a way that (as he
suddenly discovers) he has not in fact been doing. If this attitude is
too strong to yield in the conflict—and let us assume that it is—then
the man can resolve the conflict only by altering his approval of X
or by altering his disapproval of Y.

Now the attitudes to X and Y may continue to compete for acceptance, but nevertheless the man may temporarily cease to give *expression*, by the words "right" and "wrong," to *either* of them. For
obviously, a man needn't express every attitude he happens to have;
and here the normal incentives for expressing the attitudes will be
absent. That is to say, if he should go on maintaining that X is right,
or alternatively, that Y is wrong, his judgments would be part of a
process in which he was actively attempting to *resolve* his conflict
one way or another; and in fact that may impress him as premature.
Both attitudes are for the moment checked by his deliberations about
the consequences of X and Y, or their points of differences, and so
forth, and only as a result of these deliberations, perhaps, will one of
the attitudes become strong enough to gain verbal expression, and
thereby, directy or indirectly, to grow still stronger. Meanwhile he is
in a state of indecision. (And it is easy to see why, initially, he would
not address judgments about the rightness of X or the wrongness of
Y to other people: he does not want to encourage *their* attitudes,
quasi-imperatively, until his own get out of their deadlock.) But all
the same we may expect him, and quite without our abandoning the
Attitude Theory, to acknowledge that he must, and *permanently*,
give up either his expression of approval of X or else his expression
of disapproval of Y. For we can readily take that as a reflection of
his inclination to resolve his conflict in a way that satisfies his third
attitude. He has suddenly come to see that this third attitude cannot
be satisfied along with *both* the others.

Note that there is nothing in my explanation that implies that the
man's first two attitudes must be immediately extinguished by his
third; they may persist in a state of conflict. So although Brandt

may be correct when he says, "There is no psychological law to the effect that when one emotional attitude becomes directed to another, the latter automatically disappears," this observation has no bearing on the example, granted my interpretation of it. And note that there is nothing that prevents the man's decision from having a certain "immediacy." When he decides, on the basis of his third attitude, that he must give up at least one of the other two, that need take him no longer than it takes him to see (cognitively) that the other two are not organized in the way that the third one requires. Immediacies of this sort have any number of simpler analogues. Thus I may express contempt for a man I see at a distance; but when I go nearer and realize that I have been mistaken in his identity, I may immediately correct my judgment, and express my liking for the man.

Let me conclude with this remark: The psychology that I have used in dealing with Brandt's examples, and which is in conformity with the Attitude Theory, has no official confirmation. It is definitely homespun. But it seems to me that the psychology that Brandt himself has brought to his examples, and which attacks the Attitude Theory, is equally homespun. And that is only to be expected so long as the machine-made psychology that is available to us can yield no definitive answer on the topics that are in question. But we can scarcely conclude, on this account, that ethical analysis should be discontinued until some happier day when psychology ceases to be controversial. I want to make clear, then, that my own version of the Attitude Theory, and my defense of it both here and elsewhere, is in need of a sounder and more complete psychological background than I have been able to provide for it. But I want also to suggest that Brandt's objections, however interesting they may be in bringing presuppositions to light, are in no way sufficient to show that the psychological background of the Attitude Theory is false, or that it is not closer to the truth than the psychological background of a Cognitive Theory.

Response by Brandt

Stevenson's interesting Comments do not contest the assertion that the truth of the Attitude Theory is a matter for observation to decide. That is, I hope, a point—and an important point—of common ground. But he proposes ways of countering the empirically based objections

I raised against the Attitude Theory. I shall comment in turn on his objections to my three "puzzles."

First Puzzle. I agree with him that one will hardly assert "X is wrong" seriously unless one is *inclined* to disfavor X *in some respects.* I think all cognitivists would agree to this. For almost everyone who comes to think something wrong will, *just as a consequence,* incline to some extent to have unfavorable reactions toward it. Insofar, the use of "is wrong" will be a clue to the speaker's attitude, even if cognitivists are right that "is wrong" essentially expresses a belief (designates, has cognitive meaning).

But will there be a correspondence between willingness to say "X is wrong" and *decidedly* unfavorable *over-all* attitudes toward X? Stevenson apparently is ready to say there may not be. Indeed, from what he says it is not clear he would object even to saying that a person may be fully convinced that X is wrong, be in no ethical doubt whatever, and yet have attitudes to X that by no means "speak with one voice."

Stevenson also thinks that such a (to my mind, inadequate) correlation between attitudes and willingness to use this ethical expression is enough for the Attitude Theory. We should note, however, that anyone who proposes that an inclination to disfavor in some respects is a sufficient condition for proper use of "X is wrong" is offering a theory different from the one I called the Attitude Theory. And I think it less convincing. For, on such a theory it would not be incorrect for a person to say that something is both right and wrong at the same time—corresponding with his conflicting attitudes. Moreover, some non-cognitivists have argued for their view by urging that ethical debates go on until the attitudes of opponents are in harmony, and that ethical deliberation goes on until a person's own attitudes are in harmony. The use of this reasoning would be inconsistent with the proposal Stevenson seems to suggest.

It would be more defensible, I think, to suggest that one can say "X is wrong" correctly only if one's *over-all* ethical attitudes are in some sense preponderantly (but not necessarily entirely) unfavorable to X. But in this case at least we need more information about the senses in which there can be conflicts, and in which some attitude can be preponderant, before we can assess the proposal. In my Essay I mentioned some examples of what might be classed as such conflicts. Further examples are: a man feeling guilty about indulging in extramatrimonial sexual relations, but not disapproving such conduct in others; a person having favorable attitudes toward some features of an act and unfavorable attitudes toward other aspects of it (for example, perjury to save one's family).

Stevenson describes how ethical terms may function in a kind of "mopping-up" process, a process in which we try to get our attitudes wholly in line. We should note, however, that a cognitivist need not object to the assertions he makes; nor, I think, do they furnish support for the Attitude Theory. On the contrary, one can most easily understand such mopping-up processes in a case like that of our hypothetical Southerner, if he has come to *believe* that X is wrong but still has a long way to go to get his attitudes in line.

Second Puzzle. The question of "relevance" is a large one. But notice it is not the cognitivist who is here on the defensive; his analysis seems to fit all the cases where we speak of a point as being "ethically relevant." The noncognitivist is the one in trouble. Stevenson proposes, as a solution for the noncognitivist, that "relevant" has different *senses*; this would explain why emotivist analyses all fail to fit important uses of the term. This proposal is one that must be considered seriously. But, as Stevenson would agree, it is not easy to decide, when an awkward counterinstance presents itself, whether we should simply say the term being analyzed has several senses, or should give up our analysis as inadequate. (And "relevant" does have a causal sense.) But I suggest it does not *seem* as if "relevant" means different things, on different occasions, in *normative* contexts.

Third Puzzle. The essence of Stevenson's reply to my proposal that the Attitude Theory cannot explain the *immediate* effect, on ethical convictions, of certain reasons is this: The Theory *can* explain immediate hesitation to *express* attitudes; and it can consistently hold that actual change in attitudes, due to such reasons, may come only later and gradually. But I do not believe that, when we find ourselves convicted of inconsistency, we merely hesitate to *express* our (unchanged) view. Quite the contrary, we are clear that at least one of our ethical convictions must be mistaken. And, however it may be with our attitudes, I should think we shall *immediately* be less certain of *both* previously held convictions than we formerly were. So I continue to doubt whether the Attitude Theory can produce a satisfactory psychology of ethical thinking.

COMMENTS BY ROBINSON

I FIND little in Lee's Essay with which to quarrel, and the things which bother me the most are by no means peculiar to him. There is also much that I like. I sympathize fully, for instance, with his trying to find sense in such expressions as "This has value," and I think he has pinned down one possible interpretation very nicely. I also agree that value judgments may be expressed in sentences where the specifically valuative reference (if I may call it that) may take either a substantive, a verbal, or an adjectival form. But although Lee apparently holds that the substantive and adjectival usages are equivalent, and recognizes that the verbal usage is at least quite idiomatic, he still maintains that the substantive usage is somehow more "basic" than either of the others, and he insists that here "a choice must be made by theory."[1]

Now I do not see that theory has to make such a choice. I grant that a *reductive* theory such as Lee is apparently attempting does have to make such a choice, but I see no necessity for a reductive theory here. I also grant that an *axiomatized* theory which attempts to show what can be done with a minimum of undefined terms must accept some usage as more "primitive" than others from the standpoint of the system adopted, even if other usages could be chosen just as suitable for alternative but intertranslatable systems; but Lee is not providing such an axiomatization. And while I feel that both reductive theories and axiomatized systems have their rightful place as revealing important special possibilities, I think there is still room for the more tolerant though less spectacular kind of theory in which one simply tries to consider all the current idioms which seem relevant to the problem in hand, and to decide which of them are equivalent and how the rest may best be distinguished.

Lee sets out to justify his own position by proposing a criterion for "semantical priority." He writes in Section II:

if the word in its most general sense—that upon which all the specific

---

[1] See Sections I and II of his Essay, pp. 178-82, above.

meanings and derivatives depend—designates an act, then the verb sense is semantically prior; but if the word most generally designates a property or characteristic, and every other meaning depends on this, then the noun sense is semantically prior. This is regardless of what part of speech the word happens to be in the syntax of any particular sentence.[2]

I am not at all sure what he means by the expression "most general sense." He might conceivably have in mind (a) the "broadest" sense —the one with the widest extension or comprehension; he might also mean (b) the sense most frequently encountered; or he may mean simply (c) the sense which is etymologically the oldest. Whatever he means, however, it is up to him to show us that his favored interpretation of "value" satisfies his criterion, and that the criterion itself deserves the exalted place he has given it. I do not think he has done so. In fact he has done something else altogether. He explicitly rejects the one kind of empirical evidence that would seem the most relevant, namely, the "part of speech the word happens to be in the syntax of any particular sentence"; and eventually he lets his cat out of the bag: "The noun meaning of the word is still primary, however, for when I value an object, I am finding value in it or ascribing value to it. The value is something that the object has. This is only a semantic statement. I am stipulating how I shall use the word."[3] Unless I have overlooked something, this strongly suggests that his appeal to the criterion of "generality" has been only a bluff, and that his sole excuse for deciding which sense of the word "value" is "semantically prior" is his own quite arbitrary decision as to how he wants to use it.

In the remainder of the paper Lee has given a very attractive account of the usage he has chosen to honor. But I do not agree with everything he says about it. He tells us, for instance, in Section III that "the semantic usage advocated in Section II is easily compatible with either a realistic or a relational theory of value, but it is not easily compatible with a subjective theory or one that is purely affective such as classic hedonism."[4] Now the most clearly germane passage in Section II is the one which I quoted in my last paragraph; and if we interpret this in the light of the broad definition of "object" which Lee gives us immediately afterwards, it seems difficult to see why his usage would not be quite harmonious with a

---

[2] P. 180, above.   [3] P. 181.   [4] Pages 182-83.

subjective or even a purely affective value theory. For he writes, "anything is an object which can have the act of attention directed toward it... A thing, an event, a situation, a state, an action, a feeling, a condition or set of conditions, a class, the defining characteristics of a class—these may all be objects in suitable contexts."[5] I have no wish to quarrel with this definition, which certainly expresses a not unfamiliar usage of the term "object"; but if a state or a feeling or a condition can be called an "object," there seems no reason why it might not be said to "have a value" in Lee's sense, and this is just the sort of thing that turns up in some of the classical subjective and affective theories.

In Section II, however, Lee has not yet brought his theory to its full development. In Section V he tells us that every value experience involves three components: an object, a conative-affective sensibility, and a rather special transaction between them (which is very likely too special to carry all the weight he requires of it). He then says that the *value* is a fourth component—"a contextual property dependent upon the first three." It is clear from other passages that he thinks of this as strictly a property of the object. It is, however, a *relational* property: the object would not have it apart from its relations with the other two components.

Now I agree that this developed theory is clearly distinguishable from those types of subjective or affective theory which make value strictly a property or an action of a subject or even of a conative-affective sensibility. But it is also distinguishable from those types of *relational* theory which would identify value with a transaction such as Lee has in mind or with some relational aspect of such a transaction; and of course it is to be contrasted very sharply indeed with those *realistic* theories which make value a *non*-relational property of the object. On the other hand, it is not hard to construct subjective, relational, and realistic theories which likewise are properly distinguishable from Lee's theory but which can be translated into it, provided that they all recognize the same components. All that is necessary is to provide different definitions-in-use with a common definiens. For instance, if we represent the object by "X," the conative-affective sensibility by "Y," and the transaction by "Z," we can write:

[5] P. 182.

"X has value" $\overset{df}{=}$ "Z is occurring between X and Y" (Lee's substantive usage);

"X is valuable" $\overset{df}{=}$ "Z is occurring between X and Y" (Lee's adjectival usage);

"Y values X" $\overset{df}{=}$ "Z is occurring between X and Y" (Subjective position; verbal usage);

"The value Z is present" $\overset{df}{=}$ "Z is occurring between X and Y" (Relational position).

Then we can enthrone the usage which we like the best, anoint it with "semantical priority" or any other unguent which we consider sufficiently sacred, and invite the other usages to render their allegiance by suitable redefinition. Of course the definitions I have listed are by no means the only ones that will do the trick, nor do they exhaust all possible types of realistic, subjective, or relational theory—certainly not the most subtle ones. But they at least suggest the kind of method one might employ.[6]

Considerations such as these make me very suspicious of Lee's retort to Lewis in the next to the last paragraph of his Essay.

Lewis says that he has no quarrel with those who insist on reserving "intrinsic value" for use such as the present paper advocates. He indicates that the choice is terminological. I think it is more than terminological. It is semantic in the way that semantics and theory are inseparable. Nevertheless, I reciprocate the tolerance of Lewis's statement.[7]

I frankly do not quite see what this means, but the courtesy of the last sentence is reassuring.

I am also troubled by some of the psychological details of Lee's theory. For instance, I am not at all clear as to what kind of "anteriority" he has in mind when he writes in Section V: "I call the attitude conative-affective because what is involved in the contexture of the value experience is anterior to the distinction between conation and affection. Cognition, conation and affection are ... factors which are analyzed out of psychological activity taken as the original whole."[8]

This primordial unity of psychological activity seems something

[6] It should be pointed out that while I have arbitrarily chosen the formula "Z is occurring between X and Y" as relatively primitive in all three cases, there is nothing necessary about this; any of the formulas on the left might just as well have been taken as primitive, with the formula on the right introduced by definition.

[7] P. 195.   [8] P. 186.

of a luxury for Lee; I am at a loss to see why he insists upon it. He takes pains to point out in Section V that "There are ways in which conation and affection are more like each other than either is like cognition, and these ways are particularly relevant to the value situation."[9] And in Section VII he writes that "cognition is involved in the attribution of instrumental value but not in the primary experience of intrinsic value."[10] But if cognition, conation, and affection are simply products of analysis as compared with the "original whole," and if Lee is willing to concede that we do have an *"experience"* of intrinsic value, it seems very strange for him to maintain that this "experience" does not have a cognitive aspect, unless he is using the word "cognitive" in a very special sense. Furthermore, in spite of all his insistence that the conative and affective aspects are integrally related, he disregards the conative aspect completely when he tries to explain how differences in the degree of intensity of values are evaluated.[11] Now if Lee were merely trying to give a modest description of one way in which the term "value" might be used, I should make no complaint; for I think he has done this very well. But his paper is obviously far more ambitious than this; and the fact that psychologists have been able to devise many different methods of measuring conative intensity which are quite independent of their methods for measuring affective intensity, makes me wonder whether Lee has not exaggerated one kind of "evaluating factor" at the expense of others. Is not this rather arbitrary?

RESPONSE BY LEE

Robinson's Comments give my Essay a thorough going over, but it seems to me that one basic misunderstanding runs throughout and lies at the bottom of most of his adverse criticisms. On reading his Comments, I get the suspicion that he wants so badly to find out what is *really* prior to what that he reads into the Essay conclusions about real priority that I do not hold and that I take some pains to abjure by saying "semantically primary," "semantic usage," and so on. If I have used the expressions "really prior," "ontologically prior," "real priority" anywhere in the paper, it escapes me. I do not conceive the Essay to be talking about such subjects. I warn several

[9] P. 186.   [10] P. 190.   [11] See Section VI, pp. 187-89, above.

times that I am not talking ontology. I do not deny the cogency of ontological speculation, but my paper is semantically oriented, not ontologically. Ontological system-building begins where studies such as I have made leave off.

It is true, of course, that we must proceed on the basis of some hypothesis. The ontological hypothesis that I make is founded on the psychological position that experience is a continuum out of which we analyze parts; it is not a synthesis of separately given parts. This suggests that perhaps reality is a continuum and is not to be conceived as made up of discrete parts. I indicate this in footnote 8, page 184, and in Section V.[12]

The semantic question is how we are going to use language unambiguously to indicate the categorial scheme of an analysis that reduces our value experience to order; that is, that enables us systematically to understand it. This is not ontological reductionism. I specifically disavow ontological reductionism in footnote 22, page 194. One's semantic scheme should indicate clearly, for example, whether "value" designates a property or an act. The language used must not confuse this point. This is all that I mean by saying that "a choice must be made by theory."[13] The semantic usage not only can be the same throughout in spite of the part of speech the word is in any given sentence, but I hold that it *must* be the same; syntactics and semantics must not themselves be confused.

Thus, in all of Robinson's definitions on page 329, the word is used semantically in the same way, and I hasten to point out that it designates an act not a property. In the usage I advocate, the definitions would have to be rephrased in some such manner as follows, but in all these cases, "value" or its cognate part of speech is used in the same semantic way. "X has value" is defined to mean "X has the relational property W when Z is occurring between X and Y." Thus, "X has value" and "X is valuable" mean the same thing. "Y values X" is defined to mean "Y is aware of the relational property W when Z is occurring between X and Y." "X has the value W" is defined to mean "X has the relational property W when Z is occurring

---

[12] A fuller statement of this position may be found in my essay "An Epistemological Analysis of Induction," in *Tulane Studies in Philosophy* (New Orleans, 1953), II, 92. The relation between ontological system building and special studies in philosophy such as the present is argued in Appendix A of my *Perception and Aesthetic Value* (New York, 1938), entitled "Metaphysics and Aesthetics."

[13] See Robinson's Comments, p. 326, and my Essay, p. 180.

between X and Y." (The third definition is defective, however, for the Y of the definiendum, which designates a conative-affective sensitivity, is not the same as the Y of the definiens, which designates the subject that has that sensitivity.)

I do not deny that "value" can be consistently used to designate an act, but in the semantic scheme I offer, it is not so used. I think that the semantic scheme I offer embodies a categorial analysis that enables us without confusion to render the field of investigation intelligible. I do not claim that it is the only true scheme. I do not know what "the only true scheme" could mean unless the reality underlying the experience is made up of discrete parts.

The kind of anteriority I mean when I say that the second component in the value-contexture is anterior to the distinction between conation and affection[14] is analytic. Out of the concrete whole of pre-analytic experience, we analyze factors. I do not know whether or in what sense this pre-analytic experience may be a primordial unity. If I insisted that it were a primordial unity, perhaps my insistence would be something of a luxury, as Robinson maintains. To insist, however, that pre-analytic experience can be analyzed, and that some of the terms of analysis are relevant to understanding and some are not is not a luxury.

Understanding depends on singling out what is relevant from what is irrelevant in our total pre-analytic experience. This cannot be accomplished until analysis is accomplished. In the theory I propose, the distinction between conation and affection is irrelevant to the determination of the value-contexture. When it comes to the understanding of the evaluating factor, however, the distinction between conation and affection is relevant. When it comes to the judgment of potential value and the attribution of instrumental value, cognition is relevant. The concrete whole of pre-analytic experience is neither purely the one nor purely the other. Purity itself is an analytic concept and is not to be found in this empirical world.

[14] See Robinson's Comments, p. 329.

COMMENTS BY BRANDT

Hartman's Essay appears to have four main goals: (a) to provide an explication of "good" when used in what has been called its attributive sense; (b) to show how all other important value terms can be explicated by reference to the concepts used in the explication of "good"; (c) to provide a classification of types of value-proposition; and (d) to draw out the implications of all this for the truth-values of certain general types of value proposition. Since it seems to me that the main interest of his discussions of (c) and (d) depends on the success with which he achieves his first two goals, I shall concentrate my critical remarks on (a) and (b).

Hartman takes "good" used in its attributive sense to be the fundamental axiological term—that is, "good" in the sense in which it is being used when we say, "This is a good horse." The general expression he uses is, "x is a good C."

His analysis of this term depends upon his distinction between the definition and the exposition (or concept) of a class term. The definition of a class term, he says, includes the properties necessary and sufficient in order for a thing to be properly regarded as a member of that class. The term "exposition" is used by him in a broader and a narrower sense. Used in the broader sense, the exposition of a class term contains the properties mentioned by the definition, but many more too. Roughly one might say (although it would be circular for Hartman to say this), it is all the properties a *perfect specimen* of the class would have. (I shall come back to this.) Used in the narrower sense, the exposition includes all the properties of a perfect specimen *over and above* and excluding those mentioned in the definition. Using "exposition" in its narrower sense, we may paraphrase Hartman's analysis as follows. "x is a *good* [really, *perfect*] C" means "x is a C and has all the properties belonging to the exposition of the class term 'C.'" Similarly, "x is a *bad* C" means "x is a C but fails to have some of the properties of the exposition." And "x is a *fair* C" means "x is a C and has some of the properties of the exposition." Likewise, "x is a *no good* C" means "x is a C but has *none* of the properties of the exposition."[1]

Hartman thinks the important axiological concepts can be defined by means of this contrast between the exposition and the definition of a class term. But before going on to query this, let us ask ourselves how we are to decide what properties are to be included in the exposition of a class term. This is an important question, for if an axiological analysis is to take us anywhere, it must make it somewhat clearer what we are asking when we ask "Is x good?"—and if it is to be a naturalistic or empiricist analysis it must make clear how we may go about confirming, by the methods of science, that the defining expression is applicable to something. In particular, I do not think Hartman's proposal is very helpful if "expositional properties" of a class term is simply a technical term substituted for the ordinary "properties of a perfect specimen" of the class. It would, in this case, be no more helpful than a self-realizationist analysis of "good" when it turns out that the only instruction for deciding whether doing something "realizes" a person is to see whether doing this thing is something it is *good* for him to do. Well, then, how are we to decide what are the expositional properties of a given class-term? It may be said that in many cases this is obvious—wherever there is universal agreement on the standard. For instance, we all know that the perfect apple has no worms, skin blemishes, is juicy, and so forth. Similarly, perhaps, for the perfect cat or a perfect outfielder. But suppose someone says, "Miss X has all the properties of the ideal American girl"—namely, all those properties belonging to the exposition of "American girl." There will likely be disagreement about this, and how shall we decide who is right? Not, it seems, by finding the qualities of the *average* American girl. I do not find a clear answer to this question in Hartman, and I fear he may think the answer is more obvious than it is on account of his occupation with natural kinds like "horse," where some of the properties (teeth)

[1] In suggesting that what Hartman really defines is at best "perfect" and not "good," I agree with W. D. Ross (*The Right and the Good* [London, 1930], p. 67) that "good" in the attributive sense means something rather more complex than what Hartman suggests: something like, "contains more properties of the perfect specimen than does the average C." I am inclined also to doubt whether the other definitions follow ordinary usage at all closely. For instance, on Hartman's showing something can be both a "bad" C and a "fair" C at the same time. I do not think ordinary usage permits this.

are functional for the survival of the organism, and others (mane) are common among horses and have a certain aesthetic appeal, so that horse fanciers would not buy a horse without them. So I am doubtful how far this analysis helps. Hartman might reply that he never intended it to be helpful in this sense, that all he intended was to show that each person uses "good" to mean "having the expositional properties of the class," whatever these expositional properties, to his mind, might happen to be. But all this would still leave us in the dark what anybody is trying to say if he says, "For my part, being athletic is *part of the exposition* of the term 'American girl.'" What *would* he be claiming?

Let us now turn to Hartman's definitions of other crucial terms by means of his basic concepts: (a) "It is a good (desirable) thing that..." and (b) "ought."

Hartman says "It is good that xRy" means "the relation R is part of the exposition of one or all of its terms."[2] Thus, "it is good that John reads Ivanhoe" means that reading Ivanhoe is part of the exposition of "John"[3] (or, perhaps, "intelligent American boy"?). In general, then, when we have an "It is a good thing that..." statement, we are to translate it into the basic schema by picking out one term such that a perfect x would have some R to y, and saying that part of the exposition of x is... Will this always work? I doubt it. Consider the following. "It is a good thing [for living beings on the earth] that water expands when it freezes." Or, "It is a good thing for criminals to be punished." (Is it part of the exposition of a criminal that he be punished? Perhaps a perfect criminal would escape detection altogether.)

Let us turn to "ought." Hartman says, "x ought to be a [good?] C" means "*either* x is a C and is or is not deficient in its C-ness, *or* ... x is not a C, but say, a B, and ... it would be 'better for' x to be a C." Apparently "better for" is to mean something like "would fulfill more of its exposition as an x" (hardly as a B). It seems certain

---

[2] P. 207, above.
[3] It is noteworthy that Hartman countenances statements like, "x is good as an x" (pp. 219 ff.). I understand him to mean that just as an individual thing has its definition—the set of properties or relations uniquely characterizing it—so also it has its individual ideal at least in the case of persons. The discrepancy between ideal properties and actual properties is what permits distinction between the definition and exposition of the individual thing, and hence proper use of the phrase, "good as an x." Possibly this view has metaphysical difficulties.

that the "ought" as thus analyzed cannot be the "ought" of moral obligation. For it by no means follows from the fact that it would be better for someone to be something that he *ought* in the moral sense. Perhaps it would be better for me if I were more intelligent, but is there a moral obligation? Perhaps it would be better for me if I learned to play the piano, but am I morally obligated? This is not to say Hartman could not possibly define "moral obligation" in terms of his scheme. It is only to say that the "ought" here in question is approximately, at least, the sense sometimes called "fittingness." But even here there are difficulties, as in the foregoing paragraph. Take, "Criminals ought to be punished" or "Promises ought to be kept." Incidentally, I do not see why he holds that what a thing ought to be is always better than what it is. We can properly say: "The memorial service was just exactly what it ought to have been." Of course, I am not denying that we can say all we want to say by way of value propositions, by means of one or two fundamental concepts. All I am questioning is the convenience or even possibility of doing this with the particular concept Hartman has picked out as the basic one.

Much of Hartman's space is taken with classifying value propositions according to the underlying assumptions about the factual connection of subject and predicate, according as the copula is "is" or "ought," and according as the predicate is a factual or a value term. He also works out various rules concerning the truth of value propositions of various types. These classifications and rules strike me as overly complex for convenient use, but this is a point best left to the individual reader. I have various objections to minor points.[4]

---

[4] For instance, I cannot see why he rules out as necessarily false statements like, "No x are good [C's?]." He rules them out for the reason that "there is no empirical class of which x is a member . . . . Such a class presupposes that at least two members fulfill the exposition" (pp. 204, 211, 226). But why should there not be a class in which no member is a perfect specimen? In fact, the class "human beings" seems to be just such a class. Notice that, even if no member is perfect, each property required for perfection might be realized by some member of the class.

He also rules out "All x are good [C's?]" as necessarily false, because it is the nature of exposition that some members fulfill it and some not. But why? It seems enough for the distinction between definition and exposition that something *could* satisfy the definition (and then be properly placed in the class) without having the additional properties specifying the exposition.

Response by Hartman

I would like to answer Brandt under two headings, (1) difficulties he sees in my Essay and (2) difficulties I see in his Criticism.

1. Brandt mentions three main difficulties in my paper. The first is my failure to treat the process of exposition, in other words, the question, what properties are to make up the exposition and how disagreements about the relevance of such properties are to be dissolved. This is a subject which, of course, must be discussed but could not be discussed within the space limit of the Essay. I have examined it elsewhere.[5] It was shown there that the production of an exposition and a definition is not as indefinite a matter as one might expect and that the possibilities of agreement can actually be mathematically computed. However, this is a matter which must be developed in much greater detail. In particular, it must be shown what, precisely, is the structure of an exposition as against that of a definition. This is the more necessary, and difficult, as the nature of definition itself is still quite obscure.

The second difficulty Brandt mentions is the definition of "It is good that..." Brandt puts this wrongly as "It is a good (desirable) thing that..." The identification of "good" with "desirable" is against the purpose of my Essay, which not only has the four goals mentioned by Brandt, but, especially, the purpose of freeing the interpretation of "good" from any psychological, ontological, deontological or similar connotations and of showing its purely formal character. Brandt questions whether the definition I give of "It is good that..." will always work. In this connection he considers the propositions "It is a good thing (for living beings on the earth) that water expands when it freezes" and "It is a good thing for criminals

---

Nor do I see the justice of his proposal conjoining being a fair or bad C with what he calls the problematical modality. For problematical modality is the assumption that x *may* or *may not* have some or all of the expositional properties of a C, whereas to say that x is a bad (or fair) C is to say it in fact lacks some of these properties (or in fact has at least one) (see p. 217).

Another consequence of the theory is that, according to Hartman (p. 229), it is analytically true that "No bachelors ought to marry." This seems to me a decidedly counterintuitive result!

[5] "Group Membership and Class Membership," *Philosophy and Phenomenological Research*, XIII (1953), 353-69. See also "The Analytic and the Synthetic as Categories of Inquiry," in *Perspectives in Philosophy* (Columbus, Ohio, 1954).

to be punished." He asks whether it is part of the exposition of a criminal that he be punished. Perhaps, he says, a perfect criminal would escape detection altogether. In the same way, I take it, he would ask whether it is part of the exposition of living beings on earth that water is to expand when it freezes. Now, these are precisely the questions that *should* be asked in an analysis of these two propositions. In other words, the material problem—whether it *is* a good thing for living beings on earth that water expands when it freezes and whether it *is* a good thing for criminals to be punished —appears in my analysis as a *formal* problem. It is precisely the purpose of the theory that its *formal* pattern leads to an analysis of such problems which are *materially* relevant. In the same way in, say, physics, it is mathematical, that is formal, analysis which is used to show up the essential *material* nature of phenomena. In our case, following the formal pattern, we ask the question whether it is part of the exposition of living beings that water expands when it freezes; and in answering this question we answer at the same time the question whether it is a good thing for living beings that water expands when it freezes. Similarly, the formal pattern leads us to ask whether it is part of the exposition of a criminal to be or not to be punished. This forces us to raise the very question which Brandt raises: whether it would be a good thing for criminals to be punished or not. Axiology does not tell us how to answer the material question, but it tells us what the answer, whatever it may be, axiologically means.

The third difficulty is my definition of "ought." Brandt rightly says the "ought" defined in my paper is not the moral "ought." I emphasize that what I discuss is not ethics but axiology, which is a purely formal discipline. Ethics is a particular application of axiology, namely, the application of axiology to persons—in the sense in which, say, astronomy is the application of mathematics to stars. Ethical "ought" is a particular application, namely, an application to persons, of axiological "ought." Axiological "ought" has three forms, the analytical, the hypothetical, and the synthetic, where the analyticity, hypotheticity, and syntheticity depend on the modality of the underlying unexpressed judgment. Therefore, Brandt's two examples, "Criminals ought to be punished" and "Promises ought to be kept" can be analyzed in all three forms, namely, analytically, if I regard "punishment" as part of the exposition of "criminal" and "keeping" as part of the exposition of "promise;" hypothetically, if the exposition does not include either the punishment of criminals or the keeping of promises; and synthetically, if "punishing" is *not* part of the exposition of "criminal" and "keeping" *not* part of the exposition of "promise," but I think they ought to be. Brandt's third example, "The memorial service was just exactly what it ought to have been"—which he uses to show that it is not always true that what a thing ought to be is better than what it is—is not an example of an "ought"-proposition in the sense of my Essay, that is, a proposition which refers to an underlying unexpressed judgment. Rather, it is a telescoping of an analytic "ought"-proposition *with* its underlying judgment itself. The underlying judgment is, in Brandt's example, neither underlying nor a judgment, but an *expressed* proposition, combined with what would *be* its analytic "ought"-proposition if it *were* an underlying judgment. An analytic "ought"-proposition, in my sense of the word, would be "[The excellent Rev. Godspeed conducting it,] the memorial service *ought* to have been dignified," meaning "And it indeed was dignified." The latter statement is the underlying judgment. In Brandt's example this underlying judgment is *expressed*, and combined with the "ought"-proposition in such a way that "dignified" is replaced by "what the memorial service ought to have been"—namely, again, dignified. The result is "The memorial service was just exactly what it ought to have been," where "The memorial service was just exactly" belongs to the underlying judgment and "what it ought to have been" to the analytic "ought"-proposition. A truly analytic "ought"-proposition does not express the underlying judgment. Rather it *states* "x ought to be φ" and *means* "and x *is* φ." In an analytic "ought"-proposition, then, it is confirmed that x is what it ought to be, or rather, that it ought to be what it is. But this confirmation does not destroy the sense of ought, which is, that what a thing ought to be is always better than what it is. On the contrary, it confirms this sense of "ought"—for if it did not, the analytic "ought"-proposition would be tautological with its underlying judgment, and so would be the two clauses of Brandt's example.

2. Now to the difficulties I see in Brandt's criticism. When I say that it is analytically true that "No bachelors ought to marry," I mean first of all not logical analyticity but axiological analyticity, that is, analyticity referring not to the proposition itself but to the

correspondence between it and the underlying judgment. The latter, in accordance with the definition of "bachelor," is "Bachelors do not marry." Therefore, analytically speaking, "Bachelors ought not to marry" is true. But this does not mean, of course, that I agree that bachelors ought not to marry. Rather I can say that in my opinion bachelors ought to marry. This, however, is not analytic but synthetic "ought." I want bachelors, who analytically are, of course, unmarried to be married. All that Brandt says, then is, that synthetic "ought" is intuitive while analytic "ought" is counterintuitive, and this may be true in many cases. On the other hand, it may only be the case when the two kinds of "ought" are confused. This shows, incidentally, the importance of the modal analysis of "ought," in spite of its seeming complexity.

Another misunderstanding arises from Brandt's identification of "good" with "a perfect specimen of." I do not believe that this identification may be made, for three reasons. "Specimen" is not an axiological, that is, a purely formal term. It rather refers to certain physiologically or otherwise perfect beings and cannot be used in, say, an aesthetic or an ethical sense. We cannot say that a picture is "a perfect specimen" of a beautiful picture nor that a man is "a perfect specimen" of a moral person. When Brandt says that the class of human beings does not seem to contain a perfect specimen, he seems to use the term morally; for there certainly are physically perfect specimens, as any moviegoer can confirm.

Secondly, even if we would accept the purely formal character of "a perfect specimen," a good C which has all the expositional properties of C is not, for that matter, the perfect C; although it may be said to be *a* perfect C. "Perfect," in other words, has two meanings, one corresponding to "good" and one to "best." I failed to make this clear. "Perfect" in the second sense is very different from "good." There is at most *one* perfect specimen in the sense of "best" but— and this leads to the third point—there are at least *two* such specimens in the sense of "good." The minimum properties of the expositional class are given by the *definition*. Any being fulfilling the definition belongs to the definitional class. In addition, each such being has other properties. Those which it has in common with other members form part of the *exposition*. This means that at least one non-definitional property must be had in common by at least two definitional class members for an expositional class to come into being.

If each definitional class member had a different nondefinitional property, or a different set of such properties, there would not be an expositional class. If at least two members had one such property in common, there would be an expositional class of two members and an exposition of one property. If two other members had two such properties in common, one of which would be the property just mentioned, the expositional class would have four members and two properties. The members having both properties would be "good" class members while those having only one property would not be so good. In general, the exposition is the maximum set of nondefinitional properties had by at least two definitional class members. Thus, there cannot be an expositional class in which no member is "good," for the two members having the maximum set are always the "good" ones. "No x are good C's," therefore, cannot be true.[6]

The last point raised by Brandt concerns the connection between the relation of badness and fairness of a C with the problematical modality. Brandt says that on the one hand the modality is the *assumption* that x *may* or *may not* have some of the expositional properties whereas on the other hand to say that x *is* a bad or a fair C is to say that in fact x *does* or *does not* have these properties. Brandt, in other words, believes that I confuse the problematical and the assertory modality. However, it seems that Brandt overlooks the distinction between the modality of the expressed proposition with that of the underlying judgment. For example, if the expressed proposition is "x is a good C," we are *not* concerned with *its* modality. We are concerned with the modality of the underlying judgment, which is *not* expressed and which is the *meaning* of the expressed proposition. In this case both the modality of the proposition and that of the underlying judgment happen to be the same—both assertory. The underlying judgment is "x has all the expositional properties of C." But when we say "x is definitely a rotten C," the two modalities are different. That of the *proposition*, with which we are usually *not* modally concerned, is assertory. That of the underlying judgment, with which we *are* modally concerned, is negatory—"x does *not* have any of the expositional properties of C." Similarly, the modality of the *propositions* "x is a fair C" and "x is

---

[6] This is a subject which must be explored in much greater detail. It is conceivable that there are different kinds of goodness, if, for example, two sets of members have the same number but different kinds of properties.

a bad C" is assertory, but that of the underlying judgments is problematical. For the fairness of x as a C *means* that x has more expositional properties of C than it lacks, or that x may or perhaps may not have some of these properties, and the badness of x as a C means that x lacks more expositional properties of C than it has or that x may not or perhaps may have some of these properties. The difference between a fair and a bad C is one of emphasis. Under one point of view a thing is regarded as fair and under another point of view it is regarded as bad—for the optimist the glass of water is half full, for the pessimist it is half empty. The theory thus simply brings out what is true in moral reality.

COMMENTS BY MOORE

LEPLEY's Essay seems to have a threefold purpose: first, to indicate in synoptic fashion the major current types of analysis of the value situation from the linguistic standpoint; second, to suggest through examplification a possible common value terminology; and third, to adduce further evidence in support of his long-standing thesis that "facts and values may be more intimately related or more extensively identical than is commonly recognized."[1] I shall confine my Comments to the second and third aspects of the paper with emphasis on the latter.

I

Lepley's proposal of a common value vocabulary has the dual intent of eliminating merely verbal debate and of highlighting existing points of agreement which may serve as a base of operations for a concerted attack on the genuine problems of the area. His method of indicating such a common terminology consists in part in the eclectic practice of appropriating terms from various sources and in part in suggesting synonymity by listing a plurality of terms now in use as semantic alternatives.

The project has a laudable end which in due time will be accomplished; but I believe that we are not ready for it. What Lepley is working toward is an area of study with a conventional technical terminology, an accepted body of facts, and a common program of research; in short, the science of values he and I both believe to be possible. It seems to me, however, that value study is still in the early stage of exploration in which it is appropriate that students indulge, as they are doing, in experimental descriptions from various individual and partial perspectives. To force a common value terminology on a field of research too early in its history is to run the risk of freezing into language conventions a mass of unclear and biased ideas. After much further study, with consequent wider agreement on the fundamental structures of the value experience,

[1] P. 238, above.

and particularly after a more perceptive inquiry into the nature and role of value language, we may expect the consolidated perspective, program, and terminology Lepley here anticipates.

II

The deeper purpose of Lepley's Essay is to heal that "bifurcation between fact and value" which has signaled the belief of many students that there can be no scientific treatment of value data. Lepley believes that to accomplish this end we must assimilate value data and value language to the data and language of the currently recognized sciences. His consequent strategy throughout this and other essays is to minimize differences and to establish a maximum of community between the bifurcated areas.

I find myself in the peculiar position of agreeing with Lepley's final conclusion, that value data can be dealt with in terms of scientific method, while disagreeing with much of the argument by which he seeks to establish this conclusion. The simplest of these persuasive devices is a tendency to favor, perhaps unconsciously, a terminology which connotes the close community of the cognitive and the affective aspects of the complex value experience. Examples are "object of interest" and object "of significance" as equivalents of *value object*.[2] These, as Lepley himself admits with regard to the first, are actually equivocal terms which in one context mean *of intellectual import* and in another *of affective consequence*. The internal mechanism of a watch and the outcome of litigation to which I am a party may both be objects of "interest" or "significance" to me but in quite different senses. Sign vehicles so diversely used are really two terms; hence nothing in the way of community of fact and value is demonstrated by their use in reference to a value situation. Nevertheless, I feel that Lepley does attempt so to use them. Even were such terms univocal his peculiar use of them here would constitute a fallacy, that of attempted proof by definition, inasmuch as no justificatory argument has preceded it.

A further device for persuading the reader of the close relation between the admittedly factual and the valuative, unargued in this essay, is Lepley's identification of *valuing* and *evaluating*. The latter is a rank-ordering procedure with regard to valuable objects, an obviously cognitive act, something over and above the valuing

[2] Pages 238-39.

involved; but by a theoretical merging of the two he gains for simple valuing the cognitive prestige justifiably attributed to the evaluating procedure. With a similar consequence he identifies intrinsic and instrumental valuings. The instrumental aspect of a complex value situation is a causal pattern, plainly cognitive, hence scientific; but this fact in itself does not make any associated valuing likewise cognitive. Lepley, following Dewey, illicitly converts the product of psychological telescoping, wherein we value the means in terms of its end, into a logical identity.

In connection with his examination of the emotive theory of values Lepley advances a novel argument from the functional overlapping of the neural mechanisms involved in cognitive and affective experiences to the close relation of fact and value. The most obvious comment on this argument is that it represents a radical departure from the avowed "linguistic standpoint" of the study. More importantly it raises the serious question of the status of evidence educed from a region whose plane is at right angles to that of the area of debate. Can we prove anything in the horizontal plane of value theory by vertical reference to the region of neural mechanisms?

With examples drawn from various levels or aspects of the total value situation Lepley makes a strong case for the pervasive commingling of the factual and the valuative, as element and as function, in first order experience and in language; but, although he may thus demonstrate close association he does not, it seems to me, prove either partial or complete identity of the two. For instance, he makes much of the fact "that the same term or sentence, whether commonly called factual or valuative, may produce or prepare behavior in either designative or appraisive mode and have either cognitive or emotive meaning."[3] This apparent amphibolous functioning of language, which Lepley believes to stem from, and thus in its occurrence to prove, the close affinity or even identity of the factual and the valuative, may be otherwise explained. A language structure may simultaneously function directly as a descriptive presentation of some object and indirectly, by virtue of the affective meaning of the object thereby imaginatively constructed, as a device persuasive to decision and perhaps to action. For example, a purely descriptive passage about the Smoky Mountains, because of the antecedent attractiveness of mountains for me, may well lead me to take my

[3] Pages 248-49.

family there for an outing. How one reacts to an instance of description depends not on the character of the language as such but rather on one's whole psychological set, including his preparation to respond to the particular object thus presented. Such complex functioning of language does not, therefore, advance Lepley's case.

Lepley's most radical essay at healing the bifurcation of fact and value consists in an attempt to prove that certain types of value and factual sentences may "be mutually translated or interchanged."[4] One of his examples is the pair of sentences: (a) "This is a better table," and (b) "This table supports weights in excess of those supported by the other tables,"[5] the first being labeled *valuative* and the second *cognitive* or *designative*. My point here is that insofar as these two sentences are mutually translatable the adjective *better* is taken simply as an indicator of a rank-ordering procedure, a cognitive process. If *better* has any connotation of simple affective reaction such disappears in the translation. Nevertheless, the response of a recipient may be the same for both sentences by virtue of the affective meaning of the imagined object, as this possibility was described above. But, sameness of response does not prove sameness of the linguistic portion of the stimuli.

III

Since I hold that Lepley's final goal is both laudable and possible of accomplishment, albeit his supporting arguments are weak, I should indicate broadly how I think he goes wrong. As I see it the only sort of assimilation of value to fact necessary is proof that the former, like the latter, yields to description.[6] If an area yields to description it is proper subject matter for scientific procedure, and, since valuings do so, there can be a science of values, and the lamented bifurcation is healed.

Why does Lepley not take this direct and easy path to our mutual goal? I believe the primary reason to be a lingering aura of behaviorism he inherits from Dewey, a perspective from which the subjective data I think to be integral to any value experience are not scientifically respectable. He, and others of this school, therefore try to locate value data within the territory already staked out by the accepted sciences, hence the tendency to merge simple values with the valuative and the instrumental, which *are* respectably cognitive.

[4] P. 255.   [5] P. 245.   [6] See my Essay, pp. 9-28, above.

Another factor preventing many students of axiology from affirming the possibility of a science of values is the prevalent assumption that the value and the moral situations are either identical or inextricably intertwined. Since the moral situation demonstrably involves an element of coercion derivative of social opinion, a code or a set of standards, a factor not amenable to descriptive rendition,[7] such identification would seem to preclude a descriptive, hence scientific treatment of the value situation. I believe Lepley's approach to be influenced by this assumption to the extent of a tendency on his part to shy away from an assertion of the completely descriptive character of value experience and a tendency to overemphasize what I consider trivial and merely incidental forms of community of fact and value. When we can bring ourselves to see the moral situation as independent of and, where it does appear in conjunction with it, superimposed upon the value situation, and when we can also overcome our feeling of guilt when dealing with subjective data, then and only then shall we be in a position to achieve the science of values Lepley has so valiantly striven for.

Response by Lepley

The sections of my Response are numbered to correspond to those of Moore's Comments.

i

As Moore observes, "value study is still in the early stage of exploration in which it is appropriate that students indulge, as they are doing, in experimental descriptions from various individual and partial perspectives." But is it not proper and important for philosophy to interpret from general frames of reference as well as to analyze and describe, and in this sense to develop a 'science of value,'[8] from more restricted purviews? I regard my Essay as a kind of broad experimental description which attempts to bring a rather wide range of value phenomena and language into better perspective than is usually achieved in more limited, minute discussions. There is, I feel sure, little ground for fear that my paper may "force a common value terminology on a field of research too early in its history."

[7] *Ibid.*, pp. 15-24.
[8] For my use of single and double quotation marks see footnote 8, p. 234, above.

II

It had not occurred to me that "the deeper purpose" of my Essay is, as Moore states, "to heal the bifurcation between fact and value." At any rate I should not think it correct to say that I attempt to do this by assimilating "value data and value language to the data and language of the currently recognized sciences." An aim of the Essay is to discern and portray in just proportion both the differences and the continuities between fact and value when these are viewed from the perspectives assumed by various significations of the terms "fact" and "value," "factual" and "valuative." I have proceeded on the general hypothesis that an inclusive experimental attitude and approach is possible and can be fruitful in dealing with perhaps all areas of human problems. The continuing actualization of this attitude and approach may go far beyond "the currently recognized sciences" in methodologies, techniques, and terminologies as well as in subject matters and frames of reference.

Moore chooses, in line with what he conceives to be common usage and common sense, to limit the term "value" to "an affective involvement" of an organism in relation to an object, an involvement which is something more than "mere attention or interest."[9] I think we must recognize many different kinds and degrees of interest, but it appears to me to be as much a fallacy of definition (if it is one) to limit "value" to instances of greater affective involvement as to extend the term to include all occurrences of interest. Possibly in a most distinctive sense, interests of any sort (including those of marked affective involvement) become or are found to be values only through a process of 'inquiry,' in somewhat the same way that "ideas," "hypotheses," "suggested solutions," and the like become or are found to be facts. By limiting the term "value" as he does, Moore perhaps feels justified in devoting all of his attention to analysis of conspicuous cases of affective involvement. Analysis in this area is certainly important and needs to be carried further, but such a definition should not, it seems to me, be used to discourage the development of value theory in its wider aspects.

Moore thinks that I have sought to persuade the reader of the close relation between the factual and the valuative by identifying *valuing* and *evaluating* and by identifying intrinsic and instrumental

[9] See his Essay, p. 10, above.

valuings. If I have made these identifications anywhere, I should like to retract them. I do not recall ever having made them, though I remember having emphasized distinctions between valuing (prizing, liking, enjoying) and valuation (appraising, evaluating) and between intrinsic and instrumental valuings.[10]

Why Moore thinks my mention of the physiological and psychological mechanisms or conditions which seem to account (at least in part) for the close and pervasive relations of cognitive and affective elements of experience and language is "a novel argument" or "a radical departure from the avowed 'linguistic standpoint of the study,'" I do not see. Are not these mechanisms as much a part of the total "pre- or non-language level" of the axiological situation as is a candy bar liked by an individual or a custom that exerts pressure in a social group, both of which Moore evidently considers proper subject matter in the present study? Here, as at other points in my Essay, the purpose is to consider and if possible to understand, not to *prove*. If consideration of neural mechanisms makes it possible to understand better the occurrence and close relation of affective and cognitive reactions and experiences, as many physiologists and psychologists appear to believe,[11] what is radical or even novel about recognition of this aspect of the situation as seen from the "linguistic standpoint" interpreted broadly? In fact Moore himself finds it helpful in the next paragraph of his Comments to cite "one's whole psychological set, including his preparation to respond" as an explanation of "the apparent amphibolous functioning of language"—which explanation, by the way, if true, seems to me in no measure to reduce

---

[10] For valuing and valuation see "The Dawn of Value Theory," *The Journal of Philosophy*, XXXIV (1937), 368-69; *Verifiability of Value* (New York, 1944), Chap. V and p. 213; *Value: A Cooperative Inquiry* (New York, 1949), p. 167; and my present Essay, p. 252 f. For intrinsic and instrumental see *Verifiability of Value*, p. 125; *Value: A Cooperative Inquiry*, pp. 171-75, 299-300; and the present Essay, pp. 242, 243, and 252, above. My use of the expressions "valuative terms," "valuative sentences," and so forth, instead of "value terms" or "valuing-evaluating terms," and so on, is in part a matter of context and convenience. To me it seems less awkward to use "valuative terms," especially in contrast with "factual terms." (One would scarcely say "fact terms" or "fact-finding terms.") I seldom use the word "valuing," because other less controverted terms, such as "liking," "enjoying," "prizing," "holding dear," "immediate value," "qualities had," or "untested values" seem in most cases to express my meaning. But the use of "valuative" does not signify that I identify valuing with valuation, or evaluation. I think valuing often occurs apart from or before valuation, but that valuing may occur both in and after valuation.
[11] See the works referred to in footnote 36, p. 250, above.

the closeness of the relation of some factual and valuative language; I have on several occasions emphasized that how one reacts to an instance of description (or indeed to any kind of sign or sign complex) depends not on the character of the language or sign(s) as such but rather on the particular situation, including what Moore calls "one's whole psychological set."[12]

Moore may have forgotten one conclusion of my Essay: "When the intents, significative or/and nonsignificative, are the same, or insofar as they are the same, the referents of any two terms or sentences, whether factual or valuative or both, are identical and the terms and sentences are interchangeable, or equivalent."[13] He says that insofar as the sentences (a) "This is a better table" and (b) "This table supports weights in excess of those supported by the other tables" are mutually translatable "the adjective *better* is taken as an indication of a rank-ordering procedure, a cognitive process. If *better* has any connotation of simple affective reaction such disappears in the translation." I would question whether a rank-ordering procedure is always entirely, or necessarily even in large part, cognitive; certainly in many contexts the term "better" produces or triggers off reactions of liking, favoring, or giving preferred status, with very little cognitive response or experience. I would agree, however, that if "better" has in sentence (a) any connotation of simple affective reaction, such disappears in any attempted translation into sentence (b)—unless (b) also carries or is accompanied by the same affective reaction, which will perhaps not usually be the case. Unless all the 'intents,' both cognitive and affective, are the same in the particular occurrence of both sentences they are not, I should think, completely translatable, interchangeable, or equivalent.

III

According to Moore, all that is needed to heal the bifurcation between fact and value is to show that value, like fact, "yields to description." But what does he mean by "yield to description"? Does he mean that valuing and value language can be described as is done, say, in his own Essay in this volume?

Few students of value theory will deny that in this sense a 'science'

---

[12] See *Verifiability of Value*, pp. 77-78 *et passim; Value: A Cooperative Inquiry*, p. 389; and my present Essay, pp. 236 and 244, above.
[13] P. 256, above.

of value is possible. Even the most extreme emotivists usually admit that it is possible to describe value behaviors and the uses of terms and sentences in connection with, and as expressions of, valuings and valuations. Some empiricists may accept the view that all forms or nodes of value language are descriptive of value experiences. Some will agree that both introspection and objective observation can and need to be utilized,[14] and others may be willing to interpret "oughts" as something superimposed upon value experiences by social pressures, which can be described but are not descriptive and therefore not true, false, or testable.

It seems to me that the descriptive science of value envisaged by Moore, while essential for value theory, omits very important problems of the relations of science and value: Can scientific method, or a point of view and procedure which embraces elements of scientific and artistic attitudes and methods, be extended and developed in dealing with our distinctly human problems, say in family life, education, management-labor relations, and government at all levels? Can 'science' be utilized in formulating and testing experimentally both ends and means, whether more ultimate or relative, more immediate or remote? What is the nature and extent of the 'testing' possible in valuing and valuation as compared with that in the various kinds of scientific and nonscientific knowing? In view of the existence and importance of these and related problems, I hesitate to subscribe to an exclusively descriptive "science of value," though I have hopes that both it and a more truly experimental value science and art may in time be more widely envisaged and achieved. The causes of my hesitancy in following Moore's "easy path" for healing the bifurcation between fact and value are not, I hope, those which he suggests.

[14] This is indicated by some of the contributors to *Value: A Cooperative Inquiry*, for instance by Jessup, p. 135; by Lee, pp. 148-53; by Lepley, pp. 168-70; and by Morris, pp. 213-14.

COMMENTS BY HARTMAN

I PROPOSE to comment on the preceding papers in terms of what may be called Levels of Value Language. These levels may be conceived of in analogy to the levels of scientific language. The levels of this language, according to Hempel's simple and lucid analysis,[1] are the empirical, the conceptual, and the systematic. In applying these levels to value language we ask, in other words, what would be the structure of ethics and other value fields if they were regarded as empirical sciences and if concept formation would take place in them as it did in the natural sciences.

According to Hempel, a science is a theoretical system applied to a set of observed events. There are, then, three parts to a science, (1) a theoretical system, (2) a set of observed events, (3) the connection between the two, variously described as the application of the theoretical system to the observations, the interpretation of the observations in terms of the theoretical system, or the subsumption of the observations under the system. Neither the theoretical system nor the observations alone are the science, but only their combination. Neither the mathematical system applied in physics nor the physical observations made, but only their combination, the interpretation of the observations in the light of the mathematical system, constitutes the science of physics. Hempel compares a scientific theory

to a complex spatial network: Its terms are represented by the knots, while the threads connecting the latter correspond, in part, to the definitions and, in part, to the fundamental and derivative hypotheses included in the theory. The whole system floats, as it were, above the plane of observation and is anchored to it by the rules of interpretation. These might be viewed as strings which are not part of the network but link certain points of the latter with specific places in the plane of observation. By virtue of those interpretive connections, the network can function as a scientific

[1] C. G. Hempel, "Fundamentals of Concept Formation in Empirical Science," in *International Encyclopedia of Unified Science* (Chicago, 1952), Vol. II, No. 7. Ex-

theory: From certain observational data, we may ascend, via an interpretive string, to some point in the theoretical network, thence proceed, via definitions and hypotheses, to other points, from which another interpretive string permits a descent to the plane of observation. In this manner an interpreted theory makes it possible to infer the occurrence of certain phenomena which can be described in observational terms.[2]

In other words, the theoretical system determines through empirical interpretation the interrelationship between the observations, and the total set of the observational data receives its unity through the interrelationships within the theoretical system.

In order to be applicable, the formal system must be precise and detailed enough to account for the interrelationships of the empirical data. A set of merely general principles does not constitute an applicable system; the key term of neovitalism, for example, "entelechy," lacks what Hempel calls *empirical import*. On the other hand, a term such as "universal gravitation" does have such import, for "to say that the regularities of planetary motion can be explained by means of the concept of universal gravitation is an elliptic way of asserting that those regularities are explainable by means of the formal theory of gravitation, together with the customary interpretation of its terms."[3] The reason that the concept "entelechy" lacks and the concept "universal gravitation" has empirical import is that the former lacks and the latter has *systematic import*, that is, it permits "the establishment of explanatory... principles in the form of general laws or theories"[4] and is the center of a network of formal relations. To frame concepts with *empirical* import is relatively easy; they "can be readily defined in any number, but most of them will be of no use for systematic purposes.... It is... the discovery of concept systems with *theoretical* import which advances scientific understanding."[5]

The threefold structure of science arises from three kinds of definitions, namely, (1) empirical analysis or real definition, by Hempel (as by Kant) called explanation or exposition (*Erklärung*);[6] (2) concept analysis, by Hempel (as by Kant) called analytic definition; and (3) stipulative construction, by Hempel called nominal definition (by Kant synthetic definition).

---

cerpts from this source are reprinted in the present section by permission of the University of Chicago Press, publishers.

[2] *Ibid.*, p. 36. [3] *Ibid.*, p. 40. [4] *Ibid.*, p. 46. [5] *Ibid.*, pp. 46-47. [6] *Ibid.*, p. 8 f.

These three kinds of definitions produce three kinds of scientific language, namely, (1) empirical language, which describes situations in everyday terms; (2) technical language, which is of two different kinds, (a) concept analysis, (b) interpretation of concepts in terms of a theoretical system (it is never "facts" that are subsumed but concepts, "ideal cases"); and (3) the theoretical system itself, systematic language, which does not describe any situation but is *applied to* situations and orders them autonomously and normatively into a whole, thus producing the total empirico-theoretical structure which constitutes the science. To use the example of physics, (1) is empirical description of physical situations, real definition of physical events, culminating in empirical concepts; (2a) is analysis of such concepts, their testing in practical and experimental physics; (2b) is theoretical physics, subsumption of the results of (2a) under (3); here physical events are defined autonomously by nominal definition, following (3) the purely formal pattern, "mathematics for physicists." This language, through the process (2b), patterns and remodels the empirico-analytic language (2a).

Turning to value language, we would have (1) empirical description of value situations, real definition of value in terms of some feature(s) of the situation, culminating in empirical value concepts; (2a) analysis of such concepts, their testing in practical and experimental ethics (casuistry); (2b) theoretical ethics, subsumption of the results of (2a) under (3); here value is defined autonomously by nominal definition, following (3) a formal axiological pattern, "axiology for ethicists." This language, through the process (2b), patterns and remodels the empirico-analytic language (2a).

Neither value language 3 nor 2b do as yet exist to any significant degree. Thus ethics today is no science. It consists largely of levels 1 and 2a; its concepts lack empirical and systematic import—they are more like "entelechy" than like "universal gravitation." On the other hand, it follows from what has been said that ethics would be a science as soon as level 3 were supplied. The present arbitrariness of its empirical value determinations—pleasure, purpose, interest, and the like, as supposedly valuational determinants—would disappear and a definition of value would take their place which would have both systematic and empirical import and would, in turn, define the precise valuational status of these empirical data.

The papers in this volume range through all three levels. We have the following kinds of Essays: five on method or classification, namely Robinson's, Adams's, Brandt's, Lepley's, and McGreal's, all of which discuss aspects of the relation between scientific and value language; five in empirico-technical value language, namely, in order of increasing emphasis on abstract elements, Pepper's, Lee's, Moore's, Garnett's, and Fingarette's; one in value semiotic, Morris's; and one in value logic, my own. I shall now comment on the Essays (and some of the related Comments and Responses) in this order and in the light of the language levels described. My emphasis will be the exact opposite of Lepley's: on the formal rather than the empirical nature of value language.

Robinson's Essay discusses two questions: (1) How does the language of value differ from other kinds of language, and (2) how is it related to the language of sign theory. I shall here confine myself to the first question, discussing the second in connection with Morris's Essay.

An inventory of value-theoretical terms such as Robinson attempts is, in my opinion, both necessary and possible. But it presupposes a logical schema which would give all these terms their precise definition and systematic position. In the light of the levels of value language one could make the classification of Robinson's "Group 1" as follows. For Robinson's "valuative terms of relatively high generality" one could write "pure axiological terms" and here classify the same terms as Robinson does (together with those discussed and defined in my own paper). These definitions could be taken as bases for the entire classification. All the other kinds of Robinson's terms could be classified under "applied axiological terms." Under this heading would appear four subdivisions. First, as "applications of the highest generality," applications of axiological terms to space and time. This would give rise to a systematic teleology and lead to Robinson's "telic" terms. For example, the application of the definitions of axiological terms to time, would lead to definitions of "a good time,"[7]

---

[7] According to I. McGreal, *The Art of Making Choices* (Dallas, 1953), p. 44, "Two o'clock would be a good time" means "Two o'clock would be a time such that, under certain specifiable circumstances, if one ... knew about it one would favor it." This is an empirical analysis, based on a first-level definition of "good"—"good" as meaning a situational element, namely favoring. I propose a definition on the third-level: "x is a good C" means that x is empirical and possesses the properties of its concept. C in this case must be the concept "time" and x an experienced "instance" of time, which has the properties of "time". To take the first of Webster's

"a bad time," "the right time," and so forth, and produce terms such as "means," "end," "goal," "goal-gradient," "valence," "requiredness," "useful," "opportunity," "occasion," and other extrinsic valuational time terms, and also intrinsic ones like "the fullness of time," "eternity," and so on. The second subdivision would be the application of the teleological value terms to *consciousness*. This would yield Robinson's "teleutic" and affective terms—the latter teleutically defined similar to the procedure of Spinoza[8]—and his nonrelational conative terms. The third subdivision would combine the two first ones, the applications of the pure axiological terms to space-time and consciousness—and result in terms for *Value Situations*. Situational terms would be either relational, that is, referring to the relation between elements of the situation, or situational in the narrow sense, that is, referring to the situation as a whole. In the former category belong all the relational terms in Robinson's conative list, such as "want," "desire," and so forth; in the latter category belong most, if not all, of his nomological terms, for the "nomos" here refers to and defines, as I understand it, the whole situation as "nomological." The fourth subdivision, finally, would be the application of axiological terms to situational elements, such as *persons, things, groups,* and *relations.* The application to persons would yield *moral* and *psychological* terms—depending on whether intrinsic or extrinsic "good" is applied—the application to things, under the same proviso, *aesthetic* and *economic* terms; the application to groups, *political* and *sociological* terms; the application to relations, *juridical* terms. These are the terms found in Robinson's "valuative terms of relatively low generality."

Adams, too, is concerned with the relation of empirical language

---

nineteen definitions, time is "the period during which an action, process, etc., continues." An instance of time, then, is a certain period during which an action, process, etc., continues. This means that the instance must be a part of the continuity of the action or process—something which is a vehicle for the action or process and which neither stops nor deflects it but carries it forward to the next instance. The next instance, then, is the *end* of the present instance, the present instance the *means* to the next. While this can be the beginning of extrinsic teleology, the definition of intrinsic "good" can lead to intrinsic teleology. "x is intrinsically good" means, in this definition, that x is the only instance of the concept and has all the properties of the concept. In this case, there is only one instance of time, but this instance contains the full continuity of time. This is, for example, the Kierkegaardian "instance" (*øjeblikket*) where temporality and eternity meet.

[8] *Ethics,* Part III, Prop. LIX.

to value language. He attacks the thesis of logical empiricism, that empirical verification is the differentia of scientific statements, and rightly holds against Feigl that purely descriptive sciences, such as paleontology, are undeveloped. A developed science is both descriptive and explanatory, that is, its statements are both empirically verifiable and subject to a conceptual schema. Adams thus emphasizes the two-dimensionality—though not the three-dimensionality—of scientific language. Only in the one-dimensional empirical view of science are value judgments excluded from the realm of science as not verifiable. In the larger view value judgments are, *like* scientific judgments, descriptive but, *unlike* scientific judgments, not explanatory. Rather, the conceptual frame is what Adams calls justificatory or axiological. Value judgments are thus descriptive-justificatory. Adams's justificatory kind of inquiry is of the teleological type—it is "all of the means-end type"[9]—especially in what Adams calls its technological form.[10] But he does not show why this kind of reasoning *is* valuational or axiological. The appearance of words like "best" and "ought" in teleological sentences, such as "Given a specific limited end to be achieved, what is the *best* way to do it? How *ought* it to be achieved?" is only one—and an arbitrary —example of the use of such words. I can frame both sentences without either "best" or "ought," for example, "Given . . . how am I to go about it? How is it to be achieved?" Neither version constitutes either the "technological," teleological, or the justificatory as specifically valuational, that is, as *the* language of value.

Apart from this, however, I cannot see how Adams's major premise, of the nature of science, can be doubted. One may not agree with his conclusion that value judgments presuppose a conceptual frame different from that of the sciences and thus are "empirical" in the wider sense of belonging to a descriptive-conceptual scheme, though not that of science—the descriptive-explanatory—but that of its own, the descriptive-justificatory. One may hold, with the value naturalists and empiricists, that these judgments are descriptive-explanatory just as are those of the sciences. But in both cases Adams's conclusion holds, that they are "factual, empirically verifiable and proper subjects of factual truth-value predicates."[11]

In order to make the justificatory (teleological) schema applicable to the variety of concrete value situations, such a schema, of course,

[9] P. 103, above.   [10] P. 103.   [11] P. 105.

must first be created, and it must be created as axiological. Again, therefore, what is needed is a formal axiology capable of defining the terms which Robinson calls telic and teleutic and which would be the ones to constitute Adams's justificatory schema. This schema would then do for value situations what the explanatory—largely mathematical—schema does for the sciences.

Brandt, in a way, discusses a question exactly opposed to that of Adams: not, what is the over-arching conceptual schema of empirical science and valuation, respectively, but what are the underlying attitudes. For Adams, the value aspect of the factual situation comes about through a conceptual pattern different from the scientific. Brandt's question is whether the value aspect may come about through an underlying emotive pattern different from the scientific— in which such a pattern does not count. Brandt denies the adequacy of the emotive theory to account for value phenomena. His Essay is more critical than constructive; he does not say what a cognitive value theory would be—except that it must be empirical, close to common usage, and governed by the logical apparatus of *Principia Mathematica*. Constructively, thus, he stands with the empirical value analysts, where we find these points developed.

His criticism seems to me very well taken.[12] But I feel Brandt lacks concepts precise enough[13] to make it stick, as a higher level analysis could do. Within the three-dimensional schema of axiology both cognitive and attitude theory would find their place. The relation between "x is good" and "I like x" would not be that of equivalence but that between pure and applied axiology. "I like ..." would be an application—namely a psychological one—of the purely axiological term "... good," just as the homonym, moral "good" would be an ethical, "beautiful" an aesthetic, or "holy" a religious interpretation of the same term. This would establish an *axiological psychology*, or psychology as a value science, and the emotive theory would fit into, or even constitute, this science. The cognitive theory, on the other hand, would, in its pure form, be the formal axiological system itself. The relation between the formal system and its appli- cation—axiological psychology—would bring out the characteristically

[12] Stevenson's rejection or reinterpretation of Brandt's example of the Southerner could easily be refuted by Brandt with a reference to G. Myrdal, *An American Dilemma* (New York, 1944), Chap. I.

[13] See the "definition" of value attitude, p. 164, which seems to define *ignotum per ignotius*.

ethical features of the attitude theory. The "attitude" of the speaker would appear as a precisely defined "value pattern" whose logical and epistemological features would be definite and whose relation to value statements would be determinate. Formal axiology would thus determine the truth or falsity of such statements in accordance with something which on the third level corresponds to Brandt's Expressive Thesis: the agreement or disagreement between what the speaker says and what he believes or is disposed to do. But the theory would formalize this "attitude" and regard it logically rather than psychologically.[14] Since the axiological pattern is normative for the psychology, the logical determinations would be definitory of the psychological value terminology and directive for the solution of its "puzzles." The exact relation between value psychology and ethics would then become clear, both having the same formal pattern, pure axiology, of which they are both applications. These applications constitute different, and exactly defined, axiological "dimensions." Brandt's puzzles all concern the relationship between value psychology and ethics. The definition of the two dimensions, therefore, would make it possible to show precisely what in Brandt's presentation belongs to ethics and what to value psychology, and thus to sort out the pieces of the puzzles.

Lepley examines the relation between scientific and value language from a fourth point of view, the relation between fact and value. He calls an object of "relatively tested interest" or of "relatively tested likes, joys" and so on[15] a value, and an object of cognition a non-value fact. Thus, he determines value empirically. Viewed in the perspective of the distinction commonly made between "physical fact" and "human value," fact and value stand in the "contrast relation"; but as referring to any object whatsoever they stand in a "parallel relation." And the question is, whether "the modes of meaning or sign response are different in the valuative as compared with those in the factual; and if there are differences in mode, are they differences of kind or of degree?"[16] Lepley does not analyze *why* an object of interest and so on is a value and what is the relation between interest and value language. But the appearance of value terms such as "good" does not necessarily have to indicate interest,

[14] See p. 215, above: "ought" as "attitude indicator."
[15] From a letter by Lepley.
[16] P. 238 f., above.

nor its absence fact. "He is a man, indeed"[17] may convey more of value than "He is a good man," which may be a merely factual statement concerning my bookkeeper. We either do not have here the contrast relation—if both are valuative judgments—or else have it reversed, in that the value judgment looks more factual than the factual judgment. Thus, unless the nature of the two kinds of judgments is *defined* it is difficult to see how either the contrast or the parallel relation can be accounted for. Rather, the lack of definition makes the shuttling back and forth between the two series of judgments so easy as to be almost lubricous. Lepley thus is right in saying that the difference between the meanings of, or sign responses to, factual and valuative terms and sentences, may be the same and it all depends on the context of the situation. But this is only one half of the story. There *are* differences between valuative and factual judgments—the question is only how to bring them out without losing the situational cross-fertilization between the two. This, it seems to me, is only possible on a higher analytic level, by adding to the empirical method of analysis—of propositions as referring to situations—the logical of propositions *as propositions*, that is, within their own logical pattern. This pattern, for *value* propositions, must, of course, be a value-logical, an axio-logical one which includes a definition of value in its own terms.

To apply this pattern to some of Lepley's examples, "This is a table" is a logical proposition—as against an axiological one—and "This is a good table" or "This table is good" is a (mixed)[18] axiological one. The two propositions may *situationally* indeed mean the same or almost the same thing. But this does not nullify the *logical* difference between the two propositions as such. Also, the dividing line between "table" and "good table" is not merely bound to the word "good" but also to its definiens, say, "to fulfill an intension." The proposition "This sure *is* a table"—meaning that this surely fulfills the intension of "table"—may then be just as valuative as the proposition "This is a good table." Similar distinctions may be made concerning Lepley's example of sulfuric acid. Lepley points to the similarities of "Sulfuric acid dissolves iron," "Sulfuric acid is a good solvent for iron," and "Sulfuric acid is an effective substance for

[17] See Shakespeare, *Julius Caesar*, 5.5.73.
[18] P. 210, above.

dissolving iron." But this similarity is situational, not analytical. Analytically, the three propositions are entirely different. The first is logical, the second axiological, the third teleological. In the second appear the axiological terms "good" or "good for," which in third-level analysis mean either that "sulfuric acid" fulfills the definition of "a solvent of iron" ("good") or that "sulfuric acid" is part of that definition ("good for"). In the third proposition appears the telic term "effective for" which will get its definition once the teleological schema presupposed by Robinson's and Adams's Essays is elaborated.

Lepley's question as to the difference in the modes of meaning or sign response of valuative and factual judgments—which is, of course, a crucial one in value theory—must therefore, not only be discussed in relation to the referent,[19] or in relation to the neural pattern,[20]— on what Moore in his Comments on Lepley's Essay calls the "vertical" plane—but also on the horizontal plane of the conceptual pattern to which the propositions in question *as propositions* belong.

McGreal on the one hand advocates an empirical analysis of value propositions—"good" refers to the capacity of things "to arouse and sustain a liking in somebody"[21]—but on the other hand his third man is not one-sidedly committed to this kind of analysis. Rather, he is a student of symbols and willing to consider *any* value theory. I do not think that McGreal's own definition of "good," based on empirical elements of the situation—favoring, liking—is one with which a third man interested in the symbolic import of value terms could be satisfied. How, for example, would he, with McGreal's definition of "good" as guide, solve some of the questions raised—for example, that of the possible values for "x" in "x is good." Are these to be the names of all, and only such, things to which a liking can be taken? Can such things be anything—empirical things, God, circles, electrons? Are there any differences in these likings? Do the truth-values of the proposition change depending on which of the values of x are selected? Does the nature of the predicate or that of the copula change with these substitutions? Another problem raised by McGreal concerns the relation between "instrumental good," "moral good," and "good of its kind." Why would it be "silly" to suppose that in

[19] P. 246.
[20] If we use the *psychology* of emotions and knowledge as an explanatory pattern for value we may be in danger of explaining *ignotum per ignotius*.
[21] P. 302, above.

"This hammer is good" "good" is used in a moral sense?[22] Third-man Fingarette does exactly this.[23] Is "No. 17031 is a good man" an instrumental, specific, or moral value judgment? What is the significance of "is"?[24] Again, I am afraid, McGreal has not provided other third men with sufficient tools to answer the questions he himself raises.

McGreal makes a suggestive appeal for value analysis on all fronts. I thus want to add to his four third men[25]—all of whom analyze the "symbolic import" of value terms empirically—a fifth who does so nonempirically. The questions raised by McGreal can, I believe, not be answered on the first nor even on the second level of value analysis, but only on the third—be it in terms of logic, of semiotic or whatever other system, which is concerned, precisely with questions of this kind: What are axiological terms? What is the role of subject, predicate, and copula in axiological propositions? What are the truth-values of axiological propositions? How do they determine reality as valuational? and so on. In this way the symbolic import of value terms would be determined deductively and not inductively. I cannot see how by a "refinement"[26] of the empirical raw material one can arrive at a system of axiology which could answer these formal questions—as little as by a "refinement" of common sense one could arrive at a system of logic or even of geometry.[27] In the sciences the most fruitful systems were those which most strikingly contradicted common sense, such as Copernicus's and Einstein's. The same may be true in value theory; one has only to think of Kierkegaard.

The emphasis on "common sense" appears more clearly in the next group of essays which commit themselves to empirical analysis, to the exclusion of any other kind. The most outspoken in this respect is Pepper's.

[22] P. 107.
[23] In a draft of his Essay.
[24] P. 108.
[25] P. 117 f.
[26] P. 301.
[27] See H. Hahn, "Geometry and Intuition," "a classic description of how 'common sense,' once accepted as the basis of physics but now rejected, is also inadequate as a foundation of mathematics," *Scientific American*, April, 1954, pp. 84 ff. See also J. S. Hadamard, *Essay on the Psychology of Invention in the Mathematical Field* (Princeton, N.J., 1945).

Pepper has "no confidence in unempirical conceptions of cognitions" but "great confidence in the empirical procedure" and believes
"value and valuations [to be] in the end as open to empirical testing
and verification as any complex field of human and cultural relations."[28] He believes, as does McGreal, that continuous refinement
of common experience will bring about the value terms and their
interrelationships, just as such a procedure has brought forth the
botanical terms. There is no doubt that with Pepper's method
impressive value-theoretical structures can be erected, as Pepper
himself has shown.[29] But is, to speak with Adams, so incomplete a
science as botany the adequate model for a science as ambitious as
axiology—encompassing as it does the whole world in its value aspect?
Furthermore, is not the procedure outlined by Pepper a Linnean
rather than a Darwinian, and was not the former inadequate even
for botany? The Darwinian procedure presupposed an independent
hypothesis—and Darwin got it not from his experiences on the *Beagle*
but from reading Malthus: from a leap of the imagination. What
Pepper calls the descriptive definition of value corresponds to the
empirical view of science which Adams attacks. There is also needed
the conceptual framework, which overarches, as an independent
structure, the empirical. Pepper's example of magnetism is a case
in point. What made magnetism into a science was the mathematical
framework summoned for this particular task by Maxwell. While
Faraday's and even Maxwell's activities may be called "refinements"
of experience—even though this seems to be stretching the point
almost to the breaking, beyond the relatively simple procedure that
leads from evergreens to conifers—the production of the differential
equations which were used by Maxwell and developed by Lagrange
almost a hundred years earlier can certainly not be called such a
refinement of any, and certainly not the Gilbertian, experience. In
Maxwell the empirical and the mathematical met;[30] but it must be
remembered that his most epochal discovery arose from *purely formal*

---

[28] P. 268.

[29] S. C. Pepper, *A Digest of Purposive Values* (Berkeley and Los Angeles, 1947).

[30] This double-edged physical science procedure is also apparent in Lenzen's
Physical Theory, to which Pepper refers. Two paragraphs after the one quoted by
Pepper begins "Chapter II. Euclidean Geometry"—and therewith a line of reasoning which only Galileo, against the obstinate opposition of Aristotelian "empiricists,"
eighteen hundred years after Euclid definitely combined with physical phenomena.

considerations.[31] Without such considerations the result of Pepper's procedure would be—and actually is in present-day value theory—a multitude of more or less elaborate empirical theories, developing in detail purpose, integration, satisfaction, interest, and so on, in large and small structures, but like the trees in the proverbial wood obstructing the view of the whole. What is needed, then, is an over-arching theory, and this is only possible on the formal level of analysis.

Lee, like Pepper, emphasizes the empirical roots of value theory, but, unlike him, presents a theory of intrinsic value. Value, for Lee, is a fact existing in a particular situation. It is a contextual property, partly objective, partly subjective. The subject's attention to the object provides the measure for the intensity and the direction of the value. The direction is positive if the object as attended to gives the subject satisfaction. Thus we have here what may be called a contextual satisfaction theory of value. An object has intrinsic value if it satisfies *as such now*—if "the positive evaluating factor is part of the actual transaction of the value contexture."[32] It has instrumental value if "the object is judged to be a cause or necessary condition of a pleasant or satisfactory transaction in the future,"[33] even if the present transaction is unpleasant.

This is a suggestive definition and the examples adduced by Lee must be accounted for by any value theory, especially the simultaneity of intrinsic and instrumental value in one and the same experienced object, the nature of moral choice, and the role of cognition in instrumental but not in intrinsic value. In these problems, I believe, the theory points toward higher than empirical levels of analysis. The primacy of intrinsic over instrumental value—a crucial subject for any value theory—is based by Lee on the reference of the evaluating factor to a future experience of intrinsic value. But the future experience of an intrinsic value is not itself an intrinsic value—or if it is, then it is not that intrinsic value for the sake of which the instrumental value is instrumental. Value becomes intrinsic only by the actual experience. An *expected* intrinsic value *is* no

[31] "Starting with four simple differential equations whose elegance and symmetry are still the delight of mathematicians, [Maxwell] was able to deduce from them all known experimental facts," H. Margenau in L. L. Woodruff, *The Development of the Sciences* (New Haven, Conn., 1941), Chap. III.

[32] P. 189, above.

[33] *Ibid.*

intrinsic value and may turn out in actual experience to be no intrinsic value at all. But how it does turn out is not the point. That intrinsic value is noncognitive does not lead to the conclusion that instrumental value depends on it, for it depends on *cognition*: a *thought* of intrinsic value, namely its anticipation, and this anticipation is itself part of the—cognitional—instrumental value.[34]

Moore is not so completely committed to the empirical method as Pepper and Lee. For him it is only the "first storey" of the future structure of scientific axiology, which must be correlated with a logical schema before we can call axiology a science.[35]

Moore sees the value situation similarly to Lee, as a "sort of polar arrangement with the organism and the gross sensory object as the two extremes of a continuous though momentary organic strand." He holds, "first, that every experiential situation is an extensive strand with its subject and object poles; second, contrary to the position of the behaviorists, that every segment of this strand, from object to subject end, may be described; third, that the distinction between value sentences and so-called scientific sentences lies in their respective points of focus along this strand, the former comprehending and emphasizing what lies near the subject and the latter reflecting almost exclusively the structure around the object pole. Both *describe*; and they describe facts, albeit not the same facts."[36] It is quite difficult, to understand the exact relationship between the sentences in question, on the one hand, and the situation which they are supposed to describe, on the other hand. It seems that the transition from fact to value along the situational pattern is repeated or mirrored in a transition from scientific to value language, equally continuous as the transition of the situational pattern itself, though in the logical rather than the ontological realm. It would be interesting to follow this transition in the two realms and to find out (1) why and in which respect the subject pole of the ontological situa-

---

[34] Lee, in a letter, comments on this point: "The reference to the intrinsic value is in the future; thus, what actually operates now is the anticipation of the future actual existence of the intrinsic value. This is where the cognition enters into the context wherein instrumental value is to be found and by means of which is to be defined. There is a *judgment* of intrinsic value possible in the future. That this is so does not raise any problem peculiar to value theory. Whatever problem it raises is inherent in any reference to the future." Compare G. E. Moore's argument against Psychological Hedonism, *Principia Ethica* (London, 1903), pp. 69 f., 74.

[35] P. 266.

[36] From a letter by W. Moore.

tion is, or should have anything to do with, value, and (2) what, if any, is the distinguishing characteristic in the realm of sentences or propositions between the description of facts on the one hand and values on the other. Perhaps—similar to what we have seen in the discussion of Lepley's Essay—it is in the logical rather than the ontological realm, in this case in the analysis of what is meant by "description," that the distinction between fact and value, as the subject matter of two different kinds of "description," is to be found. This would lead in the direction of G. E. Moore's analysis of intrinsic value, with "description" being the differentia that distinguishes factual from value statements.[37] Such an analysis of description, with reference not merely to testability but to logical structure, would raise Moore's argument to the third level. The same may be true for his analysis of imperatives, which transcends, as Moore himself agrees, his situational procedure, and for his interesting analysis of "x is good" as "a sort of shorthand fashion" for "everybody likes x."

Most of the Essays so far—both the empirical and some of the methodological—have found the value criterion in some layer of the human psyche: Pepper in purpose, Lee in contextual satisfaction, Moore in affective involvement, Lepley in relatively tested interest, McGreal in liking, Brandt in desire. Garnett adds to these the criterion of intelligence. But his analysis differs from the foregoing in that he gives his empirical value definition so to speak with an ulterior motive—he wants to account empirically for the normative. Garnett's problem is how to account for the normativity of value-judgments not by entailment, as when value is defined in normative terms—"right," "ought," "duty,"—but when value is defined in non-normative terms, such as "good."

The question then is, how can "good" be empirically defined in such a way that the definition, as part of a first premise in a syllogism, can yield a normative conclusion. Garnett's solution is ingenious. "x is good" is equivalent to "x is a reasonable object of a favorable attitude." This is a non-normative and empirical definition, in terms of intelligence or reason. Now, says Garnett, although "the term 'good' does not, of itself, entail a normative concept," there "enters through the word 'reasonable' a material implication of normativity into the definition; for it is generally assumed that 'one ought to be

---

[37] G. E. Moore, *Philosophical Studies* (London and New York, 1922), p. 274; P. A. Schilpp (ed.), *The Philosophy of G. E. Moore* (New York, 1952), p. 592.

reasonable.'"[38] Hence, if x is a *reasonable* object of a favorable attitude, then x *ought to be made* the object of a favorable attitude. Everybody has the obligation to use his intelligence.

Thus, although the obligation to be reasonable is not established by the *definition* of "good" and neither this nor any other obligation is *asserted* by use of this term, there does arise an assertion of obligation by reason of "an independent synthetic proposition assumed by people who use the term." The assertion of reasonableness *is* not normative, but it is generally *assumed* to be so. Garnett's definition claims "to clarify ordinary usage and point out why statements about what is 'good' are generally understood as implying propositions containing an 'ought.'"[39] Garnett's definition of "good" is an empirical one designed to show *that* element—"reasonable"—which materially implies "ought."

One can well agree with Garnett that the definition of "good" contains an element which implies an "ought." But this statement— that the definition of "good" contains an element which implies an "ought"—is a formal one—dealing with a *definition*—and there is no reason why it should be rendered in empirical terms. Indeed, such rendering robs the definition of its formal power. For none of its empirical terms—neither "object of a favorable attitude" nor "reasonable"—is necessary in order to bring about the material implication of normativity. The former term—"object of a favorable attitude"— is unnecessary, for the implication attaches to "reasonable." The syllogism[40] would be just as valid if we would write:

Whatever is a reasonable A ought to be an A

x is a reasonable A

Therefore,

x ought to be an A

If we want to define "a reasonable A" in such a way that "x is a reasonable A" is equivalent to "x is good," we can now use the various empirical definitions of "good" proposed in the literature and substitute for "A" any of them—"object of pleasure," "object of desire," "object of satisfaction," "object of approval," "object of interest," "object of purpose," and so on. All of these would fill the bill, and there are just as many "good" reasons for Garnett to use his

[38] From a letter by Garnett. See p. 128, above.
[39] From Garnett's letter.
[40] P. 128, above.

definition for "good"—reasons, I presume, which are "reasonable objects of a favorable attitude" on his part—as there are "good" reasons for other ethicists to use *their* definitions of "good"—reasons which are "reasonable objects of pleasure," "reasonable objects of satisfaction," and so on for them.

But also the other part of Garnett's definition—the word "reasonable"—shares the arbitrariness of all empirical definitions of "good." Garnett states that there is an "assumption that one ought to be reasonable." How, if another ethicist would say that there is an assumption that one ought to be pleased? Or satisfied? Or purposive? In other words, would not any other of the empirical definientia of "good" do just as well for the assumption of oughtness? I might well say that to be reasonable counts for nothing if one has no goal— since, as Garnett himself says, in refuting G. E. Moore, "ought" refers to responsible human actions. Thus it is purposive rather than reasonable that, in my opinion, it is generally assumed everyone ought to be. Also, I might say, I prefer satisfaction to a favorable attitude as the characteristic of good. Hence, I define "x is good" as "x is a purposive object of satisfaction," and say "whatever is a purposive object of satisfaction ought to be an object of satisfaction." Then, if x is good, that is, a purposive object of satisfaction, the conclusion is that it ought to be made an object of satisfaction. Or again, I can use the two characteristics of "good" in the reverse order and define "x is good" as "x is a satisfactory object of purpose" assuming that everybody ought to be satisfied. In other words, the arbitrariness of the empirical level adheres also to that characteristic of "good" to which, according to Garnett, attaches the assumption of normativity: *any* such characteristic may imply normativity. The definition then becomes "x is good" is equivalent to "x is φ and x is A" where it is implied that if x is φ x ought to be A.

But this, actually, is similar to the definition given, in my Essay, on the third level of analysis. According to this definition, x is a good A if x has all the properties entailed by the concept A. Suppose A entails the properties α, β, γ, or, in general, φ (φ being the variable of which α, β, γ are the values). Then, if x has all the properties φ, x, of course, ought to be an A, where "ought" is the analytic ought; if John is manly in every respect he ought to be a man. And indeed, if he is thus manly he will be a good man, in this sense of "man"— a good specimen of manliness. If, on the other hand, John did *not* have all the properties of manliness, that is, were not manly in every respect, then he ought not to be a man in this same sense. Here "ought" is again analytic because John actually *is* not a man in this sense. On the other hand, although John is not manly he *ought* to be manly in every respect. Here "ought" is synthetic, for John is *not* manly in every respect and hence ought to be what he *is not*. As is seen, "ought" here arises, analytically or synthetically, out of a third-level non-normative definition of "good." Garnett's definition is of the same general nature.[41]

We have, thus, in all, four cases, two for "x is good" (I and II) and two for "x is not good" (III and IV) as follows:

I. "x is φ and x is A," where "x is φ" *materially implies* "x ought to be A." (Third-level version of Garnett's definition.)

II. "x is φ and x is A," where "x is φ" *entails* "x ought to be A."

III. "x is not φ and x is not A" where "x is not φ" *entails* "x ought not to be A."

IV. "x is not φ and x is A," where "x is not φ" *materially implies* "x ought to be A."

Fingarette has in common with Garnett the emphasis on rationality; but instead of coupling it with approval he couples it with *choice* as the criterion of value. Again, Fingarette does not say *why*, of all the situational elements, rational choice is this criterion and how it is related to the other empirical criteria proposed by other ethicists. Like Garnett, Fingarette uses the element of rationality to propose a logical instrument—in this case not a norm-producing assumption but a theory of "judgmental functions." Ethical terms, says Fingarette, have three functions: (1) to elicit the act of rational choice, (2) to express a certain phase of the act of rational choice, (3) to refer to an act of rational choice. Obviously, if all three functions refer to one and the same choice they may be interpreted as a temporal sequence—from bringing about the choice (1) to choosing (2) to judging the choice made (3) or as functioning in, respectively, the choice to be made (1), the making of the choice (2), and the choice made (3).

While these are useful distinctions and Fingarette makes impressive use of them a great deal of elaboration will be necessary for this function to account for truly moral choices—such as, say, those

---

[41] To get a more comprehensive view of Garnett's meaning of "good," see "Different Kinds of Good" in *The Moral Nature of Man* (New York, 1952), pp. 122 ff.

discussed by Kierkegaard—and to serve as conceptual schema, in Adams's sense, for moral phenomena. In particular, the function does not seem capable—at least not in its present form—to stake out the aspect of the moral as against other situational aspects. Some of Fingarette's examples can be called moral only by a stretch of the meaning of this word which not only for some of McGreal's third men seems prohibitive.[42] What difference, for example, does it make *morally* whether I travel in a hard or a soft coach or whether I arrive sooner or later? What difference does it make *morally* whether I use a spike or a nail in my house? There *may* be moral significance to such choices, but the fact that I decide such relative trivialities rationally does not make these choices moral, just as little as an irrational decision would make them immoral. There seems to be more to morality and immorality than eliciting, making, or judging choices rationally or irrationally. The *content* of choice seems to have something to do with its moral character. In other words, I do not think that Fingarette has successfully disposed of his own objection, "is not 'rational choice' too broad in scope as compared with 'moral'?" I answer Yes, and find the ground of the trouble in Fingarette's neglect of the distinction between the moral and the axiological, that is, of the levels of value language. When value terms such as "good," "right," and so forth are used with reference to hammers, tires, and driving-in of nails then they are *not* used "morally" but instrumentally. To drive in a nail in a wall is not only "not a 'typical' moral" situation, it is no moral situation at all. But to drive a nail through a man's hands on a cross is a moral situation.

We have here again the relation between the formal nature of terms, which is a matter of value logic, and the application of these terms, which is a matter of the lower language levels. Formally axiological terms such as "good" become in a certain application—to persons—moral, but in certain other applications—to nails, tires, hammers—instrumental (technological), economic, and so on. The goodness of a hammer, as McGreal rightly says, has nothing to do with morality. But it has to do with axiology, just as has moral goodness. Both, the hammer's goodness and moral goodness are interpretations of axiological goodness. Fingarette uses the term "moral" in the sense of "axiological." If this latter term is substituted

[42] P. 362, above.

for his "moral," "rational choice" becomes an axiological or, since it always takes place within a process, a teleological term—it should be included among Robinson's telic or teleutic terms and become part of Adams's schema—and moral choice a specific such choice, namely, in the human dimension and in humanly relevant situations. Instead of saying, then, that "examination shows that moral *terms* are always appropriate where rational choice is made, even though not every rational choice [like the choice to fix a flat tire] is considered a *typically* moral one," we could simply say that "rational choice" is a teleological term, which would mean, after what was said in the discussion of Robinson's Essay, that "rational choice" belongs to a language level higher than the empirical—including the moral—but that *a certain kind* of such choices is moral, others being nonmoral— yet all belonging to the realm of values. The hammer is then not "good by courtesy" but good by axiology. Fingarette's judgmental function thus presupposes, like Robinson's linguistic inventory and Adams's justificatory schema, the elaboration of a formal axiological and teleological systematic.

Morris distinguishes between the signification and the significance of terms—their sign and their value character. By signification of a sign he means

the properties something must have for the sign to apply to it . . . Thus if a given person applies the term 'banana' to an object if and only if the object has properties *a*, *b*, and *c*, then the set of properties *a*, *b*, and *c*, constitutes for him the signification of the term, 'banana.' In that case if he is told that there is a banana on his desk he will expect to find there . . . an object with these properties. Under this criterion for signification it is in principle, and often in practice, possible to find out by objective methods the signification which a sign has for an individual or group of individuals.[43]

Morris uses this analysis of signification for determining the signification of such words as "good" and "bad." "These words signify not merely in a context of significance, they signify significance directly." He calls such terms appraisive signs.

We can interpret Morris's analysis in terms of formal axiology. Signification is the translation into situational terms of the logical notion "subjective intension." This notion, combined with the formal definition of "good," enables us to *define* value-significance in terms

[43] P. 59 f., above.

of signification. Morris, as Robinson suggests, does not do this. He simply opposes significance to signification, without any systematic connection between the two.[44] Using the definition of "good"—as the predicate of a subject which possesses all the intensional properties of its concept—we find that the intension of the term "good" is its reference to the total set of intensional properties of a subject. Translated into Morris's language this means that the signification of "good" is the signification of the term to which "good" refers plus the assertion that a particular thing actually has the properties signified. In other words, "good" signifies *signification plus the fulfillment of the corresponding expectation.* This two-dimensional signification of "good" is—in our interpretation though not in Morris's— *"significance."* Thus, value terms do indeed "signify significance directly"; but they do so by signifying signification plus a state of its fulfillment.

We shall now interpret this result in terms of Morris's experiment. Morris's experimental subjects were asked to correlate liking expressions and goodness expressions. The former were called P-ratings (preference-ratings), the latter A-ratings (appraisal-ratings). The result of these experiments was, that 19 of the 20 paintings were signified as *both* aesthetically good *and* aesthetically bad. From this Morris rightly concludes "there can be no observable property or properties of the paintings alone, which would constitute the signification of 'aesthetically good' or 'aesthetically bad.'"[45] But then Morris continues: "The analogy for the term 'banana' would be a situation where 19 out of 20 objects were signified as being bananas and also signified as not being bananas." From this "analogy" Morris concludes that the signification of "good" and "bad" cannot possibly involve reference only to the object reacted to and not to the actor. This conclusion of Morris's, in the light of our interpretation, is not justified. The result may equally well be taken as illustrating an important relation in realistic value theory—where value resides in

---

[44] "In my terminology the signification of 'significance' cannot in any way be derived from the signification of 'signification'—though this may well be possible in your semiotic. For me something can have significance (or value) without being signified; and whatever is signified may or may not have significance (value). In my terminology 'signification' is a semiotical term (i.e., a category within semiotic) while 'significance' is not. So in my semiotic, but not in yours, there is no necessary relation between the signification of the two terms" (from a letter by Morris).

[45] P. 63, above.

the object—namely, the relation between a thing and its properties. Morris rightly says "the term 'good' apparently does not signify objects in the way the term 'banana' does. Either it has no signification, or it is very ambiguous in its signification (differing from person to person), or it signifies in some different manner than does a designative word such as 'banana.'"[46] But does this mean that "good" does not reside in the object?

According to G. E. Moore, "good" is not a natural intrinsic property, that is, a property, which is part of the description of a thing, but a non-natural intrinsic property, which is not part of the description of the thing. This can mean that "good" can be interpreted as referring *to the total set of all* the natural intrinsic properties of an object. In the light of this interpretation, Morris's result can be taken to show that an object appears differently when judged descriptively, that is, by analysis of its properties, and when judged nondescriptively, that is, when these properties themselves are being judged. For, whereas there would be very little difference in the answers if the question had been whether these were *pictures*, there were differences in the answers to the questions whether these were *good* pictures or whether the subjects *liked* them. Both these questions referred *not* to the descriptive nature of the pictures—their properties *a, b, c* which make them *pictures*, or their signification—but to the signification of these significations, plus the fulfillment or nonfulfillment of the corresponding expectations. But whereas the first question—"How do you like the picture?"—puts the emphasis on the *fulfillment of the expectation*, the second question —"How good is the picture?"—puts it on the *signification of the signification*. In this connection it is well to remember Willis Moore's analysis of the relation between "I like x" and "x is good." The latter is more objective and tends toward universal agreement. That we are here reminded of Moore's Essay is no accident, for what we are concerned with here is description—Moore's key term.

Thus there are three levels of decreasing objectivity or increasing subjectivity to be distinguished in Morris's questions: (1) "Is this a picture?" This question, which is implied in the other two, is a question of signification. Although it presupposes a subjective synopsis of the properties of the thing, only the minimum definition of "picture" must be known to answer it. (2) "Is this a good picture?"

46 P. 63.

Here a higher knowledge of the properties of a picture is needed, not only of the descriptive properties but also of the signification of these properties. It is a question of the signification of signification. This, in the case of pictures, constitutes aesthetic knowledge.[47] Fewer persons have this kind of knowledge than the kind of knowledge relevant to question (1). (3) "Do you like this picture?" Here those who have no knowledge in the sense of (2) will be arbitrary, while those who do have this knowledge will guide their answer by it. This explains the higher correlation between (2) and (3) among those who have aesthetic "interest," that is, a kind of aesthetic knowledge. It also explains why the correlation was not higher—because quite a few did not have such knowledge—and why it was not lower—because some of those who have no aesthetic knowledge were statistically bound to choose as if they had. Thus the experiment—especially if it were conducted with a larger number of persons—by its very nature tends toward correlation, even though there is a considerable factor—the ignorance in (2)—tending towards no correlation.

In my own Essay I try to outline a third-level theory. Since I have used it throughout these Comments, I believe its relative position in this book and its function as an analytic instrument for axiology have been sufficiently illustrated.

It was my endeavor throughout to correlate the various Essays into one pattern, and the relative emphasis given to the individual papers was exclusively dictated by this integrative endeavor. It seems to me that each of the Essays makes a significant contribution to the study of value language. The papers in their totality give an idea of the tremendous scope and complexity of the task before us.

---

[47] In the case of persons it would constitute moral knowledge, in the case of groups political knowledge, and so on. See p. 200n, above.

COMMENTS BY LEPLEY

M Y COMMENTS are written from what may be called an inclusive experimental standpoint. From this perspective it appears that the preceding pages of this volume deal with important aspects of the linguistics or 'semantics'[1] of value theory, that they make significant contributions to this theory, and that the limitations and weaknesses of the several papers result at least in part from failure of the authors to view their problems in a sufficiently inclusive experimental perspective. The nature of this perspective may become more apparent as we note briefly what from this standpoint are some of the main contributions and limitations of the several Essays, of some Comments and Responses which accompany them, and of Hartman's Comments over all the Essays.[2]

In making my appraisals from this perspective I do not of course imply that it is the only possible or fruitful one. Also, the 'weaknesses' to be noted no doubt result, in some instances and to some extent, from limitations of space in the present volume. Mention of additional tasks which from an inclusive experimental standpoint I think should be undertaken is intended as a challenge to further study or explication, not as adverse criticism. Such criticism is properly addressed only to treatments the inherent qualities of which are adversely affected by failure to approach problems or issues from a sufficiently broad, dynamic, analytic, and integrative point of view; and this is perhaps in some measure true of all the papers. I trust that my colleagues in the present study and other readers will

[1] For my use of single and double quotation marks see footnote 8, p. 234. The meaning of "semantics" as here used is indicated in the Introduction, pp. 4-5.

[2] Brief accounts of what is here meant by "inclusive experimental perspective" are presented by "The Dawn of Value Theory," *The Journal of Philosophy*, XXXIV (1937), 365-73; and "The Current Status of Value Theory," *Educational Theory*, IV (1954), 158-65. A more extensive development of this point of view is contained in *Verifiability of Value* (New York, 1944); *Value: A Cooperative Inquiry* (New York, 1949), pp. 167-83, 381-92; and my present Essay, pp. 232-57, above.

recognize that the somewhat assertive, sweeping quality of the following summations and evaluations results in no small part from limitations of space to which the present Comments also are subject.

Moore's Essay recognizes that value experiences and language occur in actual physical, personal, and social contexts. There is, as Moore says, "a value situation both chronologically prior to and logically independent of the use of language of any kind."[3] This of course, as Adams comments, does not mean that value situations can be studied or described without the use of language. But many aspects of value situations (including language) are what they are, quite apart from language or metalanguage. As Moore says in his Response, "Were this not so, man could neither get started in this project of describing value experience nor subsequently correct the errors that admittedly infect his descriptions."[4] Still it must be recognized, as Moore perhaps does, that value descriptions (and other value formulations) can safely be regarded only as tentative hypotheses subject to further testing, which includes continuing interaction with various 'independently existing' aspects of the value situation.

Moore observes that value experiences, or affective involvements of a subject with an object, appear to vary in "depth" or distance along a continuum from object to subject and that various sorts of sentences and terms rise to express and describe the experiences characteristic of the various "nodes" along the continuum; and he finds that "I like X" is a typical first-level value sentence. There appears, however, to be little explicit recognition of, or at least slight emphasis on, the actual and possible continuing interaction between subjects and objects and on the fact that expressions (sentences, terms) at whatever node and in whatever context can be treated as tentative formulations which come to have a status of valuative (or factual) signs in a most distinctive and objective sense only as they emerge transformed (as Dewey saw) by a process of inquiry. Failure to recognize the possibilities for the extension and development of experimental procedures in value matters may appear to be indicated by Moore's statement, in his Response, that though standards of excellence "may be shown to derive of the very structure of nature

[3] P. 9.
[4] P. 265.

and of man as a part of it," *"this is as far as a science of such standards can go."*[5]

Robinson's Essay, by presenting and classifying examples of "value-theoretical terms" such as occur in "writings which might plausibly be counted as contributions to 'value theory,'"[6] achieves a somewhat empirical and independent standpoint from which to consider the role which these terms play in the language of value theory and the language of sign theory, with particular attention to Morris's semiotical system. The study yields a number of interesting observations with regard to various phases and levels of value language. Robinson concludes (and Morris in his Comment agrees) that semiotical value theory differs from the rest of sign theory, or semiotic, in its subject matter rather than in its techniques or procedures. Both men recognize the limitations of an ostensive approach, and Robinson continues through his Response to find the relations of

---

[5] P. 267 (italics added). Moore replies to these comments as follows: "Lepley is correct in saying that in my Essay I neglected those intellectual procedures whereby a person's affective reactions to a given type of object may be modified even to the point of reversal. One reason for this neglect was lack of space. A more important one was my belief that at least some of our disagreements in axiology may be cleared up if we can be brought back to the relatively simple, initial value experience, out of which this admittedly complex current type of value situation has grown. Such men as Dewey, Geiger, and Lepley have seemed quite reluctant to admit even the existence of value experiences unclad in intellectual garb. I have been insisting that it is with such raw data that we begin our value experiences. I hold that even at the end, after any and all intellectual manipulations have been carried out, there confronts us still something which simply occurs for us.

"All this is not to deny the reality of what Lepley keeps emphasizing as the role of experimental intelligence in manipulating and modifying these experiences. As I see the role of intelligence in this area it is essentially that of a tool for extending and expanding our experiential horizons so as to give us a more adequate grasp of the affective consequences of a commitment to some object of present value. In terms of this more adequate awareness of the situation the present object becomes a cue to a more extended, more complex object and, normally, the affective reaction to the initial object becomes correspondingly more complex, even perhaps quite different in character.

"I avoid the use of such language as might suggest that the use of experimental intelligence somehow transmutes or exorcises the affective reaction to the original and simpler object. More accurately, such intellectual procedures enlarge, extend, and bring out more detail in the initial object; but this more complex object must still be reacted to affectively, must, so to speak, have an immediate aspect of value. There is no magic in language level manipulation or in scientific procedure which can metamorphose or translate the immediacy of the raw value data into something which renders this same initial data outmoded or unimportant. Scientific manipulations are external to and not constitutive of values."

[6] P. 30.

sign theory and value theory to be, if not "in a tangle," at least in some respects "obscure."

Despite Robinson's warnings that his classification of value-theoretical terms "is a bad one," that many of the words listed are "ambiguous enough to warrant placing them simultaneously in more than one subdivision," and that "many are so vague as to defy exact classification,"[7] the fact that his ostensive definitions assume or may appear to assume the prior or independent existence of subclasses may—unless the listing and study of terms is done within the framework of an inclusive experimental perspective—encourage the common view that signs are valuative (or factual) without regard to the contexts in which they occur. The effect may thus be to perpetuate the notion that facts and values, and factual and valuative terms and sentences, constitute or fall into distinct and fixed classes, or that they do so in most cases. When viewed within the actual personal and social situations in which they rise and function dynamically to mediate or assist courses of adjustment or problem solving, it is evident that terms commonly have, as Robinson emphasizes, many meanings (stimulus-effects, significations, uses).

Morris's Essay acknowledges the pervasive parallel occurrence, or possible occurrence, of signification and significance ("anything may have significance and anything may be signified"),[8] and it recognizes the hypothetical, probable character of the signification of even such a 'concrete' designative term as "banana." Morris sees that all signs signify in a context of significance, but he decides to call *appraisive signs* those which (such as "good" and "bad") "signify not merely in a context of significance" but also "signify significance directly."[9] His problem is then formulated as that of the determination of the signification of appraisive signs, and particularly that of finding "the unique features of appraisive signification needed to differentiate it from other signs (such as the term 'father') which also require an objective relativist analysis."[10] Study of preference-ratings and appraisal-ratings of paintings leads him to conclude that "appraisive signs do not signify objects in isolation from persons or persons in isolation from objects, but objects in their capacity to satisfy need."[11]

But has Morris thus succeeded in differentiating appraisive (from,

---

[7] Pages 32-33.   [8] Pages 69-70, above.
[9] P. 60.   [10] P. 65.
[11] P. 67.

say, designative) signs? In his essay in *Value: A Cooperative Inquiry* he states:

To say that an object is brown is to signify certain characteristics of the object discriminable by effects on the sense organs or other objects, while to say that an object is good is to signify either that it falls in the upper range of a series of objects ordered in terms of the preferential behaviors accorded to them by the interpreter of the sign, or to signify that the object reduces the need of some organism. "Good" in the first sense is an appraisive term and not designative; in the second sense it is as designative as the term "brown."[12]

It appears, however, that in his present Essay, Morris either has assumed that "good" and "bad" always signify as appraisive signs, or has extended the meaning of "appraisive" to include (at least in the case of "good") the signification of both "appraisive" and "designative" as these terms were used in the earlier book. By his present philosophic and statistical analyses Morris may have 'found' the distinctive subject matter or referent of what he here calls "appraisive signs," but it may be questioned whether this throws much, if any, light on the problem of *how* appraisive signs signify. For, as he recognizes, even some designative terms, such as "father" (and "brown"?), signify a relation of object and subject; and it appears that in some cases "good" may, as he said earlier, be as designative as "brown." In analyzing the difference between signification and significance in his present Essay, Morris seems to have selected a designative sign, "banana," the referent of which may appear to be 'in' objects, and to have selected instances of "good" and "bad" (paintings judged good or bad as works of art) in which the referent appears to lie largely, though not wholly, in subjects. There would seem therefore to be need for study of more truly comparable instances of designative and appraisive signs at more points along the whole scale of variation from the most concrete and certain objects to the most abstract and uncertain ones. It may also prove fruitful to study experimentally, and with similarly inclusive orientation, the extent to which different signs or ascriptors, both "factual" and "valuative," are or are not mutually translatable, interchangeable, or equivalent.[13]

[12] *Value: A Cooperative Inquiry*, pp. 217-18.
[13] In response to these comments Morris says: "It seems to me that you are quite right in pointing out that my paper in the present volume, taken alone, does not *fully* differentiate the appraisive from the designative. And you are right in

Pepper's Essay holds that descriptive definition, refined by continuing inquiry, is or can be the basis for responsible definitional criteria and that the facts described in descriptive definitions of value are selective systems which become natural norms. "The evaluative standards come out of the facts themselves."[14] By the care with which he develops this point of view Pepper may have attained, with respect to definition and the basis of value and norms, a more complete naturalization of value theory than has been achieved heretofore. Of course, some critics of this view will insist, as does Lafleur in his Comments, that "this treatment, suitable only to extrinsic values, leaves no answer available to the question whether terminal goals are good except on psychological or sociological grounds, and these can only affirm that such terminal goals do actually exist."[15] It may be that Pepper leaves himself open to misinterpretation and criticism by saying, "If a subordinate goal brings about a superordinate goal, it is good; if not, it is bad," but he emphasizes, in the last paragraph of his Response, a very important point with regard to the empirical derivation and testing of terminal satisfactions, or intrinsic values.[16] We shall return briefly to the problem of norms in considering Garnett's Essay and his Comments on Fingarette's Essay.

Adams's Essay is notable as a study of the relation of man's attempts "to make reflective intrapersonal and interpersonal adjustments among conflicting interests" as contrasted with attempts "to make reflective adjustments to a problematic environment,"[17] the latter giving rise to science and descriptive-explanatory conceptual systems, the former giving rise to axiological inquiry and descriptive-justificatory conceptual systems. Feigl finds Adams's distinction between scientific description and truth and axiological description and truth to be

---

pointing out a certain difficulty in reconciling what is said in the present paper with what was said in the preceding volume. This stems in part from a change in my use of 'need' in the interval—instead of contrasting 'need' and 'preferential behavior' I have now become convinced that 'need' is ultimately to be defined in terms of preferential behavior. I do not think that there is any basic opposition between my two papers; they seem to me to be supplementary. But neither tells the full story." And perhaps Morris will agree that the two papers *together* do not tell the full story—which is a most essential point of my comment, though not intended as an adverse criticism.

[14] P. 89, above.   [15] P. 283, above.
[16] For the quotation see p. 89; for the last paragraph of the Response see p. 286.
[17] P. 101.

"'mistaken," and concludes that value judgment, unlike descriptive knowledge, consists in more than its empirical content: "the stamp of approval, the accent of endorsement, the force of encouragement, in short the motivative appeal is part of the life process itself, and while as such open to empirical study, is not by itself anything that could conceivably be true or false."[18]

Both Adams's Essay and Feigl's Comments show clearly the extent to which logical positivists have come to recognize the hypothetical, probable nature of even scientific formulations. But though they disagree in the analysis of scientific sentences and with regard to the possibility of axiological truth, they seem to agree in viewing fact and value mainly in the contrast relation.[19] Though Feigl sees that when values are instrumental or ends are granted or agreed upon value sentences become strictly factual, he does not appear to recognize that 'scientific' (or experimental) method can in very important respects be more than descriptive or descriptive-explanatory—that even interests (likes, desires, approvals, endorsements, encouragements) which spring from and are a part of the life process can be treated as hypotheses subject to inquiry and testing in terms of how they work out in fact, how they 'stand up' *as* facts in relation to a myriad of other personal, social, organic, and inorganic facts.[20] Adams explicitly states that value formulations may be empirically 'verified,'[21] but he too gives slight indication of the potentialities for extension and development of experimental procedures in value affairs, though

[18] P. 294.
[19] "Contrast relation" is here used in the sense indicated on p. 238.
[20] With regard to these comments, Feigl says: "While there is nothing in the way of misrepresentations of my position against which I might violently protest, I am still somewhat amazed that after nearly twenty years of discussion of the issue, either the positivists or the pragmatists have failed to make their position sufficiently clear to be understood by the other party to the dispute. Let me say just this: If, as you say, interests (likes, desires, approvals . . .) can be treated as hypotheses subject to testing in terms of how they work out in fact, how they 'stand up' as facts, etc., I would be the first not only to grant but to insist that such inquiry or testing is of a factual-cognitive-empirical kind. But is it not obvious that one must have a value standard up one's sleeve in order to tell as to whether these interests 'stand up,' etc.? J. S. Mill saw this a long time ago and made a very succinct statement of it, to this effect: without value premises, no value conclusions from empirical propositions." But I would ask, cannot value premises and value standards, even when "up one's sleeve," be tentative, hypothetical formulations capable of some measure of 'test' and 'correction' through continuing experimental procedure? And what are the alternatives to such procedure?
[21] P. 104.

his position may appear to imply or be compatible with recognition of such potentialities.

In his Essay, Adams holds that the verification of axiological or means-ends formulations is in relation to the satisfaction of interests, not in relation to the (a?) descriptive-explanatory conceptual system. In his Response, he admits that "the same property may be selected and designated by terms in both the descriptive-justificatory and descriptive-explanatory languages," but insists: "However, being designated by a term from one language places the property in one set of conceptual relationships different from that established by being designated by a term in the other."[22] But he appears to compare the relations of the descriptive-explanatory and the descriptive-justificatory conceptual systems mainly at points of their most distinctive *present differentiation,* not at points of potential development in dealing with all subject matters. There is need, it seems to me, for further consideration of the close parallel (and possible identity) of scientific and axiological systems when both are most highly developed with reference to representative instances along the entire gamut of actual and possible objects.

McGreal's Essay makes a sensitive analysis of the factors which affect the signification of a word (such as "good") considered by itself, in relation with other words (as in the sentence "X is good"), and in the contexts of different purposes and perspectives. It stresses the fact that the point of view and the interest and intent of the interpreter or user determine the mode in which "good" and other signs signify. McGreal recognizes that "a thing does not necessarily become good because it is called good,"[23] and that "a thing is good only if it can win, or retain, favor upon examination."[24] He does not, however, explicitly emphasize the point that valuative as well as factual formulations may be treated as hypotheses and that the outcomes of experimental inquiry are not wholly or necessarily determined by the point of view of the 'experimenter.'[25]

[22] P. 295.

[23] P. 116.

[24] P. 117, above.

[25] In connection with correspondence on other matters, McGreal says: "Incidentally, for your reassurance, I certainly believe—though I may not explicitly have emphasized—that value formulations may be treated as hypotheses (and if true are factual), and that the 'outcomes of experimental inquiry are not wholly or necessarily determined by the point of view of the experimenter.'"

Garnett's Essay, by considering various types of sentences which have been and are currently proposed as equivalents of "X is good," brings into sharp focus the issue as to whether "good" is or is not normative, has or has not normative implications or entailments. In accepting "X is a reasonable object of a favorable attitude," "an attitude such as would arise from enlightened understanding of the object and of oneself and of the relation of the object to oneself," as the equivalent of "X is good,"[26] Garnett recognizes that the good, so far as we may be able to know it, has to be discovered through processes of inquiry. But intelligence, reason, and ought are interpreted as something within the personality; there appears to be only partial recognition that impulses, constraints, and suggestions which rise or are felt 'within' the person can be, and indeed for maximum safety and creativity need to be, critically studied in view of effects, some of which are not evident apart from inclusive personal and social interaction.[27]

[26] P. 128, above.

[27] As indicated in recent correspondence, Garnett feels that this Response (pp. 307-9, above) explicitly recognizes the need for critical study of effects, some of which become evident only through inclusive personal and social interactions. He does indeed at that point place very strong emphasis on the need for study of effects as far as the good is concerned, though his statement makes no mention of the possibilities and needs for extension and development of experimental procedures even with regard to the good; and "the standard of obligation" is apparently regarded as "absolutist," though there seems to be here, as in some of his previous writings (see that cited in footnote 30, below), recognition that the "ultimate and absolute standard" is "difficult to find" and that the most that a person can do is to try his very best to know and fulfill his obligations. But how is this to be done? By reason and intuition alone? With or without study of effects? With or without efforts to extend and develop experimental attitudes and procedures in matters of norms, oughts, and obligations as well as in matters of the good? At one point in his Response, Garnett says: "In considering which action is right (that is, what we ought to do) we consider perhaps some deontological grounds (such as W. D. Ross refers to) but, for the most part, the value (good or bad) of the consequences" (p. 308, above). He seems to have gone a long way in developing an inclusive experimental viewpoint and he emphasizes an important datum: "a remarkable consensus of moral genius endorsing as the basic principle that of an impartial concern for the welfare of all" (p. 308, above). But may we accept this or any other principle, or make particular applications of it, without careful and continuing inquiry? What Garnett has now said concerning the text of my Comments would seem to indicate that he agrees that the answer to this question should, in general, be "No." (See footnote 37, p. 386, below).

As noted before, we shall return to the matter of norms, obligations, and oughts in considering Garnett's Comment on Fingarette's Essay, in the text below.

Fingarette's Essay, a study of judgmental functions performed by ethical terms with particular attention to the nature of moral choice or decision, holds that value utterances are not merely expressions of arbitrary choice, but that they elicit new acts of choice based on reasons for and against some alternative(s). Fingarette finds nowhere in the process of rational choice "an essential, irreducible moral element" which may not sensibly be questioned. His position is thus basically empirical and perhaps in a broad sense 'experimental'; but since his present purpose is "to find, state, and analyze the *common* ground with respect to a variety of naturalistic positions and some non-naturalistic positions,"[28] he stops short of considering the view that "the rational structure" possible in value matters is essentially the same as that discernible in matters of fact, on the ground that this view is still controversial.

In his Comments, Garnett insists that Fingarette's analysis of ethical terms, though applicable to "good," is inapplicable to 'right," "obligation," and other terms referring to *norms*. But this, Garnett emphasizes in subsequent correspondence, does *not* imply that norms are beyond question. In his own Essay, he maintains that the constraint of the ought which operates as sense of obligation to be reasonable "involves no intuition of an essence but simply the recognition of a psychological fact which becomes clear to the individual when he calmly and unemotionally reflects on his conduct. It is just as natural, and 'naturalistic,' as the operations of feeling and intellect that are referred to by the non-normative term 'good.'"[29] And, although he states elsewhere, "The subjective standard of morality..., which is ultimate for each person, can be described with complete clarity, exactness, and fullness," the nature of this subjective obligation is indicated by the further statement that "the most that a person can do to fulfill his obligation is to try his best, with an open mind and all available information, to find out what his obligations are and then make his best effort to fulfill what his inquiry leads him to think are his obligations." And he adds, "The objective standard of morality... is determined by the facts of existing obligations....

[28] From a recent letter from Fingarette. He says further: "I would hold, and have written elsewhere, that the structure *is* essentially the same." See his paper "Inquiry as Behavior," presented to the Third Inter-American Congress of Philosophy, Mexico, 1950.
[29] P. 129.

The important point . . . is the need for full, critical, and open-minded inquiry into the facts that constitute objective obligation."[30]

From these statements and from recent correspondence it would appear that Garnett is almost as much an experimental empiricist as are Fingarette or Dewey, whom he criticizes as not able adequately to elucidate "the fact that ethical discussion, through all its history, has asserted the existence of duties that are not dependent upon (and even run counter to) counsels of prudence."[31] Says Garnett:

Dewey's analysis of judgments of value . . . has done naturalistic ethics the service of distinguishing between valuing and evaluating. . . . He has also shown how each person evaluates his valuings by inquiry into their relations to the further possibilities and probabilities of his interests. But Dewey leaves us with the assumption that, if a person has correctly decided what, in view of this calculation of his interests, is *best* for him to do, that this is what, as a moral being, he ought to do.[32]

But Garnett thinks Dewey has not given sufficient attention to obligations, for he (Garnett) continues:

The emotivists have performed the service for naturalistic ethics of recognizing that this assumption is not in accord with ordinary usage of ethical language, that is, that normative terms such as 'ought' and 'right' are used to set up requirements that are independent of such calculations of interest. . . . The emotivists, however, have not recognized that the term 'good,' unlike 'ought' and 'right,' does not set up a requirement or norm.[33]

Space permits me here only to recall that some who are essentially and ultimately empiricists (as contrasted with rationalists, mystics, or revelationists) conceive norms, obligations, and oughts as more or less accidental or arbitrary social accumulations and pressures superimposed upon value experiences,[34] and that other empiricists view

---

[30] "Distinctions and Definitions in Ethics," *Philosophy and Phenomenological Research*, XII (1951), 73; reprinted by permission of the editors.
[31] P. 311, above.
[32] P. 313.
[33] Pages 313-14.
[34] See, for example, Charner M. Perry, "The Relation between Ethics and Political Science," *The International Journal of Ethics*, XLV (1936-37), 163-79. The main emphasis of Moore's Essay, pp. 16-24, may appear to put him in this group, but his statements on pp. 25-26 seem to place him in the second group mentioned, below.

them as rising from interrelations of physical, social, psychological, logical, and/or linguistic facts.[35] It appears that Garnett is a member of this latter group, but that he more than some others feels that norms, obligations, and oughts are somewhat independent factors which need to be given central importance in value inquiry and choice. In my opinion Garnett is stressing an important point, though I should wish to emphasize more than he the importance of treating historically derived norms and intuitions of inner feelings and perceptions as subject to question and inquiry in the light, as Dewey said,[36] of all we can know, which from the perspective of an inclusive experimental empiricism includes much more than calculation of "personal interests" or even "rational decision or choice" in the usual, restricted meanings of these terms.[37]

Brandt's Essay, which considers the soundness of attitude (emotive) theories of value, favors the view that value statements can be reformulated in empirical language in a way that does justice to their essential point; for example, "The statement that Mr. A's act is reprehensible" can be construed "as roughly the statement that an informed and impartial person would disapprove of Mr. A for doing it."[38] Value statements are regarded therefore as in principle empirically confirmable. Three difficulties ("puzzles") lead Brandt to conclude that an attitude theory, which interprets value terms and sentences as "essentially imperative," "expressive of attitudes, or freighted with emotive meaning," does not adequately construe the

---

[35] See, for instance, Pepper's Essay, pp. 85-93, above.

[36] For example, in "Ethical Subject-Matter and Language," *The Journal of Philosophy*, XLII (1945), 701 and 710; and in *Value: A Cooperative Inquiry*, p. 77.

[37] On this point Garnett says in a recent letter: "I agree with your insistence upon more rigorous critical examination of 'historically derived norms and intuitions of inner feelings' in the light of 'all we can know.' What I want to stress is that this does include, as you say, 'much more than the calculation of personal interests or even rational decision or choice, in the usual restricted meaning of these terms.' The big problem is as to what is included in this 'much more.' I would stress that we can only get at it from an intimate study of the life of moral man at his classically recognized best. It certainly cannot be derived from mere biological theory or behavioristic psychology. My *Moral Nature of Man* is an attempt at this which I hope will be followed up by other studies which will critically improve upon it." To which I add the hope that in choosing *among* and possibly *improving upon* classically recognized best conceptions of moral man we shall feel free to make judicious use of data and concepts derived from all psychological and other viewpoints.

[38] P. 155.

ordinary meanings of value statements. But Stevenson in his Comments seeks to show that the objections thus raised can be better interpreted as supporting an attitude theory.

Brandt is perhaps correct in saying that judgments such as "That is right" or "That is wrong" are made (at least sometimes) in the absence of attitudes of favor or disfavor; that is, the ascription of rightness or wrongness does not appear in all cases to be dependent upon attitudes of favor or disfavor. But it needs to be recognized, as Brandt perhaps does, that attitudes may operate at different levels: there may be an attitude of intellectual-felt approval or disapproval even though the person's dominant, action-determining attitudes may be such as to permit doing at a 'lower' level what at another, 'higher,' level has been condemned; for example, a person may recognize and say that "Stealing is wrong," yet indulge in shoplifting occasionally in 'small' things. It is just possible, indeed probable, that attitudes are determinants, or among the determinants, of valuing and valuation at all levels.

Brandt in his Essay and Stevenson in his Comments agree that both cognitive and affective (attitudinal, emotive, feeling) elements are somehow involved in or with value statements; but they appear (here and in previous discussions)[39] to disagree as to whether value statements are more adequately construed as essentially expressing one of these or the other, and as to whether value judgments are significantly corrigible: Brandt holding that the cognitive is basic or ultimate and that value judgments are corrigible; Stevenson holding that emotive elements are basic or ultimate and that value judgments are, in the last analysis, incorrigible. Both may be correct in that in some cases cognitive or nonemotive factors of the value situation (including the language employed) are predominant determinants; whereas in some other cases the attitudes of particular individuals (and language) are ultimate and sometimes even capricious determinants; though perhaps in still other instances both cognitive and emotive factors are about equally determinants. Moreover, whether an attitude theory or a cognitive theory is correct or more adequate (if either one actually is correct or more adequate), it is important to recognize, as both Brandt and Stevenson may, that expressions of attitude affirm or imply the correctness or adequacy of lines of conduct as ends and/or as means, and that experimental

[39] See especially *The Philosophical Review,* LIX (1950), 291-318 and 528-40.

inquiry and action can often (possibly always) in some measure test their correctness or adequacy. Even individual tastes, likes, and preferences are testable to some extent in terms of the particular individual's pattern of needs, interests, and ideals, in relation to what most sensitive and discerning individuals prefer and continue to prefer "in the long run and the broad view," and in the light of possible and actual outcomes.[40]

Lee's Essay, by utilizing semantic concepts and distinctions in an attempt to discover and describe the locus and nature of intrinsic value, specifically recognizes that in the situation of the occurrence (and experience) of value there is a transaction between a conative-affective sensitivity (an attitude of an organism) and an object. Lee holds that what is involved in the contextual property of this transaction—the experienced intrinsic value—is anterior to the distinction between conation and affection. Judgment, he thinks, is not a necessary component in a value contexture, though we make judgments about values. The evaluating factor underlies judgment of *more or less* value; the degree of pleasantness-unpleasantness (or satisfaction-dissatisfaction) of the conative-affective component of the value contexture is the measure (in consciousness) of intrinsic value.

Although Lee thus achieves a rather dynamic conception of the value situation, it is a conception such as may for the most part be formed by a single individual studying introspectively a single instance of value experience. It is evident from his other writings, however, that Lee clearly recognizes the hypothetical, experimental nature of value formulations.[41] The present purpose of painstaking semantic analysis and the space limits set for each Essay apparently precluded mention here that transactions in "the value situation" frequently extend across many instances and embrace one individual with many others in an on-moving personal, social, physical process (made up of many subprocesses), and that it is possible as a result of these wider more inclusive interactions-transactions to treat even the most immediate and private feelings and conditions as well as

---

[40] "Your comments," says Stevenson, "so far as they apply to my paper, impress me as being entirely faithful to what I said."

[41] See especially his "Ethics as Hypothesis," *The Journal of Philosophy*, LVI (1947), 645-55; and "The Hypothetical Nature of Historical Knowledge," *The Journal of Philosophy*, LI (1954), 213-20.

the most rudimentary perceptions and cognitions as subject to inquiry and test—a process from which may result purifications and enhancements of immediate qualities, qualities which thus become or evidence facts and values in a most distinctive sense. From the standpoint of the larger interactions-transactions which Lee evidently assumes, it may appear not so much that he has in his present Essay overemphasized the affective as compared with the conative (as suggested by Robinson's Comments)[42] as that he has underemphasized the important roles which can usually be played in the discovery and creation of intrinsic as well as of instrumental values by reflective thinking and overt action within continuing processes of personal and social problem solving and adjustment.

Hartman's Essay is a part of his larger research effort "to find a logic of value judgments, or 'axiology'"; to build on simple axioms a formal, universal system which will constitute "the logic of the social sciences, just as mathematics is the logic of the natural sciences."[43] Value terms, propositions, and judgments are viewed as logical classifications analogous to subsumptions in law. "Depending on how we classify a thing it is either good or bad."[44] But how does Hartman conceive the nature of classes and the methods by which they are discovered and by which subsumptions are made? Are the classes "real" as conceived, say, by Plato, Aristotle, or Thomas Aquinas, or are they such as conceived by the nominalists or the empiricists? In identifying goodness with the possession of expositional properties and in holding that *x is a good C* means that *x has all the expositional properties of C*, or that *x fulfills the exposition of C*,[45] Hartman may appear to assume that the goodness of anything is determined by its 'real' or 'logical' concept per se and can be ascertained by sheer logical analysis of expositional properties. But does a good horse (the best horse) necessarily possess *all* the expositional properties of

---

[42] P. 330.

[43] R. S. Hartman, "Research in the Logic of Value," *Main Currents of Modern Thought*, Vol. VIII (1952), No. 3. (Excerpts from this source are reprinted in the present Comments by permission of the editors.) Other papers which express Hartman's point of view and purposes are cited in footnotes 1 and 2 of his Essay, pp. 199, 200, above. See especially his Comments, pp. 352-74. For earlier writings, which emphasize empirical concepts and methods, see his "The Moral Situation: A Field Theory of Ethics," *The Journal of Philosophy*, XLV (1948), 282-300; and "Is a Science of Ethics Possible," *Philosophy of Science*, XVII (1950), 238-46.

[44] P. 197, above.

[45] P. 199, above.

horses or of some 'ideal' horse, or does it possess only (or especially) those properties which are selected relative to some purpose or goal —so that a good draft horse is not a good race horse, or vice versa? And in the choice of goals as well as in finding the best means for achieving them (thus determining which expositional properties need to be emphasized) is there not at best an experimental empirical procedure?

It is evident that Hartman's Essay develops an interesting phase of what must certainly be included in any fully formulated treatment of the language of value theory or of the general theory of signs; but considered alone in isolation from the personal and social contexts in which value terms and propositions rise and classifications occur, the logical structures of pure axiology may appear cold and impractical indeed. Viewed in their larger actual and potential contexts and in relation to Hartman's larger purposes it is possible to share, at least in some measure, his enthusiasm for a research which seeks to unravel the basic logic of value terms, such as "good" and "ought." For, he believes, "On these simple foundations the science of axiology can be erected, leading to a calculus of extrinsic and intrinsic value, value classes, value relations, truth values of axiological propositions, a calculus of choices, of agreements and disagreements, of polls and parliamentary procedures, and a systematic of the social and humanistic sciences."[46] Though I share the hope for the actualization of an axiology which may help achieve at least some of these results (and others), I feel sure that much more recognition must be given to the empirical contexts and processes through which classes as well as classifications are or can be formulated and tested.[47]

---

[46] R. S. Hartman, "Research in the Logic of Value," *Main Currents of Modern Thought,* Vol. VIII (1952), No. 3. Another interesting recent study of the formal, logical aspects of value theory is reported by D. Davidson, J. C. C. McKinsey, and P. Suppes in *Outlines of a Formal Theory of Value, I* (Stanford, Calif.: Stanford University, 1954).

[47] In response to these comments, Hartman remarked: "What you say about my contribution is quite true. The relation between the empirical and the various classes I construct is not clear enough in the Essay." To a further suggestion that in a broad sense experimental inquiry may include all systematic or formal developments of thought as well as what is usually considered empirical study and that it is very important to regard all judgments, intuitions, and so on as subject to experimental testing both on the level of the most formal logical system and by interactions at less formal levels of experience, Hartman replied: "I well understand your mistrust against any logical schema. But I do not mean a schema in the

My own Essay attempts to discern and summarize the functions performed by valuative as compared with factual signs and problem-solving processes, giving particular attention to the various relations in which "fact" and "value," "factual" and "valuative," may be compared, to the presence and roles of emotive and cognitive factors in the occurrence of factual and valuative signs, and to the translatability, interchangeability, or equivalence of signs of the same or different kinds. In correspondence Morris says, perhaps too generously, of the Essay: "It seems to me to be excellent for the volume, since it puts the various emphases into a sensible perspective." In pointing out weaknesses he says, however, that "to carry out fully your point of view would require a whole theory of signs—and that of course could not be constructed in an essay of this size. I am bothered by 'sign responses' and their relation to 'meaning.' The introduction of 'awareness' as a criterion of difference seems to me to raise more problems than it solves." And he continues, "I have a feeling that you should distinguish more sharply 'sign' from 'sign-vehicle.' When you stress the difference of meaning of the same sign in various contexts, I often feel it would be better to speak of different meanings of the same sign-vehicle." These comments and those received from other members of the study group[48] make it appear that though my Essay is an attempt to view factual and valuative signs (terms, sentences) in contexts of the larger social and personal situations in which they arise and to consider instances of their occurrence which are representative of different kinds and degrees of relationship between the factual and the valuative, the attempt has not been entirely successful. Perhaps all that may be claimed is that it too makes a beginning at tasks which need to be done, and perhaps will have to be redone many times, in the development of the semantics or linguistics of value theory.

As perspective for an interesting and suggestive classification and discussion of all the Essays, Hartman's Comments sketch an overarching conception of the various levels of scientific and value

authoritarian sense at all but as a thought experiment—not an empirical one, though!—of which many similar are possible. If I would give myself a label, I would call myself an axiological positivist. I insist on precise analysis of value propositions, but since logic is not adequate for such analysis I have to look for another equally formal instrument, namely, 'axiologic.' "

[48] Especially from Moore, pp. 343-47, and from Hartman, pp. 359-61.

language, from the empirical to the formal, with particular emphasis
on the latter. They reaffirm the view, noted above,[49] that a formal
level of value theory (a third-level value language) can be developed
wherein operates "a formal axiological pattern"—a pattern which,
when discovered and further elaborated by logic or "axiologic," will
"autonomously" yield a "precise" definition of value, thus remodeling
empirico-analytic language and enabling value theory to escape from
the "arbitrariness" of empirical theories.

Hartman rightly stresses the role which more formal and systematic
sorts of analysis and language must perform if any very inclusive
general theory of value is to be achieved. There is a basic issue,
however, with regard to the nature of analysis and language, especially at this 'level.' If interpreted in one way—which may be the
way Hartman intends, there can of course be little or no objection
to speaking of "third-level analysis and language" and referring to
it as "systematic" or "formal." Though it may not be possible even
with or in a symbol system to escape from at least initial or ultimate
arbitrariness, it seems clear: (a) that in such a system, especially at
the most abstract levels, language and inference often go far beyond
their "empirical origins," in the usual restricted meanings of this
term; (b) that *within* the system operations are often demonstrably
valid or invalid, and in this sense "precise"; and (c) that conclusions
reached within the system itself may constitute or give rise to predictions or other judgments which "create" language and direct
action at less abstract, less symbolic levels. But if—as often appears
to be the case—Hartman means by "formal" or "systematic" that at
the third level of value language (or any language) analysis (a) ceases
to be empirical in the sense that inference no longer utilizes elements
of form as well as of content which derive from experience (albeit
experience in some cases largely at the "formal" level), or (b) ceases
to be capable of and in need of testing by experimental operations
both on the "horizontal plane" of the symbol system itself and in the
"vertical plane" of interaction with "lower levels" of experience, it
would appear that "third-level language" has become, or may easily
become, another dubious quest for certainty—certainty sought by
flights of "pure" "logical" or "axiological" inference. If inferences of
such high-level abstraction are not to be unduly dogmatic and sterile,

---

[49] Pages 5 and 389.

they must, I suspect, be kept in intimate interrelation with other levels and phases of experience and inquiry.[50]

In conclusion, it will be evident that my Comments do not attempt to present a complete summary or an exhaustive evaluation of the papers in this volume. The several Essays, Comments, and Responses can of course best speak for themselves, and each contains points of interest not mentioned here. The present aim has been to draw attention to some of the chief respects in which the papers, especially the Essays, have made contributions that appear important from what I have called an "inclusive experimental perspective" and to note weaknesses which result from failure to treat problems or issues from this perspective. A first draft of my Comments was sent to the respective authors of the several Essays and other papers. From reactions received it is clear that in concentrating attention upon one or a few problems in "the semantics of value" the authors found it necessary, for the most part, to assume and leave unexpressed or unstated the larger, more general standpoints from which they wrote. It is also evident from the correspondence occasioned by my Comments that many elements of an inclusive experimental perspective are more widely accepted than was apparent from the several papers themselves or from previous correspondence. Some reactions have led to revisions, which I hope make my Comments (so far as they go) more correct as summations and more just as evaluations; other reactions which may be of particular interest appear in footnotes. I wish to emphasize, however, that the extent of consideration given in my Comments to the various items of correspondence and to the several Essays, Comments, and Responses in no way indicates my sense of their relative importance. Each may correctly be said to be as important as the others insofar as each contributes to the further development of value theory in its linguistic aspects.

---

[50] It may appear, indeed, that analysis of value language in terms of *levels* rather than in terms of more inclusive interactions and 'total' adjustments proves almost unavoidably more confusing and distortive than helpful. But despite the dangers and difficulties of the concept of "levels," it may be that the two modes of study—the "total interactive" and the "formal analytic"—can be fruitfully combined; this I believe is in fact Hartman's objective.

APPENDIX

THE QUESTIONS, topics, references, and comments submitted by members of the study group as it was initially constituted were organized, supplemented, and summarized by the editor and sent to the members in essentially the following form.

SOME QUESTIONS ON THE SEMANTICS OF VALUE

I

What is or should be the aim(s) of semantical study in axiology? the aim(s) and scope of the present study?

Can and should semiotic be developed prior to axiology? Or can (or must) the two be of mutual assistance?

May it be helpful to adopt, as tools of analysis and as objects of criticism, a common semiotical terminology—say, Stevenson's, Kaplan's, or Morris's, or some combination of various semiotical systems or concepts? What system or set of concepts appears to be most penetrating and fruitful?

May it help to adopt, as subject matter for study and for illustration, a common set of value and nonvalue signs, terms, sentences, and situations? What signs, terms, sentences, and situations may adequately represent all the matters that should be considered?

"*Value judgments and descriptive axiology and axiological theory* See an article by Wienpahl, *The Journal of Philosophy*, XLV (1948), 57-67. The distinctions made here with reference to ethics have analogues in theory of value. The point made is that Dewey and R. B. Perry *thought* that they were making statements in the sphere of ethical theory when they were actually making moral judgments." L. Garvin, in a letter, July 9, 1950.

"How are semantical *questions* made precise? How are hypotheses formulated and tested (that is, the proposed answers to the semantical questions)?" I. McGreal, in a letter, July 17, 1950.

II

A. What is a sign? What kinds of reactions are made to or with signs? Are the "modes of signifying" exhaustively differentiated in Morris's *Signs, Language, and Behavior*? Are expression, commitment, and motivation (stressed by Kaplan as characteristic functions of valuative signs; see his "Are Moral Judgments Assertions?" *The Philosophical Review*, LI [1942], 280-303, and The Language of Value, his Ph. D. dissertation, U.C.L.A., 1942) adequately recognized in *Signs, Language, and Behavior*? Is the term "signifying" confusing here—as suggesting meaning in only a cognitive or intellectualistic sense? Or would the recognition of expressive, committive, and motivative modes involve a confusion between the meaning (signifying) and the use of signs?

"As you can see, I think the central issue is that of differentiating the modes of signifying. *The question is how that is to be done.* I am convinced that, among other things, *an empirical study of actual value utterances* is important. I am making in the case of *paintings* a study of the relation of likings to appraisals and both to the persons who like and appraise. As things develop I will report on this." C. Morris, in a letter, July 21, 1950.

"How may observation of a person's linguistic behavior be used to determine the designation of his ethical terms? Must such observations be only such as a behaviorist would permit? What conceivable empirical observations (for example, of children's learning of ethical terms) would be relevant to the analysis of ethical language? Does psychological theory have any implications for the theory of ethical language?" R. B. Brandt, in a letter, August 1, 1950.

"I should like to see an authoritative *answer* to such an epistemology of truth and valuation as Cassirer's (outlined in his *Language and Myth*). He has hit upon the fundamental issues, especially the various forms of expression, prescientific and scientific, each with its own criterion of intelligibility and validity. His own solution is, to me, in too special a vein (Kantian), but the questions concerning valuation in myth, art (including poetry), and science are fundamental. It is these that I should like to see pursued further, and am willing myself to make an effort in this direction. Such a concept as Stevenson's 'emotive meaning' is, as I see it, inadequate to this task. In the *Kenyon Review* is a sample of my thinking on the subject; 1949, summer issue." V. C. Aldrich, in a letter, August 1, 1950.

Should the term "meaning" be used in a restricted sense to denote only cognitive elements in sign-reactions, or in a broad sense to include all elements in or of sign-reactions? Or should "meaning" be discarded as a confusing term? (For various views on this and the matter of "emotive meaning" see E. M. Adams, "A Critique of the Emotive Theory of Ethical Terms," *The Journal of Philosophy*, XLVI [1949], 549-53, and "Word-Magic and Logical Analysis in the Field of Ethics," *The Journal Philosophy*, XLII [1950], 313-19; H. D. Aiken, "Emotive 'Meanings' and Ethical Terms," *The Journal of Philosophy*, XLI [1944], 456-70, and in *Value: A Cooperative Inquiry*, pp. 298-99; M. Black, C. L. Stevenson, and I. A. Richards in "A Symposium on Emotive Meaning," *The Philosophical Review*, LVII [1948], 111-57; R. B. Brandt, "The Emotive Theory of Ethics," *The Philosophical Review*, LIX [1950] 305-18, and "Stevenson's Defense of the Emotive Theory," *The Philosophical Review*, LIX [1950], pp. 535-40.)

Can signs signify apart from a context which includes interest and intent—"use" in a broad sense? Can the same sign signify in different modes? Can different ascriptors in different modes be translated into or interchanged with one another? (See *Value: A Cooperative Inquiry*, pp. 183, 239-41, 382-90, 397-99.)

B. What if any justification or basis is there for the distinction frequently made between valuative and factual signs? Do different standpoints, or frames of reference, disclose different relations of facts and values? (See "Three Relations of Facts and Values," *The Philosophical Review*, LII [1943], 124-30.) Is the distinction between factual and valuative basic, real, artificial, convenient?

What, according to the system of semiosis or the set of semantical concepts that appears most penetrating or fruitful, is the character of valuative as compared with factual signs? Is it true that value terms or sentences, in their "characteristic uses," are essentially or mainly emotive, expressive, committive, incitive, motivative, appraisive, and/or prescriptive, but not essentially or mainly cognitive, descriptive, designative, or assertive? Or are they sometimes assertive and other times not assertive? And are the "characteristic uses" ultimately basic and necessarily final?

"Evaluative language and descriptive language are different in important respects, that is, the interpretant of one is a disposition to preferential behavior, while the interpretant of the second is a disposition to expect objects with certain causally efficacious properties." C. Morris in *Value: A Cooperative Inquiry*, p. 218.

"Whether there is or is not a difference [between designation and appraisal] depends upon more careful work in semiotic than has yet been done." *Ibid.*, p. 395.

Is a pluralistic analysis of value judgments (for example, along the lines suggested by *Value: A Cooperative Inquiry*, pp. 176-83, 383-88, and by H. D. Aiken, "A Pluralistic Analysis of Aesthetic Value," *The Philosophical Review*, LIX [1950], 493-513) needed to clarify value phenomena?

In sentences of the form "X is good," "X is better than Y," or "X is best," do *good, better,* or *best* have a referent or referents? In some contexts but not in others? Does pluralistic analysis help here?

"The controversy [over 'emotive meaning'] has been concerned not with this point [whether or not emotive meaning is present in ethical terms] but rather with the importance of their emotive meaning. Is it to be mentioned only to be put to one side, so that it will not distract us from what is really essential; or is it itself an essential factor?" C. L. Stevenson, "The Emotive Conception of Ethics and its Cognitive Implications," *The Philosophical Review*, LIX (1950), 299.

"Is the meaning of evaluations, as well as their causes, uses, and effects, emotive or prescriptive, or is it, qua evaluation, purely descriptive?" Aiken in *Value: A Cooperative Inquiry*, p. 298. "The question is not whether emotion and cognition are both present, but how and if they are related; it is not whether signs are emotive in their effects but how they are so ... Is the emotive effect of valuational statements an independent mode of meaning or is it not?" *Ibid.*, p. 299.

What is "the relation between the emotive and what Stevenson calls the 'empirical' element in value definitions? Does the presence of an emotive factor make it impossible to arrive at an objective, adequate, and sharable definition of the empirical element, as Stevenson seems to assume in practice, even though he does not state explicitly that this must be the case? That is, does and should the empirical factor control the emotive, or vice versa? Or are they independent of each other?" P. B. Rice, September, 1950.

"*The sufficiency of cognition in establishing values.* It seems to me that Geiger, Ayres, & Co. (the 'orthodox instrumentalists') have just not taken up Rice's challenge to them to reply in detail to criticisms of their position that goods are 'actually instituted by a specific act of judgment.' Incidentally, a valuable recent discussion of the relation of feeling and judgment, bearing both on the present question and that of emotive theories in general, is contained in A. N. Prior's *Logic and the Basis of Ethics*, pp. 68-94." L. Garvin, in a letter, July 9, 1950.

In the process by which inquiry and appraisal of relevant information aid in resolving ethical issues (as the process is portrayed by Stevenson, following Dewey and others; see "The Emotive Conception of Ethics and its Cognitive Implications," *The Philosophical Review*, LIX [1950], 291-304) what are the relations of the more designative, or cognitive, and the more emotive operations or aspects of the process? Is either the cognitive or the emotive basic, the other subordinate? Or may both cooperate to assist the other as means toward achieving conclusions or creations which are objective in a sense other than being merely the expression or projection of wish or feeling?

Do valuative sentences remain, regardless of the thoroughness of inquiry, essentially volitional (that is, expressions of wish or attitude), as Parker held? (*Value: A Cooperative Inquiry*, pp. 233-44, 382-88, 395-99.) Is Dewey also correct in saying: "As far as non-cognitive, extra-cognitive, factors enter into the subject-matter or content of sentences purporting to be legitimately ethical, those sentences are just that much deprived of the properties sentences should have to be genuinely *ethical*"? (Quoted from J. Dewey, "Ethical Subject-Matter and Language," *The Journal of Philosophy*, XLII [1945], 709; by permission of the editors.)

III

What consequences have answers to the questions in Section II, above, for the following?

1. The general syntax of value language (for example, Rice's formulation in "Toward a Syntax of Valuation," *The Journal of Philosophy*, XLI [1944], 309-20, with additions suggested in *Value: A Cooperative Inquiry*, p. 174)

"What is the relationship between pleasure, happiness, want, desire, interest, together with their opposites, and behavior? In part this is a psychological question, but it is partly semantic, and in any case very basic." L. J. Lafleur, in a letter, November 19, 1950.

"*Satisfaction vs. interest as determinants of value.* Though I incline to agree with Aiken in his preference for the former, I believe that he creates confusion by treating satisfaction ambiguously as identical with 'value' and as testing the 'value' of objects of desire. See Lee's criticism of Aiken on this point (*Value: A Cooperative Inquiry*, p. 368). Aiken's rejoinder does not seem to me to meet the criticism completely. Also, in this connection, the lack of a rejoinder by Rice to Geiger's point that satisfactions themselves need testing for 'satisfactoriness' (*Value: A Cooperative Inquiry*, pp. 328-29) leaves an interesting loose end that might be worth picking up for further analytical examination." L. Garvin, July 9, 1950.

"I also consider important the question of 'basic sentences' or protocols grounding valuations, on the scientific level where the demand for confirmations becomes relevant. Some problems of definitions of value-terms also appear in this dimension of expression." V. C. Aldrich, August 1, 1950.

"Is it worth while settling on some definitions of technical terms, and if so, which ones and which definitions?" R. B. Brandt, August 1, 1950.

2. The nature of appraisal, or evaluation, as compared with description, or factual judgment

3. The nature and extent of the truth, validity, adequacy, and testability of valuative signs

4. The nature and status of intrinsic, extrinsic, and inherent values of the various kinds: aesthetic, moral, economic, religious, educational

"*The definition of 'intrinsic value.'* This is the focal point of most disagreement in theory of value and if semantical analysis could promote any agreement as to the best usage here it would be a long step in the direction of clarifying many issues. I know of no better starting point for discussion of the meaning of intrinsic value than the article by J. W. Smith, in *Ethics*, LVIII (1947-48), 195-208." L. Garvin, July 9, 1950. (See also *Value: A Cooperative Inquiry*, at points cited under "intrinsic value" in the Index; I. McGreal, "A Naturalistic Analysis of Value Terms," *Philosophy and Phenomenological Research*, X [1949]; and G. Williams, "Individual, Social, and Universal Ethics," *The Journal of Philosophy*, XLV [1948].)

5. The nature of the objectivity-subjectivity of intrinsic, extrinsic, and inherent values

6. The translatability of factual and valuative sentences, and the ultimate (logical and ontological) relations of value and nonvalue facts

7. "What implications has the semantics of value for particular moralities—for criticism?" I. McGreal, July 17, 1950.

The Summary of Issues formulated on the basis of the above questions, topics, references, and comments appears in the text on page 4, above.

INDEX

Obligation (*Continued*)
greatest possible good, 307-8; standard of, is at once naturalistic, perfectionist, and absolutist, 308, 383*n*; not given sufficient attention by Dewey, 313, 385-86; what is needed to fulfill, 384; conceptions of, held by empiricists, 385-86; *see also* Ought

Observation protocols, in empirical knowledge, 292

Occurrents, 32

Ogden, C. K., 38

"On the Logic of Imperatives" (Hofstadter and McKinsey), 39

Ordinary meanings, *see* Common usage

Organization of Behavior, The (Hebb), 67

Osgood, C. E., 280

Otto, M. C., 165*n*

Ought, as coercive, 16-25; factually justified, 90-91; extended by metonomy, 125; obligation and, 125-26; fittingness and, 125-26; as personal demand, 126-28; of moral obligation, 128, 163, 265; naturalistic conceptions of, 129, 313; always better than what is? 208, 336, 339; analytic, hypothetical, and synthetic, 215-16, 338-40; not entailed by scientific language, 295; hypothetical and categorical, 311; moral, confused by Dewey with self-interest? 313, 386; axiological (formal), distinguished from moral, 338; importance of modal analysis of, 340; *see also* Ought, term; Ought, or hortative, sentences; Ought propositions

Ought, term: root meaning of, 22-23; may be nomological, telic, valuative, or teleutic, 33; as conditional, 121; as normative, 122; as axiological copula, 207; modal analysis of, 214-16, 338-40; as valuative, 233, 242, 246; as modal, 264-65, 267; as descriptive, 301; as ambiguous, 310; paradoxical sense of, 314; importance of modal analysis of, 340; arises out of third-level non-normative definition of "good," 369; *see also* Ought

Ought, or hortative, sentences, 19-25, 207 ff., 338-40, 366-69; a special case of means-ends sentences, 20; both descriptive and persuasive? 21 ff.; referent of, 22-23, 264-65; verifiability or testability of 23-25; cannot be confirmed or disconfirmed in second-level function, 24; *see also* Ought; Ought, term; Ought propositions

Ought propositions, symbolized, 211; analytic, hypothetical, or synthetic, 215-16; analysis of, 220-24; truth and falsity of, 227-31; moral and axiological, 335-36, 338-40; *see also* Axiological propositions; Ought; Ought, term; Ought, or hortative, sentences

Ought statements, 104*n*, 160, 161; *see also* Ought propositions

"Ought to be," as equivalent to "good," 125

Paintings used in study of preference and appraisal ratings, 61, 70, 74; comments by professional art critics on groups of, favored by endomorphs, mesomorphs, and ectomorphs, 66, 75

Pap, Arthur, 38

Parallel relation of facts and values, 238 ff.

Parker, D. H., subscribed to attitude theory of value, 159, 162*n*; things do not have value, 179*n*; value as satisfaction, 186; judgments *about* value and judgments *of* value, 232*n*; value terms emotive, 234

Parsons, Talcott, 71

Pepper, Stephen C., 38, 181, 232*n*; "Evaluation and Discourse," 77-93; comments on, by Lafleur, 281-83; response, 283-86; comments on, by Hartman, 355, 362-64, 366; comments on, by Lepley, 380

Perfect, term, 33, 205, 334, 334*n*, 340

Perry, Charner M., 385*n*; challengeability of definitions, 132; quoted, 147-48

Perry, R. B., 181, 186, 395; quoted, 80-81

Personality: needs of, reveal them-